JAVA **WITHDRAWN**

Also by Colin McCormack (with David Jones)
BUILDING A WEB-BASED EDUCATION SYSTEM (Wiley)

Java

GETTING DOWN TO BUSINESS

COLIN MCCORMACK

palgrave

First published 2002 by
PALGRAVE
Houndmills, Basingstoke, Hampshire RG21 6XS and
175 Fifth Avenue, New York, N.Y. 10010
Companies and representatives throughout the world

PALGRAVE is the new global academic imprint of
St. Martin's Press LLC Scholarly and Reference Division and
Palgrave Publishers Ltd (formerly Macmillan Press Ltd).

ISBN 0–333–79185–1 paperback

This book is printed on paper suitable for recycling and
made from fully managed and sustained forest sources.

A catalogue record for this book is available
from the British Library.

10 9 8 7 6 5 4 3 2 1
11 10 09 08 07 06 05 04 03 02

Printed and bound in Great Britain by
Antony Rowe Ltd, Chippenham, Wiltshire

For my family, Ann, Ellen, Kiara and Matt

Contents

Preface

AUDIENCE

The book is intended mainly for four types of students:

1 First year IS/BIS/BIT students
2 Masters or diploma conversion students in computing or information systems
3 First year computing students
4 Non-computing students taking a programming module.

With these four groups in mind, I take more time than usual at the start of the book to explain programming concepts. I also take a slower approach to introducing syntax. Most significantly, I introduce a library which the students will initially use to program, this hides some of the programming detail from them for a number of chapters.

The reasons why I follow this approach are that in my experience (teaching Computer Science and lately Business Information Systems), I find that even if students have previous programming experience, it is forgotten by the time they start a new course. I also find that some programming language environments do such a good job of hiding from the student what is going on that the student may make it through the course not understanding the basics and expecting an Integrated Development Environment to be able to do everything for them.

The focus in the book is on simple, straightforward examples with a business flavour. This is so that the audience, whatever their background, will be able to relate to the problems and appreciate how the solution works.

The material covered can be varied depending on the required duration of the course. Chapters 1–7 cover all the Java material necessary for a single semester introductory course while Chapters 8–13 cover advanced material suitable for a two semester course.

JUSTIFICATION

Why do students need to learn Java? There is no one convincing reason why Java is a better language to teach than other, more mature, languages. Java is however a language that students are more likely to have indirect experience of and a favourable opinion of (C and C++ come with a certain intimidating reputation). Java is also useful for students wishing to study further programming languages such as C and C++ and thus can be presented as a good introductory language.

The main reasons why Java can be justified are that it is:

▶ *Object Oriented* – From a pedagogical point of view teaching students Object Orientation is necessary to give them the best start in programming (and understanding the best practice for programming). The object-oriented features of Java facilitate this.

▶ *Popular* – Java is recognised by students unfamiliar with programming and is also associated with employment opportunities. This definitely acts as a motivating factor.

▶ *Easy to learn/Easy to use* – Compared with some of the other popular programming languages and environments, Java is easy to learn and use without being too easy. For instance, a common problem with Visual Basic programming is that students often get no further appreciation of what is needed to create a program other than drag and drop (a bit like teaching cookery and having students leave with just a knowledge of how to fire up the microwave).

STRUCTURE

The book is split into two sections:

1 Introduction to programming
2 Software Design

The introduction to programming section is intended to provide a gentle introduction to the language and the main principles behind Object Orientation. The introduction to Object Orientation is not comprehensive as I feel some principles are best left to more advanced courses. The section covers the more practical areas of software design including a short introduction UML. It may be worth pointing out that this chapter and the elements of UML are not integrated into the rest of the book as it may distract students from the core areas.

APPROACH

A major component of the introduction to the programming language is the use of libraries. As mentioned above, libraries will be used to keep some of the irrelevant detail from students.

Libraries will be used in the following chapters:

Chapter 3 – How to program
Chapter 4 – Choices, objects and scope
Chapter 5 – Input/output, loops and data
Chapter 6 – Classes

The purpose of the libraries is twofold. To get the students programming as quickly as possible and to hide all but the necessary details from them initially. Once the chapter on applets is introduced, this approach will be abandoned as the students are introduced to what is behind the code they are using.

The reason why the library approach has been used is to address the important factors in a successful programming course, namely:

▶ *Motivation* – keeping the students interested. This can be done by establishing the relevance of the topic (i.e. that problem solving and project management will stand to them in contexts other that Java), by making the subject as easy as possible and by providing students with tasks to engage them and keep them occupied.

▶ *Rapid start* – the sooner students start to program the better, using libraries reduces the time needed to get students in a position to write a program.

▶ *Appreciation of the important concepts* – by eliminating some of the unnecessary detail, it makes it easier for a student to appreciate the current concept being taught.

▶ *Simplicity* – for example, to provide a program to perform simple output, you need to go through a rather complicated explanation (either via applet or application). If all you want to do is to show the output of an expression, you have overcomplicated the process as far as the student is concerned by explaining every statement. By not explaining each statement the students are left without a sense of full understanding.

Against libraries there are a number of arguments. One of them is that students could be confused by the operation of the libraries when it comes to writing their first programs. However, students are nearly always introduced to programming in a supervised tutorial setting and so can be brought through the steps to use the libraries relatively easily. The use of the libraries will be explained in Appendix B.

The other common argument is that by making the syntax too easy, it causes problems when the students reach the point when they no longer need the libraries. Education is a process of building and moving from simplified concepts to the big picture. In many courses, a simplified (and sometimes not wholly accurate) version of topics is taught to students first to prepare them for further detail. I believe programming is no different and it is my experience that students adapt from their simplified language to the real syntax relatively easily. I have also perhaps oversimplified some of the other material in the book to the point where its accuracy may be questioned. Again the idea is to inculcate the concept as easily as possible, any inaccuracies can be addressed in more advanced programming courses.

EXAMPLE PROGRAMS

There are over 100 example programs to illustrate each of the statements introduced. The example programs are deliberately written to be as simple as possible so that in most cases they illustrate one single concept clearly.

WEBSITE

Support material can be found on the books website at:
http://www.palgrave.com/resources

Acknowledgements

My heartfelt thanks goes to all the people who contributed to this book. In particular, I wish to thank my wife Ellen, my parents Ann and Matt, my sister Kiara, the staff of the Department of Accounting, Finance and Information Systems, University College Cork, the staff at Palgrave, in particular my editor Tracey Alcock for her patience and courtesy, and my students, in particular, my MBS in Electronic Business and Commerce classes.

Chapter

Introduction to programming

Introduction   2

INTRODUCTION

This book is about a programming language, Java, and a way of writing programs, Object Oriented Programming. The first thing to point out is that programming is often viewed as a very difficult topic. I do not believe that it is difficult to learn the right phrases needed to write a program, the problem is learning how to think in the particular way necessary to solve the problem the program is intended for. Programming is mainly about problem solving, which is never easy. A programming language is merely what you use to express a solution, like a set of symbols is used to express an equation (e.g. $E = mc^2$). If you can learn how to solve problems, you can learn how to program, the process is the same. Remember it is not how you express the solution to a problem but the solution itself that matters and learning all the relevant phrases of a language will not automatically solve problems for you. To succeed as a programmer you need to be patient and meticulous. You also need to practice, no matter how gifted you are in other areas it is unlikely you have acquired the skills you need (unless of course you have already completed a programming course). These are qualities that do not come easily to anyone but which can be useful in areas other than programming. Why they are useful will become clear, a single semicolon in the wrong place can stop a 10 000 line program from working and drive its programmer insane trying to find it. The trick is not to make mistakes, and if mistakes are made then you need experience to track them down. The more experience you have of mistakes and what causes them, the faster you can find them when they occur. So, learning programming is not just about the language itself, it is also about how it is used and how you deal with problems which arise.

This book is intended to help you in your task, it is not a magic book and I am not your fairy godmother. Even with all the help I provide, you must still practice hard and learn to take care. I advise you to try out all the examples that you can.

Ideally a programming language like Java should help us out in writing a solution to a problem. It should help us to write the solution in a way which prevents us from doing anything which could cause problems (such as upsetting the operating system) and if we do something silly, it should enable us to track down the problem as quickly as possible. Java is quite a helpful environment but there is still no substitute for experience.

Imagine the software you are building is a car. The more cars you've built the more you know about how they work and what to keep an eye out for. You learn to take care and use quality parts. If you build a car in a hurry from scrap parts, you won't be too keen on driving it. Software is the same, you need to take time to make sure it is done properly, otherwise you and your customers could be in for a nasty shock.

This chapter is intended as an introduction to programming in general and Object Oriented Programming in particular.

1.1 WHAT IS THE POINT OF A PROGRAMMING LANGUAGE?

What will you be doing with a programming language?

▶ Solving a problem (the solution to a problem is known as an algorithm)

▶ Writing that solution in a programming language (in a form called a program)

▶ Correcting the program or the solution.

A programming language is a means by which you indirectly communicate your wishes to the computers Central Processing Unit (CPU). Since you can't speak binary (the language of the CPU, expressed in 1's and 0's) and the CPU can't speak English you need to meet somewhere in the middle and this is where programming languages come in. Programming languages are really a compromise, a means of representing instructions without getting too far away from either of the native languages of the parties communicating. It is because programming languages are imperfect attempts to model communications that there are so many of them. A programming language is a restricted form of language and the terminology and grammar used is usually based on a particular application area, such as science or business. Programming languages were originally written for special groups of people, such as engineers and mathematicians, so you have programming languages written to do specific tasks, like fly planes, run a company's accounts or manage a computer. You even have programming languages that were developed to help people to learn how to write programs so they would find it easier to learn more advanced languages (such as the PASCAL and LOGO languages).

Most of us who program dream of the day when we don't need a programming language, when you simply need to lean over to your microphone and tell the computer what to do. Why doesn't it work like that now? Quite simply the problem is context. To understand anything you need to be aware of context, if I ask you to 'pick up the blue folder' you will understand the context (what a folder is, what it means to pick it up, what blue looks like). If you don't understand the context, we can't communicate and you can't do what I ask. This is why programming is often a frustrating experience, because you must explain to the computer the context of every little thing you want it to do. Want the computer to add up all the years sales figures? You have to tell it where to find the sales figures, what number format is used to store them in and what to do with them when it has added them up (print them out, store the results for later, etc.). This is also why people have such trouble learning to program, because they assume the computer knows what they mean, it doesn't. Anyway, even if we can verbally issue the machine with plain English instructions, we will still have to go to the effort of creating these instructions (i.e. problem solving).

Java is yet another programming language that people can choose to use and more and more people, of differing needs and abilities, are choosing it. Why? Well, different people have their reasons, everything from ease of programming to the ability to recycle what you have written. We take a look at Java's characteristics and what makes it attractive later.

1.2   HOW CAN YOU WRITE A PROGRAM?

When you are writing a program you are trying to do three things: (i) solve a problem; (ii) produce a program which allows the computer to efficiently implement our problem solution; and (iii) produce a program that people can use.

When writing the program you need to write instructions to do the following:

1   Hold the information that the program needs
   ▸ Use what are called *Variables* to hold the information the program needs (day of the year, amount to add).

2   Interact with the person using the program
   ▸ Use a *User Interface* (UI) to interact with the person using the program (tell them what values to supply the solution with, give them the answer).

3   Carry out the steps which solve the problem
   ▸ Use an *Algorithm* (a set of instructions) to solve the problem.

Programming involves writing instructions that take one or more pieces of information and work on them until you get a result. Often programming is likened to cooking, you take your raw materials, apply your recipe and produce your meal. Like cooking there are a lot of variables involved, temperature of the oven, amount of ingredients, and so on. You need to get these variables right and you often need to prepare these variables before use (peel the potatoes, crush the garlic). So, if we look at the steps involved in cooking first we can get an idea of the things we need to keep in mind when writing a program.

First, you need to decide what you want your recipe to produce (i.e. what problem do you want to solve). Next you need to figure out the ingredients needed. Then write your recipe to use these ingredients. Finally you carry out (or execute) the instructions in your program which will:

▸ setup your ingredients (peel the apples, squeeze the oranges)
▸ apply your recipe to the ingredients.

You can then eat the result. If the result isn't what you expected, then you need to look either at the recipe or the ingredients. Whatever is responsible for a bad meal is sometimes obvious (if your meal sets off the smoke alarm then its most likely the cooking length part of your recipe is wrong), sometimes it is not. Just like with programming, the more experience you have with cooking the faster you can figure out the problem. Let's look at the complete process, from start to figuring out what went wrong.

To make a pie, we look at the ingredients involved and the recipe. We do not separate the ingredients (apple, sugar) from the aspects of the recipe that can vary (temperature, amount of sugar), we call them all variables. They are different types of variable though (one an actual physical fruit, the other a numeric quantity).

▶ Ingredients: Apple, sugar and pastry

▶ Recipe (Instructions)

  • Prepare ingredients

  • Cut pastry in half, roll out each half and cut circle out of each rolled out half. Put 1 circle in a dish

  • Put 5 apples, 2 spoons of sugar into dish

  • Cover dish with other pastry circle

  • Cook for 30 min at 200 °C.

▶ Variables to setup

  • Amount of apple to add in (measured in grams)

  • Amount of sugar to add in (measured in grams)

  • Amount of pastry to use (measured in grams)

  • Length to leave pie in oven (measured in minutes)

  • Temperature of oven (measured in °C).

The variables have a name (such as 'Amount of apple to add') and they have some sort of a unit of measurement (such as grams or minutes).

The person using the algorithm must understand what the variable names refer to (there are going to be problems if they do not know what an apple is, for example).

Next we look at finding out what went wrong (known as debugging) and correcting it. Debugging is often a trail and error process since the source of the error may not be obvious and it make take several attempts to solve the problem.

For example, if the pie discussed above did not turn out as planned, we can fall back on our experience with problems to try and identify what went wrong and solve it. Some of the possibilities are listed in Table 1.1.

Table 1.1

Problem which happened	Suggested solution
Pie is black	Oven temperature set too high
Pie is hard as rock	Pie left in oven too long
Pie tastes bitter	Not enough sugar added

▶ User friendliness

  The recipe, also called the algorithm, is fine for our own use but what happens if we want someone else to be able to use it? We can add a little bit extra to it in the form of comments, notes or remarks to make life a little easier for the reader.

Example remarks may be:

- Use fresh apples
- Mind the dish when it comes out of the oven as it is hot
- Add cream for extra flavour
- Use a glass dish for more even cooking.

Recipe and ingredients are usually kept separate. You get the recipe in a bookshop and the ingredients in a food shop. You use the same recipe each time but the exact ingredients (apples, sugar) and the final product will change. This makes life a little difficult sometimes, for example, if you have the ingredients but no recipe. What happens if we put all of these together so that life is more convenient for the user? What we do is put into a packet all the ingredients and a recipe, rather like instant soup. We write our recipe on the packet. So each packet contains:

- Ingredients: apple, sugar
- Recipe (including values for amounts of ingredients, temperature, etc.).

So, now you have everything you need to make pie all in one container and package. This can be transported around. So, at a factory the worker takes the list of what goes in each packet and produces a packet containing everything needed to make an apple pie.

These individual packets are what we refer to as objects. An object is a real physical item. An object has instructions and data (variables). The list of what we want in each packet is known as a class definition, it defines what will be in each object. A class definition is not an actual object but a description of what will be in each object. So, at the factory we can have lots of different class definitions, one for each product object that we produce:

▶ Class definition for Cherry pie

- Ingredients: cherries, sugar
- Recipe for cherry pie.

▶ Class definition for Banana Cream pie

- Ingredients: Banana, Cream, sugar
- Recipe for Banana Cream pie.

The important thing to remember about an object is that it is the physical ingredients (the data) and the recipe (the instructions) combined. The class is just the list of ingredients. The class is not edible, you use the class to create an object which is.

We don't have to confine ourselves to class definitions for pies, we can also produce a main course:

▶ Class definition for curry

- Ingredients: Curry powder, vegetables, rice
- Recipe for vegetarian curry.

We can now manufacture curry dinner objects using the above class definition.

Even more interesting is the fact that we can use existing class definitions in a new class definition. So, for example, if we wanted to manufacture a complete dinner product we could define the class used as:

▶ Class dinner

- Class definition for curry
- Class definition for Banana cream pie.

When the worker goes to make a dinner object they simply make an object from each of the class definitions for curry and Banana cream pie and put it in a dinner object (packet) with instructions on how to open each of the contained objects. This combination is known as inheritance because the class (dinner) uses other class definitions (curry and Banana cream pie).

1.3   A MORE DETAILED LOOK AT ALGORITHMS

Remember algorithms are the solutions to problems, sometimes algorithms are simple to deduce, sometimes they need a lot of thought. An algorithm to add two numbers together is simple, an algorithm to check a company's accounts for fraud is not.

1.3.1 Example algorithm: multi-digit addition algorithm

Everyone over the age of six can add two multi-digit numbers without thinking about it, for example, 751 + 255. But how would you explain to a small child how to do this? By breaking down the problem into simpler problems and explaining how to solve the simple problems. This is what we need to do for the computer, it has the comprehension of a very small child and needs to have everything explained carefully and in small steps. Like a child it also takes what you say very literally. Let's create an algorithm which will solve the above problem.

To add two multi-digit numbers you need to move one step at a time. We divide the problem up as follows:

▶ Adding two multi-digit numbers is the same as adding several single digit numbers

▶ Adding a single digit number (7 + 5) is the same as adding one to a number a specific number of times (7 + 1 + 1 + 1 + 1 + 1).

If we can solve the two smaller problems (adding 1 to a number and adding two single digit numbers), then we can solve the problem we are interested in.

First of all, let's see how to add one to a number, for example, 7 + 1.

Algorithm to add one to a number:

▶ Take the number

▶ Find the next number in the sequence, where the rules for the sequences have been previously defined (i.e. the person carrying out the instructions knows that the number 8 comes after 7 and so on), which is 8

▶ Write out this number.

So, the answer to $7 + 1$ using the algorithm above is 8. As you can see the user did have to have contextual knowledge about our number system but fortunately some contextual knowledge is built into every programming language so we do not have to start from square one. Knowing how to add one to a number, we can now see how to add more than one to a number, for example, $7 + 3$.

Algorithm to add two single digit numbers:

▸ Take one number x and another number y

▸ Add one to x, y times.

So to add 7 to 3 we add 1 to 7 three times, that is, $7 + 3 = 7 + 1 + 1 + 1 = 10$. What we've done is reduced our problem (adding two numbers) to one we have previously solved (adding one to a number), therefore we've not only solved our problem but saved effort by recycling a previous algorithm. Saving effort is a big part of programming, you should never expend unnecessary effort finding a new way to do something that's already been done. Such a blunder is called 'reinventing the wheel'.

We've almost got the algorithm we want, all we have to do is figure out how to use our previous algorithms to add two multi-digit numbers.

Algorithm to add multi-digit numbers ($123 + 45$):

1 Align the two numbers to the right so that one numbers rightmost digit is above the others (3 is above 5)

2 Get the rightmost two single digit numbers (3 and 5)

3 Add the two numbers

4 If the sum exceeds 9 then print out the first digit of the sum AND add 1 to the number to the left of the current digits being examined

5 Print out the answer

6 If there are any numbers to the left then move left, select the next two numbers and go to step **3**.

This algorithm is a little more advanced in that we are using a test (step **6**) to decide if we have any more numbers left (called selection) and a statement (also in step **6**) to continue the addition process until we run out of numbers (called iteration).

So, if we apply the above algorithms to our original data we can now add two multi-digit numbers, for example, $751 + 255 = 1006$.

So, what seems simple to us is not really that simple after all. To carry out multi-digit addition you need to have some context (the number system we use) and the various algorithms that deal with addition.

The above instructions were written in a form called 'pseudocode'. Pseudocode is intended as a way of expressing solutions to problems that a person can easily understand but which is easier to translate into a programming language than if the solution were just written out as a story. Pseudocode 'programs' usually break solutions up into parts, or steps, and use simplified English. There is no real pseudocode 'language', the words used and the structure can vary from person to person. Some pseudocode programs are very close to a programming language while others are much closer to plain English.

1.3.2 The number system

Now would be a good time to point out that in computer terms we start counting at the number 0 instead of the number 1. Therefore 0 is recognised as a valid number.

EXAMPLE Count to the number 10 (remember your count starts at the number 0)

0, 1, 2, 3, 4, 5, 6, 7, 8, 9, 10

How many numbers are shown above?

11.

A mistake which results from confusion over a starting point reference is known as an 'out by one' error, that is, when the user assumes one number is being used and the computer actually uses a different one. For example, the user may think the next number is 4 when the computer is using the number 3 (which is the same as the number 4 to it).

1.3.3 Problem solving

The most common way of introducing problem solving is to discuss Polya's four phases. George Polya was a mathematician who, among other things, discussed how to go about breaking down a problem and approaching it. He devised four phases for solving a problem:

1 Understand the problem
2 Plan your solution
3 Carry out your plan
4 Check that the plan worked.

The last phase is of particular importance for programming as mistakes in programming sometimes don't appear unless you look very carefully for them.

Let us look at the four phases in more detail.

1.3.3.1 Step 1: understand the problem

Understanding the problem is a big part of programming and is commonly called Systems Analysis. It involves talking to the people who have the problem to understand exactly what is involved, what the elements of the problem are, how they know when the problem has been solved and how they deal with the unexpected.

For example, if your problem is to produce a program that will automatically track stock and print out a message if stock needs to be reordered, then you will need to talk to the person who has done this job. They will tell you what to put in the order and you can decide how the user can enter information in the system (item sold, new shipment of items has arrived, etc.). They will tell you that the program works when stock levels are enough to meet demand but do not exceed available storage space or budget.

1.3.3.2 Step 2: plan your solution

So, one solution to the problem of keeping your stock levels managed is to write a program which prints out a complete order form when the stock level for an item drops below a preset level. We could also have gone with a solution whereby the computer automatically faxes the relevant supplier with the order but let's keep it simple.

1.3.3.3 Step 3: carry out your plan

Put your plan into action. Check to see that your solution is solving the problem. This involves writing your program and training the people to use it.

1.3.3.4 Step 4: check that the plan worked

Go back over the solution. Check to see that everything worked. For example, we could find out that sometimes stock items are not reordered if the season is changing (no sandals needed in wintertime). This is not something that we noticed or were told about when we set out to solve the problem but then it is often the case that the people who we are solving problems for do not realise that they haven't told us everything. We therefore add a part to our solution which asks if an item is seasonal and notes this on the reorder printout so that the clerk can make a decision.

The above looks simple and straightforward but sometimes it takes people years to solve problems. How can problems be solved in the shortest time? Well, first it is vital that the problem is understood. If you can't understand the problem, you can't solve it. Sometimes the problem might not be clear and you will have to make assumptions when you are writing the solution for the problem. Later on you can check if these assumptions are correct.

Next you must see what the problem consists of. Often problems are made up of smaller problems. You can solve these smaller problems and combine them to solve the larger problem, like we did with the multi-digit addition problem. This idea, using smaller problems, is a driving force behind object orientation. The idea is that if you solve a problem you can reuse the solution to the problem later on with the minimum of alteration. Using another technique, called inheritance, you can adapt a previous solution to your purpose without having to change the previous solution. For example, you could use code from a shelf life monitoring program that monitors how long items are kept on a shelf and reorder them if their expiry date elapses to solve the stock management problem discussed above.

Problems are rarely impossible to solve, sometimes they may seem unsolvable but this is because you may not have seen anything like it before. This is why it is important to look at many different types of problems and examine how they were solved. Working in a group also helps as people come up with different approaches to problems.

Another point to remember is that you don't rigidly have to follow each step. You can try and solve one problem and find that you need more information and have to go back to step 1. You could get to step 4 and find you need to take account of some extra information and end up back at step 1. This mirrors writing a program as this also may require many refinements and involve more than one false start.

1.4 FUNCTION OF A PROGRAMMING LANGUAGE

1.4.1 Rationale

The purpose of a programming language is to represent the solution to a problem in an easy way, that is, as near to English like statements as it is possible to get.

Problems are solved using algorithms and data structures.

▸ *Algorithm* – a set of instructions written from an extremely basic viewpoint. Algorithms ultimately will need to be written in a programming language but can be written in plain English in the beginning.

▸ *Data structure* – the form that data is stored in: a list, numbers in a particular format, an organisation of data.

1.4.2 Example of a data structure

Individual data elements such as:

▸ A *String* – a group of alphanumeric characters (the small letters a to z, capital letters A to Z, numerals 0 to 9, and other characters such as #@!).

▸ A *number* – floating point (3.14, 2.0913), integer (4, 100, −9).

These can be combined to produce a collection of elements which have some relevance to the problem.

For example, in a program which keeps track of employees a collection of the following information will be useful:

Employee record

▸ Name: (String)

▸ Address: (String)

▸ Phone number: (number)

▸ Hours worked: (number)

This type of collection of information relevant to a particular purpose is called a 'data structure'. Data structures are usually specially developed for particular problems and they are built using simpler data elements and can even use other data structures.

1.4.3 Programming styles

Various styles of programming have evolved over the years.

▸ *Monolithic* – Code is all in one block. Algorithms and data structures are mixed up together.

▸ *Procedural* (Modular/Structured) – Code is divided into sections, algorithms and data structures are kept in different sections.

▸ *Object Oriented* – Program is broken up into relevant objects. Algorithms and data structures are kept together but away from other unrelated algorithms and data structures.

1.4.4   How are programs produced and executed?

The CPU in each computer is capable of a number of different operations mainly involving:

▸ Comparison

▸ Computation

Instructions to the central processing unit to perform an operation are extremely basic and so we must find a way of making the instruction easier for people to understand.

Instruction for person: Add the numbers two and five and display the result.
Instructions for computer: LDX 2
                      ADD 5, etc.

The two different parties meet in the middle using a programming language. Remember there is nothing stopping people from writing in the native language of the CPU except it is very time consuming.

The programming language can be translated by a person into something intelligible to them and by the computer into something intelligible to it. So the programming language compromise for our adding instruction is:

```
Print(2+5)
```

The function of a programming language is not just to save you a little typing effort (instead of having to write 'Add the numbers two and five and display the result' you just say `Print(2+5)`) it should also remove any ambiguity so that it has only one possible meaning (output the result of the number 2 added to the number 5).

As another example of how the means of expression changes, look at the command: "If the numbers 5 and 4 added exceed 6 then printout the word 'Bigger'."

Its equivalent in a programming language is:

```
if((5+4)>6)
    Print("Bigger");
```

1.4.5   Executing the program

The process of carrying out the instructions in a program you have written is called execution. Execution involves giving the instructions in your program to the computer's CPU so that it can carry them out. Remember that the CPU uses a particular language and the programming language is intended to act as a means for us humans and the computer to meet half way, so you cannot simply give the CPU your programming language instructions, you must translate them into the language of the CPU. The file that your programming language instructions are stored in is called the 'source code' and the file containing the instructions that the CPU can understand is commonly called a 'binary' or 'executable'. You can usually tell the contents of files by their file names, source code files usually have an extension which indicates the programming language they are written in, such as .java or .c for the C language and .bas for the BASIC language. Executable files have the extension .exe (this is on a Windows based operating system, it will vary from one operating system to the next). It doesn't matter what programming language was used to write the source code which produced the executable file, the CPU doesn't care, all it cares about is that it can understand the file. This is like a person reading a document which was originally written in a foreign language, they don't care what the original documents language is because they can't understand it, they just care about what is in the document they are reading.

1.4.6 Areas of use

Programs are written for a variety of different problems or uses, some common uses are:

▶ *Front end* – Graphic User Interface (GUI), for example, a web browser, an email reader, a stock market graph.
▶ *System Software* – Software useful for dealing with a computer system. Utilities, operating system components, and so on.
▶ *Application* – Software of direct use to people. Wordprocessors, databases, and so on.

1.4.7 Characteristics of a language

Each programming language has its own particular set of characteristics, let's take a look at some of them.

Power – The 'power' of a language generally refers to how flexible the language is, that is, can the programmer interact with the operating system or directly with devices such as the printer.

Portability – Can the language be used on different types of computer and operating system (known as platforms).

Reusability – How easy is it to reuse portions of the code in other programs.

Syntax – The words or symbols used to perform actions, that is, the vocabulary of the language.

For example, the word 'print' can be replaced by the programming language phrase `System.out.println`. The word 'add' will be replaced by the symbol ' + '.

Syntax also governs the rules dictating the formatting of these words and symbols (i.e. the grammar of the language). For example, the rules for the two replacements we discussed are:

▶ the ' + ' symbol must be placed between the two numbers to be added, for example, 2 + 4

▶ The phrase `System.out.println` must be before the element to be output

▶ `System.out.println` can only be placed before a string and the string must be contained within brackets `()`. The start and end of the string must be indicated using a quote `"`. For example, `System.out.println("Result is:")`.

1.4.8 Control structure

How does the computer know which instruction to carry out next? Well, the sequence of execution is that instructions are carried out one at a time, one after the other. Just like you read one word and one line at a time. The next instruction that is executed (carried out by the computer) is not always the one following the current one. The order can be changed using:

• *Selection* – the ability to decide what statement should be executed next, or

• *Iteration* – the ability to repeat a single statement or a group of statements as many times as needed.

Don't think of a program like a book that follows one page from the next, think of it more like an encyclopaedia or a web page where you might jump from one part to another depending on the circumstances.

How does a program start?
Every programming language defines an entry point (or entrance). This is an agreed place to start executing statements. Different programming languages have different agreed places but the entry point is always clear (like the onramp for a road). If no entry point can be found, then the program won't work as it cannot be started (just like if the chapters in a novel were not arranged in order and you could not find the first chapter).

How does a program end?
Every program will usually have an exit point which it reaches when there are no more instructions to execute or it receives a specific instruction to stop (like running out of road or seeing a red traffic light) has been reached. If there is no exit point, then the program will run forever (known as an infinite loop).

1.5 FUNCTION OF A COMPILER

The function of a compiler is to act as a proof-reader and a translator for the instructions written in a programming language file. These instructions will be translated into a language your CPU will understand.

A compiler will take as input your program (the source code), which you will have written using some form of text editor. A text editor is defined as a computer application which is used to create and edit a file of characters. There is a limit to the range of characters you can use in most text editors, non-English language characters, for example, are usually absent. Essentially all the characters you need to write are in text editors; the letters of the alphabet, the mathematical operators (+ , –, /, *), numbers and other symbols that are directly useful such as .[]();”;<>. There are also some characters which the compiler won't understand but you might like to use for messages for yourself or for your users, such as £$@. Wordprocessors, such as Word and Wordperfect are not usually used as text editors as they do not save their contents as text files by default, they save them using their own special format which is unreadable by most other programs.

So, the compiler program takes the file that you have typed in and goes through it one line at a time. Usually near the start of the program are the list of definitions of what variables are used and what they contain. The compiler makes a note of any references and it will check the rest of the program to see that you have explained everything it needs to know (like when you read a novel you make mental note of each character as you encounter them so you can recall their details when they are mentioned later in the book). If you refer to any variables without having defined or introduced them, the compiler prints out an error. Most compilers will continue reading the rest of your file but will not produce an executable program if they find errors, the reason they read the rest of the file once they find one error is to find other errors so you can correct several errors at one go. You should note that not every error reported is 'real', sometimes one error will have a knock on effect on other parts of the program causing several other errors that would not be reported if the first error was fixed. This is why you should always try to fix the first errors reported first and then recompile the program if the other errors cannot be easily found as they could have been caused by the mistake now fixed.

The compiler reports an error if it finds any variable which has not been defined because it does not understand what to do with them. It's as if a character in a novel you are reading, who has never been introduced, is suddenly vitally connected to the plot, you can't place the unknown character in context and therefore you will get confused as to what meaning to take out of the passage of text.

A compiler translates code written in a programming language into a set of instructions which can then be read into the Operating System and executed on the CPU (like a foreign language interpreter will translate a book into a foreign language book). Programs produced from compilers are usually dependant on one operating system.

Operating Systems are usually dependant on one processor or 'family' of processors. This is why if you look at the instructions for installing a piece of software, such as a game, you see details such as 'Needs Windows 95/98'.

Interpreting An alternative to a compiler is an interpreter which translates a programming language file statement by statement and sends this translation to the operating system to execute as it translates (like a foreign language interpreter will translate a conversation word for word).

Therefore, if you use an interpreter you need to use it every time you want the computer to perform (or execute) your program. If you use a compiler, all you need is the file created by the compiler. This file contains machine language which is directly executable by the computer.

Java compilation and execution process As discussed in this chapter, the purpose of a compiler is to translate a programming language into code which the CPU (and the operating system which uses it) can execute. This means that each executable file produced is specially made for a particular type of computer. This is fine if every computer in the world is the same but this is not the case. It means that if you want your program to work on different types of computer you must run it through different compilers which will produce instructions for that particular platform. This is time consuming and often does not work well. Ideally you would like your compiler to produce an executable which is understandable by every type of CPU but this is not as easy as it sounds, instead of doing this the makers of Java did the next best thing.

They decided to have a Java compiler produce a standard type of executable (called 'bytecode') no matter what computer the compiler was running on. This executable is not directly usable by any CPU but can be used by another program called a Virtual Machine (VM) which will translate it into a form which can be used by the CPU (i.e. it interprets it).

The process of taking the source code and translating it into byte code is shown in Figure 1.1. The editor program is used to prepare and save the source code. The compiler processes the source code and produces a bytecode file if it approves of the code. If it does not approve, it's back to the editor to fix the code and try again.

Any computer for which a VM program exists can run Java bytecode which has been produced from any other computer. The bytecode file will always have the extension .class.

The VM's job is to read the bytecode file from the disk drive (or from a remote web server) and translate it into a form that can be understood by the operating system (see Figure 1.2).

There are two main types of program produced using Java:

1 An applet is a program, commonly run in an Internet browser, which is intended to solve simple problems, for example, to do a mortgage calculation.

2 An application is a program which is run on a persons computer outside the browser and is intended to perform more complicated tasks, such as acting as a Wordprocessor.

A different type of VM is used for each type of program since they are intended to do different things. Each type of program is also written in a slightly different way (more on that later). You can download relevant VM programs from the Sun Java Web site (www.javasoft.com) or if you already have an Internet browser on your computer it is likely that it installed a Java VM for Applets automatically.

Furthermore the makers of Java decided to make life easier for people using the Internet. One of the big problems with the Internet is that it is sometimes difficult to tell who you are dealing with. For example, you could access an Internet site using your browser and, unknown to you, the maker of the site could have written a program which transmits your credit card information to them. In order to prevent this type of event taking place, Sun has written VMs that will not allow Java applets downloaded from the Internet to get access to your private files unless you give them explicit permission to do so. There are no restrictions on applications so these run at your own risk. Applications will not run in browser windows.

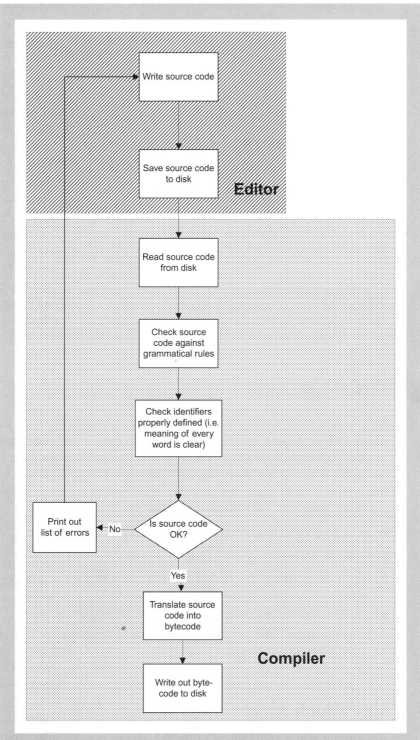

Figure 1.1

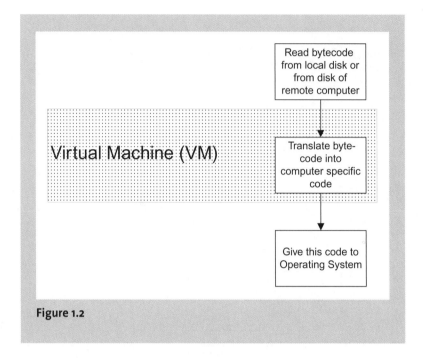

Figure 1.2

Let's look at the types of error we're likely to encounter when we start writing programs and algorithms. It's inevitable that errors occur and they happen to even the most experienced programmer, however the more practice you have at programming the easier it is to track down errors. Remember though, that it's better to take as much time as you need to get your algorithm right as errors in the algorithm can be the most difficult to spot. The types of error that will arise are:

▶ *Algorithmic error* – error in the algorithm or solution to the problem

▶ *Syntax error* – error in the programming syntax

▶ *Logic error* – syntax correct but the statement is used in a way other than that intended

▶ *Run-time error* – error produced when the program is being run, either through incorrect input values or due to a mistake in the program. Run-time errors may cause the program to stop.

1.6.1 Algorithmic error

Algorithmic errors are the hardest to spot, unless you test your program properly or you are lucky. An algorithmic error is a mistake in the algorithm, the program will compile and run perfectly but will not perform the function for which it was written exactly as planned. For example, if a program is written to output a company's results for every month and the program outputs only eleven figures, then this is an algorithmic error.

1.6.2 Syntax error

A syntax error means you have tried to do something that the programming language cannot facilitate. Most common syntax errors are mistakes in spelling which mean that your source code cannot be understood by the compiler reading your program. Sometimes a syntax error is something which sounds sensible to you but which the programming languages grammar rules are unable to cope with. A syntax error is usually easy to spot because your compiler refuses to accept the statement with the syntax error in it.

EXAMPLE   'My cat sah on the mat'. Syntax error because no one knows what 'sah' means.
The grammar mistake form of syntax error is sometimes called a semantic error and occurs when you use a word in the wrong context.
Tell the cat to fetch me the paper. Syntax error because cats don't fetch papers.
What you meant to say was:
Tell the dog to fetch me the paper. The dog is capable of processing this command.

1.6.3 Logical errors

Logical errors are a little more difficult to spot. They occur when you say something in code that you really didn't want to say. This means that the compiler will process the statement with the error in it because as far as it is concerned the statement is correct. But as far as your overall program is concerned the logical error will cause the program to go wrong. For example, if you get a testing sentence wrong, that is, if you want to check whether the user had finished supplying information so that the program could process that information. Your testing sentence might never stop causing the program to enter a state where it can never finish (called an infinite loop).

1.6.4 Run-time error

A run-time error is one that occurs when the program you have compiled is actually being executed. Sometimes your program can do things that the operating system doesn't like, such as trying to access a restricted area, and the operating system will stop the program. You then have to figure out what happened, because your program compiled and executed fine, but it just didn't work.

We will examine the areas where these types of errors can occur as we look at example programs.

SUMMARY

The purpose of a programming language is to find a way of representing your instructions to a computer that both you and the computer can understand.

Algorithms are like recipes in that they are lists of ingredients and instructions used to transform raw material into a useful product. Algorithms are intended to be written in the form of source code so that instructions can be provided to a computer which will solve a problem. To solve a problem you must develop one or more algorithms which will need to be describable in basic terms because a computer does not possess the same level of experience that a person does.

A Java compiler will translate a Java program into a form known as bytecode. This bytecode is translated into instructions which a computer can carry out by using a program called a Virtual Machine.

Different errors can occur when solving a problem. Errors can be due to a mistake in the solution of the problem, a mistake in the way the solution is written or can be due to the person using the solution.

KEYWORDS

▶ *Algorithm* – The name for the series of instructions that solve a particular problem. The source code is an implementation of one or more algorithms.

▶ *Bytecode* – The form that Java source code is translated into. Bytecode is translated into a form that a computer can execute using a Virtual Machine. Bytecode is independent of a computer and an operating system.

▶ *Class* – A written description of what the contents of an object will be. A class is used as a sort of mould for creating objects.

▶ *Compiler* – A computer program for translating source code into a more usable form. Compilers are specific to certain computers and operating system.

▶ *Execute* – The process of carrying out the instructions in a program.

▶ *Object* – An object is a means of storing information and instructions which act on that information. Objects are specialised for particular areas which are modelled on the way things are done in the real world.

▶ *Pseudocode* – A 'program' or series of instructions written so that a person can easily read and understand them. Pseudocode programs will be translated into a programming language once they have been checked and approved.

▶ *Source Code* – A Java program, written by a programmer. Source code must be translated so that the instructions contained within it can be carried out by a computer.

▶ *Virtual Machine* – A program for translating bytecode into a form that can be executed by a computer. A Virtual Machine is specific to a particular computer and operating system.

EXERCISES

1 Java uses bytecode that requires a Virtual Machine on each computer. What do you think are the advantages and disadvantages of this approach?

2 Programming languages were designed to be compact and unambiguous. For the multi-digit algorithm develop a 'programming language' that adheres to these rules, i.e. write out the all commands you would need and specify the form that these commands would take. Your commands can be in plain English.

3 Using the algorithm developed above for multi-digit addition write out the algorithms which will perform multiplication and division.

4 Other programming languages preceded Java (Smalltalk, C++, C), find out a little of the history of these languages using the Internet and see if you can determine why people switched to Java for some applications and failed to do so for others.

5 Look at the source of the Java programming language (http://www.javasoft.com). This site features a bulletin board for various Java issues as well as a considerable amount of documentation. Explore this site and try to discover what other aspects there are to Java.

Solutions to exercises and interactive exercises can be obtained at:
http://www.palgrave.com/resources

Chapter

Object orientation

INTRODUCTION

In Chapter 1, we looked at the reasons why we need a programming language. In this chapter we see that there are a number of ways to arrange the various parts of a program. We shall see that while there is a choice for a programmer about how to arrange their program some formal arrangements will be more beneficial than others.

We look also at some of the aspects of Object-Oriented Programming and discuss what makes it attractive.

2.1 PROGRAMMING METHODOLOGIES

A methodology is a set of rules used to write something (book, instructions, research paper, article, program). A methodology may not be necessary but using an appropriate one makes the process of program development easier and the solution easier to alter.

Essentially a methodology governs how you arrange and group your algorithms and variables. We look at three different methodologies.

1 Unstructured programming

2 Procedural programming

3 Object-Oriented Programming

2.1.1 Unstructured

The essence of an unstructured program is that one large body of code is written which has access to a specific group of variables called global variables. A global variable is one that can be seen everywhere in the program. Think of it as an unlocked filing cabinet that everyone can access.

Unstructured programming means you can just sit down and write out your program without thinking about how to arrange it. This works well if your program is short but as your program becomes more complicated it becomes more difficult to manage.

For example, imagine someone has written a manual for a Television set. The way s/he has written it is to write out the instructions as s/he thought of them, so for instance you read how to change the volume before you read how to plug it in. There is no index or table of contents supplied, you just have to plough through the whole manual to find what you want. This manual is unstructured. Note that all the information you need to operate your television is there, it's just not in a very convenient format. This is true for all the different ways of writing a program whether it be structured, unstructured or object oriented, the result is the same but the organisation of the instructions is quite different.

To execute an unstructured program, the computer will start at the first instruction and follow the instructions until it is told to stop or runs out of instructions.

2.1.1.1 Advantage

Easy to program (since you don't have to think about how to arrange your program).

2.1.1.2 Disadvantages

- Large programs become impossible to follow
- Maintaining (fixing) and reusing code is difficult
- Teams can have trouble working on the same program because its difficult to decide what parts are what.

2.1.2 Structured or procedural

To make life a little easier for programmers, the structured approach has been developed. The idea is to break programs into self contained, well-defined parts with specific names called 'procedures'. All of these procedures will still use global variables to hold the data being worked on.

To execute a structured program, a particular method is always called. This method is like a contents page or books preface, the reader will always look for this section first. This particular method is called a 'main' or supervisor procedure and it will 'call' (tell the computer to execute the instructions in) other procedures. Each procedure has a unique name, so we can tell them apart, and normally contains instruction for one particular purpose (e.g. calculate taxes, store information on disk). The main program is usually short and easy to read so we can understand what the whole program does in a few lines.

Procedural programming means we still keep the data global but break up the problem solving parts into procedures.

If we go back to our television manual, structured programming is the equivalent of dividing up the manual into specific sections (procedures) such as:

1 Unpacking your television
2 Plugging it in
3 Tuning it
4 Using the remote control
5 Connecting to a sound system

6 Connecting to a Video Cassette Recorder

7 Connecting to a DVD

8 Troubleshooting

All information present in the unstructured manual is here, but is arranged in such a way as to make it easy to find what we are interested in.

2.1.3 Object-oriented approach

Object-Oriented Programming was developed because there were still problems writing programs with the structured approach. The main problem was that the data was kept separate from the instructions which operated on it. For example, our television manual is separate from the television itself. Someone may not see the manual and can fiddle with the settings without consulting the manual thus causing a malfunction.

To overcome this problem and to try and make it easier to write and reuse programs the object-oriented approach has been developed. Basically this means that data and the instructions which operate on it are kept in the same place. If instructions for operating the television are kept by the side of the television, nobody can alter the settings on the television without seeing the manual and therefore they can alter them correctly.

The various groups of subprograms in an object are called 'methods' (they are the same as procedures but are given a different name because we are working with a different methodology).

Data and functions are said to be **encapsulated** into an object, that is, they are grouped together.

If you want to access a data item which is contained within an object, you call the method inside the object which will access the data and return it to you. This means data cannot be inadvertently altered. This is known as **hiding** the data (more in Chapter 4, Section 4.4).

An Object is a concrete instance of a particular **Class**. A Class is a plan of what methods and data an object will contain.

So, for our television example the class will contain the manual and a description of the model of television.

2.1.4 Analogy for the different types of methodology

Imagine a company. A company requires a lot of different departments to operate (e.g. sales, personnel, accounting, etc.). Each department will have its own workers, procedures (the way they do things, how they make a sale, hire a staff member, etc.) and data (who works for them, how much they are paid, who is acting as receptionist today, what products were sold, etc.).

Let's look at how the company can be arranged in an unstructured, structured and object oriented manner. Again it's worth emphasising that all of these organisational structures will work, but some are more suitable than others because they may be easier to manage, change or understand.

2.1.4.1 Unstructured

Everyone in the company works in the same large room and uses the same filing cabinets. Nobody has a name tag and there are no signs to indicate who does what.

How do you know who does what (Personnel, Sales)? There is no visible organisation, everything still works its just difficult to figure out how it works.

How do you get someone in sales to do something new? For example, to sell a newly introduced product, use a new accounting system. First, you have to find them and then you have to retrain each person necessary. As the organisation is unclear, it takes more time to find out what is happening and to change things.

How are you sure the data in the filing cabinets are correct? Everyone has access so people can make changes to their salaries, other people's sales results, and so on if they want to. Therefore changes I make to the files may have an impact on other people who may not realise that I am the cause of the chaos. This is another major problem with this organisation.

2.1.4.2 Structured

If the company is arranged in a structured fashion, everyone will still work in the same large room but each different section has their own particular area of the room marked off by partitions and identified by signs. Each person will have a job description sign on their desk (Sales Manager, Secretary Sales Department). This makes life easier for people who want to use or alter the company but one problem still remains. Each section still relies on central (global) file cabinets. So, for example, if I want to alter someone's personnel file I just go to the relevant filing cabinet and make the change. Nobody guards or protects the data in case I make changes I shouldn't. Therefore the data in the filing cabinets are still not reliable.

2.1.4.3 Object oriented

If the company is structured in an object-oriented fashion, then each part of the company has its own floor, personnel on the 1st floor, and so on.

Each part of the company keeps their own information in locked filing cabinets on their floor.

If you want information relating to personnel, you go to a specific person in the personnel department who will unlock the filing cabinet and give you the information you requested (if you are allowed to see it). They therefore 'hide' or protect their data.

If you want to change that information, you must tell the relevant person who will check whether the change is correct or not and it is allowed. We are now assured that the data which the company keeps are correct since no unauthorised changes to the data are permitted.

Each department is therefore an object. The objects are created from class descriptions developed by managers when they are creating the company. The class descriptions can contain requirements for information such as, department name, location, phone numbers, employees and methods, such as procedure for submitting a budget.

This of course is how the majority of companies operate. It takes more effort than other approaches but makes life easier in the long run. This is why programmers decided to mimic the system of organisation used in the real world, because it will have real benefits for them writing programs to model the real world. Though it is still not enough to write your program in an object-oriented fashion, you have to take care with your code and also you should document the code as you write it. Documenting code is known as commenting. Commenting helps anyone reading the code to understand it better by explaining the computer code in more English-like terms.

2.2 OBJECTS AND CLASSES ANALOGY: THE JELLY MOULD

Imagine a jelly mould, a shaped bowl made of glass or plastic into which a jelly mixture is poured and after the mixture cools out pops a shaped jelly (see Figure 2.1).

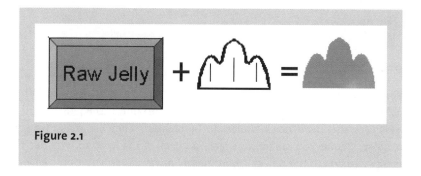

Figure 2.1

The jelly mould itself is like a class, you cannot do anything with it except make jellies, you can't eat it, for example, or put a cream topping on it. It only exists in order to make jellies but jellies cannot exist without it (because they will have nothing to shape them).

Jellies are like objects. Once they are created from the mould (the class), they are real and individual. You can change individual jellies, put different toppings on them for example. You can eat any one jelly you have made without affecting any of the other jellies (or the jelly mould). Each jelly, like each object, is a separate entity even though they have their initial appearance (shape) in common (see Figure 2.2).

Jellies, the objects, are created from a jelly mould, the class. The jelly mould contains the description of what an actual jelly should look like but is not a jelly itself. You need the jelly mould to make the jelly.

Each jelly contains all the bumps, shapes and gaps that are present in the jelly mould. Remember we can't use (eat) the jelly mould bumps, shapes and gaps because they do not exist in a form we can use. They exist merely to give shape to a jelly created using the mould. We can use (eat) the jelly created by these shapes, bumps and gaps of the mould.

The jelly mould can make hundreds of jellies and not change. Each jelly it makes can change, can be eaten or altered.

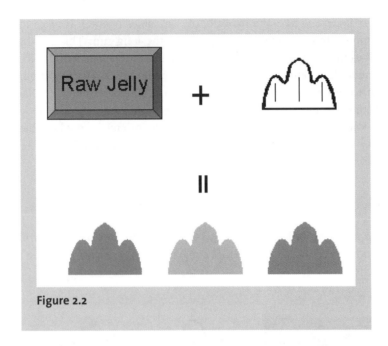

Figure 2.2

Jellies are physical, they are made from hot water and a jelly mix. When you want to make a jelly you must have jelly mix available to put in the jelly mould.

Objects also need raw material to be created. They are made from the computers memory. Before you create an object a check is made as to whether there is enough memory to create the object (there nearly always is so you don't have to worry about what happens if there isn't for the moment).

Each object contains all the methods and variables that are present in the class. These methods and variables are copied out of the class definition and given a place in the memory, just like a bump in the jelly mould is given a place in the jelly produced using the mould.

You can have many different moulds each of which are suitable for different occasions and each of which creates different shapes of jellies. Likewise, you can have many different classes in your program, each of which creates different objects.

2.3 OTHER ASPECTS OF OBJECT-ORIENTED PROGRAMMING

While Object-Oriented Programming is valuable alone for the concept of keeping instructions and data together, there are two other improvements that are made to structured programming and included as part of the object-oriented methodology. These are:

1 *Inheritance* – the ability to take code that someone else has developed and reuse it with the least possible disturbance to that code.

2 *Polymorphism* – a feature that allows a number of different methods to have the same name but to do different things.

We will look at polymorphism in detail in Section 6.4, at the moment let's look at some examples of inheritance.

2.3.1 Inheritance

Inheritance allows us to take shortcuts when writing code by reusing someone else's code. We can either write all the code we need from scratch or we can use code that has been written previously by making use of inheritance.

How does this help us write programs? Well, it will remove the need to continuously rewrite the same solutions to cope with a new problem thereby saving time and money.

2.3.2 Jellies and inheritance

Say you want to construct a really spectacular jelly, a shaped jelly on a square base. Say you already have the mould for the top part of the shaped jelly (see Figure 2.1), you can use this to help you make the overall combined jelly. That way you won't have to go to the trouble of remaking an entirely new shaped mould.

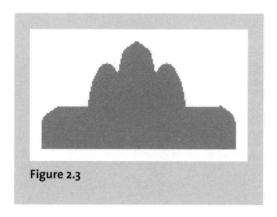

Figure 2.3

The steps you would go through are:

1   Make your square jelly mould but leave a square space in it
2   Put the shaped jelly mould in the square space
3   Pour the jelly mix into the two joined moulds.

You have now made your desired object (a shaped jelly on top of a square one) by making use of a previously defined class (a shaped jelly mould). Thus you are inheriting the qualities of the shaped mould but creating a new object which combines the two classes (moulds).

You can take the shaped mould off (this is called the parent or super class in object oriented language terms) and create new shaped jellies but the square mould will not work without having access to the shaped mould (this is called a child or subclass).

In the same way classes which extend other classes will not work without having access to their parent class and the parent class can operate independently.

2.4   OBJECT-ORIENTED ANALOGY: THE BANK

Let's look at how a bank works and explain its operations in object-oriented terms.

- *Data hiding* – only the teller can get access to the accounts, you cannot alter the balance of your own account directly, you must go through someone who has authority to do so, such as a teller or a manager.

- *Inheritance* – We can create a bank teller class and bank manager class to hold the functions and data related to these types of employees. However, tellers and managers have certain information and methods in common so they can also both inherit a common employee class.

We need to define the following classes to model the necessary bank staff:

- Bank teller
- Manager
- Employee

2.4.1   Bank teller class

A bank teller class would contain the following:

Variables

▸ Each teller has an amount of money

▸ Each teller has a hatch number

Methods

▸ Take deposit( )

▸ Make withdrawal( )

The class definition can take the form of a manual that prospective tellers are given. The manual is used to form or create a bank teller object (a person trained with all the procedures from the manual). Each bank teller object is unique and contains information (money in cash register, hatch number) as well as the procedures that each teller needs to know to do their job (take deposit, process withdrawal).

When the new teller object is created using the class definition, they have the variables they are supposed to and can execute certain methods. The new teller is the same as the other tellers concerning these methods but is unique regarding variables.

If you want to change the tellers behaviour, you have to rewrite the manual and retrain the tellers (i.e. recreate the objects).

The manager has a different set of functions and therefore must be derived from a different class definition.

2.4.2 Manager class

Variables

▶ Secretary's name

▶ Phone number

▶ Office number

Methods

▶ Make loan( )

▶ Give overdraft( )

▶ Send threatening letters( )

If you want to create a manager object, you take a person and train them with the manager manual, they then become an object of the class type bank manager. Remember the manual (the class definition) cannot do anything, it is there simply to create the relevant employee (the object).

Obviously a manager object is a different object to a teller. They have different variables and different methods.

As mentioned above they may share some characteristics though, for example each of them can be said to be an employee of the bank and thus will be paid and have personal information kept about them.

So each of them can use an employee class.

2.4.3 Employee class

Variables

▶ Name

▶ Date of birth

▶ Address

▶ Salary

Methods

▶ Request transfer( )

▶ Notify change of address( )

▶ Calculate salary( )

and so on.

Again the contents of the variables are not fixed forever, the salary or address can change for example.

Both manager and teller inherit the same class employee. So, our definition for our bank teller and manager classes can be as follows.

Bank teller class which inherits employee class:

Variables

▸ Each teller has an amount of money

▸ Each teller has a hatch

Methods

▸ Take deposit( )

▸ Make withdrawal( )

Manager class which inherits employee class:

Variables

▸ Secretary's name

▸ Phone number

▸ Office number

Methods

▸ Make loan( )

▸ Give overdraft( )

▸ Send threatening letters( )

Now, when you create a bank teller object it automatically creates an employee object as well, likewise when you create a manager object. You are therefore making use of someone else's work to avoid having to rewrite the methods and variables contained in the employee class.

So, a teller object looks like this:

```
Employee object
Variables
— Name
— Date of birth
— Address
— Salary

Methods
— Request transfer()
— Notify change of address()
— Calculate salary()

Bank teller object
Variables
— Each teller has an amount of money
```

```
— Each teller has a hatch

Methods
— Take deposit()
— Make withdrawal()
```

The bank teller object not only contains the methods and variables defined in the class 'bank teller' but also those in the class it inherited, that is, 'Employee'.

Likewise the manager object looks like this:

```
Employee object
Variables
— Name
— Date of birth
— Address
— Salary

Methods
— Request transfer()
— Notify change of address()
— Calculate salary()

Manager object
Variables
— Secretary's name
— Phone number
— Office number

Methods
— Make loan()
— Give overdraft()
— Send threatening letters()
```

The manager object contains an object of type employee as well as an object of type Manager.

2.5 SO WHAT?

So, what matters is how each company organises itself. You can find many examples of companies that function with an unstructured methodology, why put any effort into changing the way the companies operate, why not just make a few procedural changes? For example, give certain people in an unstructured company keys to the filing cabinet? There are a number of reasons why programmers move to Object Orientation (OO) and while data protection is important it's not the only valid reason for using object orientation in place of other methodologies. The reasons we look at in more detail are:

▸ Reusability

▸ Development

2.5.1 Reusability

Reusability refers to the ability of a programmer to take another programmer's code and make use of it or make additions to it to enable them to do something slightly different. It means that when a programmer writes a piece of code for a particular problem that piece of code can be easily and reliably used again by anyone else. Obviously to be reusable the programmer has to write their code in a certain way so it is clear how it works and it must work without being too closely tied to any other code. Reusability is tremendously important in software development. Software used to be written on a custom basis, each problem had code specially written for it. Object Orientation makes it easier to reuse software by forcing the programmer to write code in a form that makes it easier to reuse. By making code reusable it gives developers a chance to make use of previous solutions thus saving them time and money. It is even possible to write pieces of code specifically for reuse and sell them.

2.5.2 Development

Many of you will not have worked on large projects which involve lots of people but you can imagine that things can get complicated. Object Orientation is designed for such an environment and allows code to be built in self-contained pieces that can be put together to form a finished product. It is intended to make the process of developing software easier and save money.

2.6   PROGRAMMING CONSIDERATIONS

As you write your program, bear in mind that:

- Other people will always read your code. People will sometimes need to alter your code or try to fix it if it does not perform the way they wish it to. You should write the code so that it is as easy as possible for readers to understand how it works.

- Your code may be reused in other code. You are usually the prime user of your old code so write it in such a way that it is easy to make further use of it.

- Your code will almost certainly contain mistakes, expect to see these mistakes and don't take them personally.

- Someone will use your program, so help them out by making your program as easy to use as possible.

Therefore when programming, the goal should not only be to produce working, correct code but also to:

- Keep a notebook containing designs, algorithms, mistakes and alternatives, that is, document the development process
- Document your code, that is, explain how it works
- Produce a user manual to assist people who want to use your program (screenshots, help facility, etc.).

SUMMARY

In this chapter, we looked at some of the styles used for writing programs. These styles have evolved in response to various problems and developments. The problem with the more recent styles is that the process of writing a program has become much more complicated with the result that novice programmers tend to ignore some of the features and rules intended to help them. This is an important point to remember, that programming using Object-Oriented techniques may seem awkward and wasteful at first but in terms of large scale programming efforts and reusability it is worth the effort.

KEYWORDS

▶ *Inheritance* – Inheritance is the ability of one piece of source code to make use of another, that is, it facilitates reuse, or recycling, of code.

▶ *Object Oriented* – A program which is written in such a way that data and the instructions which use that data are placed in the same area in the source code. The term also refers to a programming language which the user can use to write Object Oriented programs (i.e. an Object-Oriented language). Note than an Object-Oriented language can be used to write structured and unstructured programs.

▶ *Polymorphism* – A programming mechanism which allows the programmer to build flexibility into their program.

▶ *Reuse* – The idea that source code is not suitable for one specific problem only. Writing code which is amenable to reuse means writing clear code and using Object-Oriented methodology properly.

▶ *Structured* – A program which has organisation but where the data and the instructions which operate on it are kept in separate parts (this may lead to problems). The term also refers to a programming language which the user can use to write structured programs.

▶ *Unstructured* – A program which has no real organisation. The term also refers to a programming language which the user can use to write unstructured programs.

EXERCISES

1   Write the pseudocode for the methods contained in the employee, teller and manager classes.

2   What other methods should be included in the employee, teller and manager classes?

3   Figure out the procedures and data involved in a school library, how will these translate to an Object-Oriented design? Remember you cannot rely on people, everything must be written down.

4   Try to think of some of the things that would make code less amenable to being reused. (*Hint*: Think general purpose)

Solutions to exercises and interactive exercises can be obtained at:
http://www.palgrave.com/resources

Chapter

How to program

INTRODUCTION

This chapter introduces some of the basic items necessary to translate an algorithm into a program. The topics covered involve the grammar of a programming language and the way it is organised. Again it is important to remember that the computer does not have your contextual knowledge so while many of the items discussed here may seem trivial it is in your best interest to pay careful attention to them as later chapters will rely on them extensively. The two main areas deal with how information is stored in a computer program and how instructions are grouped and executed.

3.1 TELLING THE COMPUTER WHAT TO DO — STATEMENTS

We have seen in Chapter 2 that to get the computer to do what we want we need to express ourselves using a programming language. This looks a lot more intimidating than it actually is. Remember the function of a programming language is to act as a reduced form of a human language so it is easier for a program called a compiler to translate your wishes into the language of the computer. Therefore, you just have to learn how to think simply and clearly as the programming language must be less ambiguous than a spoken language.

Instructions in a programming language are written as statements. A statement is like a sentence, or a command. Like an English sentence, each statement has its own rules of formatting and its own permitted vocabulary.

The first thing to learn is how to finish a statement. The rule is that all statements in Java must be ended by a semicolon ';'. This has the same meaning as ending a sentence with a full stop, it tells the compiler that the author has finished his command. Full stops are not used in programming languages because they were difficult to see on early computer screens. Forgetting the semicolon is the equivalent of forgetting a full stop in a piece of text. In the same way as you get confused if there are no full stops to tell you where the sentence ends, the compiler also gets confused if it can't separate its sentences and it won't be able to understand your meaning. The compiler will therefore stop with an error message if you forget a semicolon. The important thing to remember about this is it isn't always clear what the matter is, often a forgotten semicolon is reported as a different error which confuses the beginner. The first rule is to always inspect your code before you finish to make sure all the semicolons are there. Too many semicolons can also cause problems in the same way that a sentence with more full-stops than are necessary is difficult to understand.

Remember that all statements can be translated into English and you should try to do this if you are confused about what they mean. For example,

```
int Amount=1; // Translation: Create a variable called 'Amount'
              // which will hold an integer value and place a
              // value of 1 in that variable


int Sum=Amount+1; // Translation: Create a variable called 'Sum'
                  // which will hold an integer value and place
                  // the result of the expression Amount+1 (which
                  // is 1+1) in that variable
```

3.1.1 Operators and operands

A statement can usually be broken up into an operator and an operand.

3.1.1.1 Operator

An operator is the part that relates what is to be done.

- Print
- Add
- Store

3.1.1.2 Operand

An operand is the part that operator works on.

- Number
- String
- List

For example: 'Shut the door' – operator is 'Shut', operand is 'the door'.

There are rules associated with each operator and its operands about where each can be placed. These rules are known as the syntax. You must remember these rules when they are introduced because if you supply the operator and the operand in the incorrect order the compiler will not be able to understand your meaning.

For example, if you use the operator + everybody knows that you put the two numbers to be added before and after the + sign (e.g. 3 + 4). You will not put the plus sign and then the two numbers as the meaning of this instruction is not clear (e.g. +3 4 could be interpreted as the number 34).

3.1.2 Groups of statements

A group of statements is usually known as a block of statements. Statements that will be repeated are usually gathered into a block. For example,

Input two numbers
Add the numbers
Print out the result

To save rewriting these statements again you put them in a block and tell the computer to keep on repeating the statements in a block until a certain event occurs. The start of a block is marked by a curly left bracket '{' and the end of a block by a curly right bracket '}'. For example, repeat the following statements until the user says stop.

```
{
Input two numbers
Add the numbers
Print out the result
}
```

Statements are also gathered into named groups called methods. Each method will have a unique name followed by the statements which carry out the purpose of the method (these are contained in a block).

| **3.2** | **YOUR FIRST PROGRAM** |

Now we shall look at writing your first program. The approach we are going to take to writing code differs to that taken in most textbooks. What I propose to do at the beginning is to write some of the code for you. This code deals with setting up a Java program and providing facilities for input and output. At the start this will only serve as a distraction, you will become familiar with the necessary code later in Chapter 8, Section 8.6 and begin to replace my code with your own. More details about how to use this code and the programs shown are contained in Appendix B.

So, the way you are going to write code at first is to make use of a class (or classes) that I have written to help you out. In other words, you are inheriting my work and adding your own work to it. You indicate that you are inheriting Java code by using the word `extends` at the start of your program. Anytime the compiler sees the word `extends`, it knows to go looking for the program named after the word `extends` and add that program to the one it is currently looking at.

In my class, I have written statements which set up the environment and then look for a method called `entryPoint` (remember to use the capital letter P and use lower case letters for the rest of the name). All you have to do in your program to get it working is to provide this method. You can then create the statements that you need to solve your problems. To output any information to the screen, you can call a method named `outputOnScreen` and supply to it the message you want to be output which you place between two sets of quotes (" = shift 2 on your keyboard).

The first program that we write will simply print out a message, however, it is important that you pay careful attention as this four line program can teach you valuable lessons which will serve you well later on. This program takes the form of an applet and so it should be loaded via a web page (see Appendix B).

First, a word about how I display programs, programs are written out in a box with a set of line numbers following each line of the program. These line numbers are there so that I can refer to specific line numbers in the text. They should **not** be typed in when you are writing the program.

```
// The purpose of this program is to output a message on the screen  1
// You must look at appendix B to get this program to work properly  2
                                                                     3
public class MyFirstApplet extends TrainingWheels               4
{                                                                    5
                                                                     6
public void entryPoint()                                             7
   {                                                                 8
   outputOnScreen("This is my first program");                      9
   } // End of entryPoint                                          10
                                                                    11
} // End of MyFirstApplet                                          12
```

The first two lines of the program are actually remarks, or comments, that are ignored by the compiler. Any sentence that is started with two / characters stuck together is ignored totally. If these two / appear in the middle of a sentence then the sentence from their appearance to the end of the line is ignored. Another way to denote a comment is to start a comment with the symbols /* and end it with the symbols */. Using these symbols you can write comments which span many lines.

Line 4 is the next line of interest, it states:

```
public class MyFirstApplet extends TrainingWheels
```

This means that I am creating a class, called MyFirstApplet, that inherits from a class called TrainingWheels. This TrainingWheels class is the one that saves you from work of typing out all the other instructions needed to manage input and output. We'll take a more detailed look at it in Chapter 8, Section 8.6. This class is being declared as public which means any object created from it is visible to any other element that wishes to use it. If you forget to make the class public, then when you run your program the following error may appear:

```
MyFirstApplet.class is not public or has no public constructor.
```

This error tells you that your program cannot be accessed.

Another important note about this line is that the name of your class must **always** match the name of your file. For example, you must store the above source code in the file MyFirstApplet.java. If you don't do this, the compiler will not process your source code and will give you an error. Say, for example, that you store your class MyFirstApplet in a file called Applet1.java. If you try to compile Applet1.java you will get the error message:

```
Applet1.java:3: Public class MyFirstApplet must be defined in a
file called Applet1.java.
```

This error indicates that you should either change the name of the class to match the file name or change the name of the file to match the class. Either way they must both match before the compiler will continue.

Line 5 marks the start of the program. The curly bracket ({ = shift [) always marks the start of a code block. For every { there must be a corresponding } which tells the compiler you have finished that code block. You therefore need to inspect your code when you have written it to make sure this is the case. You can make life easier for the inspection by aligning each opening { with a closing }. This means that if you follow the alignment of the bracket in line 5 you will see that it matches up to the bracket on line 12, that is, they are both pushed in (or indented) the same amount. It is now easy to see if your brackets are paired correctly if each opening { can be easily visibly matched with a closing }. Pairing brackets is very important, a missing or misplaced bracket can cause a lot of problems both for the compiler and any person reading the program. Another example would be the brackets on lines 8 and 10, they are also paired and can be found in line with each other. One other hint is to type a closing } immediately after you type an opening {. You can then move the cursor back between the brackets with your cursor keys and type in the relevant code block. Following this hint means you don't have to remember to close the block after you have written the code.

The final hint for bracketing is to put a comment after each closing } which details what the } is closing. For example, in lines 10 and 12, I put in a comment detailing the name of the block of code that the bracket is ending. Like the other hints, this is not an essential part of coding but it does make life easier in the long run.

Line 7 shows how a method is written. A method is a way of grouping a related set of instructions. In this case the method holds all the instructions that we want our program to execute. The method we declare, called `entryPoint` (don't forget to get the capitals right) is the one which is started when this program starts (is executed), that is, it acts as the entry point or entrance for the computer.

Line 9 is the only instruction in the method and it instructs the system to look for another method called `outputOnScreen`. This method is found in the class `TrainingWheels` that I have supplied to you so you don't see it in the above program. The instruction sends a message to that method which prints the message out on the screen. The message is a string, a collection of characters, and is placed between two double quotes (") so it is recognised as a string. You can change the string (This is my first program) to read anything you want as the compiler does not try to understand what is between the ".

Line 10 marks the end of the method `entryPoint`. Any further instruction you want to write must be put into a new method. If you want this method to execute then you must call it by name from the method `entryPoint` (more on this is discussed later in this chapter).

Line 12 marks the end of the class `MyFirstApplet`.

An example of a HTML file which will cause this applet to execute is shown below:

```
<applet code = MyFirstApplet.class height = 250 width = 350>      1
</applet>                                                         2
                                                                  3
```

When the program is executed (via the HTML file which contains instructions to load it into the browser) it looks something like the screenshot shown in Figure 3.1 in p. 44.

3.2.1 Reading a program

Programs (source code) always have certain rules associated with them. These rules will help you when you are trying to read and understand the source code. The rules are:

1 Every program must have a starting or entry point – This is where the computer goes to when it starts to execute your program. It's the programming equivalent of a front door. Every programming language has its various starting points defined. These starting points are usually blocks of code with particular names, such as `main`, `init` and `start`, and when reading the code, if you search for these method names you will find your starting point for following the code. The starting point we will be using for the next few chapters is the method called `entryPoint`.

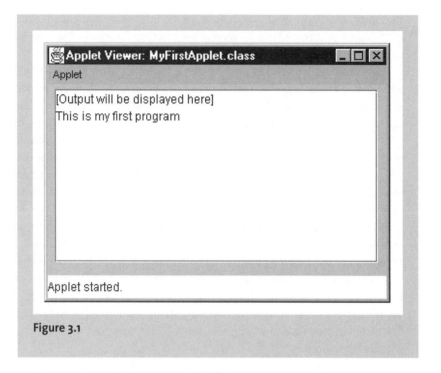

Figure 3.1

2   Instructions usually execute one after the other, that is, in sequence – Once you have established your starting point you can follow what instructions are executed by moving from one line to another. Programming languages allow the programmer to write instructions which execute a different line from that next on the screen, this is known as changing the flow of control of the program. Unless you see one of these instructions, you can assume that the next line executed is the line following the current one. The next instruction may cause the program to jump to a different part of the page, when this happens remember when the instructions at the location it jumps to run out it will come back to the point that it left off (i.e. it will return to the next line after the line which caused it to jump to a different point).

3   Instructions are executed until the program stops – Your instructions will always be executed by the computer until it runs out of instructions or it is told to wait on a particular event (such as the user pressing a button).

3.2.2 Your first errors

Be careful when typing in the program otherwise you will get your first errors before you get your first program executing. The things to be especially careful of are:

- *Brackets* – does every { have a matching }? The error 'missing {' appears if you have one more } than you have { (and vice versa).

- *Spelling* – are all the words (names of methods, names of classes) spelled correctly? The error 'unknown identifier' appears if the compiler can't understand you.

- *Capital letters* – are all the statements in their correct case? Again the error 'unknown identifier' appears because a mistake in capitalisation is equivalent to a mistake in spelling.

3.3 HOW INFORMATION IS STORED

Before we continue to look at how to write in a programming language, we should take a look at how the computer stores information. This has no direct relevance to how we program since it's not really our business how the computer does things, but it is useful to know.

As well as the CPU every computer has areas which it uses to store information. This information can be kept in two places, the primary memory which the computer can access instantly or the secondary memory which takes a little more time to access (most secondary memories are disk drives). In both the primary and secondary memories information is kept in little boxes all of the same size. If you want to keep more information than a single box can accommodate then your information is split into box sized pieces and stored in several boxes. All the information you need to do your current work is held in the primary memory. For example, when you open up a web browser it is executing instructions stored in the primary memory, when that web browser downloads a page that page is stored in primary memory. Primary memory therefore contains all the programs that you are using and each programs instructions and data. How does it tell the difference between them? That's not its job, it's the job of the operating system to keep track of what is where.

To keep track of where the information that you need is going every box has a number, called an address. This works in the same way as your home address, it is unique and enables the computer to locate whatever it wants, provided it has the correct address.

Everything you have on your computer is stored in these boxes, also called memory locations, that is, the information on your screen, the programs you have running, and the operating system that manages the programs and the data that your programs use.

It is the operating system that is responsible for keeping track of memory. If you need memory (e.g. if you want to execute a program) the operating system checks its list of locations and finds free boxes to put your program in.

So, if there are 10 000 boxes available in primary memory the operating system must manage them. If you look at an example of a particular computer's primary memory you get a breakdown of the box usage as follows:

Operating System (yes it needs memory too as it is a program itself)	Boxes 100–2000
Browser	Boxes 2500–3600
Wordprocessor	Boxes 4000–6000

Note that the above explanation is a gross simplification of what happens but will suffice for the moment.

3.4 VARIABLES

Note that the following explanations are simplifications of what occurs and are intended to start you off as opposed to provide a definitive account of storage management.

We have seen that to write a program we need to deal with data and the instructions that operate on that data. We therefore write our solution in such a way that it is easy to translate it into a programming language.

For example, say the problem was 'compute the total sales for this month'.

Data:
  Sales transactions, total
Instructions:
  Set aside a piece of paper to record the total (this will be blank at the start)
    Select Sales transaction item
    Add that Sales transaction to total
    Repeat the above two instructions until no more Sales transactions
  Print out total.

The way the solution is expressed above is close to a programming language but we're not quite there yet. One of the most important aspects of a programming language is how we store data. As we have seen in Chapter 1, a record was kept of certain information (temperature of the oven, etc.). So, as to avoid confusion we give each piece of information that we want to keep its own unique name (which we called a variable name). Therefore when the recipe refers to 'oven temperature' we know exactly what value it's talking about. In the example above we created a variable called total to hold the total sales transactions for the month.

This idea of variable names is used by the programming language as well with one extra dimension, you must introduce (or declare) a variable before you use it and when you are introducing a variable you must indicate what information the variable will be storing.

This must be done because whereas the type of data (known in programming terms as a data type) held in a variable is usually clear to us from the name of the variable it is not clear to the computer because it does not have our knowledge. For instance, we know that 'name' means a collection of characters and 'price' is a set of numbers. But computers don't have such contextual information. They don't understand the meaning of 'name' and 'price' so you have to explain to them that 'name' means a collection of characters and 'price' means a collection of numbers.

3.4.1 Data types

All programming languages have the types of data that they will store built into them. These are known as fundamental, or primitive, data types.

These data types are usually quite simple and while they may not be able to hold all the information that we want straight off they can be used to build up more complicated data types.

With a fundamental data type you do not need to explain to the programming language what its composition will be as it has been defined by the people who wrote the programming language.

Some of the main data types we use are:

- *Integer* – any whole number (i.e. no fractions/decimal places). The value of the number can be between $-2\,147\,483\,648$ and $2\,147\,483\,647$. The word used by the programming language to indicate an integer data type is int.

- *Character* – a single letter of the alphabet (upper (A) or lower case (a)) or a number or symbol (*!£$, etc.). Characters are usually represented using single quotes in case they are mistaken by the compiler as variable names. The word used by the programming language to indicate a character is char. Example: 'a', '%', '2'. Remember a character is a single letter, number or symbol, 'Hi there' is not a character.

- *Boolean* – the value true or false. Boolean values are often used to represent the results of a test, for example, 'is the number less than 5?', Yes: then answer is true, No: then the answer is false. The word used by the programming language to indicate a boolean data type is boolean.

- *Floating point* – a number which can contain a fraction, for example, 12.412. The word used by the programming language to indicate that a variable will hold a number which can contain fractions is double.

A String (a collection of characters) is not a simple data type and will be examined later in Section 3.7.

3.4.2 Declaring a variable

As we have seen a variable is a piece of data of a specific data type which can change, for example, age, address.

The amount of information that can be stored in each variable depends on the data type that the variable belongs to. For example, char can only store a single character. If you try and store more in a variable than it can accommodate, then the 'spare' information will be discarded or the compiler will refuse to accept such a statement.

Before you make use of a variable, you must tell the compiler that you are going to use this variable in your program to hold a particular type of value. This notification usually occurs near the start of the program and is called a 'declaration'. By declaring a variable you are enabling the compiler to recognise the variable when it sees it later (like introducing a character in a novel). Declaring a variable is your way of explaining the context of the variable to the compiler so that you and the compiler now share a common understanding which you can build on. If you don't declare or introduce a variable and the compiler sees you referring to it in your program, it will not understand what the variable represents, that is, it has no context, and so the compiler will output an error message. In essence, you are creating a new word that both you and the compiler (and therefore the computer that solves your problem) will understand.

Do not forget that not only do you tell the compiler what you intend to call the variable but also what type of information you expect to put in it (this description of what the variable will hold is called the variable type).

So, the declaration of a variable will have the following syntax (remember the syntax is the rule for the ordering of your instruction):

```
TypeOfDataHeld variableName;
```

where TypeOfDataHeld can be any valid data type (e.g. `int`, `char`, `boolean`) and the variable name can be any valid name (we will look at all the rules for variable names later in Section 3.4.4).

Example of creating a variable which will hold a value of type integer:

```
int number;
```

In the example above, we have introduced the name 'number' to the compiler as a variable which will hold an integer value.

Example of creating a variable which will hold a value of type character:

```
char myInitial;
```

Example of creating a variable which will hold a value of type boolean:

```
boolean todayIsFine;
```

Multiple variable names can be declared in the same line if necessary but this is not recommended as you should try to follow each variable declaration with a comment to describe its purpose and having multiple names on the same line can cause confusion. Example of a multiple variable declaration:

```
int firstNumber,total,sum;
```

3.4.3 Naming a variable

Each variable should be given a name which makes its purpose clear: for example, totalSum, priceOfItem. This makes it easier for you to remember the name of the variable when you want to use it and the closer your program is to English the easier it is for people to read it.

Variable names are called identifiers (identifier is the term used to refer to any name made up by the author of a program).

For example, t13 or jk aren't good identifiers because it is unclear what they are used for. Remember identifiers are primarily for you and your fellow programmers' benefit, the compiler or computer does not care what the variables are called provided the rules given below are followed. Using suitable identifiers helps enormously when trying to understand a program.

3.4.4 Rules for variable names (identifiers)

You must follow certain rules when creating identifiers:

- Identifiers (names) should be unique, that is, nothing else can have the same name.
- Identifiers should begin with a letter but can contain digits (e.g. ResultsForMonth1, ResultsForMonth2).
- Names can contain the character '_' to separate words. Note this character is an underscore (shift-minus on most keyboards) not a minus sign (–) as the minus sign is reserved by the compiler for representing subtraction.
- Identifiers should not correspond to 'reserved words', for example, int. Reserved words are the programming languages vocabulary. (The English equivalent would be deciding you (personally) wanted to refer to a chair as a table, it results in confusion).
- Variables must be declared before they are used. We will see in Section 3.4.6, how to use a variable but we should remember that we cannot use a variable without declaring or creating it.

3.4.5 Coding convention

A convention is not a rule in that failure to follow it will not cause problems in compiling and executing a program. A convention is rather a set of guidelines for programmers to follow so that programs are written consistently and therefore there is less possibility of confusion. The convention for Java programs can be obtained at Suns Java site (http://www.javasoft.com) and will be followed in this book. The part of the convention that applies to variables is that variable names should begin with a lower case letter. The two other parts of the convention that should be mentioned are that all class names should begin with a capital letter and all method names should begin with a lower case letter. Another convention that is often followed is to include the type of a variable along with the name. For example,

```
double doubleInterestRate; // For a variable called interestRate
int capital_int; // For a variable called capital
```

Some programmers find this convention useful as it means variables are easier to understand, others feel it overcomplicates a program. This particular convention will not be used in this book.

3.4.6 Putting a value into a variable

Variables are useless unless we can use them. By using a variable we mean that we can put a value into a variable and/or extract the value contained within the variable. For example, we saw how to create an integer variable:

```
int number;
```

To put a value into the integer variable you have created, simply type the following (don't forget to put in a semicolon to end the statement):

```
number = 5;
```

This is known as an assignment, you are 'assigning' or placing a value in a variable. The above assignment statement will place the value 5 inside the box which is being used to store a variable referred to as `number`.

You can perform a declaration and an assignment all in one line if you wish. For example,

```
int startingValue = 7;
```

will create a variable called `startingValue` and put the value of 7 in it.

Let's do the same for a character, first we declare the variable:

```
char myInitial;
```

To put a value into the character variable you have created, type the following (don't forget the single quotation marks '):

```
myInitial = 'c';
```

And for a boolean variable again you declare it first:

```
boolean todayIsFine;
```

And then place either the value true or false (no other value can be placed in a boolean variable). Don't forget that you must use lowercase letters to represent either of the allowed boolean values.

```
todayIsFine = false;
```

You can extract the contents of the variable by simply typing its name, for example, `myInitial`. A variable name on its own does not do much, but if it is used in the context of a statement that can make use of the contents of the variable, then something can happen. For example, if you type:

```
outputOnScreen(myInitial);
```

the contents of the variable `myInitial` will be printed out on the screen.

In the above examples, we created variables and then placed values in them. Placing a value into a variable once it has been created is called 'initialisation' and should be done before the variable is used.

Let's write a program to create variables and put something in them. In lines 8, 17 and 25, three variables which will hold different types of values are declared. Values must be placed in these variables before they can be used. The use of the variables in this example is to obtain their contents and print the contents of the variable onto the screen.

```
// The purpose of this program is to declare a number          1
// of variables, put values into them and output them          2
                                                               3
public class AppletShowVariables extends TrainingWheels        4
{                                                              5
public void entryPoint()                                      6
   {                                                           7
   int number;    // Declare the variable called Number as     8
                  // an integer                                9
   number = 5; // Place the value 5 inside this variable       10
                                                               11
   outputOnScreen("The value for Number after = is");          12
   outputOnScreen(number); // Output the contents of the       13
                           // variable 'Number'                14
                                                               15
   // Looking at a character variable                          16
   char myInitial; // Declare the variable called MyInitial    17
                   // as a character                           18
   myInitial='c'; // Place the value 'c' inside the variable   19
                                                               20
   outputOnScreen("The value for MyInitial after = is");       21
   outputOnScreen(myInitial); // Output the contents of        22
                              // the variable 'MyInitial'       23
                                                               24
   boolean todayIsFine; // Declare the variable called         25
                        // TodayIsFine as a boolean            26
   todayIsFine = false; // Place the value false               27
                        //inside the variable                  28
                                                               29
                                                               30
   outputOnScreen("The value for TodayIsFine after = is");     31
   outputOnScreen(todayIsFine);   // Output whats              32
                                  // in the variable           33
                                  // 'TodayIsFine'             34
                                                               35
   } // End of entryPoint                                      36
                                                               37
} // End of AppletShowVariables                                38
```

The above program sets up the variables which we have discussed, assigns values to them and then prints their contents out as shown in Figure 3.2 in p. 52.

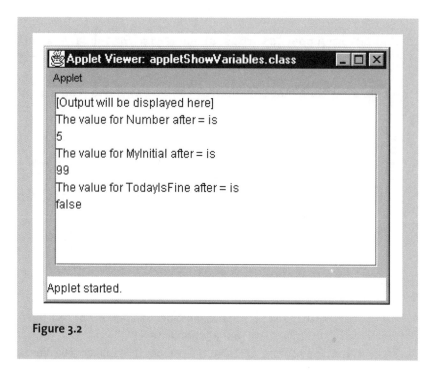

Figure 3.2

3.4.6.1 Possible error situations

Let's look at the two possible error situations that can arise when dealing with variables. They are:

1 **The variable is used before it is declared**

The first type of error is often made, even by experienced programmers. It means that a particular variable is used but the programmer has forgotten to declare it. Type in the following program to see an example.

```
// The purpose of this applet is to show that not        1
// declaring a variable will cause an error              2
// message to be generated when you compile it           3
                                                         4
public class AppletShowErrorNoDeclaration extends        5
TrainingWheels
{                                                        6
                                                         7
public void entryPoint()                                 8
```

```
{                                                                    9
number = 5;                                                         10
outputOnScreen("The value for Number after = is ");                11
outputOnScreen(number);    // Output the contents of the           12
                           // variable 'Number'                     13
                                                                    14
} // End of entryPoint                                             15
                                                                    16
} // End of AppletShowErrorNoDeclaration                            17
```

As you can see in the above program, we try and put the value of 5 into an identifier called number in line 10 but we never introduce the compiler to the variable named number, therefore the compiler complains with the message:

```
Undefined variable: number
```

2 **The variable is used before it is initialised**

Let's look at what happens if we try and use the variable before we put a value into it, that is, before it is initialised. Type in the following program to see the relevant error message.

```
// The purpose of this applet is to show that not putting          1
// a value into a variable will cause an error message             2
// to be generated when you compile it                             3
                                                                    4
public class AppletShowErrorNoValue extends TrainingWheels         5
{                                                                   6
                                                                    7
public void entryPoint()                                           8
   {                                                                9
   int number;     // Declare the variable called Number          10
                   // as an integer                                11
                                                                   12
   outputOnScreen("The value for Number is ");                    13
   outputOnScreen(number); // Output the contents of the          14
                           // variable 'Number'                    15
                                                                   16
   number = 5;                                                     17
   outputOnScreen("The value for Number after = is ");            18
   outputOnScreen(number);    // Output the contents of the       19
                              // variable 'Number'                 20
```

```
                                                                        21
        } // End of entryPoint                                          22
                                                                        23
    } // End of AppletShowErrorNoValue                                  24
```

The problem is in line 14, there we try to output the value of number after we declare the variable called number but at this point in the program there is no value in the variable called number to output and the compiler will spit out the following error (or an equivalent):

`Variable number may not have been initialised.`

To fix the program you need to remove line 14.

3.4.7 How are variables stored by the computer?

Let's look at how the computer stores variables and their values. This will be important later on as we look at more complicated types of variables such as objects.

By declaring the variable you are asking the computer to reserve a storage location for that variable under the name you have given it, it is the same as getting a locker number and writing your name on it or obtaining a phone number and having your name recorded as being associated with that number.

The amount of storage (or boxes) it keeps for the variable depends on the size of the variable you want to keep. For example, when we say `int vat`, we are asking for 32 bits of storage to be associated with `vat`. A bit is a binary digit, binary digits are the number system of the computer and consist of numbers expressed using just two digits 1 or 0.

Note that one useful aspect of Java is that data types are exactly the same no matter what computer you use. If you use a language other than Java, there could be 16, 32 or 64 bits used to store an integer depending on the computer.

A computer keeps many thousands of boxes, each box has its own address so the computer can find it if it needs it, just like a hotel having thousands of rooms with a naming system for the rooms. The computer will associate a location in memory with your variable's name and will stop anyone else using that location, just like a hotel manager will associate a person with a room number and not rent anyone else that room.

If your variable needs more than one location, then the computer will allocate more locations after the initial location, like a hotel manager will give you a room and then give the rooms next door to the rest of your group. Anytime you refer to a name the computer will lookup the address it has given to the name and go to that address. In the same way, if you go into a hotel and ask for 'Joan Smith', the manager will check their register for the name and give you the corresponding room number which you can access to talk to Joan Smith.

EXAMPLE Say we declared a variable called `vat`. The operating system associates a location with the variable called `vat`. This location is, for example, address 0232. (This location will change every time the program is run as the operating system allocates space as it is asked for it so no specific area is reserved for your program or its parts.)

The number of boxes allocated should be enough to hold a value of ±2 147 483 647 (which is 32 bits) as that is the amount of space which an integer can occupy. If you try and put more than a box can hold into a variable some of the number will 'fall out' and the actual value stored will be changed.

When the statement `int vat;` is executed, the memory looks as follows:

0200	
0232	← 32 bits → ← `vat`
0264	

As far as the computer is concerned, anytime you refer to the word `vat` it takes this to mean location 0232. The identifier `vat` is only for the benefit of the programmer as the computer system works entirely in numeric addresses.

Any other variables you declare have space reserved for them too but they don't have to be in the same place in memory.

When the statements `int costPrice;` and `int itemPrice;` are executed, the memory looks as follows:

0200		
0232		←`vat`
0264		←`itemPrice`
0296		
0328		←`costPrice`
0360		

where `itemPrice` is stored at location 264 and `costPrice` at location 328.

When you create integer variables, they are either assigned a default value of 0 or they are marked as being uninitialised. This means that the contents of the memory location referred to by the variable name is 0 or 'nothing'. The safest thing to do is to assume that all variables contain 'nothing' when they are declared first and you should initialise every variable before you use it. This policy may be inconvenient but is almost guaranteed to prevent syntax errors and algorithmic errors.

0200		
0232	0/Uninitialised	←vat
0264	0/Uninitialised	←itemPrice
0296		
0328	0/Uninitialised	←costPrice
0360		

You can put values into these locations, that is, you assign a value to variable costPrice=4;. This assignment statement tells the computer to put the value 4 into the location that is associated with the name costPrice. What the computer will eventually translate this into is 'Put the value 4 into location 0328'. Likewise the statement vat=25; is taken to mean 'Put the value 25 in the location 0232' which corresponds to the name vat.

When you assign values to variable names the compiler will check whether you are assigning values of the correct type, for example, you are putting an integer into a box reserved to hold an integer. If you are doing something which goes against the rules of the language, the compiler will not translate your program. For example, if you say vat=21.43; it is incorrect as the location used to hold the information for the variable called vat will only accommodate an integer and integers do not have fractions. If you wish to store the value 21.43, then you should declare a variable capable of holding it, for example,

```
double vatValue;
vatValue = 21.43;
```

To give you an analogy of the above, recall the pie making program seen in Chapter 1 and two of the variables involved, namely temperature of oven and number of apples. Can you put in the value for temperature of oven into the variable number of apples? No, each variable stands for a totally different aspect of the problem and it makes no sense to do this. An error message of the form Incompatible type for= will be displayed by the compiler to inform you of your mistake if you try and compile a program with this statement. The error indicates that you are not following the rules and so you must rewrite the assignment so that it assigns an integer value to the variable location, for example, vat = 21;

Our primary memory locations now look like this:

0200		
0232	25	←vat
0264	0	←itemPrice
0296		
0328	4	←costPrice
0360		

Programming languages have been originally written to perform basic arithmetic so naturally a programming language can do mathematical operations. There are a few differences to the way we usually work though. The main ones are with the symbols. The symbols + and − are the same but the multiplication sign × is too like the letter x so to avoid confusion multiplication is represented by an asterix * (shift-8 on your keyboard). Division (÷) could be confused with subtraction (−) on a fuzzy screen so it was replaced by the symbol / (don't get it mixed up with the \ symbol which means something different). So, our mathematical table is as follows:

Operation	Java symbol	Example
Addition	+	4 + 5
Subtraction	−	6 − 2
Multiplication	*	3 * 9
Division	/	4 / 2

```
// The following program will output the results of some      1
// calculations                                                2
                                                               3
public class AppletArithmeticExample extends TrainingWheels    4
{                                                              5
                                                               6
public void entryPoint()                                       7
    {                                                          8
    outputOnScreen(4 + 5); // Addition                         9
    outputOnScreen(6 − 2); // Subtraction                     10
    outputOnScreen(3 * 9); // Multiplication                  11
    outputOnScreen(4 / 2); // Division                        12
    } // End of entryPoint                                    13
                                                              14
} // End of AppletArithmeticExample                           15
```

When an expression is finished (e.g. when 4 has been added to 5 in the expression 4 + 5), it is said to give a result or to have 'evaluated'. So when the expression 4 + 5 is evaluated the result is 9. It is the evaluated expressions that are used by the program and the evaluations will effectively replace the original statements, for example, in the above program the four expressions are evaluated and replaced so what the computer executes is:

```
outputOnScreen(9);  // Addition
outputOnScreen(4);  // Subtraction
outputOnScreen(27); // Multiplication
outputOnScreen(2);  // Division
```

You can also combine expressions, however if you are doing so you should enclose the expressions in brackets in the order you want them evaluated. The expression which has the most brackets around it (known as the deepest expression) is evaluated first. For example, if you want to subtract 2 from 4 and multiply the result of this by the result of 3 subtracted from 6, then your expression will be: $(4-2) * (6-3)$. This prevents confusion, not on the computer's part as it knows how to do simple maths. It's just that if you give the expression $4-2 * 6-3$, the computer may not come up with the answer you expect because it has a particular set of rules about what order to compute expressions. This set of rules is called precedence. We will not be looking at the rules of precedence as if you use your brackets correctly they are not really needed.

Try it out for yourself:

```
// The following example will show that two expressions,      1
// which may look the same will produce different             2
// results since the order in which their parts are           3
// evaluated is different due to the use of brackets          4
                                                              5
public class AppletBracketsExample extends TrainingWheels     6
{                                                             7
                                                              8
public void entryPoint()                                      9
  {                                                          10
  outputOnScreen(4 - 2 * 6 - 3); // The answer to this is -11  11
  outputOnScreen((4-2) * (6-3)); // The answer to this is 6   12
  } // End of entryPoint                                      13
                                                              14
} // End of AppletBracketsExample                             15
```

EXAMPLE Let's use the variables we have declared in the last example in a calculation. Don't forget to bracket the expressions so we're sure of the order that the calculation is made in (it is evaluated from the innermost, or deepest, bracket to the outermost). The expression is:

```
itemPrice = costPrice + ((costPrice * vat) / 100);
```

This is saying that the contents of `itemPrice` should be set to the result of the contents of `costPrice` plus (the contents of `costPrice` multiplied by the contents of `vat` divided by 100).

How does the computer do the calculation?

Step 1: First it replaces the variable names by the values at their location. So our expression now becomes:

`itemPrice = 4 + ( ( 4 * 25 ) / 100 )`

Step 2: Then it does the calculation that is deepest in brackets first (`4*25`) and replaces it by its result (`100`). So now we have:

`itemPrice = 4 + ( ( 100 ) / 100 )`

Step 3: Then the next calculation in brackets is executed (`( 100 ) / 100`) and is replaced by its result (`1`). So now we have:

`itemPrice = 4 + ( 1 )`

Step 4: The final calculation is now done giving us:

`itemPrice = 5`

Step 5: Finally the result of the expression (5) is put in the variable referenced

`( itemPrice )`

The memory now looks like this:

0200		
0232	25	←vat
0264	5	←itemPrice
0296		
0328	4	←costPrice
0360		

Let's look at the above in program form.

```
// This applet performs a basic calculation to show the      1
// order in which an expression is evaluated                  2
                                                              3
public class AppletComputeVat extends TrainingWheels          4
{                                                             5
```

```
                                                              6
    public void entryPoint()                                  7
        {                                                     8
        int itemPrice;                                        9
        int costPrice;                                        10
        int vat;                                              11
                                                              12
        vat = 25;                                             13
        costPrice = 4;                                        14
                                                              15
        itemPrice = costPrice + ((costPrice * vat)/100);      16
                                                              17
        outputOnScreen("The price is");                       18
        outputOnScreen(itemPrice);                            19
        } // End of entryPoint                                20
                                                              21
    } // End of AppletComputeVat                              22
```

Will this program generate an error if we use `itemPrice` before we have assigned a value to it (line 16)? No, we are actually assigning the result of the expression to the variable `itemPrice` so that when we refer it in line 19 it contains a value.

3.5.1 Increment and decrement

Two operations that we will perform quite frequently as we progress are incrementing (or increasing) a value by 1 and decrementing (or decreasing) by 1. You have enough knowledge to represent this in expression form, that is:

To increment a variable use the expression:

variableName = variableName + 1;

To decrement a variable use the expression:

variableName = variableName − 1;

Java, however, provides you with a shortcut for incrementing and decrementing. This short cut involves using two plus symbols to represent incrementing and two minus symbols to represent decrementing.

To increment a value by 1 (equivalent to variableName=variableName+1) use a statement of the form:

variableName++;

To decrement a value by 1 (equivalent to variableName=variableName−1) use a statement of the form:

variableName−−;

There is no need to assign the result of the above increment, the compiler will automatically put that in for you, all you have to do if you want to increment or decrement is to use the variable name and put ++ or −− after it.

If you use a variable as you are incrementing it the value contained in the variable will be the current value and not the incremented value, for example, if the statements:

```
int variable=4;
outputOnScreen(variable++); // output would be 4
outputOnScreen(variable); // output would be 5
```

are executed the value for the first use of the variable will be the 4 and the value for the second use will be 5. The rule is that if the ++ or −− follows a variable then the variables value will only change for the following statements.

If you want the value to change straight away then put the ++ or −− in front of the variable you want to change. For example,

```
int variable=4;
outputOnScreen(++variable); // output would be 5
outputOnScreen(variable); // output would be 5
```

Variable++ and Variable−− are commonly known as post-increment and post-decrement because they change the variables value after (post) the statement. −−Variable and ++Variable are known as pre-increment and pre-decrement.

3.5.2 Assignment

You can also reduce the typing needed to perform basic mathematical operations. The basic idea is that if you have a statement of the form:

variableName = variableName + value;

You can replace it by the following:

variableName += value;

One way to remember this is to note that the expression above evaluates to variableName+value which is then placed in the variableName (i.e. by visualising the statement with the = removed you get the actual expression being carried out).

The symbols in Table 3.1 can replace typing in the whole statement for the other mathematical operators.

Table 3.1

Symbol	Example	Which is equivalent to

+=	```int result;```
	```result = 3;```
	```result += 5; // Value of result```
	```// is now 8```
		```int result;```
		```result = 3;```
		```result = result + 5;```

-=	```int result;```
	```result = 3;```
	```result -= 5; // Value of result```
	```// is now -2;```
		```int result;```
		```result = 3;```
		```result = result - 5;```

/=	```int result;```
	```result = 6;```
	```result /= 3; // Value of result```
	```// is now 2```
		```int result;```
		```result = 6;```
		```result = result / 3;```

*=	```int result;```
	```result = 3;```
	```result *= 3; // Value of result```
	```// is now 9```
		```int result;```
		```result = 3;```
		```result = result * 3;```

3.5.3 Casting

What happens if you have a situation where an arithmetic operation results in a value which cannot be contained in the variable it is being assigned to?

For example, the statements

```
int divisionResult;
divisionResult = 5/2;
```

indicate that the evaluation of 5/2 should be placed in an integer variable. But the result of 5/2 is 2.5 which is not an integer. Will this result in an error? No, what will happen is that the integer part of the result will be placed into the integer variable and the floating point part (.5), which cannot be accommodated, is thrown away. Therefore the two statements above will result in the value 2 being placed in the variable divisionResult.

The process by which one type of value is converted to another is known as a 'cast' or 'type conversion'. Java will automatically cast from related types if it can accommodate the result. You can explicitly ask for a cast by placing the type that you want the cast to be made to in brackets before the variable or expression which you want converted. For example,

```
double pi = 3.14;
int piInt = (int)pi;
```

3.6 METHODS

As we have discussed before, you break up problems into smaller parts to solve them. How do we represent these smaller parts, how do we cause them to execute? Well, we give each part a unique name and when we want to execute that part we give its name. This causes the computer to look for the instructions associated with the name mentioned and execute them.

We work with a very similar system in everyday life, imagine you want to buy something from a company, you ring them up and ask for a 'salesperson'. The salesperson will talk to you about the product and if you have any questions will call an 'expert'. When you want to buy the product the salesperson calls an 'accountant'. You have referred to different people and their associated functions by name. You have called the methods 'salesperson', 'technician' and 'accountant' and each of these methods have done their specific task and finished. Some of these methods will give you information, some will need information and some will need information and give you information. In the same way as people have different titles in a company, in a program methods are statements grouped under a relevant title or name. This name (identifier) should be chosen by the user to be easy to understand (e.g. you know what someone does if they are called an accountant).

The terminology in our program is similar to that used in ordinary life. If you want to carry out the instructions in a method, you 'call' it, just like if you want someone to do some work for you, then you 'call' them. If a method gives you back information, we say it 'returns' information. So for example, if I call the 'accountant' to tell me the current tax rate the accountant will 'return' the current rate to me. Information passed to the method is called a 'parameter'. For example, different goods have different tax rates so to give the accountant the information they need to give me the vat rate. I will supply a 'parameter' describing the class of goods (book, car, food, etc.) when I call the accountant. The accountant will take this information, use it and return the result to me.

For example, if we want to write a program that will make a phone call we write out the instructions we use when making the call. We will then start this set of instructions with the phone number that we want to call phone(903339);. This instruction means with we are calling the phone method with a parameter value of 903339. The method that carries out our phone call instructions is as follows:

```
phone(int thePhoneNumber)
{
Find a free phone;
    {
    Lift receiver;
    Dial thePhoneNumber;
    If you hear engaged tone then put receiver down;
    }Repeat the above block until there is no engaged tone;

Talk;
Put receiver down;
}
```

The above algorithm assumes that you have defined instructions like `Lift receiver` somewhere else either in the program or the person performing the program knows what these instructions mean.

This is a simplified method, if you want it to work for every type of phone you have to do other things like check for payment method, wait for user to insert coins or phone card, and so on.

You 'call', or start, the method and give it the phone number. This process of giving the method a value is called passing a value. The value is known as a parameter. This gets put into a variable called `thePhoneNumber` which is used throughout the method.

So, to summarise what we have learned is that when declaring a method you give the following:

- *The return data type* – what form of data the method will be sending back (use the word 'void' if no information is returned, void means empty or nothing in this context). A method can only return one value but it can be of any type. Any information returned can be used later on in a calculation, stored, output, and so on.

- *The name of the method* – the rules for the name are the same as the rules for naming variables.

- *Declarations for the parameters* – the method will need to store the parameters somewhere so you supply the declarations for the variables when writing the declaration for the method. A method can be declared to take no parameter or several and they do not all have to be the same type.

Example of method declarations:

```
void phone(int areaCode,int thePhoneNumber)
   {.....}

int accountant (String goodsDescription)
   {.....
   return integerValue;
   }
```

Don't forget that each method is a separate block of code and so must have a { marking its start and a } marking its end.

Example of calls to these methods is:

```
phone(021,903339);

int vatRate = accountant("Book");// Take the value returned from
                                 // the accountant method and put
                                 // it in the variable vatRate
```

Methods declarations can begin with the word public or private (the exact word depends on how you wish your program to work). You usually declare all methods as public unless there is a convincing reason (more in Chapter 4, Section 4.4).

3.6.1 Example: using a method to compute vat

EXAMPLE The old instruction we used to compute the value of itemPrice was:

itemPrice = costPrice + ((costPrice * vat) / 100);

The new instruction (which calls a method which contains the original instruction) is:

itemPrice = computeItemPrice(costPrice);

The method computeItemPrice will take an integer value. It places this integer value in a variable called receivedCostPrice. It then uses this variable to calculate what value should be placed in the variable result. At the end of the method the instruction return result is carried out. This tells the system to finish the method and send back the value contained in the variable result. No instructions following a return statement are executed. Once a return statement is encountered, no matter where in the method it is, the method will immediately stop and return the value to the point of the program from where the method was called.

```
public int computItemPrice(int receivedCostPrice)
    {
    int vat = 25; // You can declare a variable and give it a value
               // all in the one line
    int result;

    result = receivedCostPrice + ((receivedCostPrice * vat) / 100);

    return result; //Send back the result
    }
```

to work out the total 1
2
3
xtends TrainingWheels 4
5
6
7
8
9
10
11
12
rice); 13

```
                                                                      14
        outputOnScreen("The price is");                              15
        outputOnScreen(itemPrice);                                   16
        } // End of entryPoint                                       17
                                                                      18
    public int computeItemPrice(int receivedCostPrice)               19
        {                                                            20
        int vat = 25; // You can declare a variable and give          21
                  // it a value all in the one line                  22
        int result;                                                  23
                                                                      24
        result = receivedCostPrice + ((receivedCostPrice * vat)/100); 25
                                                                      26
        return result; //Send back the result                       27
        } // End of computeItemPrice                                 28
                                                                      29
    } // End of AppletMethodComputeVat                               30
```

EXERCISE

1 Try leaving out the return statement in line 27 and see what the compiler says.

2 Try putting some statements after return and see if they are executed.

   For instance put the statement `outputOnScreen("After return");` .

You can use statements like exercise 2 to track your program, this is quite useful when it comes to following the progress (or otherwise) of your program. For example, you can have an output statement every few lines, each one of which outputs a different message. You can then deduce from your output what statements have been executed and what have not been. This is known as tracing your program.

For example, I could have added a trace to the program above so that progress through it is reported regularly, this improvement is shown below.

```
// This program will use a method to work out the total     1
// price of an item                                         2
                                                            3
public class AppletMethodComputeVat extends TrainingWheels  4
{                                                           5
                                                            6
public void entryPoint()                                    7
    {                                                       8
    outputOnScreen("Started program");                      9
                                                            10
```

```
    int costPrice;                                          11
    costPrice = 4;                                          12
                                                            13
    int itemPrice;                                          14
    outputOnScreen("Calling computeItemPrice");             15
    itemPrice = computeItemPrice(costPrice);                16
                                                            17
    outputOnScreen("The price is");                         18
    outputOnScreen(itemPrice);                              19
    outputOnScreen("Ending program");                       20
                                                            21
    } // End of entryPoint                                  22
                                                            23
  public int computeItemPrice(int receivedCostPrice)        24
    {                                                       25
    outputOnScreen("Started method ComputItemPrice");       26
                                                            27
    int vat = 25; // You can declare a variable and give    28
              // it a value all in the one line             29
    int result;                                             30
                                                            31
    result = receivedCostPrice + ((receivedCostPrice * vat) /100);  32
                                                            33
    outputOnScreen("At point before return");              34
    return result; // Send back the result                 35
    } // End of computeItemPrice                            36
                                                            37
  } // End of AppletMethodComputeVat                        38
```

3.6.2 The order of methods

Does it matter what order methods are declared in? For example, will the above program work if the method computeItemPrice is written before entryPoint? No, it does not matter what order methods are declared as long as they are present in the program. It is better to put the method which is executed first at the start of the program, which is why the entryPoint method is at the start. This makes the program easier to read.

3.7 STRING

If you want to keep a group of characters in a single variable, you can use a data type called 'String'.

3.7.1 Declaring a string

The syntax for the declaration of a data type of String is the same as that for the other variable types that you've seen, namely,

String newStringName;

3.7.2 Assigning values to a string

You can assign a group of characters to the string variable by putting the group between two double quotes (") and using the = symbol.

newString = "This is a message contained in a string";

```
// The purpose of this program is to declare, initialise      1
// and output a string                                        2
                                                              3
public class AppletStringExample extends TrainingWheels       4
{                                                             5
                                                              6
public void entryPoint()                                      7
    {                                                         8
    String myString; // Declare the string                    9
                                                             10
    // Assign a value to the string                          11
    myString = "Hello, this is what is contained in the string  12
    MyString";
                                                             13
    // Output the contents of the string variable            14
    outputOnScreen("The contents of MyString is: ");          15
    outputOnScreen(myString);                                16
    } // End of EntryPoint                                   17
                                                             18
} // End of AppletStringExample                               19
```

3.7.3 Initialising a string

It is best to initialise a string after setting it up. When a string variable is created it contains a value called 'null' which can cause problems with the rest of your program. If you try and call the method outputOnScreen with a string containing null, the program will stop with an error message. One of the ways of heading off these problems is to make sure to declare the string and initialise it to empty, all on the one line, like so:

```
String nameOfEmployee = "";
```

The empty string is actually two double quotes (") put together without any space in between.

You can use this one line form of declaration for other variables as well, for example:

```
int value = 12;
```

EXERCISE   Try the program `AppletStringExample` after removing the line:

`myString = "Hello, this is what is contained in the string myString";`

3.7.4   Combining strings

Strings can also be combined (joined) with other strings and with other data types using the symbol we previously associated with addition (+). For example, I can create and initialise two strings and then join those strings using the following instructions.

```
String firstString = "This is the First string";
String secondString = "This is the Second string";
firstString = firstString+secondString;// Combine firstString and
                                        // secondString and place
                                        // the result in firstString
```

After executing the above instructions `firstString` will contain the string:

```
"This is the First string This is the Second string"
```

How can the same symbol be used to mean two different things (combining strings and adding numbers)? This is an example of the ability called polymorphism mentioned in Section 2.3 as one of the components of Object-Oriented Programming. Polymorphism allows symbols and identifiers to have more than one possible series of actions associated with them. How does the computer know what to do when presented with a symbol which has several possible meanings? Well, like us it will examine the context in which the symbol is used. For example, if I say 'Light the fire', 'Switch the light on' and 'Get some light milk' its clear that the word 'light' has three different meanings and you will use the appropriate one. If the + symbol is used with a string it is taken by the compiler to mean combine two strings, if + is used with two numerical data types it is taken to mean addition.

3.7.5   Converting non-strings to strings

You can also combine another data type with a string to produce a string, for example, if you have an integer and want to join it to a string. All you have to do is to make sure one of the elements in your + operation is a string and the compiler will do the rest for you. This facility is provided as most inputs and outputs (the information coming from the user and going to the user) are in the form of a string so other data types must be converted into a string before they can be displayed.

For example, combining an integer data type with a string:

```
int total=4;
String answerString = "The answer is ";
answerString = answerString + total;
```

The variable `answerString` now contains: "The answer is 4". What happens is that the contents of a variable which is being combined with a string are converted into a string for you. So, the contents of the integer variable `total` are fetched and converted into a string which is combined with the contents of `answerString`.

So, the running program will see the following instruction after the conversion.

```
answerString = answerString + "4";
```

Try it out in the following example.

```
// This program will convert an integer into a string      1
// and combine it with another string                       2
                                                             3
public class AppletStringJoinExample extends TrainingWheels  4
{                                                            5
                                                             6
public void entryPoint()                                     7
   {                                                         8
   String answerString = "The answer is ";                  9
   int total = 4;                                            10
                                                             11
   answerString = answerString + total;                     12
                                                             13
   outputOnScreen("The contents of AnswerString is ");      14
   outputOnScreen(answerString);                            15
   } // End of entryPoint                                    16
                                                             17
} // End of AppletStringJoinExample                          18
```

EXERCISE Try to combine boolean, double and character variables with a string, does this work?

3.7.6 Empty strings and combination

You often see an empty string used in combination, for example,

```
String resultString = "";
resultString = resultString + 4;
```

The empty string is used to make sure that the string being combined with the integer is a valid string (i.e. it has been initialised). The result of the above will be the empty string contained in the variable `resultString` combined with the string `"4"` which will be the string `"4"`.

Try combining an integer with a string which has not been initialised and see what happens, for example,

```
String output;
output = output + 6;
```

3.7.7 **Mathematical expressions and combination**

You can even combine the results of an expression with a string, however you must be careful that your statement is not misunderstood.

```
String resultString = "";// Setup a string and put in an empty
                         // string to make sure it is initialised
```

```
resultString = "Result: " + 3 + 5;
```

The compiler reads the above statement as:

join the string "`Result:`" with the string 3 and the string 5, i.e.
```
resultString = "Result: " + "3" + "5";
```

which means that the string `resultString` will end up containing:

`"Result: 35"`

This combination is not what you intended but this is one of those examples where what you think should happen and what the computer does are different. It is very important that you make yourself aware of these areas as they are introduced since they can be a source of confusion.

To separate different expressions you need to bracket each expression so that the compiler deals with them in the order you want. So to add two numbers and combine the result with a string you will write a statement such as:

```
resultString = "Result: " + (3 + 5);
```

The above statement does what you expect, namely that the contents of `result-String` after the expression has been evaluated will be:

`"Result: 8"`

If we automatically follow the guideline 'When in doubt bracket' we will not encounter this problem.

ARRAYS

How can you store a group of similar variables? For example a set of monthly sales figures: 12, 34, 19, 40, and so on.

You can create variables to hold each figure:

```
int salesFigureMonth1=12;
int salesFigureMonth2=34;
int salesFigureMonth3=19;
int salesFigureMonth4=40;
// and so on...
```

A program to output them will look like this:

```
outputOnScreen("Results for month 1 are "+salesFigureMonth1);
outputOnScreen("Results for month 2 are "+salesFigureMonth2);
outputOnScreen("Results for month 3 are "+salesFigureMonth3);
outputOnScreen("Results for month 4 are "+salesFigureMonth4);
```

This is a little awkward to use in practice as you have to identify each variable by name if you want to use it. It would be easier if we have a group of locations assigned to us that we can use, for example, if we are given the equivalent of a filing cabinet with a particular number of drawers. We can now refer to drawer numbers instead of referring to variable names.

We can say 'sales cabinet, drawer number 2' instead of having to write salesFigureMonth2. Such a means of grouping locations is possible in Java. Variables can be created which represent a filing cabinet and a reference for accessing the desired drawer can be used.

The way of referring to a drawer number in a programming language is to give the name of the filing cabinet and then give the number of the drawer that you want. This number is placed between square brackets, for example, salesCabinet[2] will give you drawer number 2 in the salesCabinet. The drawer number will always be a positive integer (you can't look for drawer –1 or drawer 23.5).

How does this make programming easier? Well, you can create an integer variable which you use to refer to the drawer number that you wish to work with. If you want to change the drawer number, just change the integer variable.

EXAMPLE Let's rewrite our results example using drawers instead of individual variables.

```
int drawerNr; // The number of the drawer that we want
drawerNr=1; // Starting off
outputOnScreen("Results for month 1 are"
+salesFigureCabinet[drawerNr]);

drawerNr=2; // Nextdrawer
outputOnScreen("Results for month 2 are"
+ salesFigureCabinet[drawerNr]);

drawerNr=3; // and the nextdrawer...
```

```
outputOnScreen("Results for month 3 are"
+ salesFigureCabinet[drawerNr]);
// and so on . . .
```

So, as you can see from the above we use the one statement (`outputOnScreen("Results for month 1 are "+salesFigureCabinet[drawerNr]);`) the whole time but change the drawer number to move from one drawer to the next.

In a programming language the equivalent of a filing cabinet and drawers is called an array.

3.8.1 Properties

There are three rules associated with these filing cabinet like structures.

RULES ▶

1 Each box has its own number and the first box always has the number o
2 All boxes must contain the same data type, that is, all the values in the array must be of the same type (int, char, String, etc.)
3 You must say when you are declaring the array how many boxes it will have. You cannot increase or decrease the number of boxes an array has once the array has been created.

For example, the array below has six boxes, accessible using the index numbers 0, 1, 2, 3, 4, 5. Index numbers are the more common way of referring to drawer numbers. we declare the array as int therefore each box must contain an integer value.

o	
1	
2	
3	
4	
5	

Just like a filing cabinet you are free to choose whatever box you like in whatever order you like. You can use only some of the boxes in your array or fill them all, its up to you.

3.8.2 Selecting a box

To select a location in the array use its box number (its index, sometimes called a subscript) and the name of the array variable:

arrayName[indexValue *or* indexVariable]

The index must be an integer or an expression which evaluates to an integer.

EXAMPLE

```
result[2];  // This instruction accesses the third location
            // (remember 0,1,2) of the array called result

int currentStudentNumbers = 3;  // Declare a variable currentStudent
                                // Numbers which will hold an integer
                                // value of 3
marks[currentStudentNumbers];   // This instruction accesses the
                                // location whose number is contained
                                // in the integer variable current
                                // StudentNumbers
```

EXAMPLE

Result for student 3 is 89.

result[3] = 89;

result

0	
1	
2	
3	89

You can assign values to relevant boxes in the array in any order.
Sales figures for the four quarters are:

```
salesFigureCabinet[1] = 19;
salesFigureCabinet[3] = 21;
salesFigureCabinet[4] = 40;
salesFigureCabinet[2] = 34;
```

The result of the above assignments will be an array with the following contents:

salesFigureCabinet

0	
1	19
2	34
3	21
4	40

3.8.3 Setting up an array

Arrays are variables so they must be declared and initialised. As with the other variable declarations that we have seen (e.g. int, char) we must declare a name and a type for an array. We also provide an indication that this is no ordinary variable, that is, it is not intended to hold one single value but a whole set of drawers each of which hold values. This is indicated by putting an empty set of square brackets after the variable name to say that more information about the array is to come later.

```
int monthlyResults[];
String studentNames[];
```

The above two statements tell the compiler that we will be setting up two arrays one of which will hold integers and another strings. These declarations are simply 'memos' to the compiler that further information is forthcoming. We don't yet say how many values we will be holding (i.e. how many drawers will need to be created).

The next stage in the process of setting up an array is to state how many drawers to reserve for the array. This can be done anywhere in your program but obviously it must occur before you try to use the array. The following statements will do just that.

```
monthlyResults=new int[20];
studentNames=new String[5];
```

The word new is used to indicate that you are setting up a new array object (more on objects in Chapter 4, Section 4.6). It is this array object that will hold the boxes for you and allow you to access them. The value in the square brackets indicates the number of boxes that will be held in the array. Note that you do not put square brackets after the array name in the above statements.

Now you can use the arrays monthlyResults and studentNames as the compiler has been given all the information it needs to recognise the arrays. If you try to use the two arrays before you enter the above instructions the compiler will give you an error message because, although it may be aware of the array names it does not have all the information it needs to deal with the arrays.

Let's formally look at the two ways to create an array. The first way is to create an array of a given number of elements as shown above. You supply:

- The type of value the array will hold (int, String, etc.)
- The identifier for the array
- An empty set of brackets to indicate that an array is being created [ ]
- The word 'new'
- The type of value the array will hold (again)
- The number of boxes in the array (contained in square brackets).

This can be done all in one line:

typeToHold nameOfArray[] = new typeToHold[NumberOfBoxes];

For example,

```
int incomeForDay[]=new int[5];
// create an integer array, called incomeForDay, containing 5 elements
```

You then put information into the array using the box numbers. You have a choice as to whether you write the declaration and creation all on one line, as above, or on two separate lines, that is,

```
int incomeForDay[];// Declaration of variable which will refer
                   // to the array
incomeForDay=new int[5]; // Creation of the array
```

Either way will work but the two separate statements are the more commonly used methods as this way offers some advantages which we will discuss further in Chapter 4.

You can use any index you want up to the number of boxes you declare the array to have, minus 1. So, for the array `incomeForDay` you can access box numbers 0, 1, 2, 3, 4 but not box number 5 because that does not exist (the array contains 5 boxes as requested in the creation statement). Most programmers will fill an array from its start (the 0 index) and you should get used to doing this as well even though it may seem strange at first to refer to a location 0. For example,

```
incomeForDay[0] = 23; // First location
incomeForDay[4] = 19; // Second location
```

In the following example program, we see an array being set up and used.

```
// This program will setup an array, place values in        1
// locations and output the contents of the array           2
                                                             3
public class AppletArrayExample extends TrainingWheels      4
{                                                            5
                                                             6
public void entryPoint()                                    7
   {                                                         8
   int salesFigureCabinet[];                                9
   salesFigureCabinet = new int[12];                        10
   salesFigureCabinet[1] = 19;                              11
   salesFigureCabinet[2] = 34;                              12
   salesFigureCabinet[3] = 21;                              13
                                                            14
   int drawerNr; // The number of the drawer that we want   15
   drawerNr = 1; // Starting off with drawer number 1       16
   outputOnScreen("Results for month 1 are"                 17
   + salesFigureCabinet[drawerNr]);
   drawerNr = 2; // Next drawer                              18
   outputOnScreen("Results for month 2 are"                 19
   + salesFigureCabinet[drawerNr]);
```

```
    drawerNr = 3; // and the next drawer..                      20
    outputOnScreen("Results for month 3 are"                    21
    + salesFigureCabinet[drawerNr] );
    } // End of EntryPoint                                       22
                                                                23
} // End of AppletArrayExample                                  24
```

The result of the above program can be seen in Figure 3.3.

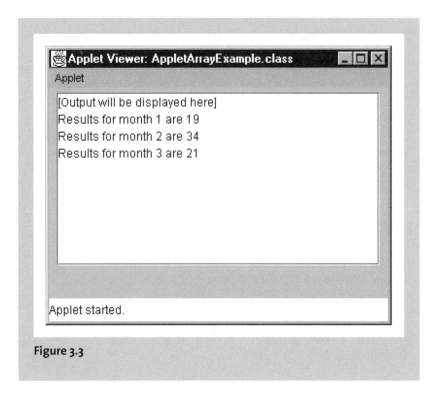

Figure 3.3

3.8.4 Dynamic initialisation

Another way to setup an array is to supply the contents of your array and get the compiler to figure out how many locations it needs and fill in the values for you. This is done using the syntax:

typeOfArray nameOfArray[] = {<listOfValuesToHold>};

This is called dynamic initialisation. You can do this only once, usually in the same line as the array declaration. Your list of values should consist of each of values the array will hold separated by a comma. The values supplied should all be of the same type, that is, the type the array is declared as holding. For example,

```
int myArray[] = {3,4,5};
```

This creates an integer array, called myArray, containing three elements: 3, 4 and 5. The values supplied will be put into the array in the order they appear in the list. Your array is now fixed at a size of three locations as there are three elements in the list.

In effect the dynamic initialisation command int myArray[] = {3,4,5} is the equivalent of the commands:

```
int myArray[] = new int[3];
myArray[0] = 3;
myArray[1] = 4;
myArray[2] = 5;
```

So, the contents of this array are now:

0	3
1	4
2	5

You can change any value that you place in a dynamically initialised array by simply giving the box that value is stored in. For example,

```
myArray[0] = 9;
```

will change the contents of location 0 from 3 to 9.

You can break up the dynamic initialisation into two statements if you want to declare the array in one part of the program and set it up in another as follows:

```
int myArray[];
myArray = new int[] {3,4,5};
```

(Make sure that you don't put in any semicolons after new int[] as new int[] {3,4,5} is part of the one statement.)

You can also dynamically initialise an array of strings by providing the list of strings which will be stored at each location.

EXAMPLE   String names[] = {"Fred","Ginger","Tom","Jean"};

The array names now looks like this:

0	Fred
1	Ginger
2	Tom
3	Jean

Let's look at dynamically initialising an array in an example program. One other thing that we should look at is tidying up array accesses a bit. We are basically repeating the same statement again and again (outputOnScreen("Contents of location 0 is " + myArray[drawerNr]);). This makes for a waste of typing. We could put this statement into a method of its own and call it with the box that we want to be output. We look at how methods work later in Section 3.9.

```
// The following program demonstrates how an array can    1
// be dynamically created and initialised. It creates an  2
// array and prints out its contents                      3
                                                          4
public class AppletDynamicArray extends TrainingWheels    5
{                                                         6
                                                          7
public void entryPoint()                                  8
    {                                                     9
    int myArray[] = {3,4,5};                              10
                                                          11
    int drawerNr; // The number of the drawer that we want 12
    drawerNr = 0; // Starting off at location 0           13
    outputOnScreen("Contents of location 0 is"           14
    + myArray[drawerNr]);
    drawerNr = 1; // Next drawer                          15
    outputOnScreen("Contents of location 1 are"          16
    + myArray[drawerNr]);
    drawerNr = 2; // and the next drawer..                17
    outputOnScreen("Contents of location 2 are"          18
    + myArray[drawerNr]);
    } // End of entryPoint                                19
                                                          20
} // End of AppletDynamicArray                            21
```

3.8.5 Out of bounds errors

Arrays are said to have limits called 'bounds' or 'ranges'. This is the number of boxes or locations that an array can hold, the capacity of an array in other words.

Since you ask that a certain number of locations be set aside for your array you are only allowed to refer to these locations.

For example, an array of size 100 is said to have a range expressed: 0...99. That means it has 100 boxes available to store information starting at box 0 and ending at box 99.

What happens if you try and access a location that no storage location exists for?

For example, if my array declaration was

```
int arrayOfIntegers[] = new int[4];
```

That means my array object holds four boxes with indices from 0 to 3.

O	
1	
2	
3	

What happens if I say:

```
arrayOfIntegers[3] = 9;
```

The box at index 3 will have the value 9 placed in it, the result of this is shown as:

O	
1	
2	
3	9

What happens if I try to set the value for location 8?

```
arrayOfIntegers[8] = 3;
```

The system will go looking for box number 8, in Java it is told that no box 8 exists and there is a mistake in the program that looked for box number 8 so this instruction will be rejected by the compiler as breaking the rules.

The Java VM will not continue to execute any program which attempts to access an array location that doesn't exist. The VM will do this because it is a specification in the Java language, other programming languages do not check for out of bounds errors but enable you to access locations that do not technically exist, this can lead to problems as you may write over another programs memory. Consequences of allowing one program to interfere with another in this way range from crashing (stopping) the other program or causing a breach of security therefore the VM will stop executing your program before it allows an out of bounds access.

This system of looking out for programs trying to access boxes that don't exist is called 'bounds checking'.

What happens if your index location is chosen by the user and the user mistakenly selects an array location that doesn't exist?

Well, the VM which is running your program will check that the location exists for you and if it doesn't it stops the program with an error message.

The facility offered by Java whereby it checks when you are running your program is called a 'runtime' check.

You do not want to have your program stop with an out of bounds error so the safest thing to do when dealing with arrays is to place the array access in an if statement which checks if the array location being accessed exists (see Chapter 4 for discussion of 'if').

So, as to get you in the habit of recognising error messages try out the following program, as you can see in line 22 it breaks the out of bounds rule by trying to access drawer number 99, take careful note of the error message that the program will give you when you run it.

In Chapter 4, we will see how to test a variable before it is used as an index so that an out of bounds error can be prevented. This is accomplished using an if statement.

```
// The following program will produce an error when it        1
// is executed                                                2
                                                              3
public class AppletArrayBoundsError extends TrainingWheels    4
  {                                                           5
                                                              6
  public void entryPoint()                                    7
  {                                                           8
    int myArray[] = {3,4,5};                                  9
                                                             10
    int drawerNr; // The number of the drawer that we want   11
    drawerNr = 0; // Starting off with drawer 0              12
    outputOnScreen("Contents of location 0 is"              13
    + myArray[drawerNr]);
                                                             14
    drawerNr = 1; // Next drawer                            15
    outputOnScreen("Contents of location 1 is"              16
    + myArray[drawerNr]);
                                                             17
    drawerNr = 2; // and the next drawer..                  18
    outputOnScreen("Contents of location 2 is"              19
    + myArray[drawerNr]);
                                                             20
    drawerNr = 99; // and the next drawer..                 21
    outputOnScreen("Contents of location 99 is"             22
    + myArray[drawerNr]);
    } // End of EntryPoint                                   23
                                                             24
  } // End of AppletArrayBoundsError                         25
```

3.8.6 Setting an array size using a variable

Programmers usually use a variable to specify array size. For example,

```
int arraySize = 10;
int results[] = new int[arraySize];
```

This means that if you want to change the size of one or more arrays you need only change the one value.

EXAMPLE

Say we are setting up arrays to hold information about customers. First we will decide how many customers we want to keep information about (say 1000) and then create arrays to keep their details.

One way will be to write out the number of customers we want to keep each time we creat an array.

```
String customerName[] = new String[1000];
String customerAddress[] = new String[1000];
int customerPhone[] = new int[1000];
```

The problem with this way is what happens when we want to change the number of customers whose information is stored from 1000 to 10 000? We must find every point in the code where we refer the number 1000 and change it to 10 000.

A more sensible way will be to create a single variable to hold the number of customers and use this variable each time we create an array.

```
int howManyCustomers = 1000;
String customerName[] = new String[howManyCustomers];
String customerAddress[] = new String[howManyCustomers];
int customerPhone[] =new int[howManyCustomers];
```

If the above guidelines are followed when the time comes to increase the number of customers whose details are kept from 1000 to 5000 all you need to do is to change a single line of the program (int howManyCustomers = 1000;) and the other lines which use this variable will change also. Using the above rule also makes it easier to understand the program because where the number 1000 appears, a descriptive variable name can be placed which enables the user to understand what is going on.

3.9 DEALING WITH METHODS

When declaring a method you have a great deal of flexibility as regards what the method can take from you and give back to you. You can get the method to accept a single parameter, multiple parameters or no parameters. Multiple parameters can consist of variables of varying types. A method can return a value of any type (you can even get it to return an object).

Table 3.2 summarises that there are four possible ways to define and use a method.

Table 3.2

Method type	Example of such a method's declaration	Example of a call to such a method
Method takes no parameter and returns no result	`void methodName()`	`methodName()`

Method takes no parameter and returns a result	`int methodName()`
	`{ return anInteger;`
	`}`
		`result=methodName()`

Method takes a parameter and returns no result	`void methodName` `(int parameter)`	`methodName(5)`

Method takes a parameter and returns a result	`int methodName(int`
	`parameter)`
	`{`
	`return anInteger;`
	`}`
		`result=methodName(6)`

A method can also accept multiple parameters, each separated by a comma	`int methodName(int` `first,int second)`	`result=methodName(5,9)`

3.9.1 Terminology

3.9.1.1 Parameter descriptions

The 'formal' parameter is the name given to the definition of the variable which holds data passed to a method (sometimes just called the parameter).

```
methodName(int formalParameter)
    {....
    }
```

The actual parameter is the name given to the value copied into the formal parameter (sometimes called the argument), i.e. the actual parameter is the value passed to the method.

```
int actualParameter = 5;
methodName(actualParameter);
```

So, in the following example the name of the formal parameter is `value` and the name of the actual parameter is `costOfGoods`. The value of both formal parameter and actual parameter will be the same when the program starts as the actual parameter is copied into the formal parameter. So, in the example below the value of 20 in `costOfGoods` is copied into the variable `value` which is created when the `computeVat` method begins to execute.

```
int costOfGoods = 20;

computeVat(costOfGoods);

public void computeVat(int value)
    {
    int vat = 25;
    outputOnScreen("vat is "+((value*vat)/100));
    }
```

3.9.1.2 Messages

When a method is called, this is sometimes described as 'sending a message'. For example, if you call the `computeVat` method above you can be said to be sending a message to `computeVat`. This term has more relevance when viewed in the context of an object, each object has its own methods and you send a message to a relevant object (i.e. you call a method in that object).

3.9.1.3 Describing method parameters

Sometimes other programmers will write descriptions of their methods, so you know how to deal with them. For these descriptions, programmers do not usually include the names of the formal parameters that they use as they have no relevance to you if all you want to do is call their method. All you need to know if you are using a method is what it does, what it will give back (return) to you and what values it requires. Such a description of a method is often known as a 'signature'.

EXAMPLE

Other programmers description	We interpret this as
`public void` `checkValue(boolean)`	The method `checkValue` is called with a single boolean value as a parameter and returns nothing
`public int` `getAverage(int,int,int)`	The method `getAverage` is called with three integer values as parameters and it will return an integer value

---

3.9.2 Methods and the rest of the program

As far as the rest of the program is concerned what is in the method (the variables declared and the instructions) is of no interest. All it knows is that, it should start executing the instructions in the method when given the methods name, create any variables the method asks it to, finish executing the method and dispose of the variables created while executing the method. Finally it returns any value it was instructed to return. So, any variable created in a method is deleted when the computer finishes executing the instructions of the method. The only contact other parts of the program have with a method is the parameters it gives to the method and the result given (or passed back) by a method.

SUMMARY

Data is stored using reference names, called variables. These names make it easier for programmers to use data. A variable name refers to an actual address in memory where a value is stored. The compiler will automatically translate these variable names into a form it can use. There are different types of data and the programmer must decide what type of data they wish to store, and declare and inform the compiler of their decision. The compiler will use this information to check the program for any incorrect use of the data.

Methods are a means of grouping related instructions. You use methods in the program to structure the execution and make it easier for readers to follow the execution of the program. Methods can be named according to the programmers' wishes and a good naming system will help readers further as the program can more closely resemble an English narration. Every program will start with a method of a particular name, in the programs seen so far that method name is `entryPoint`.

Data is passed to a method for it to work on, this data is known as a parameter. Methods create a temporary variable to hold the parameter. This variable disappears when the method finishes. Data generated in method can be stored in a variable or can be 'returned' (sent back) by the method to the point in the program from where the method was called.

Data can be grouped in structures called arrays. These arrays resemble filing cabinets as they are separate and hold individual pieces of data in drawers or 'index locations'. Two statements must be used in order to create an array. One statement declares the array and the other creates it.

KEYWORDS

▶ *Array* – a way of grouping a number of elements of a similar type using one name.

▶ *double* – indicates a variable, whose name follows, will hold a floating point value.

▶ *boolean* – indicates a variable, whose name follows, will hold a boolean value (true or false).

▶ *bound* – the limit of an array.

▶ *calling* – executing the contents of a particular method (a method is 'called').

▶ *char* – indicates a variable, whose name follows, will hold a character.

▶ *expression* – a collection of operators and operands that will produce a result when evaluated.

▶ *evaluate* – when an expression is computed, that is, the result of an expression is calculated by the computer.

▶ *int* – indicates a variable, whose name follows, will hold an integer value.

▶ *operator* – a function which will be applied to operands.

▶ *operand* – a piece of data which is used in an expression.

▶ *method* – a way of naming a group of instructions. This group will be executed when the name of the structure is encountered by the VM (i.e. the method is called).

KEY CONCEPTS

▶ Every program begins with a declaration of a class

```
public class NameOfProgram
```

This program must be saved in a file which has the same name as the class (e.g. `NameOfProgram.java`).

▶ Every statement ends with a semi-colon ';'.

▶ A class consists of methods and variables.

▶ Variables are declared following the declaration of the class and take the form:

```
variableType variableName;
```

where `variableType` can be one of the following: `int`, `boolean`, `char`, `double`. Each type is associated with a different sort of value, a variable declared with a particular type cannot hold values of any other type.

▶ Value can be placed in a variable using an assignment statement:

```
variableName = value;
```

A value can be another variable (provided it is the same type) or an actual value which is compatible with the type of a variable (e.g. you do not try to put a character into an integer variable).

▶ Declaring a method

```
modifier returnType methodName(parameter declarations);
```

where `modifier` is public or private.

▶ Java is sensitive to the case of words (i.e. capital and small letters).

▶ Methods introduced

```
outputOnScreen(value);   // Method used to output values on
                         // the screen
public void entryPoint();   // Method where the program
                            // always starts executing
```

▶ Creating an array

```
arrayType arrayName[];// Declaration
arrayName = new arrayType[numberOfElements]; // Creation of
                                             // array
```

▶ Accessing a location

```
arrayName[location];  // Note the maximum value for
                      // location is numberOfElements-1
```

▶ Calling a method

```
nameOfMethod(parameters);  // If no parameters then leave
                           // brackets blank
```

▶ Mathematical operations

Operation	value <symbol> value	variable <symbol> value	value <symbol> or <symbol> value
Addition	+	+ =	+ +
Subtraction	–	– =	– –
Multiplication	*	* =	
Division	/	/ =	

▶ Creating a string

```
String identifier = "StringContents";
```

▶ Joining two strings

```
StringOne = StringOne + StringTwo;
```

▶ Joining a string and another type

```
StringOne = StringOne + variableName;
```

▶ Single line comment

```
// The compile will ignore this sentence
```

▶ Multi-line comment

```
/*
All these lines will be
ignored by the compiler
*/
```

EXERCISES

1 Update your notebook with what you have learned (see Section 2.6 for a discussion of what the notebook should contain). As you complete the exercises below enter what you learn into your notebook.

2 Write a program which will return the average of three numbers. The result should be combined with a string and output.

3 Take the code developed in the previous exercise and place it in a method which returns the average of the numbers.

4 Identify the mistake in the following program (*Hint*: type the program in and compile it).

```
class Exercise4 extends TrainingWheels
{
public void entryPoint()
    {
    outputOnScreen("This is Exercise4");
    } // End of entryPoint

} // End Exercise4
```

5 Identify the mistake in the following program.

```
public class Exercise5 extends TrainingWheels
{
public void entryPoint()
    {
    char value;
    value = 5;
    outputOnScreen("The value in the variable is " + value);
    } // End of entryPoint
} // End Exercise5
```

6 Rewrite the computeItemPrice method from the AppletMethodCompute-Vat class so that instead of declaring the vat variable inside it, the value of vat is passed to the computeItemPrice method when it is called.

7 Rewrite the computeItemPrice method from the AppletMethodCompute-Vat so that it uses values of type double instead of type integer (int).

8 Write a program which will create an array of five integers and five strings. The contents of the array of integers, called itemPrices, will be the cost price of a number of items. The contents of the array of string, called stock, will initially be the names of the five items whose prices are stored in the itemPrices array. The actions of the program are as follows:

(i) Compute the retail price of the elements by calling a method computeItemPrice which returns the methods price. Replace the cost price by this new value in the array itemPrices.

(ii) Join the actual price of the item with the item name in the array stock and replace the item name with the result in the stock array.

(iii) Output the contents of the array stock.

Example
For a vat rate of 20.
The original contents of itemPrices are 10, 20, 30.
The original contents of stock are: 'plate', 'cup', 'bowl'.
The final contents of stock (and therefore the output) would be 'plate 12', 'cup 24', 'bowl 36'.

Solutions to exercises and interactive exercises can be obtained at:
http://www.palgrave.com/resources

Chapter **4**

Choices, objects and scope

INTRODUCTION

This chapter is divided into four distinct sections. The first section introduces the idea of scope which relates to the position that variables are declared in a class. Scope is discussed further towards the end of the chapter. The second section deals with how choices are made so that different actions can be taken depending on the value of a particular variable or the result of an expression. The third section discusses the words 'public' and 'private' which control how variables within an object are accessible to other objects. Finally we look at how classes are written and turned into objects.

4.1   SCOPE

In this section, we look at why the position at which variables are declared in a program is important.

Let's have a look at an example program.

```
// The purpose of this program is to show how variables      1
// have scope                                                2
// The program will calculate the retail price of an item    3
                                                             4
public class AppletVariables extends Training Wheels         5
{                                                            6
public void entryPoint()                                    7
    {                                                        8
    int itemPrice;                                           9
    int costPrice;                                          10
                                                            11
    costPrice = 4;                                          12
                                                            13
    itemPrice = computeItemPrice(costPrice);               14
                                                            15
    outputOnScreen("The price is");                        16
    outputOnScreen(itemPrice);                             17
    } // End of entryPoint                                 18
                                                            19
```

```
private int computeItemPrice(int receivedCostPrice)        20
   {                                                       21
   int vat = 25; // You can declare a variable and give    22
   // it a value all in the one line                       23
   int result;                                             24
                                                           25
   result = receivedCostPrice + ((receivedCostPrice * vat)/100);   26
                                                           27
   return result; //Send back the result                  28
   } // End of computeItemPrice                            29
                                                           30
} // End of AppletVariables                                31
```

What happens to the variable vat and result declared inside the method com-puteItemPrice (lines 22 and 24)? Are these public or private?

Well, these variables are not part of the class itself and need only exist for the life of the calculation. Therefore, they are created once the method is called and discarded when it is finished. It also means that no other method can access these variables since they no longer exist after the method is finished. Consequentially there is no need to declare them as private or public.

This type of a variable is known as a local variable as it is local to the method which contains it. If you want to create a permanent variable (one which lasts for the life of the program), you must put it outside all the methods so that it, like the methods, belongs to the class. This type of variable is called a global variable, because it is there for the whole world (where the world is the class) to see. This global variable can be seen and modified from all the methods in the program. Global variables are usually declared right after the class is named. Global variables are generally declared as being private. In object orientation global variables are usually referred to as instance variables.

What we are dealing with here is the issue of visibility of variables. Some variables are visible to all parts of the object, some only to particular parts. The topic of variable visibility is called 'scope'. When programmers refer to the 'scope' of a variable they refer to the variables' visibility.

For example, look at the following program. The variable vat (line 26) can only be used in the method computeItemPrice because it is declared inside that method. Likewise, the variables itemPrice (line 9) and costPrice (line 10) can only be used in the method entryPoint. Any attempt to access them outside these methods will result in the compiler outputting an error message. For instance, in the program below we try and print out the value of vat in the method entryPoint (line 20). If you try and compile this program, the compiler prints out the message:

```
Undefined variable: vat
```

This is because it has no definition for vat at line 20 in the method entryPoint. According to the rules of scope the only place the variable vat can be used is in the method computeItemPrice.

```
// The purpose of this program is to show how variables          1
// have scope                                                    2
// The program will calculate the retail price of an item        3
                                                                 4
public class AppletVariables1Wrong extends TrainingWheels        5
{                                                                6
                                                                 7
public void entryPoint()                                         8
    {                                                            9
    int itemPrice;                                               10
    int costPrice;                                               11
                                                                 12
    costPrice = 4;                                               13
                                                                 14
    itemPrice = computeItemPrice(costPrice);                     15
                                                                 16
    outputOnScreen("The price is");                              17
    outputOnScreen(itemPrice);                                   18
                                                                 19
    outputOnScreen("The value of Vat is"+vat); // This would     20
    // result in an error being generated by the compiler        21
    } // End of entryPoint                                       22
                                                                 23
private int computeItemPrice(int receivedCostPrice)              24
    {                                                            25
    int vat = 25; // You can declare a variable and give it      26
    // a value all in the one line                               27
    int result;                                                  28
                                                                 29
    result = receivedCostPrice + ((receivedCostPrice * vat)/100);  30
                                                                 31
    return result; // Send back the result                       32
    } // End of ComputeItemPrice                                 33
                                                                 34
} // End of AppletVariables1Wrong                                35
```

As discussed above, to have a variable such that it can be seen (accessed and used) from every method in your object you must declare the variable outside all the methods. In the following example program, the vat variable is now declared as a global variable so it can be seen by all the methods. Line 20 (which accesses `vat` in the `entryPoint` method) will now compile without errors because the `entryPoint` method can see the variable `vat` (as can the `computeItemPrice` method).

So remember the rule, variables that you want every method to see are declared globally, these variables exist as long as the object exists. Variables that only one method needs should be declared inside that method and will therefore exist only as long as that method is running.

```
// The purpose of this program is to show how variables    1
// have scope                                              2
// The program will calculate the retail price of an item  3
                                                           4
public class AppletVariables1Right extends TrainingWheels  5
{                                                          6
private int vat = 25;                                      7
                                                           8
public void entryPoint()                                   9
   {                                                      10
   int itemPrice;                                         11
   int costPrice;                                         12
   costPrice = 4;                                         13
                                                          14
   itemPrice = computeItemPrice(costPrice);               15
                                                          16
   outputOnScreen("The price is");                        17
   outputOnScreen(itemPrice);                             18
                                                          19
   outputOnScreen("The value of Vat is" + vat);           20
                                                          21
   } // End of entryPoint                                 22
                                                          23
private int computeItemPrice(int receivedCostPrice)       24
   {                                                      25
   int result;                                            26
                                                          27
   result = receivedCostPrice + ((receivedCostPrice * vat)/100);  28
                                                          29
   return result; // Send back the result                 30
   } // End of ComputeItemPrice                           31
                                                          32
} // End of AppletVariables1Right                         33
```

What happens if the value of vat in the above program is changed within one of the methods? Well, since the variable is global any change to it can be made in any method and that change will be visible in any other method. If there is more than one change, for example, if you change the value of vat in the computeItemPrice method and the entryPoint method, then the value of vat will change each time. The new value of vat will apply until it is changed again.

Note that the only statement that can occur outside a method is a variable declaration (e.g. private int total). You can combine a variable declaration with an initialisation (e.g. public String description = "This string holds the result";) but you cannot put any other statement, including an assignment outside a method. For example, if I declare the variable vatRate as a global variable

```
private int vatRate;
```

and then follow this declaration with an assignment

```
vatRate = 20;
```

the compiler will indicate that this statement is the cause of an error. It is perfectly permissible to put any value you want into a variable provided it is done either in the same line that the variable is declared or in a method. The method executed first is commonly used to initialise variables (the entryPoint method is the one executed first in our introductory programs).

4.2   DETAILED LOOK AT PASSING PARAMETERS

In this section, we look at passing the contents of variables to a method and examine what happens to those variables throughout the process.

First of all, you need to know that there is a difference between how an object and a non-object (e.g. an integer) are passed as parameters. We look at how passing an object as a parameter works in Chapter 6, Section 6.1.3.2.

Let's have a look at an example program and the contents of its variables at different points in its execution. When the following program is executed by the VM it will setup a variable vat as a global variable and place a value into it (line 3). This variable can be seen by all the methods in the program and can be altered at any point in the program. The VM then executes the method entryPoint. This method sets up a variable called itemPrice and places a value in it. This variable is only valid within the method entryPoint. The method computeItemSalePrice is then called with itemPrice as a parameter (line 12). The value for itemPrice (the actual parameter) is copied into the formal parameter variable in computeItemSalePrice (priceOfItem). The variable priceOfItem is a new variable which can be seen only within computeItemSalePrice, if it is altered it does not affect any other variable in the program, that is, the actual parameter is not affected if the formal parameter is changed.

```
public class CalculateSalePrice extends TrainingWheels        1
{                                                              2
private int vat = 25;                                         3
                                                             4
public void entryPoint()                                     5
    {                                                        6
    int itemPrice;                                           7
                                                             8
    outputOnScreen("(entryPoint) vat rate is "+vat);         9
    itemPrice = 100;                                         10
    outputOnScreen("(entryPoint) itemPrice is "+itemPrice);  11
    computeItemSalePrice(itemPrice);                         12
                                                             13
    // Output ItemPrice to see if its changed               14
    outputOnScreen("(entryPoint) itemPrice is "+itemPrice);  15
    } // End entryPoint                                      16
                                                             17
public void computeItemSalePrice(int priceOfItem)           18
    {                                                        19
    // The contents of itemPrice are copied into priceOfItem 20
    outputOnScreen("(computeItemPrice)                       21
    priceOfItem is "+priceOfItem);

                                                             22
    outputOnScreen("(computeItemPrice) vat rate is "+vat);  23
    // Add the vat to the priceOfItem                        24
    priceOfItem += (priceOfItem * vat)/100;                 25
                                                             26
    // Output the new priceOfItem value                      27
    outputOnScreen("(computeItemPrice) The total price is"  28
    +priceOfItem);
    } // End computeItemSalePrice                           29
                                                             30
} // End CalculateSalePrice                                  31
```

The output of the program is shown in Figure 4.1 in p. 96. Let's trace the execution of the program in more detail, we'll keep a note of the variables which have been created and their current value as we go along. So, the program starts off, an object is created from our class definition for calculateSalePrice and the class variable vat is created and given the value 25. So, our variable list so far is:

Variable name	Value	Type	Scope	Created on line
vat	25	integer	Class variable (visible in all the methods)	3

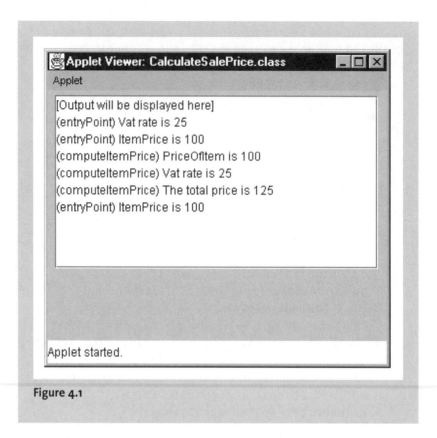

Figure 4.1

The method `entryPoint` is then started automatically. That creates the variable `itemPrice`. This is a local variable and is empty initially. A value is placed in it in line 10. So, at line 11, we have the following variables:

Variable name	Value	Type	Scope	Created on line
vat	25	integer	Class variable (visible in all the methods)	3
itemPrice	100	integer	local variable visible in entryPoint method only	7

We then call the method `computeItemSalePrice` (line 12). This method is called with the actual parameter `itemPrice`. The formal parameter `priceOfItem` is created and the contents of `itemPrice` are copied into it. So, now we have:

Variable name	Value	Type	Scope	Created on line
vat	25	integer	Class variable (visible in all the methods)	3
itemPrice	100	integer	local variable visible in entryPoint method only	7
priceOfItem	100	integer	local variable visible in computeItemPrice method only	18

In line 25, we alter the value of priceOfItem using a calculation. The new value of priceOfItem at line 28 is 125.

Variable name	Value	Type	Scope	Created on line
vat	25	integer	Class variable (visible in all the methods)	3
itemPrice	100	integer	local variable visible in entryPoint method only	7
priceOfItem	125	integer	local variable visible in computeItemPrice method only	18

The method computeItemPrice then finishes and the VM goes back to line 12 in the entryPoint method which executes the remaining instructions. The priceOfItem variable disappears when computeItemPrice finishes, so the variables we have at line 12 are:

Variable name	Value	Type	Scope	Created on line
vat	25	integer	Class variable (visible in all the methods)	3
itemPrice	100	integer	local variable visible in entryPoint method only	7

Notice that when the computeItemPrice method finishes and its variable (priceOfItem) disappears, the variable which is the actual parameter is not affected.

When the entryPoint method is finished our program contains only one variable:

Variable name	Value	Type	Scope	Created on line
vat	25	integer	Class variable (visible in all the methods)	3

4.2.1 Returned values

We now look at an example which deals with what happens when values are returned from a method.

```
public class ReturnSalePrice extends TrainingWheels        1
{                                                          2
private int vat = 25;                                      3
                                                           4
public void entryPoint()                                   5
   {                                                       6
   int itemPrice;                                          7
                                                           8
   outputOnScreen("(entryPoint) Vat rate is "+vat);        9
   itemPrice = 100;                                        10
   outputOnScreen("(entryPoint) itemPrice is "+itemPrice); 11
   computeItemSalePrice(itemPrice);                        12
                                                           13
   // Output ItemPrice to see if it is changed             14
   outputOnScreen("(entryPoint) itemPrice is "+itemPrice); 15
   } // End entryPoint                                     16
                                                           17
public void computeItemSalePrice(int priceOfItem)          18
   {                                                       19
   // The contents of itemPrice are copied into priceOfItem 20
   outputOnScreen("(computeItemPrice) priceOfItem is       21
   "+priceOfItem);
                                                           22
   outputOnScreen("(computeItemPrice) vat rate is "+vat);  23
   // Add the vat to the value of priceOfItem              24
   priceOfItem += computeVat(priceOfItem);                 25
                                                           26
   // Output the new priceOfItem value                     27
   outputOnScreen("(computeItemPrice) The total price is"  28
   +priceOfItem);
   } // End computeItemSalePrice                           29
                                                           30
public int computeVat(int finalPrice)                      31
   {                                                       32
   int result;                                             33
   result = (finalPrice * vat) / 100;                      34
                                                           35
   outputOnScreen("(computeVat) Result is "+result);       36
                                                           37
```

```
    return result;                              38
  } // End computeVat                           39
                                                40
} // End ReturnSalePrice                        41
```

What happens when you want to pass a value back from a method? Well, first you declare the relevant method. In the above example we have declared the method computeVat to take an integer parameter, call it priceOfItem and return as a result an integer.

If we go through the same process again of examining the variables created (done in the previous example), we see that by line 11 in the method entryPoint we have the following list of variables:

Variable name	Value	Type	Scope
vat	25	integer	Class variable (visible in all the methods)
itemPrice	100	integer	local variable (visible only in the method entryPoint)

When we get to line 12, computeItemSalePrice(itemPrice);, we see that a call is made to the method computeItemSalePrice so now that method is executed. We also see that we pass this method the contents of the variable itemPrice (currently 100). The first line of computeItemSalePrice (18) indicates that it will create a variable called priceOfItem and copy into it the value of the actual parameter (itemPrice which is 100). We now have:

Variable name	Value	Type	Scope
vat	25	integer	Class variable (visible in all the methods)
itemPrice	100	integer	local variable (visible only in the method entryPoint)
priceOfItem	100	integer	local variable (visible only in the method computeItemSalePrice)

computItemSalePrice will call the method computeVat (line 25) and the rest of the statement indicates that the result of that method is to be added to the variable priceOfItem.

The declaration for computeVat indicates that it will return an integer value and take a integer parameter which it will place in a variable it creates called finalPrice. So, at line 31, we now have the variables:

Variable name	Value	Type	Scope
vat	25	integer	Class variable (visible in all the methods)
itemPrice	100	integer	local variable (visible only in the method entryPoint)
priceOfItem	100	integer	local variable (visible only in the method computeItemSalePrice)
finalPrice	100	integer	local variable (visible only in the method computeVat)
result	0	integer	local variable (visible only in the method computeVat)

The value from the itemPrice variable in computItemSalePrice is copied into the new variable finalPrice created when computeVat starts. Again remember that these are two distinct variables whose only relationship is that one is created by copying the contents of the other, therefore changes to either variable after the copy is made will not affect the other variable.

At line 34, the value for result is calculated (25) and at line 38 this value is passed back by the method computeVat which then disposes of its variables (finalPrice and result). So, just when the computeVat method is finished we have the following variables:

Variable name	Value	Type	Scope
vat	25	integer	Class variable (visible in all the methods)
itemPrice	100	integer	local variable (visible only in the method entryPoint)
priceOfItem	100	integer	local variable (visible only in the method computeItemSalePrice)

We now return to line 25 where we can replace computeVat(priceOfItem) by the result of the call to the method computeVat, that is 25. The variable priceOfItem has this value added to it and the contents of priceOfItem are output in line 28.

The method computeItemSalePrice now finishes and disposes of its variables. When we return to the entryPoint method following the completed computeItem-SalePrice method (line 12), we have the following variables:

Variable name	Value	Type	Scope
vat	25	integer	Class variable (visible in all the methods)
itemPrice	100	integer	local variable (visible only in the method entryPoint)

4.3 MAKING CHOICES

As we have seen when discussing how to program, one of the things you need to be able to do is to make choices. Once a choice is made you can then act accordingly. This is accomplished in Java by using the if statement. The if statement works by phrasing the questions in a form which yields one of two answers, yes or no (where the value of yes equates to the value 'true' and the value of no equates to the value 'false' in computer terms). Every question can be phrased to ultimately yield one of these answers. The if statement can then carry out a set of instructions in response to either of the results. The question is usually known as a 'condition'.

There are two versions of the if statement, in one version we can test just to see if a condition is true and do something if it is. In the other version we can test to see if a condition evaluates to a true (yes) or false (no) answer and have a set of actions performed in response to either possible answer.

The if statement tests a condition to see if it is true or false, that condition can be a single variable (for example a boolean variable) or it can be a more complicated expression (e.g. $(5 + 4) < 10$).

EXAMPLE   Question: what do we do if the weather is rainy?
Action: if it is rainy weather put up an umbrella

The computer won't understand decisions expressed in plain English (such as the question asked above) so we have to translate the question into a form it can cope with. What you do is write your question in a form which evaluates to a yes or a no answer. You then provide the action (or actions) which will be carried out if the answer to the question is yes (true). You have an option as to whether you provide an action or actions to be carried out if the answer to the question is no (false). So we can rephrase the question and action above to the following:

Question: is it raining?
Action if answer is yes: put up an umbrella.
Action if answer is no: put on sunscreen

This is usually known as an if-then-else statement.

What this means is that a question is evaluated (i.e. the result of the questions, true or false, is obtained) and IF the answer to the question is true THEN one statement is executed ELSE another statement is executed (i.e. a different statement is executed as the answer must be false).

4.3.1 Syntax

The if statement can have two forms.

Form 1: else condition provided
```
if(condition)
    action(s) if condition is true;
else
    action(s) if condition is false;
Rest of program...;
```

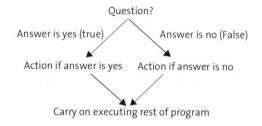

Form 2: else condition omitted

```
if(condition)
    action(s) if condition is true;
Rest of program ...;
```

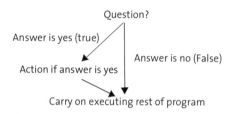

Note the following:

- The word 'then' (in if-then-else) does not appear in the syntax. It does appear in other programming languages versions of the if statement though.

- The semicolon occurs at the end of the action, not after the 'if (condition)' portion of the statement. Putting a semicolon directly after an if statement will not cause a syntax error but will almost certainly cause a logical error as the if statement will not have any action associated with it. For example,

```
if(condition);
    action statement;
```

In the above the action statement will always be executed because the action, associated with the condition being true is the statement which is between the end of the condition and the first semicolon encountered (which is blank, i.e. ');').

The correct form of the statement will be:

```
if(condition)
    action statement;
```

- Your action does not have to be a single statement. If there is more than one action, you should enclose the action statements in a block of statements (i.e. contained within brackets { and }).

- The condition must either contain the value true or false, or be an expression which must evaluate to true or false.

- The statement executed when the condition is true is called the **then clause**.
- The statement executed when the condition is false is called the **else clause** (this is optional).

EXAMPLE 1

Say you want to attend a concert. You need to check if there are tickets left to buy and the variable `ticketsLeftForSale` will be true if tickets remain and false otherwise. If you can't go to the concert then you will go to the theatre (i.e. the value of `ticketsLeftForSale` is no (false)). Your actions if the value of `ticketsLeftForSale` is yes (true) are to buy a ticket and enter the concert.

```
boolean ticketsLeftForSale=true; // There are currently tickets left
if(ticketsLeftForSale)
    {
    buyTicket();
    enterConcert();
    }
else
    goToTheatre();
```

You can provide multiple `if` conditions to check for various situations.

EXAMPLE 2

```
boolean itIsRaining = true;
boolean itIsSnowing = false;
boolean itIsSunny = false;

if(itIsRaining)
  takeUmbrella();

if(itIsSnowing)
  takeSnowShoes();

if(itIsSunny)
  takeSunGlasses();
```

We now have three separate statements associated with three conditions.

EXAMPLE 3

In this example we perform an action only if the contents of the boolean variable `itIsRaining` is true.

```
// This program will output a message if a boolean      1
// variable is true                                     2
                                                        3
    public class IfExample1 extends TrainingWheels      4
    {                                                   5
                                                        6
    public void entryPoint()                            7
        {                                               8
```

```
        boolean itIsRaining = true;                          9
                                                             10
        if(itIsRaining)                                      11
            outputOnScreen("Bring your umbrella");           12
        } // End of entryPoint                               13
                                                             14
    } // End of IfExample1                                   15
```

The result of the above program will be to output the message 'Bring your umbrella' as the content of ItIsRaining is the boolean value true.

Add an else clause to the above program to remind the user to bring their sunhat if it isn't raining.

In the program IfExample2, if the first if condition (that is the value of ItIs-Raining) evaluates to true we print out the message 'Bring your umbrella'. However, if the value of itIsRaining evaluates to false, we then test the value of sunIsShining, that is, we perform another if test which is placed inside the first one. Writing one if statement so that the statement it executes is another if statement (as in this program) is called 'nesting'. If the second if (the one nested inside the if(itIsRaining)) evaluates to true, we output a message 'Bring your sunhat', if it evaluates to false we do nothing (since there is no else clause supplied).

```
// Perform a test on a boolean variable, if the test is false    1
// then perform another test on another boolean variable         2
                                                                 3
public class IfExample2 extends TrainingWheels                    4
{                                                                 5
                                                                 6
public void entryPoint()                                          7
    {                                                             8
    boolean itIsRaining = false;                                  9
    boolean sunIsShining = true;                                  10
                                                                 11
    if(itIsRaining)                                               12
        outputOnScreen("Bring your umbrella");                    13
    else                                                          14
        if(sunIsShining)                                          15
            outputOnScreen("Bring your sunhat");                  16
    } // End entryPoint                                           17
                                                                 18
} // IfExample2                                                   19
```

The output of the above program will be 'Bring your sunhat' as this is the conclusion that is reached based on the contents of the variable ItIsRaining and SunIsShining.

4.3.2 Summary

So, any if-else statement you write must take the form of one of the following varieties:

Leaving out the else the two forms you can have are:

1 Single statement executed:

```
if (condition)
    statement;
```

2 Multiple statements executed:

```
if (condition)
    {
    FirstStatement;
    SecondStatement;
    }
```

With an else clause included you can have:

1 Two single statements executed:

```
if (condition)
    statement;
else
    statement;
```

2 Multiple statements and a single statement:

```
if (condition)
        {
        FirstStatement;
        SecondStatement;
        }
else
    statement;
```

3 Multiple statements for both if and else clauses:

```
if (condition)
        {
        FirstStatement;
        SecondStatement;
        }
else
        {
        FirstStatement;
        SecondStatement;
        }
```

4   Multiple statements for the `else` clause only:

```
if (condition)
    statement;
else
    {
    FirstStatement;
    SecondStatement;
    }
```

where statement, FirstStatement and SecondStatement are any valid statements. A valid statement could include another `if-else` or an empty statement (;). For example, the following `if-else` will output a message only if the `else` clause is executed, the `if` clause has an empty statement associated with it:

```
boolean stop=false;
if(stop)
   ;// An empty statement
else
   outputOnScreen("Keep going, stop is false");
```

4.3.3   Relational operators

What other conditions can you have for your `if` statement apart from a single boolean variable? Well, you can check relationships between numbers and use the answer to the relationship question to carry out an action. We use symbols called relational operators to figure out how information is related to each other (such as, the contents of one variable equal to a particular number, the contents of one variable bigger than the contents of another). We therefore write expression which phrase the questions we wish to ask, these expressions are evaluated to a boolean value which will be used by the `if` statement.

To compare two elements we pick the relevant symbol from Table 4.1 and put the elements at each end of the symbol to create a question. The expression that we have constructed is then evaluated by the computer which gives us an answer, true if the expression is valid (e.g. the answer to the question 5 < 9? is yes (true)) or false if the expression is invalid (e.g. the answer to 2 > 4? is no (false)). You can use actual values or variables.

Table 4.1

Symbol	Meaning	Example
>	Greater than	4 > 5 (is 4 greater than 5? This will evaluate to false because it is not)
<	Less than	2 < 3 (is 2 less than 3? This will evaluate to true because 2 is less than 3)

>=	Greater than or equal to (there is no space between the symbols). You are essentially getting two tests in one, the answer will be true if one number is greater than the other, or one number is equal to the other	1 >= 4 (is 1 greater than 4 or equal to 4? It is not greater or equal so we get an answer of false)
<=	Less than or equal to, like the above you get two tests in one	3 <= 3 (is 3 less than or equal to 3? This will result in an answer of true because whereas 3 is not less than 3 it is equal to it)
==	Equal, is one number equal to the other. Note the two = symbols put together without a space in between	9 == 9 (is 9 the same as 9? Yes so the answer is true)
!=	Not equal, different. Is one number not the same as the other	8 != 8 (Is 8 different to 8? no so the answer is false)

VERY IMPORTANT!

If you are using an equality test make sure that you use the correct symbol (==) instead of the = symbol (which most people automatically choose).

EXAMPLE The expression (value = 1) means assign 1 to the variable value. The compiler will report this error as:

```
Can't convert int to boolean
```

which is its way of saying that the result of value = 1 is an integer which cannot be used (it expects to see a boolean so it can test whether the value of the boolean is true or false).

Note there is a difference between < and <=, < will test whether a number is less than a particular number while <= will test whether a number is less than or equal to another number. People sometimes get confused and end up being out in their calculations by a value of one.

EXAMPLE The maximum occupancy for a club is 90. Let people into the club unless the number in there exceeds 90. So your test would take the form:

```
if(numberOfPeopleInside <= 90)
    outputOnScreen("Admit person");
else
    outputOnScreen("Sorry, club full");
```

You can also write the above test in the form:

`if(numberOfPeopleInside < 91)`

There is usually several different expressions which could be used to achieve the desired question, the main criteria when choosing the one to use is how easy it is to understand for the reader.

EXAMPLE   Try the following example program and see if you can guess what the output is.

```
// The purpose of this program is to show the results of         1
// some relationship tests                                       2
                                                                 3
public class AppletRelationshipExample extends TrainingWheels    4
{                                                                5
                                                                 6
public void entryPoint()                                         7
   {                                                             8
   if(4 < 2)                                                     9
      outputOnScreen("The answer to 4 < 2 ? is true");          10
   else                                                         11
      outputOnScreen("The answer to 4 < 2 ? is false");        12
                                                                13
   // Your expression does not have to be placed               14
   // inside an if, you can see its result                      15
   // (true/false) directly by simply stating the              16
   // relationship test (as below)                             17
                                                                18
   outputOnScreen("The answer to 4 < 2 ? is "+(4 < 2));        19
                                                                20
   if(0 != 0)                                                   21
      outputOnScreen("The answer to 0 !=0 ? is true");         22
   else                                                        23
      outputOnScreen("The answer to 0 !=0 ? is false");       24
                                                                25
   } // End of entryPoint                                      26
                                                                27
} // End of AppletRelationshipExample                          28
```

The output of the program is shown in Figure 4.2 in p. 109.

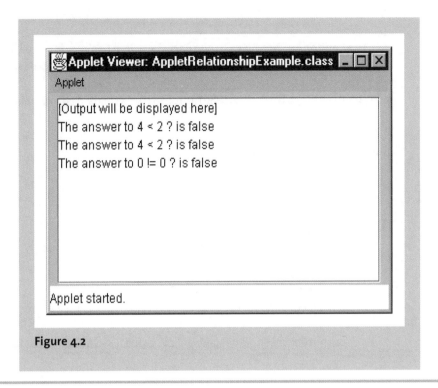

Figure 4.2

4.3.3.1 Testing strings

In Chapter 3, you were introduced to a `String`. `String` type variables should not be tested for equality using the == symbols but instead the test should take the following form:

```
String testString = "example";
String dataString = "test";
if(testString.equals(dataString))
    outputOnScreen("both strings contain the same characters");
else
    outputOnScreen("Strings are different");
```

Using an expression of the form `if(testString == dataString)` will always return a false answer even if both strings are the same. The reason for this will be covered in Chapter 6.

4.3.3.2 Variables

Note that you won't usually have values written into your program explicitly as in the program above, you will use variables to hold the values. Here is a program which tests the relationship between variables.

```
// The purpose of this program is to place some values in        1
// variables and then test the relationship of those variables   2
                                                                 3
public class AppletVariableRelationship extends TrainingWheels   4
{                                                                 5
                                                                 6
public void entryPoint()                                         7
    {                                                            8
    int value1;                                                  9
    int value2;                                                 10
                                                                11
    value1 = 5;                                                 12
    value2 = 9;                                                 13
                                                                14
    if(value1 < value2)                                         15
        outputOnScreen("The answer to value1 < value2 ? is true");   16
    else                                                        17
        outputOnScreen("The answer to value1 < value2 ? is false");  18
                                                                19
    if(value1 == value1)                                        20
        outputOnScreen("The answer to value1 == value2 ? is true");  21
    else                                                        22
        outputOnScreen("The answer to value1 == value2 ? is false"); 23
                                                                24
    if(value1 > value2)                                         25
        outputOnScreen("The answer to value1 > value2 ? is true");   26
    else                                                        27
        outputOnScreen("The answer to value1 > value2 ? is false");  28
                                                                29
    } // End of entryPoint                                      30
                                                                31
} // End of AppletVariableRelationship                          32
```

Remember that you should use methods whenever possible to break up solution into easily understandable and readable sections. Let's use a method with the above so that we can vary the value for value1 and value2 without having to rewrite the test statements.

```
// This program will use a method to test the relationship between   1
// various values which will be passed to it as parameters           2
                                                                     3
public class AppletRelationshipMethod extends Training Wheels        4
```

```
{                                                               5
                                                                6
public void entryPoint()                                        7
   {                                                            8
   int value1;                                                  9
   int value2;                                                  10
                                                                11
   value1 = 5;                                                  12
   value2 = 9;                                                  13
   // Call the testRelationship method with the two parameters  14
   testRelationship(value1,value2);                             15
                                                                16
   // Change the values and try again                          17
   value1 = 12;                                                 18
   value2 = 4;                                                  19
   testRelationship(value1,value2);                             20
                                                                21
   // And again...                                              22
   value1 = 6;                                                  23
   value2 = 6;                                                  24
   testRelationship(value1,value2);                             25
                                                                26
   } // End of entryPoint                                       27
                                                                28
public void testRelationship(int value1Passed, int value2Passed) 29
   {                                                            30
   outputOnScreen("The contents of value1 is "+value1Passed);  31
   outputOnScreen("The contents of value2 is "+value2Passed);  32
                                                                33
   if(value1Passed < value2Passed)                             34
      outputOnScreen("The answer to value1 < value2 ? is true"); 35
   else                                                        36
      outputOnScreen("The answer to value1 < value2 ? is false"); 37
                                                                38
   if(value2Passed == value2Passed)                            39
      outputOnScreen("The answer to value1 == value2 ? is true"); 40
   else                                                        41
      outputOnScreen("The answer to value1 == value2 ? is false"); 42
                                                                43
   outputOnScreen(""); // Output a blank line                  44
   } // End of testRelationship                                45
                                                                46
} // End of AppletRelationshipMethod                           47
```

Remember that the value passed to the method is copied into the variables in the method declaration. So, the contents of `value1` and `value2` are copied into the variables `value1Passed` and `value2Passed` each time the method is executed.

The results of the above program are shown in Figure 4.3. Use the scroll bar on the right hand side of the window to see the rest of the results.

Relational operators can only compare certain data types (`int`, `char`). If you want to compare objects you must use other means (we'll see in Chapter 6).

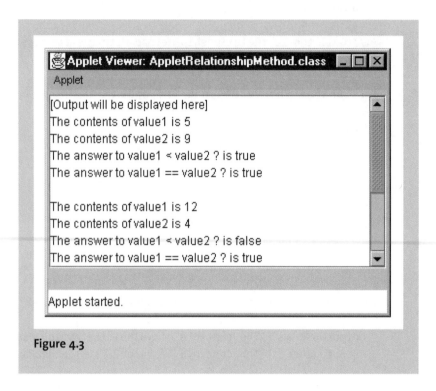

Figure 4.3

EXAMPLE 1

```
int result;
result = 50;
if(result >= 40)
    outputOnScreen("You passed");
else
    outputOnScreen("You failed");
```

EXAMPLE 2

```
int yearsResult;
int expectedResult;
yearsResult = 40;
expectedResult = 50;

if(yearsResult < expectedResult)
```

```
        outputOnScreen("The result was lower than expected");
    else
        outputOnScreen("The result was above or equal to expected");
```

As `yearsResult` is less than `expectedResult` the output for the above will be 'The result was lower than expected'.

EXERCISE   What is the output of the above if the following values apply?
```
yearsResult = 30;
expectedResult = 20;
```

4.3.4 Checking boolean variables

Sometimes in `if` statements you see an inexperienced programmer checking the value of a boolean variable, for example,

```
boolean finished = true;
if(finished == true)
    statement;
```

The `== true` part of the statement is redundant as the contents of the boolean variable can be used directly without having to compare them with true or false. So, the above `if` statement is more accurately written as:

```
if(finished)
    statement;
```

4.3.5 Dangling-else problem

The situation where you can supply an `else` if you feel like it can cause a problem called the **dangling-else** problem. This occurs because you as the programmer can lose track of what the code is actually doing and so your program could end up not working as you intended.

EXAMPLE   You are asked to write a test to see if a customer can partake of a fairground ride. The customer is only allowed to ride if they are greater than one meter tall. If they are less than one meter tall but are over 18 years of age, they can still take the ride.
We can write the above decision as follows:

```
if(height < 1)                              1
    if(age > 18)                            2
        allowCustomerToRide();              3
else                                        4
    allowCustomerToRide();                  5
```

Note that the indentation is intended to reflect the logic of the decision.

You may think the above statements carry out the decisions asked for. Is this actually the case? Look carefully to see if you can figure out which if-then-else clause is associated with. The answer is that the else on line 4 is associated with the if on line 2 not the if on line 1 as can be assumed from the indentation. The rule is that an else is associated with the first preceding if (which in the above case is the if in line 2), but this may not always be what we want. Using this rule, we see that what our statements above actually do allow people who are under 18 and under 1 meter tall to take the ride. This is not consistent with the original logic and means the program is incorrect.

In other words, in the above example what we have really said is:

```
if(height < 1)
    if(age > 18)
        allowCustomerToRide();
    else
        allowCustomerToRide();
```

RULE ▶ An else is associated with the closest preceding 'free' unattached if (i.e. one without an else).

One solution to potential confusion is known as the if/else blocking rule. It states that for any if statement that requires more than a single line or an else clause always use curly braces to enclose in a separate block the statements under the control of the if statement. Once you put an if statement in curly brackets the compiler assumes that the if statement is finished when it sees the } bracket. Therefore, any subsequent else will not be associated with the if in brackets but with the if which caused the bracketed statements to be executed.

So, our if-else example becomes:

```
if(height < 1)                          1
    {                                   2
    if(age > 18)                        3
        allowCustomerToRide();          4
    }                                   5
else                                    6
    allowCustomerToRide();              7
```

The if statement in line 1 is closed or ended by the bracket in line 5, therefore the else in line 6 is associated with the if on line 1 which is the required one to properly implement the decision. In other words the compiler sees:

```
if(height < 1)
    statement1;
else
    statement2;
```

and executes `statement1` (the block) in response to the condition evaluating to true.

RULE ▶ When in doubt, bracket all relevant statements.

4.4 HIDING OR PROTECTING VARIABLES AND METHODS

Let's take a closer look at the first program we have written in Chapter 3.

```
                                                          1
public class MyFirstApplet extends TrainingWheels        2
{                                                         3
                                                          4
public void entryPoint()                                 5
  {                                                       6
  outputOnScreen("This is my first program");            7
  } // End of entryPoint                                  8
                                                          9
} // End of MyFirstApplet                                10
```

We have already seen what it does, now it's time to look at why it is written the way it is.

The word `public` appears before the declaration of the class and the method `entryPoint`. What does this word mean? Well, public is an instruction that says that other parts of the program have permission to use the part labelled public. Public is the equivalent of making something publicly available, for example, publishing it on a web site or in a newspaper. Phone numbers are usually public, other people can look it up in a phone directory. Placing 'public' before a variable or a method makes the element a public property, anyone can use it or alter it. The opposite of public is of course private. Your bank account balance is private, only you and the people you authorise (spouse, bank manager, etc.) are allowed look at it. You can make your phone number private by asking for it to be removed from the directory.

The example programs you have seen so far did not discuss private elements because there is no need for them. Where is the need to have private elements in other programs? Well, there are parts of your program which you may not want other people to have access to in the same way there are aspects of your own life you do not want people to know (home address, personal telephone number, ATM code, etc.).

Another example of public and private would be the company example we have looked at in Chapter 2. If you want to get access to the files belonging to a particular department, you must go through a person in that department, you are not allowed to access the files directly since they are private. You can make contact with the person since they are public but only they are allowed to access the files which are private.

Private methods and variables can only be accessed by methods within the object (e.g. the personnel manager can only access the personnel files because they are in the personnel department object). Public methods (and occasionally variables) can be accessed by anyone, whether they are in the object or not.

This can be seen from Figure 4.4. If you have data about yourself (you take the form of an object) you can access all your data. But other people can only access parts of you that you choose to make public. Any part of your data or life that you choose to keep private cannot be accessed. This is the same idea for an object.

For example, look at the contents of a bank account object:

▶ Account Holder: will be a <variable>
▶ Balance: will be a <variable>
▶ Withdraw Money: will be a <method>
▶ Lodge Money: will be a <method>
▶ Check Balance: will be a <method>

What parts of the bank account object will be public and what parts will be private? We can make all the methods public and all the variables private. That way people will have to go through a method in order to access our balance and we can use the method to check if we want to give this person access to our private balance amount (equivalent to a bank checking if you own an account or have power of attorney over someone else's account).

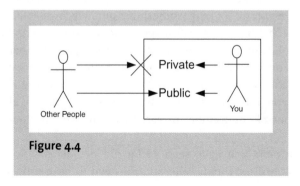

Figure 4.4

Why have a method to check at all? Why not make the variable `balance` publicly accessible? The reason is that if `balance` is public it will be like writing it on a wall, once it is public, people can view it and alter it without being subject to checks or controls. Therefore we make it private so you have to go through another method to get to it. You can use this method to control who has access to the variable. For instance, the `CheckBalance` method can be carried out by a bank clerk who will verify that it is the account holder who is asking for the balance, any one else will be refused permission to view the balance.

Therefore while the methods which access private variables are public, they can have built into them a check to make sure that only the correct person can get at the private information.

So, why are the class and the `entryPoint` method in the example below declared as public? Who else needs to see them? Well, the VM creates an object from the class definition and then calls various methods. The VM has a list of these method names and attempts to call these methods. If the methods are private, the VM is not allowed call them, if they are public it can call them. If the VM cannot access the class or methods it needs, your program will not run (try it and see for yourself). Denying the VM access to a method it wanted to execute will be a bit like putting your name in for a competition but not your phone number or address, you have no way of being contacted.

Public and private are known as 'visibility modifiers' (or more often just modifiers) since they modify the default access that is permitted. If you use no modifier then a default modifier is used the result of which resembles the private modifier.

Note that there is a distinct difference between the scope of a variable and its modifier. Local variables do not need modifiers as they can never be seen outside the object since they are contained within a method. The method that contains the local variables will need a modifier. Global variables do need modifiers as they are outside all the methods and therefore are part of the object thus needing a indication as to whether they are public or private.

4.5 CREATING A CLASS

Let's create a new class to give you an example of public and private.

Our program will create an object of this class type and we will attempt to use that object.

Let's create a class type which models a bank account. A bank account's variables are usually the name of the account holder and the amount kept in the account. We'll use a String to hold the name and an integer to hold the amount (remember int holds whole numbers only, so it's not the most suitable variable type to represent monetary amounts but it is easy to work with, so that is why it is used). Will these variables be public or private? I think that it's best they be private. That means that if we want to get access to the variables, we need to go through a method in the same class.

Once we have the variables, we need to decide on the methods. For our example, let's assume that we need only two methods namely (i) `lodgeAmount`, which takes a value and adds it to the variable `balance` and (ii) `getBalance`, which returns the value of the variable `balance`. Obviously we need more methods than that, otherwise how can we put the account name in the variable `name` or withdraw money, but we leave those out to keep the example simple.

```
class BankAccountClass                                    1
{                                                          2
private int balance;                                       3
private String name;                                       4
                                                           5
public String lodgeAmount(int amountToLodge)               6
    {                                                      7
    if(amountToLodge < 0)                                  8
        return "Error, cannot lodge negative amount";      9
    else                                                  10
        {                                                 11
        balance = balance + amountToLodge;                12
        return "Lodged money";                            13
        }                                                 14
    } // End of lodgeAmount                               15
                                                          16
public int getBalance()                                   17
    {                                                     18
    return balance; // Send back balance                  19
    } // End of getBalance                                20
                                                          21
// Note we have left out some methods for the moment,     22
// for instance methods to deal with the Name string      23
                                                          24
} // End of BankAccountClass                              25
```

Why does the above class not begin with the word public in the same way that our other programs did? Well, the class defined above is intended to be used by another class and is not a class which can be executed on its own. If you place more than one class in a source code file only one class, the one used as the main program, should have the word public in front of it, otherwise the compiler may get confused as to which is the main part. We look at classes in more detail later in Section 4.5.

We can see why we will use a public method to get at a private variable in the example above. Say the teller made a mistake entering the data and told the program that you were lodging a negative amount in your account. The `lodgeAmount` method in the above program checks to see if the amount being lodged is less than 0 and returns an error message if it is and does not alter the balance of the account. Therefore any possible incorrect alterations to the balance variable are caught in time.

Let's look at another example, let's create a class which will hold details about a person, their name and address. Again the only way to get at the variables is through the methods.

```
class PersonClass                                      1
{                                                      2
private String address;                                3
private String name;                                   4
                                                       5
public String getAddress()                             6
    {                                                  7
    return address;                                    8
    } // End of getAddress                             9
                                                      10
public String getName()                               11
    {                                                 12
    return name;                                      13
    } // End of getName                               14
                                                      15
public void setName(String nameSupplied)              16
    {                                                 17
    name = nameSupplied;                              18
    } // End of setName                               19
                                                      20
public void setAddress(String addressSupplied)        21
    {                                                 22
    address = addressSupplied;                        23
    } // End of setAddress                            24
                                                      25
} // End of PersonClass                               26
```

The above class definition does not do any testing but is an example of a class which will create objects whose data are accessed through their methods. The only way to change or gain access to the variables address and name are through the public methods. This may seem like a waste of effort in the above example since no test is performed to see if alterations or accesses meet certain requirements but it is better to write code in the spirit of OO so that when you need protection and verification you are used to writing such programs.

4.6 CREATING AN OBJECT

Once the class definition has been written, then we can declare variables of that particular class type, for example, `PersonClass john;`. We must do one more task before we can use objects and that is to create a new object. You see, declaring a variable name for your object is only stage 1 of the process of creating an object. Stage 2 involves you telling the system to create a new object for you and to put it in the variable you have declared in stage 1. The reasons why this is done will be explained later in Chapter 6, Section 6.1.1, but for the moment it is important that you remember that an object cannot be used without going through the two stages. For example,

```
PersonClass john; // Stage 1 – declare the objects name
john = new PersonClass( );// Stage 2 – create the object
```

The above statements can be placed in different parts of your program. Occasionally you will see both stages combined in a single statement:

```
PersonClass john = new PersonClass( );
```

You can check if an object has been created yet by checking if it is equal to the value 'null'. If you try and use an object before stage 2 has completed properly, you will get an error message since you cannot use an object which does not exist yet. Sometimes the compiler will pick up these errors for you but it's advisable not to take any chances. This statement checks to see if the variable `john` (which holds an object of type `PersonClass`) has been initialised yet. If it has not been initialized, that is, an object has not yet been created, a message is printed out. You can substitute a statement which uses the object created in the place of the message.

```
if(john == null)
    outputOnScreen("Object John has not yet been created");
```

The following program creates an object of a particular type and checks to see if it has been created correctly (i.e. it does not contain the value null).

```
public class AppletCreateObjectJane extends TrainingWheels    1
{                                                             2
private PersonClass jane;// Declare that an object called     3
                        // Jane of type PersonClass will      4
                        // be created in the program          5
                                                             6
public void entryPoint()                                      7
    {                                                         8
    // Check to see if the object is created yet              9
    checkIfObjectJaneCreated();                               10
                                                             11
    // Create the object                                      12
```

```
    jane = new PersonClass();                                13
                                                             14
    // Check to see if the created object is ok              15
    checkIfObjectJaneCreated();                              16
    } // End of entryPoint                                   17
                                                             18
public void checkIfObjectJaneCreated()                       19
    {                                                        20
    if(jane == null)                                         21
       outputOnScreen("The object Jane has not been created");  22
    else                                                     23
       outputOnScreen("The object Jane has been created");   24
    } // End of CheckIfObjectJaneCreated                     25
                                                             26
                                                             27
} // End of AppletCreateObjectJane                           28
                                                             29
// Insert the text for PersonClass discussed previously here  30
```

The output of the above program will look like the Figure 4.5.

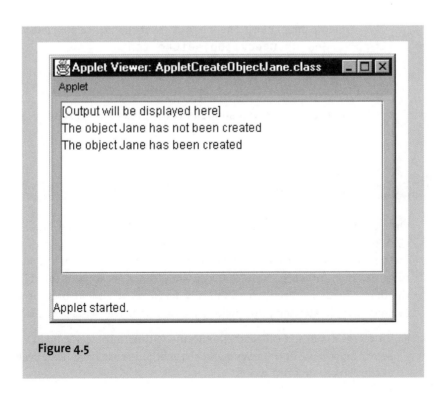

Figure 4.5

Objects can be passed as parameters too and so it will make more sense to rewrite our example program so that parts of it can be reused.

```
// Program to create an object and pass it as a              1
// parameter to a method which will check if it exists        2
                                                               3
public class AppletCheckObject extends TrainingWheels         4
{                                                              5
private PersonClass jane;                                     6
                                                               7
public void entryPoint()                                      8
   {                                                           9
   checkIfObjectCreated(jane);                                10
   jane = new PersonClass();                                  11
   checkIfObjectCreated(jane);                                12
   }                            // End of entryPoint          13
                                                               14
public void checkIfObjectCreated(PersonClass objectSupplied) 15
   {                                                           16
   if(objectSupplied == null)                                 17
      outputOnScreen("The object tested has not been created"); 18
   else                                                        19
      outputOnScreen("The object tested has been created");   20
   }  // End of CheckIfObjectCreated                          21
                                                               22
} // AppletCheckObject                                        23
                                                               24
// Put the text for PersonClass discussed previously in here 25
```

4.7   ACCESSING AN OBJECT

Once an object has been created how do we access the variables and methods within it? We simply give the name of the object followed by the name of the variable or method that we want to use. You separate the object name from the method you want to access by a full stop. Note that you should not access any variable from outside the object because, although technically possible, it should only be done for good reasons as it violates the principle of encapsulation. The syntax is as follows:

▶ To access a method called methodName within an object called ObjectName (the object must have been created and the method must have been declared as public in the class definition) write:

ObjectName.methodName();

This statement means that we are asking the system to go and find the object ObjectName and run the code it contains for the method methodName (which takes no parameters). For example,

```
jane.getName();
```

▶ To access a variable called variableName within an object called ObjectName (which must have been declared as public) write:

ObjectName.variableName;

This statement means that we are asking the system to go and find the object ObjectName and access the variable called variableName contained within it. Note that you do not often see statements like this as variables are usually declared as private and are therefore inaccessible from outside the object.

The possible errors are:

▶ If you try and access an object that has not yet been created then you get the runtime error 'Null pointer exception' (remember runtime means it happens when your program is running).

▶ Sometimes people use the class name instead of the object name. Remember each object is the creation of a class and is present in the computers memory. Classes represent only a set of definitions and cannot be used directly to store or execute methods unless there are special circumstances.

EXAMPLE Let's look at a very simple example. We define a class called `BusinessCardClass` which will hold the name of the representative for a particular company. We then create two different objects from this class. We use one to hold the name of the representative of the copier company we employ and one to hold the details for the water company. We can then access the information contained in these objects any time we want.

```
// The following program will setup two objects and use them     1
                                                                 2
public class AppletUseBusinessCardObject extends                 3
TrainingWheels
{                                                                4
                                                                 5
public void entryPoint()                                         6
    {                                                            7
    BusinessCardClass copierSalesPerson;                         8
    copierSalesPerson = new BusinessCardClass();                 9
                                                                10
    // Place values in the object just created                  11
    copierSalesPerson.setupObject("John Smith","Copiers Inc");   12
                                                                13
```

```
    BusinessCardClass waterCompany;                        14
    waterCompany = new BusinessCardClass();                15
                                                           16
    // Place values in the object just created            17
    waterCompany.setupObject("Jane Jones","Water Suppliers Plc");  18
                                                           19
    outputOnScreen("Your copier representative is");       20
    outputOnScreen(copierSalesPerson.getName());           21
                                                           22
    outputOnScreen("Your water company contact is");       23
    outputOnScreen(waterCompany.getName());                24
    } // End of entryPoint                                 25
                                                           26
} // End AppletUseBusinessCardObject                       27
                                                           28
// Above this line is your program, below is the class     29
// that your program will use to create the objects        30
// to store and access information                         31
                                                           32
class BusinessCardClass                                    33
{                                                          34
                                                           35
private String name;                                       36
private String company;                                    37
                                                           38
public void setupObject(String nameSupplied,String         39
companySupplied)
    {                                                      40
    name = nameSupplied;                                   41
    company = companySupplied;                             42
    } // End setupBusinessCardObject                       43
                                                           44
public String getName()                                    45
    {                                                      46
    return name;                                           47
    }// End getName                                        48
                                                           49
public String getCompany()                                 50
    {                                                      51
    return company;                                        52
    }// End getcompany                                     53
                                                           54
} // End of BusinessCardClass                              55
```

The output of the above program is shown in Figure 4.6.

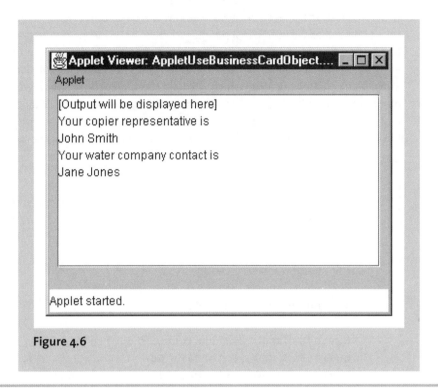

Figure 4.6

1   Try accessing the object `copierSalesPerson` before it is used, for example, put
          the statement `copierSalesPerson.getCompany();` in between the current
          lines 10 and 11.

       2   Try accessing the variable `Name` in one of the objects and see what the
          compiler says, that is put in `copierSalesPerson.Name` or `waterCom-`
          `pany.Name`.

4.7.1 Arrays of objects

Just as we have declared arrays to hold variables of type `int`, `String`, and so on, we
can also hold objects in arrays. The declaration syntax and the syntax for accessing an
element in the array are the same. What you must remember though is that the element accessed is an object and so must be used in the same way a single object variable must be used, that is, you give the name of the method you want to be executed.
You also need to remember that before an object is placed in an array location it must
be created (using `new`).

Let's rewrite the entryPoint method from the previous example so that instead of
using two separate variables to hold the details for the business cards we use an array
with two locations. In each of those locations will be an object which we can use to store
the details just as we used the separate variables. So in line 9, we state that we are going
to be using an array of objects of type BusinessCardClass. In line 10, we setup the
array to hold those objects. Note that this line does not create the objects that go in the
array, it just creates the array which will hold these objects. In line 12, we create the first
object and put that in the array location 0. In line 15, we create the second object and put
that in location 1 of the array. We can use the object in the array by writing the name of
the object (businessCardObjectArray[0]) and then putting the syntax for calling
a method within an object (.setupObject(String,String)).

```
public class AppletBusinessCardObjectArray extends        1
TrainingWheels                                            2
{                                                         3
                                                          4
public void entryPoint()                                  5
    {                                                     6
    int numberOfBusinessCards = 2;                        7
                                                          8
    BusinessCardClass businessCardObjectArray[];          9
    businessCardObjectArray = new                        10
    BusinessCardClass[numberOfBusinessCards];

                                                         11
    businessCardObjectArray[0] = new BusinessCardClass(); 12
    businessCardObjectArray[0].setupObject("John Smith", 13
    "CopiersInc");

                                                         14
    businessCardObjectArray[1] = new BusinessCardClass(); 15
    businessCardObjectArray[1].setupObject ("Jane Jones", 16
    "Water Suppliers Plc");

                                                         17
    outputOnScreen("Your copier representative is");     18
    outputOnScreen(businessCardObjectArray[0].getName()); 19
                                                         20
    outputOnScreen("Your water company contact is");    21
    outputOnScreen(businessCardObjectArray[1].getName()); 22
    } // End of entryPoint                               23
                                                         24
} // End of AppletBusinessCardObjectArray               25
                                                         26
// Code for BusinessCardClass would be placed here      27
```

EXAMPLE In the following example, we use the `BankAccountClass` which we discussed above. We create an object from that class called `johnsAccount`. We then use the method `lodgeAmount` to add a value of 10 to the balance in the account (line 14). As discussed above the method `lodgeAmount` in the object `johnsAccount` will check to see that this is a valid lodgement (line 32) and will return a message to indicate whether the transaction has been carried out or not. This message is stored in the variable `resultOfLodge10` (line 14) and then printed out on the screen (line 15). Following this we print out the current balance of the account. We also try a lodgement of –50 (line 18) but in this case the method `lodgeAmount` will not permit such an alteration to the balance and an error message is returned and printed out.

```
// The purpose of this program is to make use of an      1
// object which will attempt to check accesses to its    2
// variables and refuse to make changes if the change    3
// goes against the rules it has been given              4
                                                         5
public class AppletUseBankAccount extends TrainingWheels 6
{                                                         7
private BankAccountClass johnsAccount;                    8
                                                         9
public void entryPoint()                                 10
   {                                                     11
   johnsAccount = new BankAccountClass();                12
                                                         13
   String resultOfLodge10 = johnsAccount.lodgeAmount(10);   14
   outputOnScreen("Result of lodgement was "+resultOfLodge10);  15
   outputOnScreen("Balance is "+johnsAccount.getBalance());  16
                                                         17
   String resultOfLodge50 = johnsAccount.lodgeAmount(-50);  18
   outputOnScreen("Result of lodgement was "+resultOfLodge50);  19
   outputOnScreen("Balance is "+johnsAccount.getBalance());  20
   } // End of entryPoint                                21
                                                         22
} // End AppletUseBankAccount                            23
                                                         24
class BankAccountClass                                   25
{                                                         26
private int balance = 0;                                 27
private String name;                                     28
                                                         29
public String lodgeAmount(int amountToLodge)             30
```

```
   {                                                31
   if(amountToLodge < 0)                            32
      return "Error, cannot lodge negative amount"; 33
   else                                             34
      {                                             35
      balance = balance + amountToLodge;            36
      return "Balance lodged";                      37
      }                                             38
   } // End of lodgeAmount                          39
                                                    40
public int getBalance()                             41
   {                                                42
   return balance; // Send back balance             43
   } // End of getBalance                           44
                                                    45
// Other methods will go in here later to deal with the  46
// Name string                                      47
                                                    48
} // End of BankAccountClass                        49
```

The result of the above program is shown in Figure 4.7.

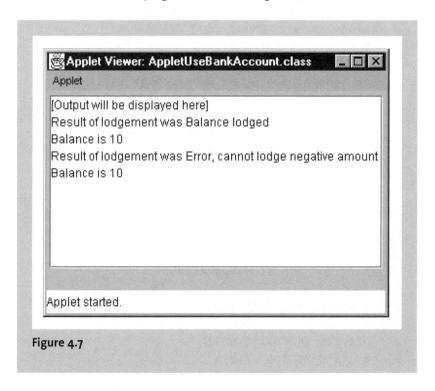

Figure 4.7

EXAMPLE   Let's take a look at an e-Commerce application. We write a class which will store details about a customer, including their balance. Now a customer's balance is sensitive so we want to put some sort of a scheme in place which will protect this information. Obviously we make the variable holding the customers balance a private variable so no one can get at without going through a method in the object. We then write the method that accesses the variable only if a correct password is supplied. The method then checks the password against one the user originally supplied and only allows access if they match. The password checking method (`checkPassword`) is declared as private since access to it outside the object is not needed.

The two characters used in line 17 (\n) are called a control character and tell the system to substitute a return for them. You need to use control characters to represent various formatting requirements (e.g. tab = '\t') since these cannot be directly placed in a string. The character '\' tells the system that the next character will be related to formatting so the character '\' cannot appear in a string on its own (if you must have a \ what you do is type two of them \\).

```
// The purpose of this program is to setup objects        1
// of class type CustomerAccountClass and use them         2
                                                           3
public class AppletEcommerceUserAccount extends TrainingWheels    4
{                                                          5
                                                           6
public void entryPoint()                                   7
    {                                                      8
    CustomerAccountClass johnsAccount;                     9
    johnsAccount = new CustomerAccountClass();             10
    johnsAccount.setUpObject("John","2468");               11
                                                           12
    outputOnScreen("Buying 50 worth of goods");            13
    outputOnScreen("Message from object is:");             14
    outputOnScreen(johnsAccount.makePurchase(50,"2468"));  15
                                                           16
    outputOnScreen("\nCheck balance"); // \n is a newline  17
                                                           18
    outputOnScreen("Message from object is:");             19
    outputOnScreen(johnsAccount.getBalance("2468"));       20
                                                           21
    outputOnScreen("\nBuying 100 worth of goods with       22
    wrong password");
                                                           23
    outputOnScreen("Message from object is:");             24
    outputOnScreen(johnsAccount.makePurchase(100,"777"));  25
                                                           26
```

```
    outputOnScreen("\nCheck balance with wrong password");   27
    outputOnScreen("Message from object is:");               28
    outputOnScreen(johnsAccount.getBalance("777"));          29
    } // End of entryPoint                                   30
                                                             31
} // End of AppletEcommerceUserAccount                       32
                                                             33
class CustomerAccountClass                                   34
{                                                            35
private int balanceOwed;                                     36
private String customerName;                                 37
private String customerPassword;                             38
                                                             39
public void setUpObject(String customerNameSupplied,         40
String customerPasswordSupplied)
    {                                                        41
    customerName = customerNameSupplied;                     42
    customerPassword = customerPasswordSupplied;             43
    balanceOwed = 0;                                         44
    } // End of setUpObject                                  45
                                                             46
public String makePurchase(int valueOfPurchase,              47
String passwordSupplied)
    {                                                        48
    if(checkPassword(passwordSupplied))                      49
        {                                                    50
        balanceOwed = balanceOwed + valueOfPurchase;         51
        return "Your purchase has been made";                52
        }                                                    53
    else                                                     54
        return "Sorry, wrong password, no purchase made.";   55
                                                             56
    } // End of makePurchase                                 57
                                                             58
public String getBalance(String passwordSupplied)            59
    {                                                        60
    if(checkPassword(passwordSupplied))                      61
        return "You owe "+balanceOwed;                       62
    else                                                     63
        return "Sorry, wrong password, no information for you.";   64
    } // End of getBalance                                   65
                                                             66
private boolean checkPassword(String passwordSupplied)       67
    {                                                        68
```

```
        if(passwordSupplied.equals(customerPassword))    69
           return true;                                   70
        else                                              71
           return false;                                  72
        } // End of checkPassword                         73
                                                          74
     } // End of BankAccountClass                         75
```

The execution of the above program is shown in Figure 4.8.

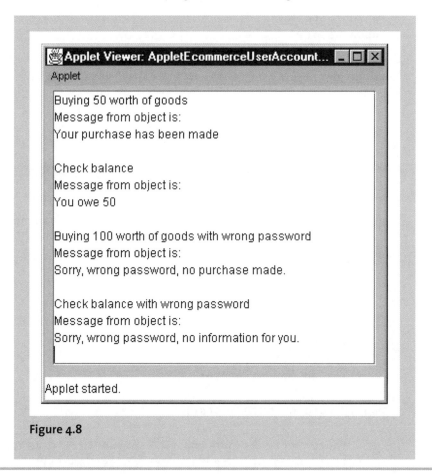

Figure 4.8

SCOPE CONTINUED

4.8.1 **Scope and objects**

Scope is the reason why the declaration of an object and its creation are introduced as two separate statements. This allows you to declare an object as a global variable and set that object up in a local method.

If you set up an object in a local method, then it doesn't disappear when the method is finished as it is not a part of that method but part of the overall program. The only variables which disappear with the method are those that are local to the method, that is, those which have been declared in the method.

In the example below, we set up our `BusinessCardClass` objects as global variables (lines 6 and 7). Next we create the objects for these variables in the method `setupObjects` and finally we use the global variables in the method `outputObjects`. Note that if we use an object in a method it must have been created at some point in the program. For example, if we change the order of the instructions in `entryPoint` to

```
outputObjects( );
setupObjects( );
```

the compiler will give an error message as an attempt is being made in `outputObjects` to use the two objects (`copierSalesPerson` and `waterCompany`) before they are created.

```
// This program shows how objects can be declared       1
// globally then setup and used in methods               2
                                                          3
public class AppletUseBusinessCard extends TrainingWheels  4
{                                                         5
private BusinessCardClass copierSalesPerson;             6
private BusinessCardClass waterCompany;                  7
                                                          8
public void entryPoint()                                 9
    {                                                    10
    setupObjects();                                      11
    outputObjects();                                     12
    } // End of entryPoint                               13
                                                         14
public void outputObjects()                              15
    {                                                    16
    outputOnScreen("Your copier representative is");     17
    outputOnScreen(copierSalesPerson.getName());         18
                                                         19
    outputOnScreen("Your water company contact is");     20
    outputOnScreen(waterCompany.getName());              21
    } // End of outputObjects                            22
                                                         23
// This method is private because we don't want anyone else  24
// setting up our objects from outside this program object   25
private void setupObjects()                              26
```

```
        {                                                    27
        copierSalesPerson = new BusinessCardClass();         28
        copierSalesPerson.setupObject("John Smith","Copiers Inc");  29
                                                             30
        waterCompany = new BusinessCardClass();              31
        waterCompany.setupObject("Jane Jones","Water Suppliers Plc");  32
        } // End setupObjects                                33
                                                             34
    } // End AppletUseBusinessCard                           35
                                                             36
    // Above this line is your program, below is the class that  37
    // your program will use to create the objects to store and  38
    // access information                                    39
                                                             40
    // Put the BusinessCardClass code in here                41
```

The output from the above program will be the same as the earlier example which used BusinessCardClass because both programs do the same thing. This shows you again that there are different ways of achieving the same goals but some ways have more benefits associated with them than others.

4.8.2 Scope: replacing global variables with local ones

In this section we see that you can replace the definition of a global variable by a local one.

```
    // The purpose of this program is to show how variable   1
    // definitions can 'override' or replace each other      2
                                                             3
    public class AppletVariablesScope extends TrainingWheels 4
    {                                                        5
    private int vat = 25;                                    6
                                                             7
    public void entryPoint()                                 8
        {                                                    9
        int costPrice = 4;                                  10
                                                            11
        double itemPrice = computeItemPrice(costPrice);     12
                                                            13
        outputOnScreen("The price is ");                    14
        outputOnScreen(itemPrice);                          15
                                                            16
```

```
    outputOnScreen("The value of Vat is "+vat); // This would        17
    // result in an error being generate by the compiler            18
    } // End of entryPoint                                          19
                                                                    20
private double computeItemPrice(int receivedCostPrice)              21
    {                                                               22
    double vat = 12.5;                                              23
                                                                    24
    double result = receivedCostPrice +                            25
    ((receivedCostPrice * vat) / 100);
                                                                    26
    outputOnScreen("The value of Vat is "+vat);                    27
                                                                    28
    return result; //Send back the result                          29
    } // End of ComputeItemPrice                                    30
                                                                    31
} // End of AppletVariablesScope                                    32
```

In the above program, we call a method, ComputeItemPrice, from the entry-Point method in order to perform a calculation. What is noteworthy about this program is that it declares a variable called vat, of type int, in line 6 and places the value 25 in it. The variable name vat is then declared again, this time as a double, in line 23 and the value 12.5 is placed in it. How can we have two variables of the same name existing at the same time? From a clarity point of view it may seem confusing but it is possible since both variables called vat have a different scope so neither can be seen by the other and therefore there is no conflict as far as the program is concerned. It's a bit like having two people with the same name in a company, so long as these people are not in the same room there is no confusion and by declaring them in separate methods you are making sure they are in different rooms.

What actually happens is the compiler will ignore (or override) the global version of vat and accept the new version of vat inside the method ComputeItemPrice. This new local version of vat can be used to store values until the method finishes. When the method finishes the local version of vat will disappear. This process will not affect the global variable vat, it just means it can't be seen in any method which redeclares (overrides) it, that is, you can only use one version of vat at a time. Which version of vat is currently in use depends on which part of the program you are in. The compiler will never allow there to be a conflict between two different versions of the same variable, so long as it can tell them apart its up to the programmer to use them correctly. This type of redeclaration is best avoided as it can lead to confusion.

The output of the above program is shown in Figure 4.9 in p. 135.

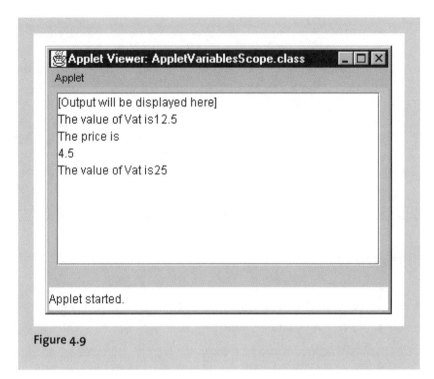

Figure 4.9

Put an object within an object, that is, within `BusinessCardClass` instead of a String holding a name use an object of type `personClass`.

SUMMARY

A variables scope determines where it can be used. A global (or instance) variable can be used throughout an object whereas a local variable is usually declared for a specific set of circumstances, such as a method, and does not need to be used elsewhere. Global and local variables are used to keep the program neat and tidy, declaring variables as global when they are only used in specific areas will make the program harder to read. Therefore when deciding to create a variable you should think carefully about whether it should be global or local.

The `if` statement is used to decide whether to execute a statement or statements. The decision is based on the evaluation of a condition. A condition can be any expression or variable as long as its result is a boolean variable (true or false). The `if` statement can execute a statement if the result is true or it can execute one statement if the result is true and another statement if the result is false (by using the `else` clause). If you are making use of an `else` clause, be careful that there is no confusion about what `if` statement it belongs to. If there is confusion about this, it could result in a dangling-else problem.

The words public and private are used to control access to variables and methods from outside an object. Variables and methods are freely accessible within an object but if any other part of the program uses an object only the public methods and variables are available to it. This allows programmers to protect certain methods and variables to make sure that no unauthorised changes can be made. This protection means that programmers can track down their mistakes more easily since they know that if a mistake occurrs in an area that no other part of the program has access to then it is their mistake and not someone misusing their code.

A class is a description of the methods and variables that an object will hold. Objects are produced by declaring a variable to hold an object of a particular class and placing an object created from a class definition (using new) into this variable. Any methods or variables declared as public can be accessed using the object variable name.

KEYWORDS

▶ *Condition* – A question, the answer to which is true or false. A condition is used to decide what to do next, that is, what statements should be executed.

▶ *Global* – A variable is available to every part of the class if it is declared as global.

▶ *Local* – A variable in only available in a small part of a class (usually a method) if it is declared as local.

▶ *Modifier* – A variable or methods visibility to other classes is controlled using modifiers (public or private)

▶ *Null* – Null is used to signify that an object does not exist. If an objects contents are null then it means that it has not been created using 'new'.

KEY CONCEPTS

▶ Decision making

```
if (conditionIsTrue)
    statement;

if(conditionIsTrue)
    statementExecutedIfConditionIsTrue;
else
    statementExecutedIfConditionIsFalse;
```

▶ Classes
Declaring a variable to hold an object

```
ClassName variableToHoldObject;
```

▶ Creating an object

```
variableToHoldObject = new ClassName();
```

▶ Checking if an object has been created

if(variableToHoldObject == null)

▶ Calling a method which has the modifier public (private methods can only be called within an object)

variableToHoldObject.publicMethodName();

▶ Accessing a variable which has the modifier public

variableToHoldObject.publicVariable = value;

EXERCISES

1 Write a program which will return the 'median' or middle number of three numbers.

2 Write a program which will find the smallest number in an array of five integers.

3 Write a program which will output a grammatically correct description of a variable. The variable describes the number of computers that are currently in stock. For example, if the number of computers in stock is 0 it should output:

```
There are no computers in stock.
```

If the number of computers in stock is 1 it should output:

```
There is a single computer in stock.
```

If the number of computers in stock is more than one it should output:

```
There are x computers in stock.
```

where x is the contents of the variable which holds the number of computers.

4 Write a method which will keep track of how many times it has been called, that is, it will output 'I have been called x times' each time it is called (where x is the total number of times it has been called).

5 Given the following narrative write a program that will implement it.
A funfair wants to run a series of checks on the people wanting to get on a certain ride. If the person wishing to ride is under 18 then they can only ride if they are not under 5 ft tall, otherwise they cannot ride. If the person has ridden the ride at least twice before then they can only ride if less than 20 people are in the queue (this gives everyone a fair chance to get a ride). Finally if the person has ridden the ride more than five times then they are not allowed ride it again because they may become ill. You can define all the relevant variables in the program, for example,

```
int age=10;
```

(*Hint*: Draw out the decision tree for the above and then use it to implement the necessary decisions.)

Solutions to exercises and interactive exercises can be obtained at:
http://www.palgrave.com/resources

Input/output, loops and data

INTRODUCTION

This chapter contains a number of quite diverse topics. A number of new commands are introduced but some important mechanisms and programming concepts are also discussed.

The first topic discussed in this chapter is how to obtain input from the user. Second, the mechanism by which more complicated conditions are constructed is looked at. Following that statements which allow you to repeat selected statements as many times as you wish are introduced. The next topic deals with several programming mechanisms which will help you solve problems and trace errors. Finally some of the more useful methods contained in the Math and String classes are explained.

5.1 INPUT/OUTPUT

Let's take a look a program we can use to enter information. The program will allow the user to type in information and we can then examine and use this information using some of the commands introduced in previous chapters.

The method in our program that will contain the instructions that we wish to perform on the input is called `processInput` (remember that the case, small and capital letters, is important). Your programs will still make use of the class called `TrainingWheels` although now you use elements of the class dealing with the Graphic User Interface (GUI) which is the name for graphical elements such as windows, icons, buttons, and so on used for input and output. This class does some of the work for you so you don't get bogged down by details at this early stage in your programming career. Later on you'll see that this is in fact the best way to write a program, to use previous classes to make life easier.

```
// This program will add an area to the screen which the      1
// users can use to type in an integer, the VM then sends      2
// this integer to the method processInput                     3
                                                               4
public class InputTest extends TrainingWheels               5
{                                                              6
public void entryPoint()                                     7
    {                                                          8
    addInputElement("Your Input");                           9
    } // End entryPoint                                       10
                                                              11
public void processInput(int inputSupplied)                  12
    {                                                          13
    outputOnScreen("Input supplied doubled is"               14
    +(inputSupplied * 2));
```

```
    } // End processInput                            15
                                                     16
} //End InputTest                                    17
```

Let us go through the above program line by line and see what it does. Line 5 gives the class the name `InputTest` and says that it is building on a class called `TrainingWheels`. This means that we can use the methods contained within the class `TrainingWheels`. We start the block for the program on line 6 (i.e. we put the opening bracket '{'). In line 7 we declare a method called `entryPoint`. This method will be executed as soon as your program will start. You don't have to do anything, just run this program and that method will be run for you (how it does this will be explained in Chapter 8, Section 8.6). That means any commands you put in this method will be run as soon as the program begins. The command we will run is in line 9 and is a call to a method named `addInputElement`. What this method (`addInputElement`) does is to create a box for you on screen to type your input into. It also places the text `Your Input` in front of the box to denote that it is an input area. Select the box using the mouse pointer and click the mouse button over it to make a cursor appear inside it. You can now type in your input (which should be an integer). You signify that you have finished typing in your input by pressing the return key. You decide what name will be displayed alongside the box to guide the user and supply it as a parameter for the `addInputElement` method. An example of a running program can be seen in Figure 5.1.

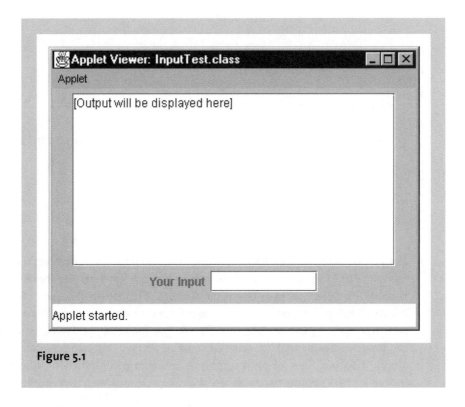

Figure 5.1

When the program is compiled and run the VM executes the `entryPoint` method and waits for the user to type in input. To signify to the VM that you want the input processed (i.e. you want the `processInput` method executed) press return when you have finished typing your input. The method `processInput` is executed by the VM to deal with this input each time return is pressed. This can continue until the VM is stopped (i.e. the browser is closed). In the method `processInput` (line 12), we have an instruction that prints out on the screen the value of the input element doubled. What is the value of the input? Well, it is passed to the method `processInput` by the program `TrainingWheels` using the parameter `inputSupplied`. Note that the input comes in the form of an integer, and so if you input any number other than an integer, this will not work. What happens if you want to supply input in a different format, for example a string? Well, you use the same method name, `processInput`, but in the parameter declaration specify that the method will take as a parameter a string variable. This method is shown on line 12 in the following program.

```
// This program places an input element on the screen and      1
// allows the user to input a string into it. When the user hits  2
// return processInput is called and the string is outputted    3
                                                                 4
public class InputTestProcess extends TrainingWheels            5
{                                                                6
public void entryPoint()                                        7
    {                                                            8
    addInputElement("Your Input");                               9
    } // end entryPoint                                         10
                                                                11
public void processInput(String inputSupplied)                 12
    {                                                           13
    outputOnScreen("Input supplied is "+inputSupplied);        14
    } // End processInput                                       15
                                                                16
} // End InputTestProcess                                      17
```

Keen eyed readers will spot that we have used two different versions of the same method name (`processInput`). The reason why we can have two methods with the same name is that each takes different parameters. This is a technique called overloading which allows you to use the same name for a method more than once, provided each similarly named method takes a different parameter. Overloading is intended to aid the programmer by making relevant method names easier to remember (e.g. output, store). This is a form of polymorphism, an example of which we also saw when we looked at the + operator and strings. We take a closer look at overloading in Chapter 6.

5.1.1 Event driven programming

The way the above programs operated was that the instructions in `entryPoint` were executed when the program started. Then the programs waited until the user pressed return while in a text box. Therefore the programs depended on the user to press return in a textbox before any other instructions were executed. When a program's execution sequence is based on what the user does next it is known as an event driven program. An event driven program is one which depends on events, which are usually created by the user. The programs in earlier chapters were not event driven as they did not depend on the user doing anything since all the data was present in the program (this is known as hardcoding a program which means that it does not require any external data). You can read these programs and follow what instructions they executed and exactly when they preformed them. With event driven programming you cannot follow the program exactly as you are not sure what exactly the user will do. For example, in the two programs seen earlier in this chapter (pp. 140–42) the user may never enter data, therefore the method `processInput` may never be executed. Writing programs in a form which facilitates event driven programming means that you decide what events the user can generate (click on a button, move a mouse, press return, etc.) and write code to handle the relevant events. You may not know what events the user will cause or in what order they will cause them but your program should be written in such a way that this does not matter. From now on, any program which involves user input is written in the form of an event driven program. The above examples are based on a single event (pressing return) but later on in the book you will see how multiple events can be handled and different methods executed depending on the event.

EXERCISE Write a program that combines the two versions of `processInput`, that is, if the user inputs a string then a welcoming message is printed out and if they input an integer then their number doubled is output.
Hint: The two different versions of the method `processInput` can be included in the same class.

5.1.2 Buttons

If you do not need to have information passed to your program by the user but require the user to send a signal to the program then you can use a button. The method `addButton` will take a string as a parameter and display a button on the screen with this string written on top of it. When the user presses the button the VM will look for a method called `public void ifButtonPressed()` which it will execute.

In the following program the user presses a button to cause a string to be written out to the output area.

```
// This program places a button on the screen and allows the    1
// user to press it. When the user clicks on it                  2
// ifButtonPressed is called and a string is output             3
                                                                  4
public class InputTestButton extends TrainingWheels            5
{                                                                6
public void entryPoint()                                        7
    {                                                            8
    addButton("Press To See a Message");                        9
    } // end entryPoint                                          10
                                                                  11
public void ifButtonPressed()                                   12
    {                                                            13
    outputOnScreen("You pressed the button");                   14
    } // End processInput                                       15
                                                                  16
} // End InputTestButton                                        17
```

The display of the above program after the user presses the button once is shown in Figure 5.2.

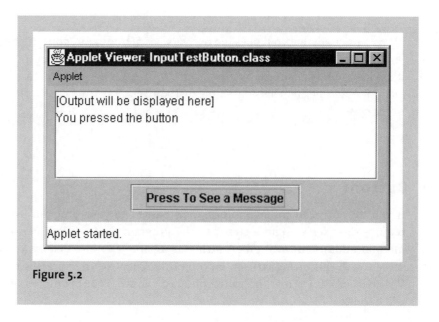

Figure 5.2

5.1.3 Input validation

Having looked at input, the next important topic is input validation, that is checking the input to see that it is valid and is what we expected.

We often hear about invalid input such as people being assigned a negative age or having their bank balances reduced instead of increased. In many cases problems arise because the input values are correct as far as a computer is concerned but incorrect with respect to their context. So, for example, when someone supplies a negative age for a person (e.g. –24) the computer will usually blindly take the data and use it in a way that human beings will regard as incorrect as the computer has not had the context explained to it.

Usually people will blame the computer for these errors when the fault is that of two persons: (i) the person who entered the mistaken data and (ii) the programmer who didn't make sure that the input received by their program was correct or valid before it was used in an expression, that is, they assumed that the user would never make a mistake (a dangerous assumption).

To prevent such misunderstandings we must build a little intelligence into the computer program (i.e. define the context in the form of rules). This intelligence can be simple or quite complicated depending on the data being handled. Let's take the age as our example. For us, a valid age for human beings must be greater than 0 but less than 200. Therefore any number we see outside this range must be an error. We can now build into any program we write that any value for age supplied by a user must be checked to see that it is in the permitted range.

To protect our program from silly people, we should always test the input received before we use it. We can do this by writing checking statements using limits and any other rules necessary for that particular piece of data. The important point to remember is what that piece of data means to us, and consequentially what will it be used for. For example, a numerical input may be a sum of money, an age, a measurement or a time period (hours, days, years). All the computer cares about is storing and operating on the number, it neither knows nor cares what it represents. But you should take care because a user making a mistake entering a number can throw out your calculations.

Looking at the age example again we have that it must be greater than 0 but cannot be greater than 200. We will just use the >0 test for the moment.

We now write our test conditions to make sure that the input is in the correct range.

```
if(ageSupplied<0)
    outputOnScreen("Error, age too low");
```

EXERCISE Write statements which will check to see if the input supplied is a valid month (where we represent Jan.–Dec. by the numbers 0–11).

5.1.3.1 Conclusion

Input validation is usually a bothersome process and often programmers don't bother with it, however, this is a mistake and you should always try and check the input as thoroughly as you can before you use it.

5.1.4 Divide by zero error

Some mistakes in input can be very harmful indeed to the program. One of the states which can result from mistaken input is called a 'divide by zero error'. This happens when the user inputs a zero instead of a non-zero number and this zero is used in a division operation. As you know any number divided by 0 is infinity and the computer cannot deal with the concept of infinity so it will commonly halt the program and notify the user that the program contains a mistake (you can check this rule by dividing any number by zero on your pocket calculator and seeing what it says).

For example, type in the following program, compile it and run it:

```
public class divByZero extends TrainingWheels
{
public void entryPoint()
    {
    outputOnScreen("Result is" + (4/0));
    }
} //End divByZero
```

When the above program is run it will cause the VM to print out the message Java.lang.ArithmeticException:/by Zero. This message indicates that our statement (4/0) is correct as far as the compiler is concerned (since the program compiled without incident) but performed an illegal operation while executing (namely dividing by zero) and was therefore halted. When the VM comes across something it doesn't expect (called an exception), it sometimes stops the program because it cannot continue executing instructions that ask it to do the impossible. Later on we look at how to deal with exceptions but for the moment you should concentrate on making sure that your program doesn't cause any exceptions, that is, you validate your important variables before using them.

EXERCISE Write a program which will input a number and check that number to see if it is zero. If the number isn't zero, then it is divided by two and the result is printed out. If it is zero, then print out an error message.

Java is in fact a little friendlier than some other languages which may cause your operating system to hang if you make a divide by zero mistake. Java merely stops running your program. Remember it's your responsibility as the author of the program to minimise the possibility of mistakes that can happen.

5.2   **LOGICAL OPERATORS**

We have seen how to test one expression at a time. But how can we test a piece of data using more than one test? Well, one way we have seen is to simply follow one `if` statement with another. Another (better) way is to combine two expressions in one `if` statement using a 'logical operator'. A logical operator is used if you want to get the result of two expressions. You can use a logical operator to check if both of the expressions evaluated to true or only one did.

Logical operators work with expressions which produce a boolean result (true or false). A logical operator will take two boolean values and produce a boolean value as a result based on a set of built in rules. For example, one rule may say that if one boolean value is true and the other is false, then the expression should give an answer of false. Another rule may take the same values and give an answer of true.

These expressions will usually contain a relational test which will produce boolean values.

Let's go back to the age example, one way of checking to see if the age entered is >0 but <200 is to write the following:

```
if(ageSupplied > 0)
   {
   if(ageSupplied < 200)
      outputOnScreen("Age just right, thank you");
   else
      outputOnScreen("The value you entered is incorrect");
   }
else
   outputOnScreen("The value you entered is incorrect");
```

There is a better way of doing the above using logical operators. First, we look at the two main logical operators AND and OR.

5.2.1 AND

The example above shows it can be cumbersome to do a relatively simple check. However, there is an easier way. All you really want to do is to have a statement which is the equivalent of the English sentence: 'if the age is greater than 0 and also less than 200, then we have a correct value, otherwise (else) the value supplied is incorrect'.

Putting our required code in program form we have:

```
if((ageSupplied > 0)AND(ageSupplied < 200))
   outputOnScreen("Age just right, thank you");
```

Well, we can do this in Java but instead of the word AND we use two symbols && (the symbol can be obtained using SHIFT 7 on most keyboards). Make sure that you put both of the & symbols together because a space between them may give an error message.

You'll see the AND logical operator explained using Table 5.1. Using Table 5.1 you can work out what the result of combining the two expressions will be.

So what will Expression_1 && Expression_2 result in? It depends very much on the boolean value resulting from Expression_1 and Expression_2. Use Table 5.1 to find the line which holds the same values as your statement. For example, the answer to the question 'if (true && false)' can be found in the entry

Yes	No	False

where we see that the answer for the expression is FALSE (i.e. the expression evaluates to the boolean value false).

Table 5.1

Is the result of Expression_1 True?	Is the result of Expression_2 True?	Then Expression_1 && Expression_2 will be
No	No	False
No	Yes	False
Yes	No	False
Yes	Yes	True

So, we can now represent our check for a correct age in the form of a single expression by combining the two checks we have used earlier.

```
if((ageSupplied > 0) && (ageSupplied < 200))
    outputOnScreen("Age just right, thank you");
else
    outputOnScreen("Value entered is wrong, should be >0 and <200");
```

Note that in the piece of code above I am giving the user one of two messages. One message tells them that they entered the right data. This sort of message is not usually found in a program as it is redundant. The other message which tells the user that they have entered the incorrect data is the important one because it should tell the user two things: (1) they have done something wrong and (2) how to go about correcting their mistake.

Often programmers ignore this second part of an error message but this can cause many difficulties for the user who may not always be very familiar with computers. Anytime you write an error message you should also put in instructions to tell the user more about the error and how to correct it. This makes your program more useful to people.

Let's work through the above piece of code for some sample values.

EXAMPLE 1   ageSupplied is 20

The statement if((ageSupplied > 0) && (ageSupplied < 200)) will now look like this (we replace the variable name ageSupplied with the actual value):

```
if((20>0) && (20<200))
```

The next step is to evaluate the expressions in brackets.

20 > 0 evaluates to true since 20 is bigger than 0.
20 < 200 evaluates to true since 20 is less than 200.

So our statement now looks like this:

```
if(true && true)
```

If we look at Table 5.1 we see when the two expressions involved in an AND are true then the result of the overall statement is true so our statement therefore evaluates to

```
if(true)
```

This causes the statement immediately following the if statement to be executed. In our example the statement to be executed is:

```
outputOnScreen("Age just right, thank you");
```

EXAMPLE 2   ageSupplied is 300

Let's try the same piece of code with a different value. Again we replace the variable name with the value:

```
if((300 > 0) && (300 < 200))
```

We then evaluate the two expressions in brackets

300 > 0 evaluates to true.
300 < 200 evaluates to false since 300 is larger than 200.

So the statement is:

```
if(true && false)
```

We look at Table 5.1 and see that if Expression_1 is true and Expression_2 is false then the result of true && false is false, so our if statement evaluates to:

```
if(false)
```

This now causes the statement following the else keyword to be executed, that is,

```
outputOnScreen("Value entered is wrong, should be >0 and <200");
```

The above process of putting in sample values and working out the solution is known as a walkthrough and you should do this with your programs. Go through them manually and put in different values and see what the next statement executed will be. This allows you to spot problems before the code is compiled, executed or delivered to the customer.

Here is the full program for you to try out with sample values.

```
// This program demonstrates the result of two test      1
// combined using AND (&&)                                2
                                                          3
public class ANDTest extends TrainingWheels               4
{                                                         5
public void entryPoint()                                  6
    {                                                     7
    addInputElement("Input Age");                         8
    } //End entryPoint                                    9
                                                          10
public void processInput(int ageSupplied)                 11
    {                                                     12
    if((ageSupplied > 0) && (ageSupplied < 200))          13
        outputOnScreen("Age just right, thank you");      14
    else                                                  15
        outputOnScreen("Value entered incorrect, must be >0   16
        and <200");
                                                          17
    } //End processInput                                  18
                                                          19
} //End ANDTest                                           20
```

5.2.1.1   Brackets

Make sure you don't forget your brackets '(' and ')'. Bracket each expression and bracket the whole expression, otherwise the compiler may get confused about what to do. For example, if you forget to bracket the whole expression you get the following error from the compiler.

Original statement:

```
if(ageSupplied>0) && (ageSupplied<200)
```

Compiler response to this statement:

```
ANDTest.java:10: Missing term.
  if(ageSupplied>0) && (ageSupplied<200)
                  ^

ANDTest.java:10: Invalid expression statement.
  if(ageSupplied>0) && (ageSupplied<200)
                  ^
```

To fix the statement simply bracket the two expressions and the && operator:

```
if((ageSupplied>0) && (ageSupplied<200))
```

Brackets not only solve confusion as regards the different parts of the expression but they also overcome a cause of programmer confusion known as precedence (mentioned briefly in Chapter 3, p. 58). In most programming languages every mathematical operator has a particular priority in an expression. For example: 2 + 4 * 3 would be run by the computer in the order 4 * 3 and then 2 + 12, that is, it evaluates any operation involving * before one involving + . This differs to the way most people work (we'd go 2 + 4 and multiply the result by 3) and can cause problems, and so the best thing to do is to always bracket your mathematical expressions in the order you want them to be evaluated. So our original expression would now be (2 + 4) * 3.

5.2.1.2   What do you do if you have more than two expressions?

Notice that we are dealing with two expressions for the AND logical operator. That is, `Expression_1 && Expression_2`.

What happens if you have more than two tests you want to perform? For example, what happens if you want to test a number to see that its not less than –10, not greater than 20 and not equal to 0.

You therefore have three expressions: `(number >= –10)`, `(number <= 20)`, `(number ! = 0)`.

Beginners often think of writing the following:

```
if(number > = –10) && (number <= 20) && (number ! = 0)
```

You can't do this, look back at the rule for AND, you can only have two expressions not three. The way to get three into two is to divide your three expressions into two groups, one group will do two expressions and the other group will do the remaining expression and the result of the first two expressions. That is,

```
if((number > = –10) && ((number <= 20) && (number !=0)))
```

Note in the above we put the second two expressions in another level of brackets. Remember the rule that the expression which is evaluated first is the one within the most sets of brackets. The first part of the above statement to be executed will be `((number <= 20) && (number ! = 0))`. This part is executed first as it is the deepest. `(number >= –10)` is only enclosed in one set of brackets while `((number <= 20) && (number ! = 0))` is contained within two sets.

We then take the result of this operation and perform the next deepest expression (the result of the previous expression would be filled in).

```
(number >= –10) && [Result of ((number <= 20) && (number != 0))]
```

This is how we execute three logical tests, by breaking the three into two separate expressions. You can apply a similar method to any number of logical tests that you wish to combine.

Also remember that when using brackets it is important that for every right bracket '(' there is a corresponding left bracket ')'. If compiler cannot match every bracket it will report an error message and you will have to go through your program to find where the bracket is missing.

5.2.2 OR

We have seen how to check if one expression AND another are true using &&. How can we check to see if one expression OR the other is true? Well, like AND a set of symbols exist in Java which indicate that an OR test is to be done on the two expressions. The symbols used are || (the symbol | is SHIFT \ on most keyboards). Again we look at the result for Expression_1 || Expression_2 in Table 5.2.

Table 5.2

Is the value for Expression_1 true?	Is the value for Expression_2 true?	Then Expression_1 || Expression_2 will be
No	No	False
No	Yes	True
Yes	No	True
Yes	Yes	True

EXAMPLE

Let's say we want to give a customer a free gift if they spend more than £100 or buy more than 30 items at a time. We need to write an expression to test if the customer satisfies one or the other of these conditions. The expression would be:

```
if((totalSpent > 100) || (numberOfItems > 30))
    outputOnScreen("Give customer free gift");
```

Try this out using a manual walkthrough or by adapting the previous example program to contain the new statements. Since you can supply only one input to the program via a parameter you will have to include a variable in your program to hold the other value necessary for the program.

5.2.3 Checking your expressions

Always ensure that your logical expression does what you think it does. If you have written the expression incorrectly, your program will be carrying out different instructions to those in your algorithm resulting in errors. For example, under what conditions do you think statement1 and statement2 get executed in the following expression?

```
if((number<5) || (number>4))
    statement1;
else
    statement2;
```

`statement1` is always executed no matter what the value of number. It is unlikely that the programmer will go to the trouble of writing `statement2` knowing it will never be executed, and so it seems likely that the author of the above has made a mistake when translating the algorithm into code.

5.2.4 Combining your expressions – decision trees

Some problems involve making a lot of decisions and it can get confusing deciding how to program them and how to check them. The most common strategy is to make out an upside-down tree like structure with all your decisions on forks and their possible outcomes at the end of a branch. This diagram can then be used to write the programming statements. You can also work backwards when you want to understand a group of complicated if statements by drawing out the relevant tree.

For example, let's look at the following instructions and try to make sense of them. A shopping chain wants to hold a special promotion. They want to hand out various types of gifts based on the profile of the customer. If the customer has a loyalty card and they purchase over £70 worth of goods, then they get 10% of their money back. If they spend less than £70, they get five points added on to their loyalty card for every £1 spent. If the customer does not have a loyalty card, then if they spend more than £50 or they buy more than 20 items, they get a £5 voucher. Otherwise they get a chocolate bar.

So, let's put the above details in graphical form as shown in Figure 5.3.

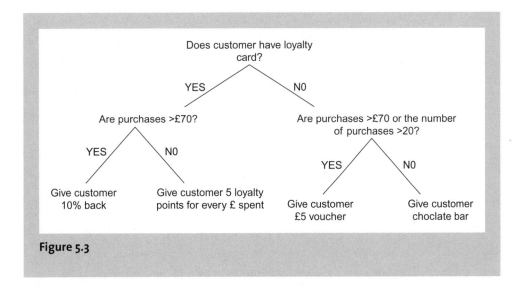

Figure 5.3

Now it's much easier to follow what is going on using the diagram and simpler to write code to implement the decisions. The code will be as follows (take the decision at the top of the tree as the first one):

```
public class ShoppingGiveaway extends TrainingWheels        1
{                                                           2
public void entryPoint()                                    3
    {                                                       4
    boolean customerHasLoyaltyCard;                         5
    int totalPurchases;                                     6
    int numberOfItems;                                      7
                                                            8
    customerHasLoyaltyCard = true;                          9
    totalPurchases = 30;                                    10
    numberOfItems = 10;                                     11
                                                            12
    if(customerHasLoyaltyCard)                              13
        {                                                   14
        if(totalPurchases > 70)                             15
            outputOnScreen("Give customer £ "              16
            + (totalPurchases/10));
        else                                                17
            outputOnScreen("Give customer "+(totalPurchases * 5)  18
            + "points");
        }                                                   19
    else                                                    20
        {                                                   21
        if((totalPurchases > 50) || (numberOfItems > 20))   22
            outputOnScreen("Give customer £5 voucher");    23
        else                                                24
            outputOnScreen("Give customer chocolate bar");  25
        }                                                   26
                                                            27
    } // End entryPoint                                     28
                                                            29
} // End ShoppingGiveaway                                   30
```

The result for the above program is shown in Figure 5.4 in p. 155.

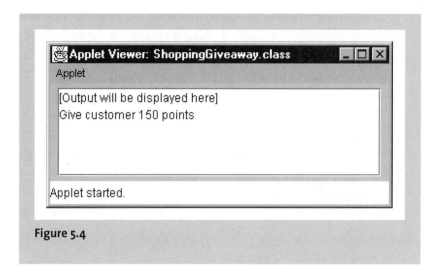

Figure 5.4

5.2.5 NOT

Another logical operator we need to look at is NOT (represented by an exclamation mark !). NOT will simply reverse the result of a single boolean expression. This is useful sometimes when you want to write your expression more clearly.

Is the expression true?	Then ! expression will be
Yes	False
No	True

So, for example, the expression value = !value; will reverse the contents of the boolean variable value.

The NOT operation allows you to translate from an algorithm to a piece of code as directly as possible. For example, say our algorithm specifies that a statement is to be executed if a particular number is not less than five. We can represent this wish using the NOT operator in the following way:

```
if(!(number < 5))
    statement;
```

The alternative to the above is to alter the algorithm so that it reads 'execute statement if number greater than or equal to five'. This is valid but we've wasted time doing it and we've had to alter the original set of instructions meaning that when the program is read through it does not match the algorithm exactly and more time is needed to check the program.

The NOT operator also allows you to structure your checking statements better. Remember when we first looked at AND we produced the following code:

```
if((ageSupplied > 0) && (ageSupplied < 200))
    outputOnScreen("Age just right, thank you");
else
    outputOnScreen("Value entered is wrong, should be >0 and <200");
```

The outputOnScreen("Age just right, thank you") part is redundant but how do we get the code to send out a message only if the user supplies the incorrect input? The answer is to use the NOT operator to rephrase the expression as follows:

```
if(!((ageSupplied > 0) && (ageSupplied < 200)))
    outputOnScreen("Value entered is wrong, should be >0 and <200");
```

Our expression now reads 'if the value of ageSupplied is not in the range 0–200 then print out an error message'.

5.2.6 Summary

!	Logical NOT (Reverse a Boolean value)
&&	Logical AND (Evaluate to TRUE if both operands are TRUE)
||	Logical OR (Evaluate to TRUE if **either or both** operands are TRUE)

EXERCISES

1 Write a program which will take a number as input. The program should use methods to check to see if the number is zero and positive and print out the relevant message.

2 Given the following narrative write a program that will implement it.
   A funfair wants to run a series of checks on the people wanting to get on a certain ride. If the person wishing to ride is under 18 then they can only ride if they are not under 5 ft tall, otherwise they cannot ride. If the person has ridden the ride at least twice before, then they can only ride if less than 20 people are in the queue (this gives everyone a fair chance to get a ride). Finally, if the person has ridden the ride more than five times then they are not allowed ride it again because they may become ill.

5.3   CONSTANT

A constant is an unchanging variable. That is a bit of a contradictory statement but that is literally the way you write the definition in your program. What it essentially means is that a constant is declared and initialised in almost the same way as a variable but it is fixed at its initial value for the life of the program. Declaring variables as constants means that the user is permitted to see their contents but not to change them. This allows you to set constants at the start of your program which can only be changed by editing your program and recompiling it.

Examples of constants: First Name, Speed of Light. As a guide to whether an element should be declared as a constant or not, ask yourself if an item of data is likely to change for the life of your program. If it won't, you should declare it as a constant. If it is likely to change, then it should be declared as a variable.

Constants are declared in that same way as variables but the word 'final' is put before the declaration. You must assign a value to a constant variable on the same line as it was declared on, otherwise the compiler will report the error:

Blank final variable may not have been initialised.

So, a statement for the creation of a constant must be of the form:

final type IDENTIFIER = initialValue;

The initial value can be an actual value (called a literal) such as 9, "Hello", or it can be another constant.

Constants can be public or private just like variables. The convention for the name of a constant is that it is capitalised, this does not mean that a constant will not work if it is not in capital letters it just makes them easier to spot.

EXAMPLE

```
private final int DAYSINWEEK=7;
```

We now have an integer variable called DAYSINWEEK that will always contain the value 7, any attempt to change that in the program will result the compiler error: 'Can't assign a value to a final variable'.

Constants are significantly underused by novice programmers but their importance cannot be underestimated. By using a constant you may save yourself from great inconvenience at a later stage in the programs life. For example, say you are asked to write a program to store and calculate an average for 30 integers. You can write your program as:

```
int values[];

values = new int[30];

for(counter = 0;counter < 30;counter++)
    inputItems

for(counter = 0;counter < 30;counter++)
    compute average
```

The above statements are quite correct but think about the implications of writing the program in this way. How often have you used the value 30? Three times in three different parts of the program. What do you do if the user asks you to alter the program to accommodate 60 numbers instead of 30? You must find those three locations in the code and change the value 30 to 60. What happens if you write a much larger program where you have many more uses of the number 30? Again you must read through the code and manually alter each value of 30 to read 60. Won't it be much easier to have written the code as follows:

```
final int MAXNUMBEROFITEMS = 30;
int values[];

values = new int[MAXNUMBEROFITEMS];

for(counter = 0;counter < MAXNUMBEROFITEMS;counter++)
    inputItems

for(counter = 0;counter < MAXNUMBEROFITEMS;counter++)
    compute average
```

The above code does exactly the same thing but it uses the number 30 only once and stores the relevant number in a constant for the rest of the program. That means that if the program needs to be altered at a later date, you only need to make one alteration and need not search through the entire body of code for instances of that number. Bear this in mind as you are writing your programs as a little planning at the start can save a lot of time later on.

Note that the values which are directly entered into code (such as the value 30 above) are known as 'literals'.

5.4 LOOPS

One of the big advantages of computers is that they are easily able to perform repetition, that is, they can do the same task over and over. In this section we look at how you go about writing your program so that certain statements can be repeatedly executed until we decide to stop.

When we look at repetition, more commonly known as looping, we need to concern ourselves with two questions: what statements do we repeatedly execute and how often should we execute those statements? You indicate to the compiler which statements are to be repeatedly executed by putting them in brackets and placing them next to the loop statement. Telling the compiler how often to execute these statements is another matter. It would be simple if the statements had to be executed forever (called an infinite loop) but this is a rare case. Loops stop under one of two circumstances, either a predefined number of repeated executions has been reached or a certain event has occurred (like the user types in 'stop'). These are known as count controlled loops and event controlled loops respectively and each type of loop has a particular statement associated with it.

We look at three loop statements, the for statement is a count controlled loop and is the most popular type of loop. The while statement is an event controlled loop and is the next most commonly used. Finally we look at a do-while loop which is a variation on the while loop and is useful in certain situations.

5.4.1 The 'for' statement

As discussed above, the for statement is a count controlled loop. That means when you setup the loop you need to indicate how many times the loop should execute. You do this by initialising an integer variable which the computer will use to keep track of how many times the loop has been executed. This variable is often known as a counter (though you can call it by any name you want). Next you need to indicate what value to stop at, this is known as a limit. Usually you compare the current value of the counter variable to the value of the limit for the loop each time the loop executes, if the counter variable exceeds the limit, then the statements in the loop are no longer executed and the rest of the program continues. If the counter variable does not exceed the limit, then the statements in the loop are executed and the value of the counter variable is altered to reflect the fact that the loop has been executed again. It is up to you as a programmer to define how much to alter the counter variable by, you can increase the counter variable by 1 after each loop or by any value you wish.

So, in summary, the programmer needs to supply:

▶ An integer variable to hold the counter (this variable can have any name you want)

▶ A test to decide if the loop can continue

▶ A statement to alter the value of the counter

▶ The statements which will be executed each time the loop goes round.

At each cycle of the loop a statement or a block of statements is executed. At each execution an expression is evaluated to see if the loop should continue. The loop continues as long as the 'testing condition' expression evaluates to TRUE.

The for statement has the following appearance:

```
for(initialisation of counter; test for loop halt condition; counter update)
{ loop_statements;
} // End of the loop
```

The three sections of the for loop are:

1 Initialisation of counter – used to set up the counter used in the for loop: for example,

```
for(counter=0;...
```

The counter initialisation can be any assignment expression (e.g. totalNumber-OfMonths=yearsRequested*12).

You can create a variable specially to hold the count

```
for(int counter=0;...
```

Remember to make your counter variable meaningful. Many programmers use names like i, j and k for their loop counter which, although valid, do not help people trying to read their programs.

2 Test for loop halt condition – This is the expression that is evaluated before the body of the loop is executed. For example, for(...;counter<10;...)

means that the body of the loop (the loop statements) will be executed if the variable counter has a value less than 10. The testing expression can be any expression which evaluates to a boolean result. You can even use a call to a method to obtain the result or combine a number of expressions using a logical operator.

3 Counter update – The counter is changed to reflect an execution of a statement. For example, we could increase the counter by 1 every time the statement is executed:

```
for( ...;...;counter++)
```

The counter update can be any expression (e.g. `counter+=value/2`). You can increase or decrease value of the counter (e.g. `counter--`).

The progress of a loop can be shown in the Figure 5.5 (start at the first box and follow the arrows).

EXAMPLE

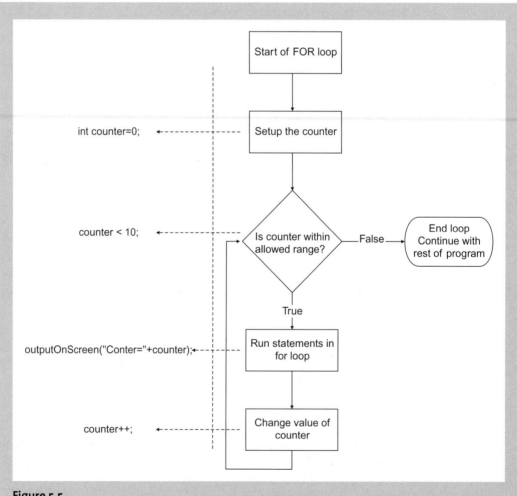

Figure 5.5

The statement executed each time a `for` loop runs can either be a single statement:

```
for(int counter = 0;counter<10;counter++)
    outputOnScreen("Counter = "+counter);
```

Or a block of statements:

```
for(count=0;count<10;count++)
    {
    outputOnScreen("Current value is "+count);
    outputOnScreen("Current value *2 is "+(count*2));
    outputOnScreen("Current value *3 is "+(count*3));
    } // End of loop 'for(count=0;count<10;count++)'
```

Notice that in the above code I put the loop statement in the comment that follows the end of the loop. This is done so that readers of the code have an easy time figuring out where the loop finishes.

IMPORTANT! Never put a semicolon directly after the `for` Statement. For example, don't do this:
```
    for(count = 0;count < 10;count++);←
        statement;
```

What you are saying if you do put a semicolon directly after the `for` statement is that the `for` loop ends at the semicolon and the `statement` you thought was being executed as part of the loop only gets executed after the `for` loop is finished. That is, in the above piece of code the `statement` is executed only once after the `for` loop has completed executing a blank statement for 10 times. Make sure you remember to check this anytime you have problems with loops as it catches out even experienced programmers. The correct version of the above is:

```
for(count=0;count<10;count++)
    statement;
```

If you are using a block of statements, then there is no need to supply a semicolon at the end at all. The compiler realises that you are associating a block of statements with your `for` loop and executes the block each time the `for` loop goes around. Each statement in the block must still be finished by a semicolon.

```
for(count=0;count<10;count++)
{
Statement(s);
}
```

EXAMPLE

```
// This program will print out the value of a counter      1
// variable as a for loop executes                         2
                                                           3
public class FORLoopTest extends TrainingWheels            4
{                                                          5
public void entryPoint()                                  6
   {                                                       7
   for(int counter=0;counter<10;counter++)                8
      {                                                    9
      outputOnScreen("Counter value is "+counter);        10
      }// end for(int counter=0;counter<10;counter++)     11
                                                          12
   } // End entryPoint                                    13
                                                          14
} // End FORLoopTest                                      15
```

The output of the above example is:

```
Counter value is 0
Counter value is 1
Counter value is 2
Counter value is 3
Counter value is 4
Counter value is 5
Counter value is 6
Counter value is 7
Counter value is 8
Counter value is 9
```

5.4.1.1 'for' and the number of executions

Since you are counting up the number of executions and comparing them, make sure that you get your sums right. For example, look at the following loop conditions and the number of times they execute:

Loop statement	Number of executions
for(count=0;count<10;count++) statement;	Statement is executed 10 times (count starts at 0 and goes to 9)
for(count=0;count<=10;count++) statement;	Statement is executed 11 times (count starts at 0 and goes to 10)

So, by putting in the = in the second loop we cause the loop to execute one more time because its limit has effectively been changed. This can be a very serious logical error, particularly if you are using the value in the counter variable to access arrays (see later in this chapter).

For loops, which are incorrect because the programmer thought they were executing the loop statements one more or one less time than they actually were, are said to be suffering from an 'out by one error'. The easiest way to avoid it is to stick to a particular way of writing loops.

Remember...

`for(count=0;count<n;count++)`   executes n times (count goes from 0 to n–1)

`for(count=1;count<=n;count++)` also executes n times (count goes from 1 to n)

EXAMPLE   You can try the following example and see what different limits result in. You supply the limit you want for the loop as input and the loop prints out the value of its counter and the limit as it's repeating statements.

```
public class FORTest extends TrainingWheels              1
 {                                                        2
 public void entryPoint()                                 3
    {                                                     4
    addInputElement("Input Limit");                       5
    } // End entryPoint                                   6
                                                          7
 public void processInput(int limit)                      8
    {                                                     9
    for(int counter=0;counter<limit;counter++)           10
       {                                                 11
       outputOnScreen("Counter value is"+counter);       12
       outputOnScreen("Limit is "+limit);                13
       }                                                 14
    } // End processInput                                15
                                                         16
 } // End FORTest                                        17
```

EXERCISE   1 Vary the limits and starting points of the loop to get an idea of the output of various values.
2 Change the above loop so that it counts down instead of up, for example, 5,4,3,2,1.

5.4.1.2   Creating variables within the 'for' loop

As we said before you can create a new variable to hold your counter when you start the loop, be careful however as this variable only lasts as long as the loop executes.

EXAMPLE   Try the following section of program which will print out the values 1 to 10 on the screen. If you try and compile it, the compiler will give you an error message as it no longer recognises the variable counter outside the loop. The counter variable is local to the loop as it is created within the body of the loop (just like a variable is local to a method if it is created in the body of that method).

```
for(int counter=1;counter<=10;counter++)
    outputOnScreen("The number is "+counter);
outputOnScreen("The last number was "+counter);
```

The error message which will be printed out by the compiler is: `undefined variable counter`.

If you want to keep a count of how many times the loop executed, use a variable which is not defined only for the lifetime of the loop.

For example,

```
int counter;
for(counter=1;counter <=10;counter++)
    outputOnScreen("The number is "+counter);
outputOnScreen("The loop ran "+counter+" times");
```

The output is

```
1
2
3
4
5
6
7
8
9
10
```

```
The loop ran 11 times.
```

EXERCISE   Why is the value of counter 11 above instead of 10? How will you get the actual number of times the loop executed?

5.4.1.3   Changing the value of the counter within the loop

You can change the value of the counter within the loop (as in the example below). You can use this to end a loop before its counter runs its course. However, this is viewed as very bad programming practice and so it is better to avoid it.

For example,

```
for(int counter=1;counter<5;counter++)
    {
    outputOnScreen("The number is "+counter);
    counter=5; // The loop terminates next time the count is checked
    }
```

EXAMPLE   This example shows you how to use a `for` loop to work your way through an array. In this example the array stores sales figures which are added together in the `for` loop.

In line 13, we create an array with four locations to hold each month's sales figures. We put each sales figure in its relevant location in lines 14–17. In line 19, we initialise the counter for the loop and set the limit to be the value of the public variable called `length` in the object `salesForQuarter`, that is `salesForQuarter.length`. To get the number of boxes in any array you just need to access the public variable in the array object called `length`. The value of `salesForQuarter.length` is the number of locations in the array `salesForQuarter`, which works out at 4, so our loop will go through the values from 0 up to and including 3 (remember < `SalesForQuarter.length` means < 4). If you are using the counter variable as a means to access your array, be very careful that you do not exceed the number of locations actually in your array. For example, if we make a mistake and say <= `salesForQuarter.length` is the limit, the loop will go through the values 0 to 4 and try and access `salesForQuarter[4]` which doesn't exist. This would result in your program stopping with the error `java.lang.ArrayIndexOutOfBoundsException` which basically says that you went outside the limit of your array.

```
// The purpose of this program is to access output an array   1
// using a loop                                               2
                                                              3
public class ComputeAverageSales extends TrainingWheels       4
    {                                                         5
    private int salesForQuarter[];                            6
    private int total;                                        7
    private final int NUMBEROFQUARTERS = 4;                   8
                                                              9
```

```
public void entryPoint()                              10
  {                                                   11
  total=0;                                            12
  salesForQuarter=new int[NUMBEROFQUARTERS];          13
  salesForQuarter[0]=242;                             14
  salesForQuarter[1]=168;                             15
  salesForQuarter[2]=52;                              16
  salesForQuarter[3]=73;                              17
                                                      18
  for(int counter=0;counter<salesForQuarter.length;   19
  counter++)
    {                                                 20
     total += sales For Quarter[counter];             21
    }                                                 22
  outputOnScreen("Number of sales was "               23
  + salesForQuarter.length);
                                                      24
  outputOnScreen("Total sales were "+total);          25
  outputOnScreen("Average sales were "+(total/        26
  salesFor Quarter.length));
  } // End entryPoint                                 27
                                                      28
}// End ComputeAverageSales                           29
```

5.5   NESTED LOOPS

It is possible to put one loop inside another. For example, if we want a set of multiplication tables we write:

```
for(int number=0;number<11;number++)
   for(int times=0;times<11;times++)
      outputOnScreen(number+"*"+times+"="+(number*times));
```

This is dealt with in the same way as a normal for loop. The first loop for(int number=0;number<11;number++) will execute its associated loop statement 11 times with the value for number going from 0 to 10. The loop statement it executes just happens to be another loop which also executes its loop statement 11 times with the value for its counter times going from 0 to 10. The statement outputOnScreen(number+"*"+times+"="+(number*times)) therefore gets executed by the loop for(int times=0;times<11;times++) 11 times which in turn gets executed by for(int number=0;number<11;number++) 11 times which gives a total of 121 times.

5.5.1 **while**

The while loop, like the for loop, will repeat a statement until an expression evaluates to true. Unlike for, while is designed to continue executing by checking a preset condition, or event. This means that there is not always a counter variable to set up and alter. Such a stopping condition might be: a user inputting an exit command, the end of input being reached or a result being calculated.

while (expression evaluates to true)
    loop_Statement;

Within the loop statements, there must be an instruction that will cause the loop to stop at some point. You do get very rare cases where the loop is not designed to stop. These are called 'infinite' loops because they will go on forever or until the program is stopped.

    An example of an infinite loop would be:

```
while(true)
    outputOnScreen("Hello");
```

The above loop will output the string Hello forever because the expression which is evaluated will always evaluate to true. Make sure that somewhere in your loop the value of the expression can be changed, that way your loop will end at some point and the rest of your program can carry on.

    The sequence for the while loop can be seen in Figure 5.6.

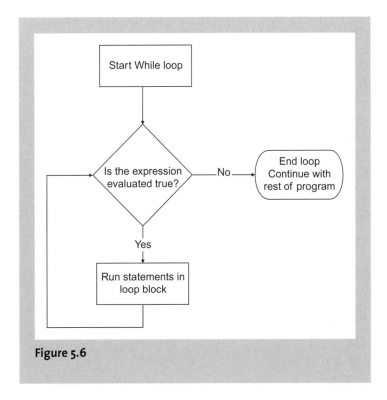

Figure 5.6

Let's write a `while` loop that will perform an interest calculation. The loop will terminate when a certain condition is no longer true.

The purpose of our program is to take an interest rate as input and then, using that interest rate, find out how long it will take for our investment to double in value. The expression which is evaluated to check if the `while` loop should continue is `while (currentInvestmentValue < (2*INITIALINVESTMENT))`. This compares the `currentInvestmentValue` with the initial investment doubled. The current investment value increases each year by the interest rate. Therefore, what your program is doing is computing the increase in the current investment value for each year, adding it to the previous year's investment value and checking that it isn't double the original investment.

```java
// The purpose of this program is to execute a while loop   1
// until a particular value is reached                       2
                                                             3
public class WhileTest extends TrainingWheels              4
{                                                            5
private final int INITIALINVESTMENT=2000;                  6
                                                             7
public void entryPoint()                                   8
   {                                                         9
   addInputElement("Interest Rate");                       10
   } // End entryPoint                                      11
                                                            12
public void processInput(int rate)                         13
   {                                                        14
   int currentInvestmentValue;                             15
   int yearsInvested;                                      16
                                                            17
   yearsInvested=0; // Initialise the variable            18
   currentInvestmentValue=INITIALINVESTMENT;              19
                                                            20
   while(currentInvestmentValue < (2*INITIALINVESTMENT))  21
      {                                                     22
      currentInvestmentValue+=(currentInvestmentValue*     23
      rate)/100;
      yearsInvested++;                                      24
      }                                                     25
                                                            26
   outputOnScreen(yearsInvested+ "yrs to double at         27
   interest rate "+rate);
   } // End processInput                                   28
                                                            29
} // End WhileTest                                          30
```

The result of the above program is shown in Figure 5.7.

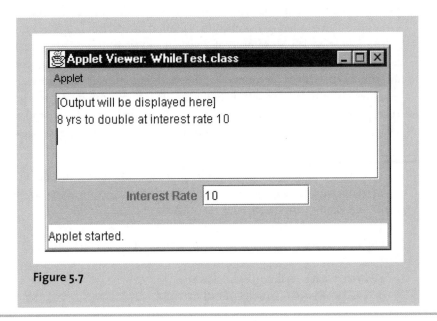

Figure 5.7

5.5.1.1   Using a 'while' loop when you should use a 'for' loop

If you want to execute for a preset number of times, then the best loop to use is the for loop. Some programmers use while to do this but that's not what it has been designed for.

For example, instead of doing

```
for(int counter = 0;counter < 10;counter ++)
    statements;
```

some programmers will write:

```
int counter = 0;
while(counter < 10)
    {
    statements;
    counter++ ;
    }
```

Both the above loops have the same result but they are phrased differently. As you can see it makes more sense to have a neat for loop to manage a count controlled loop as opposed to making a messy while loop.

5.5.1.2 Writing a searching algorithm using a 'while' loop

While is often used in algorithms which search for a particular value or values. The purpose of while in this type of algorithm is to go through a set of elements until either the element being searched for is found or you run out of elements to search.

The following is an example of a search program in which we search an array for a particular number. Each number in the array represents an employee ID number for an employee who is currently in the building. If we want to see if a particular employee is in today, we simply enter the ID into our input box and program searches through the array of present employees. The while loop will stop searching either when it runs out of things to search or when it finds the name we are looking for.

```
// This program will search through an array until it finds    1
// the value it is looking for or it runs out of array         2
// to look through                                             3
                                                               4
public class SearchForID extends TrainingWheels             5
{                                                              6
private int employeesPresent[];                             7
private final int NROFEMPLOYEES = 5;                        8
                                                               9
public void entryPoint()                                   10
   {                                                          11
   addInputElement("Employee ID to search for");           12
                                                             13
   // Create an array to store the IDs of employees present 14
   employeesPresent = new int[NROFEMPLOYEES];               15
   employeesPresent[0] = 242; // Put ID 242 into location 0  16
   employeesPresent[1] = 168;                                17
   employeesPresent[2] = 52;                                 18
   employeesPresent[3] = 73;                                 19
   employeesPresent[4] = 124;                                20
   } // End entryPoint                                       21
                                                             22
public void processInput(int employeeToLookFor)            23
   {                                                          24
   boolean found = false;                                   25
                                                             26
   int currentIndex = 0;                                    27
                                                             28
   while((currentIndex < employeesPresent.length) && (!found)) 29
      {                                                       30
      if(employeesPresent[currentIndex] == employeeToLookFor) 31
         found = true;                                       32
      currentIndex ++;                                       33
```

```
        }                                                 34
                                                          35
    if(found)                                             36
        outputOnScreen("Employee is present");            37
    else                                                  38
        outputOnScreen("Employee is not present");        39
    } // End processInput                                 40
                                                          41
  } // End SearchForID                                    42
```

How does the above program work? Well, the first thing we do is to set up the contents of the array we will be searching in lines 15–20. Next in the `processInput` method we take the input given by the user, which is in the variable `employeeToLookFor`. In line 25, we set up the variable `found` which will hold the state of the search. We haven't started the search yet so we set the contents of the variable found to be false indicating that we haven't found the employee name yet. In line 27, we set the value of the `currentIndex`, that is the array element that we are currently checking, to see if it matches the `employeeToLookFor`. Since we are starting the search we set the value of `currentIndex` to be the first array location namely location 0. In line 29, we set the condition for the `while` loop. The `while` loop will continue as long as there are array elements to examine and the variable found does not change to true. The `while` loop therefore continues until we run out of elements to look at or we find our sought for element. In line 31, we check to see if the current array element is the same as the element we are looking for. If we change the value of found to true (line 36), the loop will stop next time round. If it isn't equal then we select the next array location (`currentIndex ++`) and go round the loop again. When the loop is finished we can check if the employee was found by examining the contents of the variable `found` (line 32). If `found` is true then the employee was located, if it is false then we went through the entire array without finding the employee.

An example output of the above program is shown in Figure 5.8 in p. 172.

5.5.2 Do-while

Sometimes you need the body of loop to be executed before the condition is evaluated. For example, if you want to test an input from a user, you have to get the input first before you test it.

What you can do in this case is to use a `do-while` statement which guarantees that the body of the loop is executed at least once. Once is enough to get the input and check that it's not what you want.

The syntax is

```
do
    {
    Statements;
    } while(condition);
```

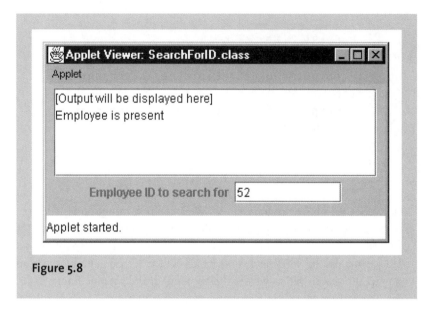

Figure 5.8

It is important to note the way that the do-while is written. The word do is always followed by an opening bracket ({), the statements to be executed and a closing bracket (}). Then the word while and the condition are supplied. Finally you must remember to put a semicolon to indicate that your do-while loop is finished. Have a look at the flowchart below to follow the progress of a do-while loop.

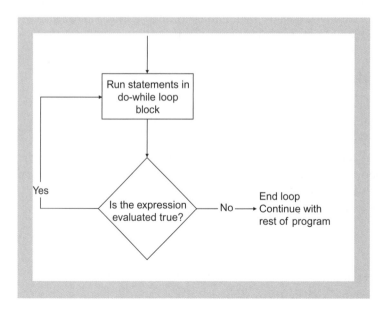

EXAMPLE   The following program will keep a list of guesses that will be compared to a value that the user has input. When the user inputs a number, the program will attempt to guess the number they have entered. If the program goes through its list of guesses without finding the number, then the user wins the game. If not the computer wins.

```
// The purpose of this program is to take the user      1
// input and cycle through a array to see if it          2
// contains a matching value                             3
                                                         4
public class GuessUsingdoWhile extends TrainingWheels    5
{                                                        6
private int[] guessList;                                 7
private final int NROFGUESSES = 5;                       8
                                                         9
public void entryPoint()                                10
   {                                                    11
   addInputElement("Your number");                      12
                                                         13
   guessList = new int[NROFGUESSES];                     14
   guessList[0] = 6;                                     15
   guessList[1] = 9;                                     16
   guessList[2] = 3;                                     17
   guessList[3] = 4;                                     18
   guessList[4] = 1;                                     19
   } // End entryPoint                                   20
                                                         21
public void processInput(int userGuess)                 22
   {                                                    23
   int counter = 0;                                      24
   boolean isNumberGuessed = false;                      25
                                                         26
   do {                                                 27
      outputOnScreen("I guess your number is "          28
      +guessList[counter]);

                                                         29
      if(guessList[counter] == userGuess)                30
         isNumberGuessed = true;                         31
      else                                              32
         counter ++ ;                                    33
                                                         34
      } while((!isNumberGuessed) &&                      35
      (counter < guessList.length));
```

```
                                                                      36
    if(isNumberGuessed)                                               37
       outputOnScreen("The computer guessed your number");            38
    else                                                              39
       outputOnScreen("You beat the computer");                       40
                                                                      41
    } // End processInput                                             42
                                                                      43
} // End GuessUsingdoWhile                                            44
```

You can see why the do-while is used in the above program. The program must make a guess before it can check to see its guess corresponds to that of the user.

An example output for the above program is shown in Figure 5.9.

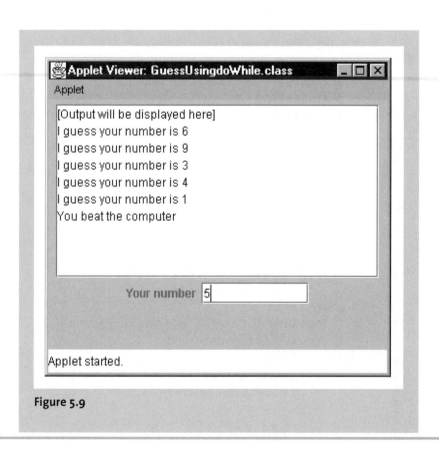

Figure 5.9

EXERCISE   Change the program to handle strings instead of integers.

5.5.3 Checklist for loops

Each time you write a loop, you should run through it with the following checklist in mind. This will help you to spot many of the common and tricky errors which are associated with loops.

- *Infinite loops*
  Make sure that your loop will come to a stop eventually (unless you want an infinite loop on purpose). You do this by checking the loop visually and by checking the data which goes into the loop. If it's a `for` loop make sure that the condition will result in the counter exceeding the limit at some point. If it's a `while` loop, then make sure that the event which causes the loop to finish has the possibility of happening. In particular, if you are using more than one condition, make sure that you have got your logical expression correct.

- *Correct syntax*
  In a `for` loop remember not to put a semicolon after the `for` statement.
    In all loops remember that if you have more than one statement that you want to be executed as part of the loop then the statements must be in a block immediately following the loop.

- *Exceeding the bounds of an array*
  If you use an array in your loop and use your loop counter to access elements in the array, bear in mind that each array has certain preset limits. If your loop counter exceeds this limit, then you are effectively trying to access an array location that doesn't exist and your program will halt with an error message.

- *Out-by-one errors*
  In `for` loops in particular, make sure that your expression is correct and so you get the correct number of repeats. One useful formula to use if starting from a non-zero number is the following:

  for(int counter = starting value;counter < (number of executions + starting value); counter + +)

  If you are using an increment other than 1 then the following formula will apply.

  for(int counter = starting value;counter < (number of executions*increment) + starting value;counter += increment)

5.6 DEBUGGING

The first step in removing a logical error from code is to find out the source of that particular error. If there are a number of statements which can be the cause of a particular error then you must find out which one it is. You can do this by using Integrated Development Environments (IDEs) and putting what are called breakpoints in code. An alternative, which is independent of any development environment program is to put in statements which output as you progress through the code. For example,

```
outputOnScreen("Reached point 1");
input = new InputClass();
outputOnScreen("Reached point 2");
input.callMethod();
outputOnScreen("Reached point 3");
```

Now you know if your program prints out the messages:

```
Reached point 1
Reached point 2
```

and stops that the problem lies with the statement:

```
input.callMethod();
```

This mechanism can also be used for tracing the execution of your program if you are unsure of what is happening. You can even output the contents of variables as you progress through the program to make sure that things are going as planned.

Remember that you should have done a visual inspection of your program and a walkthrough before embarking on this course of action. Its better to find the error as early as possible in the life of the program rather than be surprised by it later on.

Another option is to use a method to output your error messages. This has the advantage that you can switch on and off the error messages using a constant so that when you finish debugging the program you do not have to remove the output statements but simply 'switch' the error method off.

For example, in the code below I define a variable `debuggingIsOn` which contains the status of debugging for the program (true = on, false = off). When I call the method `outputError` to printout my message, I test to see if I am still in a debugging mode and print out the message if so. Otherwise no message is displayed.

```
private final boolean DEBUGGINGISON=true;

outputError("The value of variable counter is "+counter);
```

```
public void outputError(String errorMessage)
{
if(DEBUGGINGISON)
    outputOnScreen(errorMessage);
}
```

5.7   FLAGS

A flag is a term used to describe a boolean variable which is used to indicate, among other things, that some event has taken place or some condition satisfied. The idea of a flag is the same as any signal which can change, for example, a traffic light. A flag can be used to 'make a note' of some event or to indicate a particular state (see Section 5.8). We have used flags without realising it when we looked at loops, found (used in the example program for the while loop) and numberGuessed (contained in the example program for do-while) were both flags.

Examples of circumstances you can use a flag value:

- To indicate that the user has supplied the correct input
- To record that an array is now full
- To mark that a value searched for has been found.

5.8   STATE

Sometimes you may like your program to perform certain actions based on particular circumstances. You can do this by using one or more flags to represent the state a program should be in, where the state is the execution of a particular group of instructions. The program can then switch state depending on the value of a flag, for example, it can switch from allowing input to computing the output, it can switch from expecting one input value (e.g. a users name) to another (e.g. the users age).

For example, suppose you want to input three strings, a name, an address and a date of birth. Three distinct operations are associated with each string, if the input is a name then put it in an array called customerName, if the input is an address then put the string in an array called customerAddress and if the input is a date of birth calculate the users age and output it. You can define three boolean state variables: inputName, inputAddress and inputDOB. Each of these boolean variables will represent a state. That is, if inputName is true then the program will be expecting a name and will perform the associated tasks, if inputAddress is true, then an address is expected, and so on. So, we need to move from one state to another, where each state will be expecting a different form of input and will perform different instructions based on this assumption. Therefore, we define a sequence for the inputs and use the state variables to force the program to follow that sequence.

We define the sequence as: name is input first, address is second and DOB third. Therefore, we set the value of `inputName` to be true in the `entryPoint` method and the other state variables to be false. When we get the name from the user, we can move on to the next input which is the address. Therefore after the name is received we set the `inputName` to false (since next time we don't expect the name) and `inputAddress` to be true (since we want the input received to be treated as an address. And so on, at the end of the process (i.e. when the DOB is input) we start the sequence all over again and set `inputName` to be true.

Therefore the `processInput` method will look like this:

```java
public void processInput(String inputParameter)
    {
    if(inputName) // Is the name expected in inputParameter?
        {
        statements which treat inputParameter as if it was a name;
        // Change the state, next value expected is the address
        inputName = false;
        inputAddress = true;
        }
    if(inputAddress) // Is the address expected in inputParameter?
        {
        statements which treat inputParameter as if it was an address
        //Change the state, next value expected is the DOB
        inputAddress = false;
        inputDOB = true;
        }
    if(inputDOB) // Is the DOB expected in inputParameter?
        {
        statements which treat inputParameter as if it was a DOB
        // Change the state, next value expected is the name
        inputDOB = false;
        inputName = true;
        }
    } // End processInput
```

EXAMPLE   The function of the program below is to check a user's name and password. To do this you need to supply two strings to the program. The problem is that the code you have been introduced to so far will only allow one input element to be placed on screen. How do you supply two input values using just one input element? The answer is to supply one piece of input at a time but to have the program in one of two states. One state will expect the input to be the username, the other state will expect the input to be the password. You use a boolean variable to indicate which variable is expected, that is, which state the program should be in.

So, in the program below, the state variable used is called `inputUserName`. When the program begins, this is set to true indicating that the first value expected is the username (line 10), that is, the state of the program is that the username will be input next. The values that should be contained in the username and password strings are then set (lines 11 and 12). We compare these values to the values input by the user to decide whether the user has satisfied our security restrictions, that is, that the strings supplied by the user match the strings defined in lines 11 and 12.

When the user supplies an input the method `processInput` is called. Depending on the current value of `inputUserName` (i.e. the state) the value supplied by the user is compared to either the `username` variable (this is done when `inputUserName` is true, line 21) or the `password` variable (this is done when `inputUserName` is false, line 32). If the value supplied matches the value it's being compared to, then the state is changed to allow the next value to be input. So, if the value expected is the username and it is correct then the value of `inputUserName` is changed to false to allow the next value to be entered and treated as a password. If the value expected is the password and it is correct then a message indicating success is output and the `inputUserName` variable is changed to true so that the next value supplied will be treated as the username and therefore the next user can try to verify themselves. This process of changing from one state to another continues as long as the values supplied are correct. If they are incorrect then the state does not change and the user is notified that they must re-enter the same expected value, that is, their username or their password.

The value `userLoggedIn` declared on line 6 is a flag. It is set to false when the program starts and indicates that the user has not passed the login test. When the user passes both tests the value of `userLoggedIn` is set to true. This variable is not made use of in the program and its purpose is to serve as an example of a flag.

```
public class StateExample extends TrainingWheels          1
{                                                         2
                                                          3
private boolean inputUserName;                            4
private String username,password;                         5
private boolean userLoggedIn; // Flag to indicate successful login  6
                                                          7
public void entryPoint()                                  8
    {                                                     9
    inputUserName = true;                                10
    username = "sue";                                    11
    password = "suespassword";                           12
                                                         13
    userLoggedIn = false;                                14
    outputOnScreen("Input Username");                    15
    addInputElement("Input");                            16
```

```
        } // End entryPoint                                    17
                                                               18
    public void processInput(String inputSupplied)             19
        {                                                      20
        if(inputUserName)                                      21
           {                                                   22
           if(inputSupplied.equals(username))                  23
              {                                                24
              inputUserName = false;                           25
              outputOnScreen("Input password");                26
              }                                                27
           else                                                28
              outputOnScreen("Incorrect username, reenter");   29
                                                               30
           }                                                   31
        else                                                   32
           {                                                   33
           if(inputSupplied.equals(password))                  34
              {                                                35
              outputOnScreen("Correct login");                 36
              inputUserName = true;                            37
              userLoggedIn = true;                             38
              outputOnScreen("Input username");                39
              }                                                40
           else                                                41
              outputOnScreen("Incorrect password, reenter");   42
           }                                                   43
                                                               44
        } // End processInput                                  45
                                                               46
    } // End StateExample                                      47
```

EXERCISE

1 The above program is not a 'safe' one to distribute to users, that is, it does not take steps to guard the user against a runtime error. Analyse the program to determine what the error is (it has been mentioned in Chapter 4) and fix the program so that the error is handled properly.

2 Alter the above program so that instead of holding the name and password of one user, it holds several names and passwords in an array. When the username is entered this array should be searched to find out the user and note what the matching password should be.

5.9 / SENTINEL

A sentinel is the term used to describe a value which is being watched for. When a sentinel value is received then something happens (e.g. input so far is processed, program stops reading from a file, program stops looking through an array, etc.). A sentinel is used to indicate when one part of the program should finish and another part should start. Sentinel values can be any type, string, integer, and so on, depending on the type of value that your program is processing when watching out for the sentinel.

An example of a sentinel value in use would be a situation where your program is continuously reading input and wants to stop when a particular input value is received. You tell the user what value they should enter in order to indicate to the program that they have finished entering their input and you tell the program to watch out for this value. Sentinel values supplied by the user are usually not treated as actual input. The sentinel value should therefore be one which the user will never need (e.g. a sentinel value of −1 could be used if positive integers are required as input since the user should never supply a negative number) or which the user will never inadvertently use (e.g. if strings are being input, a value of 'end' can be used provided the user never wants to supply this string as an input).

Another example of a sentinel value is the `while` loop searching program discussed in Section 5.5.1. In this program the sentinel value is supplied by the user and the program searched through its list of values looking for the sentinel variable (`employeeToLookFor`).

Sometimes programmers use the words sentinel and flag interchangeably as a flag can be used as a sentinel. For example, in the search program illustrating the `while` loop the boolean variable `found` is used as a flag in line 32 and a sentinel in line 25.

EXAMPLE   The following program is an example of a program using a sentinel value of − 1. The program will receive input continuously and add that input to a variable `totalSoFar` (line 19). It also keeps track of how many inputs have been supplied in `totalValuesInput` (line 20). If the user supplies an input of −1 then the program computes the average of the values supplied, outputs this result and then sets the variables back to 0 so that it can start the process all over again.

One extra feature to note in this program is that another version of `processInput` is provided. This version of the method will take a string as input. The function of this specific version of `processInput` is to guard against the user supplying non-integer input (e.g. a string). If the user does supply a string by mistake then the `processInput(String)` method is called and their error is pointed out to them.

```
public class SentinelExample extends TrainingWheels        1
{                                                          2
// Variables used to store input and information           3
private int totalSoFar,totalValuesInput;                   4
private final int SENTINEL = -1; // Sentinel value         5
                                                           6
public void entryPoint()                                   7
   {                                                       8
   resetValues();// Initialise the input and information variables 9
                                                          10
   outputOnScreen("Input integers, (input -1 to stop)"); 11
   addInputElement("Input");                              12
   } // End entryPoint                                    13
                                                          14
public void processInput(int inputParameter)              15
   {                                                      16
   if(inputParameter != SENTINEL)                         17
      {                                                   18
      totalSoFar += inputParameter;                       19
      totalValuesInput ++;                                20
      outputOnScreen("Value supplied "+inputParameter);   21
      }                                                   22
   else                                                   23
      {                                                   24
      int averageValue = totalSoFar/totalValuesInput;     25
      outputOnScreen("Average Value "+averageValue);      26
      resetValues(); // Reset the variables to 0          27
      }                                                   28
   } // End processInput(int)                             29
                                                          30
public void processInput(String inputParameter)           31
   {                                                      32
   outputOnScreen("Error: you must supply an integer      33
   \nplease reenter");
   } // End processInput(String)                          34
                                                          35
private void resetValues()                                36
   {                                                      37
   totalSoFar = 0;                                        38
   totalValuesInput = 0;                                  39
   } // End resetValues                                   40
                                                          41
} // End SentinelExample                                  42
```

The output of the above program is shown in Figure 5.10.

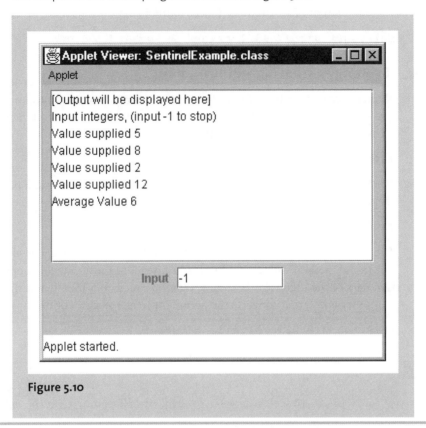

Figure 5.10

5.10   ADVANCED MATHEMATICAL OPERATIONS

This section deals with some advanced mathematical operations.

5.10.1   The Math class

The following operations are available in the `Math` class. This class does not have to be imported since it is imported by default. When using the static methods contained in the class, you must however give the name of the `Math` class. (See Chapters 6 and 7 for discussions of `import` and `static`)

All the methods discussed return a value of type `double`.

5.10.1.1   Power

Raising one number to the power of another can be done in Java by using the pow method. It takes as parameters the number which you want to operate on and the number of times you want the number multiplied by itself. For example, '2 to the power of 3 (2^3)' is given as:

```
Math.pow(2,3);
```

5.10.1.2 Square root

The square root of any number can be found using the sqrt method. For example,

```
Math.sqrt(4); // Will return 2
```

5.10.1.3 'Evening' a floating point number

Numbers can be rounded up or down before being converted into integers or output. The ceil method will return the next highest number if the argument supplied has a fraction (i.e. it will round a number up). For example,

```
Math.ceil(4.13); // Will return 5
```

The floor method will return the argument supplied with the fraction removed (i.e. it will round the number down). For example,

```
Math.floor(3.42); // Will return 3
```

The value of the fraction has no influence on the result (i.e. it can be either .99 or .01). The round method will return the closest integer to the argument supplied. If the fraction part of the argument is greater than or equal to .5 then it returns the argument + 1, otherwise it just converts the argument to an integer. For example,

```
Math.round(9.32); // Will return 9
```

EXAMPLE

Number	Output for Math. ceil(number)	Output for Math. floor(number)	Output for Math. round(number)
12.49	13	12	12
3.51	4	3	4
5.01	6	5	5
9.999	10	9	10

Reducing the accuracy of a floating point number

You can use round if you want to reduce the accuracy of a floating point number. For example, say you want to round the value of PI to two decimal places,

```
double pi = 3.142857;
```

Multiply the number by 1 followed by the number of zeros you want represented.

```
pi = pi * 100;
```

This gives you 314.2857. Round off the result:

```
pi = Math.round(pi);
```

and divide it by the number you just multiplied it by

```
pi = pi / 100;
```

which results in `pi` having a value of 3.14 (i.e. to two decimal places).

5.10.2 Remainder

In addition to +, – and so on, there is another operator, %. This is known as a modulus operator and will produce as its result the remainder of the division of its arguments.
  For example,

`4%2` will result in a remainder of 0 as 4/2 is 2 even.
`5%2` will result in a remainder of 1 as 5/2 is 2 with a remainder of 1.

5.10.3 Absolute value

A call to the method `abs` will return the absolute value of the parameter, that is, if the parameter is negative, it will return its positive value, otherwise the same value is returned. The `abs` method will accept `int`, `float` and `double` parameters. For example,

```
Math.abs(-5423); // Will return 5423
Math.abs(4.523); // Will return 4.523
```

5.10.4 Trigonometric operations

The following are the trigonometric oriented methods supported together with their parameter and return types.

▶ double cos(double) // Returns trigonometric cosine of the supplied angle (which
   // should be supplied in radians)

▶ double sin(double) // Returns the trigonometric sine of the supplied angle (which
   // should be supplied in radians)

▶ double tan(double) // Returns trigonometric tangent of the supplied angle (which
   // should be supplied in radians)

▶ double asin(double) // Arc sine (the range is –pi/2 to pi/2)

▶ double acos(double) // Arc cosine (the range is 0.0 to pi)

▶ double atan(double) // Arc tangent (the range is –pi/2 to pi/2)

▶ double toDegrees(double) // Convert from radians to degrees

▶ double toRadians(double) // Convert from degrees to radians

For example,

```
Math.tan(90);
```

The value of PI is stored as a double in a static variable `PI` in the `Math` class, that is, `Math.PI`.

5.10.5 Logarithmic operations

The value of E is stored as a double in a static variable E in the math class, that is, `Math.E`.

The following are the logarithmic oriented methods supported together with their parameter and return types.

▶ double exp(double) // Returns the exponential number e raised to the power
// the supplied parameter

▶ double log(double) // Returns the natural logarithm (base e) of the supplied
// parameter

5.11 ADVANCED STRING OPERATIONS

This section introduces some of the other methods present in an object of type `String`.

5.11.1 length()

The length( ) method will return the number of characters in the string which contains it. For example,

```
String example = "TestString";
```

`example.length()` will return an integer value of 10.

Note that while the same name is used to get the number of items in an array, the name `length` refers to a variable in an array while it refers to a method in a String. Therefore a common mistake for a programmer to write is:

```
String example = "TestString" ;
example.length;
```

which will return an error of: `"Invalid expression statement"` or

```
int myArray[] = {2,4,5};
myArray.length();
```

which will return an error of:
`Method length() not found in class java.lang.Object.`

5.11.2 Getting characters in a string

A call to the method charAt with an integer value as a parameter (this represents the character at that index position) will evaluate to character at given index position. Like arrays, strings start at index location 0.

For example,

```
String exampleString = "abc";
char exampleCharacter;
```

```
exampleCharacter = exampleString.charAt(0);  // exampleCharacter
will now contain 'a'
```

You can get the last character in a string by calling the `length` method and taking the value 1 from it (the `length` method will return how many characters in the string but this is not the same as the number of locations in the string).

```
exampleCharacter=exampleString.charAt(exampleString.length()–1);
// exampleCharacter set to 'c' (exampleString.length()=3, 3–1=2)
```

You can assemble a string using characters by creating an empty string and concatenating characters to it. For example,

```
String finalString = "";
finalString += exampleString.charAt(0);
finalString += exampleString.charAt(2);
```

The string `finalString` now contains the string "ac".

5.11.3 endsWith

The endsWith method takes a string as its parameter and tests the string which the endsWith method was called in, to see if it ends with the string supplied. If it does end with the supplied string, then it returns a value of true otherwise it evaluates to false. For example,

```
String Name = "Fred Jones:";

if(Name.endsWith(":"))
    outputOnScreen("String ends with colon");
```

5.11.4 equalsIgnoreCase

This method performs the same test as the `equals` method but it will ignore the case of both strings (i.e. if the strings are the same but contain different cases then this method will report them as equal whereas the `equals` method will not). For example,

```
String FirstString = "Tuesday";
String SecondString = "tuesday";
```

`FirstString.equalsIgnoreCase(SecondString)` would return a value of true.

5.11.5 indexOf

The indexOf method will take a string as parameter and search the string which is called in for this string. If it finds the string then it will report the location at which it finds the beginning of the string (i.e. what character the string starts at).

indexOf will return a positive integer if it finds the string supplied and a value of – 1 if the string can not be found. The indexOf method can therefore be used for searching through large strings for key words. For example,

```
String stringToSearch = "This is an example of a string";
stringToSearch.indexOf("an") will return an integer value of 8
stringToSearch.indexOf("the") will return an integer value of −1
```

5.11.6   replace

If you want to replace one particular character with another in your string then you can call the replace method with the old character and the character you wish to replace it with. It will return a new string which has the specified characters replaced. For example,

```
String replaceExample = "This.is.a.string.with.full.stops";
String newString = replaceExample.replace('.','-');
```

The contents of newString would be This-is-a-string-with-full-stops

5.11.7   substring

To get a particular section of a string, call the substring method. You supply as parameters the character numbers at which the substring should start and end. The substring method will result in a new string which is a substring of the original string.

```
String mainString = "This is the main string";
String sectionOfMainString = mainString.substring(5,10);
```

The string sectionOfMainString now contains: "is the"

5.11.8   toLowerCase

The toLowerCase method will produce a new string which is equal to the old string except all the upper case letters replaced by their lower case equivalent.

5.11.9   toUpperCase

The toUpperCase method is the same as toLowerCase except all characters in the string it generates are in upper case.

5.11.10   compareTo(String)

The compareTo method is used to compare one string with another to establish their lexical relationship (i.e. whether one string comes before another by reason of the alphabetical order of their characters). It is a valuable method when it comes to sorting strings. It will take as a parameter a string object. A call to the `compareTo` method of a string object will return an integer. That integer will be >0 if the string supplied as a parameter appears before the string object which `compareTo` is called in. It will be negative if the parameter string comes after it and 0 if both strings are exactly the same.

One way to read `compareTo` will be: if the left string compared to the right string is <0, then the left string precedes the right. For example,

```
String first = "Apple";
String second = "Banana";

first.compareTo(second); // Will return -1 (Apple comes before Banana)
second.compareTo(first); // Will return 1 (Banana comes after Apple)
```

Example: Using `compareTo` to sort strings

One of the uses of `compareTo` is to take an array of unordered strings and sort them. For example, the following program will take an array of unordered strings and output the strings in alphabetical order. There are textbooks full of algorithms for sorting strings, new algorithms are developed to increase the speed at which the sorting takes place. In this example no account is taken of the speed of processing as the idea is to introduce you to a simple sorting algorithm in as straightforward a manner as possible.

The algorithm used will take an array of strings as input (let's call the array unsorted). It selects the first string from this array and puts it into a new array (call it sorted) in the first available location (location 0). It then selects the next string from unsorted and puts it into the next location in sorted (location 1). To make sure that the array called sorted is in alphabetical order, the algorithm compares the string in location 1 to the string in location 0. If they are in the wrong order then it swaps them. The next string taken from the unsorted array is placed in the next available location in the sorted array (location 2). Again the algorithm compares it with the first string in the array (location 0) and swaps them if they are out of order. Next it compares the string in the last location to that in location 1 and swaps them if necessary. The algorithm continues adding in new strings and comparing the last string added to all the other strings, swapping the strings in the sorted array until it runs out of elements in the unsorted array. The sorted array will now contain the same strings as the unsorted array but stored in alphabetical order.

How are elements swapped from one array location to another? Well, you cannot do a direct assignment as this would wipe out one of the elements. What you need to do is, put one element somewhere safe, replace it with the other element and then put it in its new location. This is what is done in the program below, one string is put in a variable called `temp` and then it is replaced. The contents of `temp` are then placed in the other location. This mechanism enables variables to be swapped.

```
public class StringSorter extends TrainingWheels            1
{                                                            2
                                                             3
public void entryPoint()                                     4
    {                                                        5
    // Call the method to sort the strings                   6
    sortStrings();                                           7
    } // End entryPoint                                      8
                                                             9
                                                            10

private void sortStrings()                                  11
    {                                                       12
    // Variable to track the next free array location       13
    int nextAvailableLocn = 0;                              14
    String temp; // Variable to temporarily hold string     15
    // for transfer                                         16
                                                            17
    // Array of strings, not in any order                   18
    String unsorted[] = {"Melon","Pinapple","Orange",       19
    "Apple","Lemon"};
                                                            20
    // Create a new array to hold strings in alphabetical order  21
    String sorted[] = new String[unsorted.length];          22
                                                            23
    // Output the contents of the unsorted array            24
    outputOnScreen("Unsorted array");                       25
    for(int counter = 0;counter < unsorted.length;counter ++)  26
        outputOnScreen(unsorted[counter]);                  27
                                                            28
    // For every element in the unsorted array              29
    for(int counter = 0;counter < unsorted.length;counter ++)  30
        {                                                   31
        // Put the next element in the sorted array         32
        // in the next free location                        33
        sorted[nextAvailableLocn] = unsorted[counter];      34
                                                            35
        // Reposition the elements in the sorted array so   36
        // that they are in alphabetical order.             37
        // This is done by comparing strings and moving them  38
        // if they are in the wrong order                   39
                                                            40
        for(int currentLocn = 0;currentLocn < nextAvailableLocn;  41
        currentLocn++)
```

```
                    {                                             42
                    // If the current string should be after the 43
                    // string in the last location               44
                    if(sorted[currentLocn].compareTo            45
                    (sorted[nextAvailableLocn]) > 0)
                        {                                        46
                        // Put the current string in temp        47
                        temp = sorted[currentLocn];              48
                                                                 49
                        // Put the last location in the current string 50
                        sorted[currentLocn] = sorted[nextAvailableLocn]; 51
                                                                 52
                        // Put the contents of temp in the last location 53
                        sorted[nextAvailableLocn] = temp;        54
                        }                                        55
                    }                                            56
                    // Have added a string so move last location by 1 57
                    nextAvailableLocn ++;                        58
                                                                 59
            } // End for(int counter = 0; . . .                 60
                                                                 61
        // Print out the contents of the sorted array           62
        outputOnScreen("Sorted array");                         63
        for(int counter = 0;counter < unsorted.length;counter ++) 64
            outputOnScreen(sorted[counter]);                     65
        } // End sortStrings                                     66
                                                                 67
    } // End StringSorter                                       68
```

The output of the above program will be as represented in Figure 5.11 in p. 192.

EXERCISE   1   How does compareTo handle capitals (i.e. does it ignore them or treat a capital letter as being before a lower case letter)? For example, what is the result of the following:

```
String capitalString = "STRING";
String lowerString = "string";
capitalString.compareTo(lowerString);
```

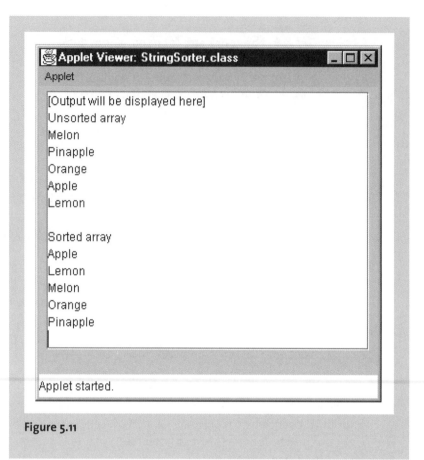

Figure 5.11

SUMMARY

A new type of program has been introduced, one which waits on the user to provide input before executing instructions. Such a program is said to be event driven.

Conditions can be combined using logical operators. These operators allow users to combine two conditions using AND and OR.

Loops are a way of repeatedly executing the same group of statements for a certain number of times. Three different loop statements are introduced namely `for`, `while` and `do-while`. The number of times a statement should be executed may be known, in which case a `for` loop is appropriate, or it may be dependant on some particular condition, in which case a `while` or `do-while` loop is appropriate.

A constant is a variable whose value is assigned to it when it is declared. The contents of a constant cannot be changed after the initial assignment. Constants are used to make life easier for programmers and for people reading programs.

A flag is a variable (usually boolean) used to indicate that some particular event has occurred. Flags are used to control the flow of execution of a program based on events.

A sentinel is a value which is being watched for. A code segment is usually written to watch out for a particular sentinel and take some action when it is encountered. Often when a sentinel value is received a flag is set to indicate this.

KEYWORDS

▶ *Constant* – A variable whose value does not change from that which is assigned the variable on its declaration.
▶ *Event driven* – A program which is written to respond to one or more events, where the events are usually input supplied by the user.
▶ *Flag* – A variable used to indicate some particular event has occurred.
▶ *Input validation* – Checking input received from the user to make sure that it is in the correct form.
▶ *Loop* – A statement which causes a group of instructions to be repeatedly executed.
▶ *Sentinel* – A value defined by the programmer as causing some sequence of actions, for example, causing a result to be calculated.

KEY CONCEPTS

▶ Input
To add an input area to the screen

```
addInputElement(ElementLabelString);
```

To process input from the user need to declare the method

```
public void processInput(inputType parameterName){}
```

where `inputType` can be `String`, `boolean`, `double` or `int`.

▶ Constants
To declare a variable whose value cannot be changed after the declaration

```
final type variableName = value;
```

▶ Logical operators

AND (symbols &&)

Expression1	Expression2	Expression1 && Expression2
True	False	False
False	True	False
False	False	False
True	True	True

OR (symbols ‖)

Expression1	Expression2	Expression1 ‖ Expression2
True	False	True
False	True	True
False	False	False
True	True	True

▶ Loops
```
for(variableName = startValue;conditionForContinuing;alteration-
OfVariableName)
    statementsExecutedWhenConditionForContinuingIsTrue;
```

```
while(conditionIsTrue)
statementsExecutedWhenConditionIsTrue;
```

Do not forget that any statement which changes the value of the condition should be contained within the while, loop. If the condition never changes from true, then the while loop will never finish.

```
do
{
statementsExecuted;
} while(conditionIsTrue);
```

Do not forget the semicolon at the end of the do-while.

PROJECTS   1   A funfair wants to run a series of checks on the people wanting to get on a certain ride. If the person wishing to ride is under 18, then they can only ride if they are not under 5 ft tall, otherwise they cannot ride. If the person has ridden the ride at least twice before, then they can only ride if less than 20 people are in the queue (this gives everyone a fair chance to get a ride). Finally, if the person has ridden the ride more than five times, then they are not allowed ride it again because they may become ill. (This is the same decision as that implemented in Exercise 5 in Chapter 4.)

Write a program that will implement the above narrative according to the conditions:

(a) Details (age, height, etc.) can be input via a text box input element (don't forget to extend `TrainingWheels` and use `addInputElement`).

(b) Values are tested as they are input to see if they are in the correct range (this is to eliminate impossible values like a negative age or 10 feet tall). An error message is displayed to the user if there is a problem with the data they supplied and the user is required to re-enter the data.

(c) Keep a record of each person who attempts to take the ride (it doesn't matter if they succeeded or not). Store this information in an individual object which is contained in an array of objects.

(d) Print out a statistical summary (the average of each of the values) of the people who attempted to take the ride (extract this information from the objects). The results should be printed out when the user is presented with the decision (can ride/cannot ride).

Suggested Approach

Implement each part of the problem separately, that is, modify the solution to project 1 so that it just solves part (a), then modify it again so that it just solves part (b). Do the same for part (c) (part (d) is really a sub problem of part (c), so that need not be separated). When each of the parts have been written and tested, incorporate them into one single program.

The reason behind this phased development is that you keep the solutions separate and focus your efforts on one problem at a time as opposed to writing an overall solution from scratch.

You should also do all you can to help the user, specific examples of this will be to output an error message and allow the user to re-enter data if the value entered is outside the range or handle the situation where the user enters a non-integer (e.g. a string).

Hints: The main problems you have to solve are the following:

• The input element which can be used can take only one input at a time. How do you enter four values (age, height, etc.) via a single input element?

• You must create objects, store information in these objects and use the objects created so far, how do you track which is the next free array location and how many objects have so far been created?

2 You are asked to write a security applet for your company. The applet will take a String as input and scan it for a list of keywords they are interested in. The words are: bribe, headhunt, sabotage and lawsuit. The program will print out the number of these terms it has found in a string. If no terms are found then no message is printed out. For example, if the string was: "I must bribe the headhunter to find me a job before the lawsuit starts." then the program will report three keywords found.

Hints: `MainString.indexOf(subString)` will return a positive number if it finds the `subString` in a `mainString`.

You can assume that all strings will be in the same case, that is, in lowercase.

3 Each patient who makes an appointment to see the doctor on a particular day is given a number. The first person that day gets the number 1, the next 2 and so on. When the patient enters the surgery, they give their number to the receptionist. The receptionist enters this number into a program. When the receptionist wants to select the next patient they ask the program to print out the numbers as they are entered, the patient next in line is then taken (no matter what their number is). They are then removed from the queue. When there are no more patients in the queue and the 'next patient' button is pressed, the program will print out all the patients who have missed their appointments, that is, the numbers which were not entered as input.

Write the program to do this.

You can assume that the maximum number of patients in a day will be 10. The program should start at patient 1 (i.e. there should be no patient 0).

Reminder: You can add a button using the `TrainingWheels` class by calling the method `addButton(String)` from `entryPoint`. When this button is pressed it will look for a method called `public void ifButtonPressed()`.

4 Write a program which will store the following information in an array of objects. You can assume the limit for the array is 100. You will therefore need to write a class which will store and access the following:

Name
Address
Phone Nr

All the above will be stored in object of a class type called `Customer`.

Your program must occupy one of two states, either it is waiting for a user to input the data for the next record or it is waiting for the user to supply a search term. You can use a button to change to a search state and the program will automatically change back to an input expected state once the search is completed.

If the mode is waiting for a search term, then the string the user supplies will be compared with each string in each object that is currently being stored. If a matching string is found then the contents of the object (Name, Address and Phone Nr) are printed out.

If the mode is data entry, then the three items will be entered one after the other. When the last item is entered an object will be created and all the items are placed in the object.

5 The StringSorter program is not as efficient as it can be as strings in the sorted array continue to be compared after an element has reached its correct position. Rewrite it using a `while` loop which will stop when the element has reached its correct place, so that no unnecessary comparisons are performed.

6 Write a computer pen pal matching applet. The purpose of this program is to allow people to input their name, age, profession and hobby. These details are stored in objects. When a person inputs their details the program will go through the people whose objects are currently stored and find the most suitable match. The most suitable match is defined as the person who is most similar to them, that is an ideal match (3/3) will be someone with the same age, profession and hobby, the next ideal match (2/3) will be someone who is the same in respect of two of the attributes, age, profession and hobby.

Solutions to exercises and interactive exercises can be obtained at:
http://www.palgrave.com/resources

Chapter

6

Classes

INTRODUCTION

We have seen that classes are used to provide a description of what an object will contain. We have created objects and used classes but we have not yet seen what lies behind this process, that is, how classes are turned into objects and how objects are stored and used. In this chapter, we look at how objects and classes are created and managed. We also take a brief look at how Java applications are created. The idea of an interface, which acts as a sort of guide book for programmers is discussed and finally an example of how classes are combined is examined.

6.1 HOW ARE CLASSES USED?

So far we have used classes in one of two ways:

1 Building on an existing class (using extends)

2 Creating an object using a class definition (using new)

In the first way we added to, or built on, an existing class. We see an example of this each time we use the `TrainingWheels` class. This is a class which you make use of to perform input and output tasks. Every time you write a program you extend this class in order to use the code it contains to perform input and output. This particular example of class use is called inheritance (first discussed in Chapter 2). Inheritance involves taking an existing class definition and adding new parts to it (more on that in Section 6.2).

EXAMPLE   `public class myProg extends TrainingWheels`

The above class definition is saying that the class `myProg` is building on the class `TrainingWheels`. Inheritance is essentially a way of combining one or more classes. When the class file that does the inheriting (for example `myProg`) is executed the definition for the class file that it inherits (`TrainingWheels`) is combined with it.

The second way we use a class is when we create a new object from a class definition. For example,

`ExampleClass ObjectName = new ExampleClass();`

We shall leave inheritance for the moment and look at what happens when you create an object.

6.1.1 What happens when an object is created?

We already know how to declare and create an object, we simply provide a declaration of the form:

`className objectName = new className();`

But what actually happens when an object is created, and how is the object stored? This is an important point because objects differ from ordinary variables in that they need much more memory space (since you need to store not only variables but also code for the methods). (Note that the same method code is not really stored many times in different objects but visualising an object in this form, as variables and actual instructions, helps when it comes to understanding the mechanics of executing methods in an object.)

What is the difference between an object and a non-object? The most obvious difference between an object and an ordinary variable (int, char, boolean) is that an ordinary variable (also known as a fundamental data type) will only need to store one value of a particular type. An object will need to store whatever variables are defined in the class definition as well as the code contained in the methods declared in the class definition. Every object created from a class will keep its own copy of the methods and variables defined in the class.

We know that variables are stored in a memory location, that is, if I say `int Total = 4;` I know that the value 4 will be stored in a memory location which will be associated with the name `Total`. The memory location associated with a variable name will therefore have stored in it an actual value of a specific type (an int, a double, a character, a boolean). A memory location can also store another type of value which we haven't seen before, an address. What we mean by an address is an actual box number in the computers memory. It may sound a bit strange at first to appreciate that we can store an address inside a box which is itself referenced by an address but it is possible and indeed is advantageous, as we shall see.

Placing an address in a memory location, which is also found using an address, is the equivalent of a forwarding address, if you are moving house, you will leave the new occupants with the address of your new house. When someone comes looking for you at your 'current' location (the address currently associated with your name), they are given the new address. Computers use this system of forwarding addresses to save time and memory (e.g. by leaving a forwarding address in a house, you save time going around to everyone you know and telling them your new address).

You do not need to worry about having to deal with the address contained in a variable as the system is able to make a distinction about what is stored in a variable based on the context of its use, that is, if it is an address then the system follows the address, if it's a value then it accesses the value.

Why are we interested in storing addresses? Well, the way objects are stored in memory is by using addresses. When you declare an object variable (e.g. `Example-Class ObjectVariableName;`) you are actually setting up a variable which will hold the address where the object is stored (so the variable `ObjectVariableName` will hold an address). We call this variable an object variable. When you create an object (e.g. `new ExampleClass();`) and assign the result of that creation to an object variable (e.g. `ObjectVariableName = new ExampleClass();`) you are putting the address for the object inside the object variable. The object address is a result produced by the `new` statement. So, when you use the object variable later on in the program (say for example to call a method) the system will actually follow the address stored in your object variable to find the code to execute.

So, where does the address stored in the object variable come from? Well, it is given to your executing program by the operating system.

Going back to a declaration of an object we see that it is commonly divided up into two parts. In the first part you create a variable to hold the address of an object. Therefore, the `NameOfObject` variable in our example does not actually hold an object, it holds the address of the object (its value is empty or 'null' when it is first declared). For example,

NameOfClass NameOfObject;

The next part of object creation is the actual creation of the object:

NameOfObject = new NameOfClass( );

which can be divided up into two stages.

The first stage, the instruction `new NameOfClass()`, will ask the VM to create a new object whose definition will come from the class `NameOfClass`. The VM will do this, that is, it asks the operating system for free memory, locates and reads the class definition for the named class, creates the variables and copies the code from the class definition. Once the VM has done this, it needs to let you know where it has put the object, so it returns the address at which it stored the object. So `new NameOf-Class()` will result in an address, that is, it evaluates to an address of an object of type `NameOfClass`. This address is then placed into the variable `NameOfObject` (the second stage). Now the variable `NameOfObject` contains the location in memory where an object of type `NameOfClass` is stored. Any time you use `Name-OfObject`, for example, `NameOfObject.printResult()` you are asking the VM to call the method contained in the object found at the location stored in the variable `NameOfObject`.

For example, say you want to reserve a hotel room, first you make space to store your room number:

HotelRoom MyRoomNumber;

Next the room is 'created' for you (cleaned, restocked) using 'new' and the number of the room is returned after this creation. You then take the resultant room number (which is the address of the room, not the room object itself) and place it in the variable you set aside to hold it.

MyRoomNumber = new HotelRoom( );

So, to sum up, if you create a simple variable, such as a integer or character, the location corresponding to that variable name will store a value. If you create a variable using a class name, then the location corresponding to that variable name will hold an address, which will be followed to get to an object.

Another analogy would be if you run a small company, there is certain information you want to keep, that is:

▶ Bank balance
▶ Bank account number
▶ Solicitor
▶ Banker

What will you put in bank balance and bank account number? Well, the amount in your bank account and its number respectively. So, you will store two values which correspond to your bank balance and your bank account number. What about your solicitor and banker? These are not treated as actual entities or values but addresses, you will store the address of your solicitor and banker so you can contact them later (it will be a bit much to expect the solicitor to sit in your filing cabinet until they are needed). The solicitor and banker are essentially objects (remember Chapter 2) so we are storing the address of these objects for later use. That way when someone says 'get the solicitor to write a contract' you get the address of the solicitor from your variable and you contact the solicitor via that address to get them to execute the method 'write a contract'.

Name of variable	Stores	Example
Bank balance	Number	1560.34
Bank account number	String	444-992-387
Solicitor	Address	BigWigs Ltd, 32 High St.
Banker	Address	Money4u Inc, 1 Cash Ave.

6.1.2 Example: walkthrough

Let's just look at a run through of the creation and use of a simple variable and an object.

6.1.2.1 Initialisation

In this example, we create two variables. A variable to hold an integer, called `Integer-Variable`, and a variable to hold an object address, called `ObjectVariable`. We use a class definition called `ExampleClass` for the object referenced in `Object-Variable`.

So, first we create the two variables:

```
int IntegerVariable=0;
ExampleClass ObjectVariable;
```

On initialisation `IntegerVariable` is associated with an example memory location and a value of 0 is placed in that location.

Variable name used	Memory address stored at	Contents of that location
IntegerVariable	0120	0

On initialisation `ObjectVariable` is also associated with a memory location (say 140 for example) and a value of null is placed in that location.

Variable name used	Memory address stored at	Contents of that location
ObjectVariable	0140	null

Since the only value `ObjectVariable` can contain is an address, we must place an address into it.

This cannot be done directly by the programmer, it is the responsibility of the operating system to decide what addresses you can have. For example, you cannot say

`ObjectVariable = 0232` because that address may be in use by another program. The operating system decides what areas of memory are free and suitable for your programs needs and gives the addresses for those areas to the VM which uses them.

To get an address to put in the variable `ObjectVariable` you must use a statement that results in an address. Furthermore, this address must be for an object of the same type as was used in the declaration of the variable `ObjectVariable`.

The statement `new ExampleClass()` will create an object of type `ExampleClass` and evaluate to an address. So,

`ObjectVariable = new ExampleClass();`

means:

The contents of `ObjectVariable` are set to the result of `new ExampleClass()` which is the address where the object which has just been created is stored at.

The result of `new ExampleClass()` is an address (say 920). Therefore at location 920 can be found stored all the variables and methods defined in the class `ExampleClass`. This address is now placed in the variable `ObjectVariable`.

Variable name used	Memory address stored at	Contents of that location
ObjectVariable	0140	0920

So, we now have, Table 6.1.

Table 6.1

Location	Contents
0140	0920
⋮	⋮
0920	Object of type ExampleClass
	methods . . .
	variables . . .

6.1.2.2   Putting a value into a fundamental data type

Putting a value into an integer variable is easy, just make sure the value you are assigning is in the form of an integer.

`IntegerVariable = 5;`

Then the memory will look like:

Variable name used	Location stored at	Contents of that location
IntegerVariable	0120	5

If you reference any other integer variable in an assignment statement, the contents of that variable are copied into your variable. Say for example, we created another variable called `SecondIntegerVariable` and put a value of 10 in it.

```
int SecondIntegerVariable;
SecondIntegerVariable = 10;
```

Memory now looks like this:

Variable name used	Location stored at	Contents of that location
IntegerVariable	0120	5
SecondIntegerVariable	0320	10

We now give the statement:

```
IntegerVariable = SecondIntegerVariable;
```

which translates to:

The contents of the memory address for `IntegerVariable` are set to the contents of the memory address for `SecondIntegerVariable`.

which means:

Copy the contents stored at location 0320 into location 0120.

So, now we have the following in memory.

Variable name used	Location stored at	Contents of that location
IntegerVariable	0120	10
SecondIntegerVariable	0320	10

6.1.2.3 Putting a value in an object variable

You can also put values into an object variable, as long as those values are in the form of an address which leads to an object of the same type. For example, if we create another object address holding variable and call it `AnotherObjectVariable` we can copy the address stored in `ObjectVariable` into it. The two variables will then hold the same address.

So, we create the variable to hold the address of an object of class type `ExampleClass`.

```
ExampleClass AnotherObjectVariable;
```

Memory now looks like this:

Variable name used	Location	Contents of that location
ObjectVariable	0140	0920
AnotherObjectVariable	0420	null
	0920	Object of type
		ExampleClass
		methods . . .
		variables . . .

So,

AnotherObjectVariable = ObjectVariable;

translates to:

The contents of the memory address for AnotherObjectVariable are set to the contents of the memory address for ObjectVariable.

which means:

Copy the contents of 0140 (location of ObjectVariable) into 0420 (location of AnotherObjectVariable).

Memory now looks like this:

Variable name used	Location	Contents of that location
ObjectVariable	0140	0920
AnotherObjectVariable	0420	0920
	0920	Object of type
		ExampleClass
		methods . . .
		variables . . .

So, as you can see both ObjectVariable and AnotherObjectVariable lead you to the same memory address (which stores an object of type ExampleClass).

This means that if you call a method in ObjectVariable or AnotherObject-Variable you are accessing the same object both times (i.e. the object stored at location 0920).

Copying addresses from one variable directly to another is not usually done in practice but the above example serves to illustrate what goes on with addresses and object variables and this concept is of great importance when we look at passing objects as parameters.

6.1.2.4   Example: object creation and access

Let's have a look at an example piece of code. We use a table to explain what is happening at each point in the code.

The code declares three object variables and manipulates them.

```
// Declare a variable to an address of an object of ExampleClass    1
ExampleClass objectVariable;                                        2
ExampleClass anotherObjectVariable; // same as above               3
ExampleClass finalObjectVariable; // same as above                 4
                                                                   5
// Point 1                                                         6
// Create an object and place the address in the variable          7
// objectVariable                                                  8
objectVariable = new ExampleClass();                               9
// Point 2                                                         10
// Copy the contents of objectVariable into anotherObjectVariable  11
anotherObjectVariable = objectVariable;                            12
// Point 3                                                         13
// Create an object and place the address in the variable          14
// finalObjectVariable                                             15
finalObjectVariable = new ExampleClass();                          16
// Point 4                                                         17
// Copy the contents of finalObjectVariable into                   18
// anotherObjectVariable                                           19
anotherObjectVariable = finalObjectVariable;                       20
// Point 5                                                         21
                                                                   22
class ExampleClass                                                 23
{                                                                  24
// methods and variables go here                                   25
}                                                                  26
```

For the above, we can produce a table showing what value each variable contains during the course of the execution (Table 6.2).

So, at point 1 all the object variables have been declared but not yet initialised. At point 2, an object of class type `ExampleClass` is created and its address placed in the variable `objectVariable`. The other variables remain uninitialised.

After point 3 is reached, the variable `anotherObjectVariable` has placed in it the address contained in the variable `objectVariable` (0960 in the example).

On reaching point 4, the variable `finalObjectVariable` has the address of a new object of type `ExampleClass` placed in it. Finally after point 5 the contents of the variable `finalObjectVariable` (1060) are placed in the variable `anotherObjectVariable`.

Table 6.2

The contents of the variable	At point	Are
objectVariable	1	null
anotherObjectVariable	1	null
finalObjectVariable	1	null
objectVariable	2	0960 (location assigned by VM)
anotherObjectVariable	2	null
finalObjectVariable	2	null
objectVariable	3	0960
anotherObjectVariable	3	0960 (contents of objectVariable)
finalObjectVariable	3	null
objectVariableVariable	4	0960
anotherObject	4	0960
finalObjectVariable	4	1060 (location assigned by VM)
objectVariable	5	0960
anotherObjectVariable	5	1060 (contents of finalObjectVariable)
finalObjectVariable	5	1060

You can see that the variable anotherObjectVariable held addresses like the other variables but these addresses were originally stored in other variables, that is, an object was never explicitly created for the variable anotherObjectVariable, it just used the addresses of other objects.

6.1.2.5 Copying object addresses: types

The only restriction on copying addresses from one object variable to another is that the address you are copying into an object variable leads to an object of the same type as that variable has been declared with. For example,

```
// Create an object of type ExampleClass and store it in a
// variable called anObject
ExampleClass anObject = new ExampleClass();
```

```
// Try to copy the contents of anObject into a variable which
// will hold an address for an object of type AnotherClass.
AnotherClass anotherObject = anObject;
```

You cannot do the above so you get an error from the compiler saying.

```
Error: Incompatible type for declaration. Can't convert ExampleClass
to AnotherClass.
    AnotherClass anotherObject = anObject;
```

The error message is telling you that it cannot convert the address of an object of type `ExampleClass` to the address of an object of type `AnotherClass`. Your variable `anotherObject` must have been declared as holding an address of an object derived from a class called `AnotherClass` in order to hold the contents of the variable `anObject`, that is, the correct statement is:

`ExampleClass anotherObject = anObject;`

EXAMPLE   In the following program, you can look at an example of what has been discussed.

```
public class ObjectCreationExample extends TrainingWheels    1
{                                                            2
                                                             3
public void entryPoint()                                     4
    {                                                        5
    CustomerInfoClass customerObject;                        6
                                                             7
    customerObject = new CustomerInfoClass();                8
    outputOnScreen("Value of customerObject is an address:");9
    outputOnScreen("" + customerObject);                     10
                                                             11
    outputOnScreen("Creating a new object gives an address:");12
    outputOnScreen("" + (new CustomerInfoClass()));          13
                                                             14
    outputOnScreen("Creating a second new object gives a     15
    new address:");
    outputOnScreen("" + (new CustomerInfoClass()));          16
                                                             17
    outputOnScreen("We can create and use a third new Object");18
    (new CustomerInfoClass()).setName("colin");             19
                                                             20
    outputOnScreen("We can use our customerObject");         21
    customerObject.setName("Jane");                          22
                                                             23
    outputOnScreen("We can retrieve information from         24
    customerObject");
    outputOnScreen(customerObject.getName());                25
                                                             26
    // Declare a new object variable called customerObjectCopy 27
    CustomerInfoClass customerObjectCopy;                    28
    // Copy the address of customerObject into               29
    // customerObjectCopy                                    30
    customerObjectCopy = customerObject;                     31
                                                             32
```

```
        outputOnScreen("The value of customerObjectCopy is"); 33
        outputOnScreen("" + customerObjectCopy);                  34
                                                                  35
        outputOnScreen("The same information is in customer       36
        ObjectCopy");
        outputOnScreen(customerObjectCopy.getName());             37
                                                                  38
        } // End entryPoint                                       39
                                                                  40
    } // End ObjectCreationExample                                41
                                                                  42
    class CustomerInfoClass                                       43
    {                                                             44
    private String name;                                          45
                                                                  46
    public void setName(String nameParameter)                     47
        {                                                         48
        name = nameParameter;                                     49
        } // End setName                                          50
                                                                  51
    public String getName()                                       52
        {                                                         53
        return name;                                              54
        } // End getName                                          55
                                                                  56
    } // End CustomerInfoClass                                    57
```

In line 6, a variable called customerObject is created to hold an address of an object of type CustomerInfoClass. The definition of this class can be found in line 43.

In line 8, an object of type CustomerInfoClass is created and its address is placed in the variable customerObject.

In line 10, the contents of the customerObject variable are combined with a string to create a string which is output (so you can see what it contains). The output of this variable will be something like CustomerInfoClass@1e29ded8 (see Figure 6.1 on p. 212 for an example). This means that contained in the variable customerObject is the address 1e29ded8 which is the address of an object created using the class definition CustomerInfoClass. The letters e and d represent the numbers 14 and 13 as the computer uses the letters a–e in its numbering system for addresses (called hexadecimal, also known as base 16). The addresses are combined with an empty string in lines 10, 13, 16 and 34 in order to get the overall expression in the form of a string so it can be output. If you try to output the address without joining it with a string, you will get an error message.

Line 13 outputs an example of what the statement new CustomerInfoClass()
returns. Again it will take the form of CustomerInfoClass@address which is
combined with a string.

Line 16 gives you another example of the creation of an object. Note that the
addresses produced as a result of the new statements in this line and in line 13 are not
assigned to a variable, so they are effectively lost, that is, no record is kept of the location of the created object. What happens to objects like this? Well, the VM will eventually see that an object is not being referenced or used and will erase it from memory.
Therefore, if an address of an object is no longer stored the object is deemed to be
unnecessary and is destroyed and its memory made available for other purposes. So,
the object created in this line and line 13 will be destroyed soon after its creation. This
process is called 'garbage collection' and enables efficient recycling of memory.

Line 19 creates a new object again but this time the new object is used, that is, the
address produced from the object creation is used to call a method in the object. This
statement is intended to show you that it is the address we are using to access the
variables and methods in an object, not the variable which holds the address. Even
though we use a method (and one variable) of the object created in this line, we do not
keep the objects address so this object will also be discarded in due course.

So, the command first creates an object of type CustomerInfoClass and returns
an address to this object (the statement new CustomerInfoClass() is therefore
replaced by an address). The next part of this statement then uses this address to
execute the code for the method setName. The address of the object is not stored so
this object is inaccessible after the full statement is executed and the object in question (and its contents) will be disposed of.

In line 22, we use the object created in line 8 and store information (the string Jane)
in the variable contained in that object.

In line 25, we execute some code belonging to the object which accesses (and displays) the variable which is stored in the object in line 22. This value is the string Jane.

In line 28, we create a variable called customerObjectCopy to hold an address of
an object of type CustomerInfoClass.

In line 32, we copy the address in the variable customerObject into customer-
ObjectCopy. Remember we are copying the address, not the object.

In line 34, we print out the address contained in customerObjectCopy (which
should have the same value as that printed out in line 10 which shows the contents of
the variable customerObject).

In line 37, we access the method getName, which contains the object whose reference is stored in customerObjectCopy. The result of this call will be the same
as the result of the call printed out in line 25 since we are accessing the same method
and the same variable in the same object in both lines (because both object variables
hold the same address). We are using different variables to hold the object address
(customerObject and customerObjectCopy).

Remember you can print out the address of an object (as done above in line 10)
anytime but there is no way to directly access the information at this address. You
must use the object variable and allow the system to access it for you (it was deemed

dangerous to allow programmers in Java to be allowed to directly access memory locations because they might change their contents inadvertently causing problems, yet another example of how Java prevents the programmer from doing harm).

An example of the above program is shown in Figure 6.1. Note that the addresses will usually change each time the program is run as the memory allocated by the OS will change.

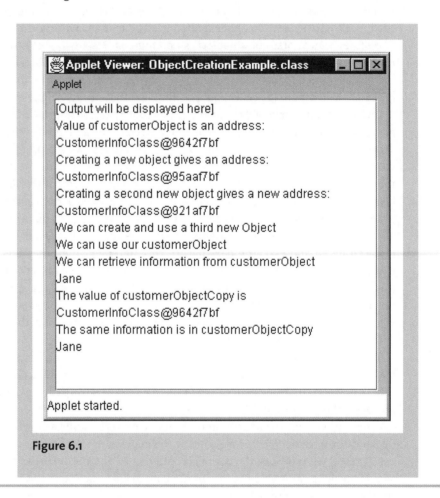

Figure 6.1

6.1.3 Parameter passing

When it comes down to passing parameters, the two types of variable that we can have, fundamental data type and object, are handled in the same way, that is, the contents of the variable being passed are copied into the formal parameter in the method which is called.

However, as the information you are passing can take the form of a value or an address we use a naming scheme to identify exactly what is being passed. The mechanism used for passing fundamental, or simple, data types such as int, double, char, and so on is known as 'pass by value'. The mechanism used to pass addresses of objects to a method is known as 'pass by reference'. In each case it amounts to the fact that the contents of the variables being passed (the actual parameter) are copied into the parameter variable (the formal parameter). Since the contents of a fundamental data type variable is a value and the contents of an object variable is a reference then passing the contents of a variable can have two different consequences. For a fundamental data type variable, it means that the original variable will not be affected as it is simply being copied. However, for a variable holding a reference to an object it means the method being called has access to the same object as the variable used as the actual parameter. It does not mean that a method has access to a copy of the object since what was passed was not a copy of the object itself but a copy of the address of the object. So, two variables (the formal parameter and the actual parameter) now contain the same address, that is, they lead to the same object. This means that any changes a called method makes to the object referenced in its formal parameter will remain after the method is finished and disposed of.

6.1.3.1 Example: pass by value

In the following example, we look at passing parameters of simple data types. This shows that the values passed are copied into formal parameters and can be altered without affecting the original values.

Table 6.3 shows what is happening at the relevant points in the code (which follows the table).

Table 6.3

The value of the variable	At point	Is
actualParameter	1	5
formalParameter	1	(has not been created yet)
actualParameter	2	5
formalParameter	2	5 (copy of contents of actualParameter)
actualParameter	3	5
formalParameter	3	10
actualParameter	4	5
formalParameter	4	(doesn't exist, method finished so deleted)

```
public class PassByValueExample extends TrainingWheels      1
{                                                            2
                                                             3
public void entryPoint()                                     4
    {                                                        5
    // Setup Variable                                        6
    int actualParameter;                                     7
    // Assign value to variable                              8
```

```
        actualParameter = 5;                                              9
        outputOnScreen("Value of actualParameter is "+actualParameter);   10
        // Point 1                                                        11
        // Call method with variable                                     12
        doubleIt(actualParameter);                                       13
                                                                          14
        // Point 4                                                       15
        // Examine contents of variable to see if changed               16
        outputOnScreen("actualParameter after doubleIt = "              17
        + actualParameter);
                                                                          18
    } // End entryPoint                                                  19
                                                                          20
  public void doubleIt(int formalParameter)                             21
    {                                                                     22
    // Point 2                                                          23
    // Copy of parameter placed in variable formalParameter            24
    // Alter value of variable                                         25
    formalParameter = formalParameter * 2;                             26
                                                                          27
    // Point 3                                                         28
    // Output current value of variable                               29
    outputOnScreen("Value of formalParameter is "                    30
    + formalParameter);
    } // End of doubleIt                                              31
                                                                          32
} // End PassByValueExample                                           33
```

So, in the above program you can see that the value contained in the variable `actual-Parameter` does not change throughout the life of the program. The value of the variable `formalParameter` (copied from `actualParameter`) is doubled (line 26) without having any affect on the value in `actualParameter`. This variable disappears when the method `doubleIt` is finished.

The result of the program is shown in Figure 6.2 in p. 215.

6.1.3.2 Example: pass by reference

This example shows what happens when you pass the contents of a variable which holds a reference to an object to a method in a parameter. Remember that the contents of an object variable are an address or reference so you are passing a copy of the location that the object is stored at, not the object itself.

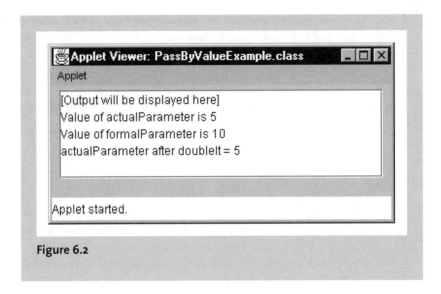

Figure 6.2

Table 6.4 shows the contents of the variables at the relevant points in the program.

Table 6.4

The value of the variable	At point	Is
exampleObject	1	Null
exampleObject	2	0420 (example location of object of type exampleObject)
exampleObject.valueString	2	"default"
exampleObject	3	0420
receivedObject	3	0420 (contents of example-Object)
exampleObject.valueString	3	"default"
receivedObject.valueString	3	"default"
exampleObject	4	0420
receivedObject	4	0420
exampleObject.valueString	4	"hello"
receivedObject.valueString	4	"hello"
exampleObject	5	0420
receivedObject	5	doesn't exist
exampleObject.valueString	5	"hello"
receivedObject.valueString	5	doesn't exist

Note that the use of the statement `exampleObject.valueString` and `received-Object.valueString` is for illustrative purposes only since `valueString` is a private variable so neither of these statements will be valid.

```
public class PassByReferenceExample extends TrainingWheels    1
{                                                              2
                                                               3
public void entryPoint()                                       4
    {                                                          5
    ExampleClass exampleObject;                                6
    // Point 1                                                 7
    // Setup the variable exampleObject to hold an address     8
                                                               9
    // Create an object and put its address in exampleObject  10
    exampleObject = new ExampleClass();                        11
                                                              12
    // Point 2                                                13
    // Access the object                                      14
    outputOnScreen("Contents of ValueString");                15
    outputOnScreen(exampleObject.getValueString());           16
                                                              17
        // Call the method changeObject with the address of   18
        // exampleObject                                      19
        changeObject(exampleObject);                          20
                                                              21
        // Point 5                                            22
        // Check to see if the contents of exampleObject have changed  23
        outputOnScreen("Contents of valueString");            24
        outputOnScreen(exampleObject.getValueString());       25
        } // End entryPoint                                   26
                                                              27
    public void changeObject(ExampleClass receivedObject)     28
        {                                                     29
        // Point 3                                            30
        // Copy the reference to an object into the variable  31
        // receivedObject                                     32
                                                              33
        // Change one of the variables in the object          34
        receivedObject.changeString("hello");                 35
        // Point 4                                            36
        // Finish the method                                  37
        } // End changeObject                                 38
                                                              39
    } // End PassByReferenceExample                           40
```

```
class ExampleClass                                          41
{                                                           42
private String valueString = "default";                     43
                                                            44
public void changeString(String receivedValue)              45
    {                                                       46
    valueString = receivedValue;                            47
    } // End changeString                                   48
                                                            49
public String getValueString()                              50
    {                                                       51
    return valueString;                                     52
    } // End getValueString                                 53
                                                            54
} // End ExampleClass                                       55
                                                            56
```

You will see if you try out the above program that the contents of the string contained in the object are changed from "default" to "hello" using the method change-Object. The variable receivedObject disappears after the method (changeObject) is finished but the object whose address it holds will still be kept in memory because the variable receivedObject also holds its address.

The output of the above program is shown in Figure 6.3.

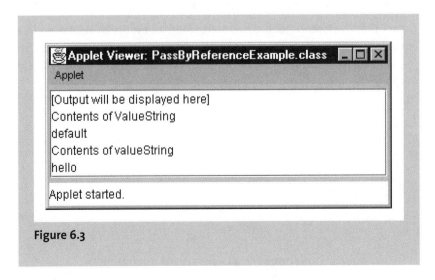

Figure 6.3

6.1.3.3   Example: string passing

String is actually a class definition though as far as definition and use is concerned we have been treating String like the other simple data types (int, boolean, etc.). Is a String variable passed by reference or by value? (*Hint*: what happens if a String is passed as a parameter, does its original value change if the parameter is altered in the method?).

6.1.3.4   Example: passing arrays

We have seen that any object can be passed as a parameter. Since an array is actually an object then we can see that passing an array as a parameter will have the same consequences as passing single objects, that is, the address of the array is passed into a formal parameter and therefore any changes made to the array declared in the formal parameter in the method are made to the same array as that used for the actual parameter.

For example, in the following program an array is declared in line 6. The contents of this array are then output using a method called `printArray`, defined in line 17.

The reference to the array is then passed to another method called `changeArray` (line 11) which changes all the values contained in the array to '99'. Since the address of the array `results` is what has been passed to the method `changeArray`, then the contents of the array referenced in the variable results also change (as both variables, `results` and `arrayOfResults`, lead to the same array). When the new contents of the array are printed out (line 14), you should see that the values have indeed been changed.

When an array address is being passed to a method you declare the formal parameter as if an array object were going to be created later, that is, you place the name of the type of value held in the array, followed by the identifier for the array and a set of square brackets. For example, the method declaration:

```
public void outputAllEmployees(String employeeNames[])
```

says that a reference to an array containing a number of strings will be passed to this method. You can use the `length` variable to ascertain exactly how many strings are contained in the array passed to the method, for example, `employeeNames.length`.

```
public class ArrayPassingTest extends TrainingWheels          1
{                                                             2
                                                             3
public void entryPoint()                                     4
    {                                                        5
    int results[] = {5,3,7};                                 6
                                                             7
    outputOnScreen("Values before change");                 8
```

```
        printArray(results);                                9
                                                            10
        changeArray(results);                               11
                                                            12
        outputOnScreen("Values after change");              13
        printArray(results);                                14
        } // End entryPoint                                 15
                                                            16
    public void printArray(int arrayValues[])               17
        {                                                   18
        for(int counter = 0;counter < arrayValues.length;counter++)  19
            outputOnScreen("Value in location" + counter + "is"      20
            + arrayValues[counter]);
        } // End printArray                                 21
                                                            22
    public void changeArray(int arrayOfResults[])           23
        {                                                   24
        arrayOfResults[0] = 99;                             25
        arrayOfResults[1] = 99;                             26
        arrayOfResults[2] = 99;                             27
        } // End changeArray                                28
                                                            29
    } // End ArrayPassingTest                               30
```

The result of the above program showing the altered contents of the array is shown in Figure 6.4 in p. 220.

EXERCISE What happens if instead of passing an entire array to a method you simply pass a location, for example, Results[4]. Will that variable be copied or will a reference to it be taken, that is, will any changes made to the formal parameter be reflected in the original array.

6.1.3.5 Example: returning objects

Since object references can be passed as parameters, they can also be returned as a result of a method. This resulting reference (or address) can then be used in the same way as a reference from an object created using new, that is, it can be accessed or it can be placed in a variable.

In the following example program we set up a variable to hold an address of an object of type CustomerInfoClass in line 6. We then call a method named getCustomerObject

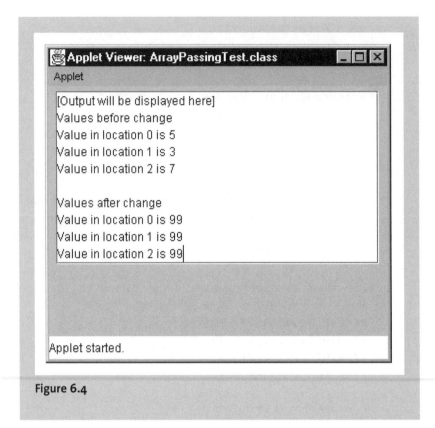

Figure 6.4

which will create a new object (line 18), put the reference to that object into a variable and return the contents of that variable (line 21). We have therefore placed the reference to the object created in the method `getCustomerObject` into the variable `customerObject` (line 8). In line 11, we use the object stored at the address contained in the variable `customerObject`.

One question which should be occurring to you at this point is regarding the variable `temporaryCustomerObject`. Should that variable, and therefore the object it refers to, not disappear when the method `getCustomerObject` is finished? The answer is that the variable `temporaryCustomerObject` does disappear but since the object that it contained the address for is in use (the variable `customerObject` now holds the address which was stored in `temporaryCustomerObject`) the object will not be erased. This is a strict rule in Java, if an object is in use by another part of the program or by the operating system it is not erased.

If, however, I was to type the statement:

```
customerObject = null;
```

and insert that statement at line 11, then the object whose reference contained in `customerObject` is now no longer usable, that is, no variable contains an address for it, and therefore the VM will erase this object in due course.

```
public class ObjectReturnExample extends TrainingWheels          1
{                                                                2
                                                                 3
public void entryPoint()                                         4
   {                                                             5
   CustomerInfoClass customerObject;                             6
                                                                 7
   customerObject = getCustomerObject("Janet");                  8
                                                                 9
   outputOnScreen("Content of object is");                      10
   outputOnScreen(customerObject.getName());                    11
   } // End entryPoint                                          12
                                                                13
public CustomerInfoClass getCustomerObject(String              14
nameParameter)
   {                                                            15
   CustomerInfoClass temporaryCustomerObject;                  16
                                                                17
   temporaryCustomerObject = new CustomerInfoClass();          18
   temporaryCustomerObject.setName(nameParameter);             19
                                                                20
   return temporaryCustomerObject;                             21
   } // End getCustomerObject                                  22
                                                                23
} // End ObjectReturnExample                                   24
                                                                25
class CustomerInfoClass                                         26
{                                                               27
private String name;                                           28
                                                                29
public void setName(String nameValue)                          30
   {                                                            31
   name = nameValue;                                           32
   } // End setName                                            33
                                                                34
public String getName()                                        35
   {                                                            36
   return name;                                                37
   } // End getName                                            38
                                                                39
} // End CustomerInfoClass                                     40
```

Note that you can use the object returned from `getCustomerObject` without having to declare an object variable. For example, you can replace line 8 by the following:

```
outputOnScreen(getCustomerObject("Janet").getName());
```

This instruction causes the method `getName` which is contained in the object returned from the call to the method `getCustomerObject` to be executed. The object will of course disappear if this form of statement is used since no reference for it exists but this example statement shows you another way of accessing objects which you will encounter later.

6.1.4 Strings

In Chapter 4, we explained that you should not test two strings for equality using the `==` symbols. You can now appreciate why this is so as since strings are treated as objects. What `String1 == String2` actually does is check if the address contained in the variable `String1` matches the address contained in the variable `String2`. The test does not check the contents of the string objects, merely the addresses at which these objects are contained.

So remember if comparing two string variables to use `equals`. For example,

```
String value = "Value";
String result = "Result";
if(value.equals(result))
  ouputOnScreen("The Strings match");
```

`equals` is a method contained in every string object. It takes as a parameter another string object, extracts the contents from the parameter string and compares it with the contents of the string object which is executing the `equals` method.

The only circumstances you can use = = is if you are comparing a string value with another value or a variable. For example,

```
if("Result" = = "Value")
  ouputOnScreen("The Strings match");
String result = "Contents";
if(result = = "Value")
  ouputOnScreen("The Strings match");
```

You can, and should, use `equals` for these operations also as it will get you into the habit of using it, so you do not inadvertently get caught out if you make a minor change to the program, that is, replace the above `if` statements with the following:

```
if(result.equals("Value"))
if("Result".equals("Value"))
```

Note: Some compilers will accept `==` as equivalent to `.equals`, therefore, sometimes `value == result` will compare the contents of both strings rather than their addresses. For the sake of correctness though you should get used to using `.equals` and not rely on `==` working.

If a String is an object, will the following code copy the contents of one String object into another or copy the address?

```
String testString1 = "TestString";
String testString2 = teststring1;
```

Is this behaviour the same for other objects? For example:

```
CustomerInfoClass customer1 = customer2;
// Where customer2 has been setup
```

6.1.5 Running a class

One element of programming that we have only briefly looked at is what happens when you run a Java program. Well, a Java program is essentially a class, that is why all the files created when you compile the source code use the extension .class. When you want to run a program what happens is that the VM will take this class definition and start to execute a specific method.

There are two types of Java program, an applet and an application and the way that the VM starts each differs. In the Java Development Kit discussed in Appendix A, there are two separate VMs mentioned, one for applets and one for applications. We look now at how each type of program is started.

6.1.5.1 Applet

For an applet the VM is started with a html page which contains the location and name of the applet class file. It also contains the information needed to decide the size of the applet. The VM locates this named file and reads the class file into its memory. The VM then creates an object from the class file (and also creates any object which the class files extends). The VM will then attempt to start some specific methods in the object it has created. The methods it looks for are called: init, start, and paint. If it cannot find these methods either in the applet object or any object that the applet inherited, then it does nothing. If it does find those methods, it executes them in turn, first init, then start and finally paint. These are the methods you will write instructions in to setup your applet (they are equivalent of the entry-Point method you have used up to now). You can call other methods from these methods so the VM is not confined to executing only these methods. We look at applets in more detail in Chapter 7. Once the VM finishes executing these methods it will usually wait for the user to stop the program, which they can do by closing the window, before destroying the objects created. This means that any display created by the program will be visible even if no more instructions in the program are being executed.

6.1.5.2 Application

When a VM reads in an application class, it does not automatically create an object from it, you must specifically request an object's creation. How do you do that? Well, the VM will always look for a method called main when it loads the application class.

If it cannot find this method, it stops and outputs an error message. If it finds the method called main, it executes the instructions contained within it. Usually one of those instructions is an instruction to the VM to setup an object using the class definition of the class containing the main method. The main method is not part of an object, it operates outside an object using a mechanism known as static. We look at applications later in Section 6.6.

6.1.6 What else happens when an object is created?

As we've seen when an object is created, the VM allocates memory for it and copies the instructions in the class definition into this memory. It also creates locations to store the variables which have been defined in the class. Before the VM finishes with the object and returns the address at which the object is stored it does one last thing. It looks for a method in the object with the same name as the class and which does not supply any type for a return value (not even void). If it cannot find this method it continues, if it does find such a method it executes it and then continues.

This method is known as a constructor because it is used to setup or construct the object. Constructors are usually written to initialise variables but can do other things such as set up other objects, access files, open communication with remote systems, and so on.

Let's look at the use of a constructor in the following example. We use one class definition with a constructor (CustomerInfoClass) and one without (Customer-InfoClassNoConstruct). The constructor in CustomerInfoClass will put a String into the name variable (line 31). This initialises the string. Other than the constructor the two classes are the same. We setup objects using the two class definitions in lines 8 and 14. We can see the results of the constructor because when we call the method getName in the object with the constructor (customerObject), it will return a value for the string which was placed in the variable Name when the constructor was executed. This shows that the constructor must have executed when the object is created, otherwise there would be no value in Name. When we call the getName method in the other object (customerObjectNoConstruct), we see that it contains a value of null (since its String variable name was not setup when the object was created).

```
public class ConstructorExample extends TrainingWheels      1
{                                                            2
                                                             3
public void entryPoint()                                     4
    {                                                        5
    CustomerInfoClass customerObject;                        6
                                                             7
    customerObject = new CustomerInfoClass();                8
                                                             9
```

```
    outputOnScreen("Name = " + customerObject.getName());      10
                                                               11
    CustomerInfoClassNoConstruct customerObjectNoConstruct;    12
                                                               13
    customerObjectNoConstruct = new                            14
    CustomerInfoClassNoConstruct();
                                                               15
    outputOnScreen("Name = "                                   16
    +customerObjectNoConstruct.getName());
                                                               17
    } // End entryPoint                                        18
                                                               19
} // End ConstructorExample                                    20
                                                               21
// Class with constructor                                      22
class CustomerInfoClass                                        23
{                                                              24
private String name;                                           25
                                                               26
public CustomerInfoClass()                                     27
    {                                                          28
    name = "Customer Name Goes Here";                          29
    } // End CustomerInfoClass constructor                     30
                                                               31
public void setName(String nameParameter)                      32
    {                                                          33
    name = nameParameter;                                      34
    } // End setName                                           35
                                                               36
public String getName()                                        37
    {                                                          38
    return name;                                               39
    } // End getName                                           40
                                                               41
} // End CustomerInfoClass                                     42
                                                               43
// Class without constructor                                   44
class CustomerInfoClassNoConstruct                             45
{                                                              46
private String name;                                           47
                                                               48
public void setName(String nameParameter)                      49
    {                                                          50
    name = nameParameter;                                      51
```

```
      } // End setName                              52
                                                    53
  public String getName()                           54
      {                                             55
      return name;                                  56
      } // End getName                              57
                                                    58
  } // End CustomerInfoClassNoConstruct             59
```

The output of the above program is shown in Figure 6.5.

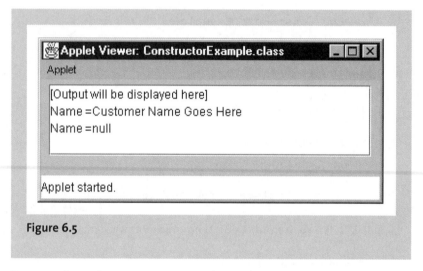

Figure 6.5

You can also write a constructor so that it will take a parameter. In the example program below, the constructor in line 22 will take a parameter supplied by the user in line 10. The form of the object declaration

```
customerObject = new CustomerInfoClass(nameToInsert);
```

indicates that the constructor code for CustomerInfoClass should be executed and the actual parameter, nameToInsert, should be passed to it. This is just like calling a method directly using its name except the constructor method will only execute once, when the object is created.

```
  public class ConstructorExample2 extends TrainingWheels     1
  {                                                           2
                                                              3
  public void entryPoint()                                    4
      {                                                       5
      CustomerInfoClass customerObject;                       6
                                                              7
```

```
      String nameToInsert = "Jane";                          8
                                                             9
      customerObject = new CustomerInfoClass(nameToInsert);  10
                                                             11
      outputOnScreen("Name = " + customerObject.getName());  12
      } // End entryPoint                                    13
                                                             14
  } // End ConstructorExample2                               15
                                                             16
                                                             17
  class CustomerInfoClass                                    18
  {                                                          19
  private String name;                                       20
                                                             21
  public CustomerInfoClass(String nameParameter)             22
      {                                                      23
      name = nameParameter;                                  24
      } // End customerInfoClass constructor                 25
                                                             26
  public void setName(String nameParameter)                  27
      {                                                      28
      name = nameParameter;                                  29
      } // End setName                                       30
                                                             31
  public String getName()                                    32
      {                                                      33
      return name;                                           34
      } // End getName                                       35
                                                             36
  } // End CustomerInfoClass                                 37
```

The output of the above program is given in Figure 6.6 in p. 228.

What happens if you don't supply a parameter when declaring the object in the above example? For instance, if you replaced line 10 with:

```
customerObject = new CustomerInfoClass();
```

Well, because you declared the constructor as taking a single parameter of type string (line 22), the compiler will expect to see you supply a parameter for the constructor when declaring the object. If you do not, it will give the error message:

```
No constructor matching CustomerInfoClass() found in class Customer-
InfoClass.
```

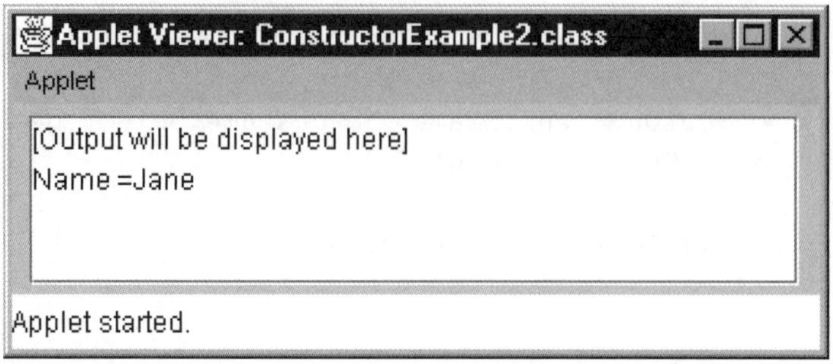

Figure 6.6

This indicates that there is a mismatch in how you declared the constructor and how you are actually using it (i.e. you have forgotten to supply the parameter). It is possible to have several constructors each taking different numbers and types of parameters (see polymorphism in Section 6.4).

6.1.6.1 Constructor analogy

Going back to our example in Chapter 2 that equated objects with jellies and classes with jelly moulds we can look at an analogy for a constructor. The main point is that even though every object created from a class is initially the same you may want to customise them slightly as you are setting them up. If we look at the jelly mould example again, we see that we may like to create jellies in lots of different colours. All we do is decide when creating the jelly what colour mix to put in. The jelly is exactly the same in contents (its shape) but differs from other jellies in its initial setup (its colour).

In the same way as we supply the colour mix to use for the jelly, we can also decide when creating an object what information to place into the object when it is created by passing it into the constructor.

6.2 INHERITANCE

6.2.1 Introduction

Inheritance is one of the most vital parts of object oriented programming. As it allows classes to be assembled by combining new code and existing code it enables not only the recycling of code but also simplification of the solution. You have seen examples of this in the customised class (TrainingWheels) which you have used to conduct input and output operations without having to write all the statements which are really necessary to setup areas of the screen for input and output.

What's the difference between inheriting and creating an object? Well, inheritance is used when you are not happy with a particular class definition and you want to adopt certain parts of it to suit your purpose. Creating and using an object as it is means that you are happy with the class definition and do not want to make any changes.

Inheriting is like going to a restaurant, you can pick an item on the menu and customise it (ask for it to be well done, extra spicy, etc.). You therefore get a new object which is a customisation of the original class. Creating an object is like a fast food restaurant, everything is the same and no customisation is permitted.

In this section we look at exactly how inheritance works and see some examples of its use.

6.2.2　How it works

You should now be familiar with the idea of inheritance, the fact that one class builds onto another (have a quick look back to the jelly analogy in Chapter 2 for a further explanation). How does this work in practice? Well, the first rule of inheritance in Java is that a class can only inherit or extend one other class. There is no limit to the number of classes you can inherit one after the other but you can only inherit one at a time. This turns out not to be a major restriction though some programmers familiar with other object programming languages which allow classes to inherit several other classes may find it a bit annoying.

So, what actually happens when you 'extend' or inherit a class? Well, one way of thinking about it is imagining that the compiler will go and get the source code for the class you inherit and attach it to your own source code.

Obviously the class you inherit will have certain methods you want to use but the code for the methods will not be in your source code but wherever the inherited class is stored. How does the compiler deal with this? Well, it goes to the file which contain the definition for the class you are extending and examines it to see if it has the relevant methods. This means that these class files must be in a place the compiler can access them, either in the same directory or where the operating system can find them (using path information).

So, the compiler will convert your code into bytecode. Among the bytecode instructions are a reference to the class you inherited.

When this bytecode is executed and the VM creates an object out of your class file, it will then look for the class file you extended. Then it creates an object from this class file and associates it with the object it created from your class.

6.2.3　Terminology

The technical name for a class which you inherit is a Parent or Super class. The name for a class which does the inheriting is a Child or Sub class. For example,

```
class StockItem extends Record {}
```

StockItem is a child or subclass of Record and Record is a parent or superclass of StockItem.

6.2.4 Example: bank staff

We have seen an example of what inheritance can do for you in Chapter 2. In that chapter we discussed employees of a bank, an ordinary employee, a teller and a manager.

Let us design the three classes which will be needed to store information about the different types of employees of a bank. The first class is Employee class, which holds details about each employee and calculates their wages. Basic employees of the bank (gardener, electrician, cleaner, etc.) can be stored using those objects. So we do not need to make any changes to the Employee class to suit these types of employees.

For other types of employees, we would like to alter the class to keep extra information. For example, for the tellers we would like a record kept of their incoming and outgoing cash. For the manager (who needs to be able to perform as a teller if things are busy in the Bank), we would like to know the amount of loans they have approved. We can construct individual classes for the different types of employee or we can analyse the information we have and decide whether it is feasible for certain classes to make use of each other, that is, we can save effort by having some classes inherit others.

In the case of the above description, we see that the information and actions associated with a basic employee are common to the other employees also, so we can inherit the class Employee when defining other type of employees class. Next let's look at the class for a tellers, we just decided that it can inherit the Employee class, so we write that it extends Employee in the definition. We also decided that we need to store other information (incoming and outgoing balances) and write methods to access and update that information, so we write those relevant variables and methods into the teller class definition.

For the Manager class, we see that it too can inherit the Employee class but we also saw that a manager must be able to act as a teller. Therefore, we need the Manager class to contain the methods and variables found in the Teller class and those contained in the Employee class. How does the Manager class accomplish this? Well, it needs to inherit both classes to make use of their methods and variables but it cannot inherit both Employee and Teller classes at the same time. However, if a Manager class inherits a Teller class the Teller class will automatically inherit the Employee class. So, by inheriting the Teller class, we also indirectly inherit the Employee class.

The descriptions for the classes we have designed can be seen below.

```
class Employee                                             1
{                                                          2
private String name;                                      3
private int hourlyWage;                                   4
                                                           5
public void setupObject(String nameParameter,int          6
hourlyWageParameter)
   {                                                       7
   name = nameParameter;                                   8
   hourlyWage = hourlyWageParameter;                       9
   } // End setupObject                                   10
```

```
                                                                    11
    public String getName()                                         12
        {                                                           13
        return name;                                                14
        } // End getName                                            15
                                                                    16
    public int calculateWages(int hoursWorked)                      17
        {                                                           18
        return(hoursWorked*hourlyWage);                             19
        } // End calculateWages                                     20
                                                                    21
    // Other methods such as changeWages,etc would go here          22
                                                                    23
    } // End Employee                                               24
```

```
    class Teller extends Employee                                    1
    {                                                                2
    private int totalLodged = 0;                                     3
    private int totalWithdrawn = 0;                                  4
                                                                     5
    public void lodgeMoney(int amountToLodge)                        6
        {                                                            7
        totalLodged += amountToLodge;                                8
        } // End lodgeMoney                                          9
                                                                    10
    public void withDrawMoney(int amountToWithdraw)                 11
        {                                                           12
        totalWithdrawn += amountToWithdraw;                         13
        } // End withDrawMoney                                      14
                                                                    15
    // Other methods such as getTotalLodged,etc would go here       16
                                                                    17
    } // End Teller                                                 18
```

```
    class Manager extends Teller                                     1
    {                                                                2
    private int loansApproved = 0;                                   3
                                                                     4
```

```
public void approveLoan(int loanAmount)              5
  {                                                   6
  loansApproved += loanAmount;                        7
  } // End approveLoan                                8
                                                      9
// Other methods such as getLoans etc would go here  10
                                                      11
} // End Manager                                      12
```

Let's look at a declaration for each class and go through what happens.

We create a new `Employee` object and store the address in the variable `Gardener`.

```
Employee gardener = new Employee();
```

When an `Employee` object `Gardener` is declared and created it will contain the methods and variables mentioned in the class description, namely:

Object of type Employee	
Variables	`name,hourlyWage`
Methods	`setupObject(String,int), String get-Name(), int calculateWages(int)`

We can therefore call any of the methods it contains, for example:

```
gardener.setupObject("John Smith",5);
```

When we create an object of class type `Teller` the system again will go looking for a description of the `Teller` class.

```
Teller tellerNumberOne = new Teller();
```

It creates an object of type `Teller` which will hold the following:

Object of type Teller	
Variables	`totalLodged,totalWithdrawn`
Methods	`lodgeMoney(int), withDrawMoney(int)`

However, the class `Teller` inherited the class `Employee` so the VM will look for the class `Employee`, create an object from that class and associate the `Teller` object created with it. So, our `Teller` object now looks like the following (i.e. it is a combination of a `Teller` object and an `Employee` object):

Object of type Teller	
Variables	totalLodged, totalWithdrawn
Methods	lodgeMoney(int), withDrawMoney(int)

Object of type Employee	
Variables	name, hourlyWage
Methods	setUpObject(String,int), String getName(), int calculateWages(int)

We effectively have two objects in one. That is, what we asked for when we extended the class Employee and that is what we got. We can now access any method in the object variable we named and the system will access the relevant part of our Teller object (either the Teller part or the Employee part). For example,

```
tellerNumberOne.setupObject("JaneJones",10);
// Access the Employee object part
tellerNumberOne.lodgeMoney(100); // Access the Teller object part
```

Next we create a branch manager object.

```
Manager branchManagerOne = new Manager();
```

Again the VM will look for a definition for the class Manager and create an object from that class definition, so we initially get the object below.

Object of type Manager	
Variables	loansApproved
Methods	approveLoan(int)

Next the VM will bring in the inherited class (Teller) and create an object from that, which in turn creates an object from its inherited class (Employee). So, a Manager object contains three objects of type Manager, Teller and Employee.

Object of type Manager	
Variables	loansApproved
Methods	approveLoan(int)

Object of type Teller	
Variables	totalLodged, totalWithdrawn
Methods	lodgeMoney(int), withdrawMoney(int)

Object of type Employee	
Variables	`name,hourlyWage`
Methods	`setUpObject(String,int), String getName(), int calculateWages(int)`

Again we are free to access any of the methods or variables stored as part of the manager object.

```
branchManagerOne.setupObject("Mary Marie",15);
// Access employee part of object
branchManagerOne.lodgeMoney(150); // Access teller part of object
branchManagerOne.approveLoan(2000); // Access manager part of object
```

All objects have three methods in common that they can call since `Teller` and `Manager` inherit the three methods in `Employee`. Here is an example of calling the `calculateWages` method contained in the `Employee` object part of the three objects created.

```
gardener.calculateWages(41);
tellerNumberOne.calculateWages(38);
branchManagerOne.calculateWages(45);
```

6.2.5 Example: using a constructor in an inherited class

In the following example, we look at creating a class to hold basic details about an item of stock. We also look at how to deal with a situation where the parent class contains a constructor which requires parameters to be passed to it. You could create a `StockItem` class as follows:

```
class StockItem
{
private String name;
private String value;

public StockItem(String newName,String newValue)
   {
   name = newName;
   value = newValue;
   } // End StockItem constructor

public String getName()
   {
   return name;
   } // End getName

public String getValue()
   {
   return value;
   } // End getValue

} // End StockItem
```

Now suppose you want to keep track of extra details about your stock items, for example, the expiry date if they are perishable, where they are stored, and so on. You can either rewrite the original class and add methods and variables to it or create a new class which contains the relevant variables and methods and inherits `Stock-Item`, and therefore all of the methods and variables within `StockItem`.

The disadvantage of rewriting the original class is that we could destabilise it or even damage it. Ideally we would like simply to use the methods and variables within it without affecting the class itself. This is an important need since by reducing the amount you have to interfere with existing code to get what you want you reduce the possibility that you introduce errors into the code (and this in turn saves you time and money). This is one of the main reasons we use inheritance.

We therefore write a new class `TrackedStockItem` which contains all the necessary additional methods and variables and which inherits `StockItem` (and therefore all its methods and variables).

```
class TrackedStockItem extends StockItem
{
private String dateReceived;
private String expiryDate;
private String currentShelfLocation;

public TrackedStockItem(String name,String value)
    {
    // need to call the constructor in the superclass using
    // the super method
    super(name,value);
    } // End RrackedStockItem constructor

public void setUpObject(String received,String expiry,String
location)
    {
    dateReceived = received;
    expiryDate = expiry;
    currentShelfLocation = location;
    } // End setUpObject

public String getDateReceived()
    {
    return dateReceived;
    } // End getDateReceived

public String getExpiryDate()
    {
    return expiryDate;
    } // End getExpiryDate
```

```
public String getCurrentShelfLocation()
    {
    return currentShelfLocation;
    } // End getCurrentShelfLocation

} // End TrackedStockItem
```

So, when an object of type TrackedStockItem is created, it will be assigned space in memory to hold the variables dateReceived, expiryDate and currentShelf-Location as well as its methods. A space will also be created to hold an object of type StockItem which will also be created. As the class StockItem contains a constructor you need to find some way of passing values to the object being created. You can do this in the constructor for TrackedStockItem by calling the method super with the variables you want to pass to the constructor for StockItem. Why do you have to do this? Well, how else will you get the parameters to the constructor for StockItem? You cannot supply them directly because you are not creating an object of StockItem, it is being created for you since TrackedStockItem (which you are creating) inherits it.

By using the word super you are indicating that you are calling the super class and that you are supplying its constructor with the relevant parameters.

The program below will create a StockItem object (line 7) and use it (line 9). It will then create a TrackedStockItem object (line 12) and pass the parameters supplied to the parent of the object (line 53) using a call to the super method. You can see that these parameters are successfully passed from the output of line 15 which contacts the StockItem part of the TrackedStockItem object to output the value of the variable name.

```
public class InheritanceExample extends TrainingWheels     1
{                                                          2
                                                          3
public void entryPoint()                                   4
    {                                                      5
    StockItem bigScreenTV;                                 6
    bigScreenTV = new StockItem("Television","999.99");    7
                                                          8
    outputOnScreen("The item name is "+bigScreenTV.getName());   9
                                                          10
    TrackedStockItem plums;                                11
    plums = new TrackedStockItem("Plums","1.99");          12
    plums.setUpObject("2/8/01","20/8/01","Isle 4b");       13
                                                          14
    outputOnScreen("The item name is " + plums.getName());  15
    outputOnScreen("The location is "+plums.getShelfLocation());  16
    } // End entryPoint                                    17
                                                          18
```

```
} // End InheritanceExample                              19
                                                         20
class StockItem                                          21
{                                                        22
private String name;                                     23
private String value;                                    24
                                                         25
public StockItem(String newName,String newValue)         26
   {                                                     27
   name = newName;                                       28
   value = newValue;                                     29
   } // End StockItem constructor                        30
                                                         31
public String getName()                                  32
   {                                                     33
   return name;                                          34
   } // End getName                                      35
                                                         36
public String getValue()                                 37
   {                                                     38
   return value;                                         39
   } // End getValue                                     40
                                                         41
} // End StockItem                                       42
                                                         43
class TrackedStockItem extends StockItem                 44
{                                                        45
private String dateReceived;                             46
private String expiryDate;                               47
private String shelfLocation;                            48
                                                         49
public TrackedStockItem(String name,String value)        50
   {                                                     51
   // need to setup the superclass                       52
   super(name,value);                                    53
   } // End TrackedStockItem constructor                 54
                                                         55
public void setUpObject(String received,String expiry,   56
String location)
   {                                                     57
   dateReceived = received;                              58
   expiryDate = expiry;                                  59
   shelfLocation = location;                             60
   } // End setUpObject                                  61
                                                         62
```

```
    public String getDateReceived()                        63
      {                                                     64
      return dateReceived;                                  65
      } // End getDateReceived                              66
                                                            67
    public String getExpiryDate()                           68
      {                                                     69
      return expiryDate;                                    70
      } // End getExpiryDate                                71
                                                            72
    public String getShelfLocation()                        73
      {                                                     74
      return shelfLocation;                                 75
      } // End getShelfLocation                             76
                                                            77
  } // End TrackedStockItem                                 78
```

The output of the above program is shown in Figure 6.7.

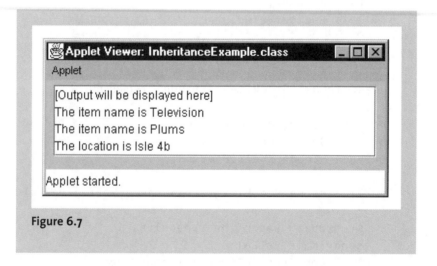

Figure 6.7

Another point to make is that you do not have to put the source code for the class you inherit in the same file as the source code for your program. The compiler will look for the source code or for the bytecode for any class you refer to and will check your interaction with that class. You can therefore put the classes into separate files, provided those class files can be found when they are needed (they are in the same directory as the class being compiled/run or are in a directory which the system automatically searches, i.e. they are part of the path). The compiler will automatically compile any of the classes that your program uses if they are not already compiled.

6.3 / PROTECTED

We have looked at the meaning of public and private in previous chapters, but there is one other word used to indicate where variables and methods can be accessed from (called a modifier) that we have not yet talked about, protected. The protected modifier indicates that a particular method or variable is available to methods only if they are defined within the same class as the protected element, or within a class that inherits the class which contains the protected element. In essence, the protected modifier exists so that variables and methods can be shared between classes which have an inheritance relationship with each other. As far as objects outside this inherited group are concerned, the protected elements may as well be marked private since no external access is permitted.

So, to sum up:

▶ *Public* – all elements marked with the public modifier can be viewed in the object and from outside.

▶ *Private* – elements marked private can only be viewed in the object. Private methods and variables are not even available to classes which inherit the class that contains them.

▶ *Protected* – protected elements can be viewed from outside an object but only by objects which come from classes which inherit the class that contains the protected element. By inherit we mean that the class is inherited at some point in the collection of parent–child classes used. For example, the parent of your parent class could contain a protected element which you could then use.

Public, private and protected mark what is called the visibility of an element. If an element is marked public, then its visibility is inside and outside the class; if protected, then the visibility is inside the class and inside any class which inherits the class containing the protected element.

EXAMPLE

```
public class ProtectedExample extends TrainingWheels      1
{                                                         2
                                                          3
public void entryPoint()                                  4
    {                                                     5
    EncapsulationEg egObject = new EncapsulationEg();      6
    outputOnScreen(egObject.publicMessage());             7
    outputOnScreen(egObject.getThePrivateMessage());      8
                                                          9
```

```
        EncapsulationEgSubclass egObjectSubclass =               10
        new EncapsulationEgSubclass();
        outputOnScreen(egObjectSubclass.getTheProtectedMessage()); 11
    } // End entryPoint                                          12
                                                                13
} // End ProtectedExample                                       14
                                                                15
class EncapsulationEg                                           16
{                                                               17
public String publicMessage()                                   18
    {                                                           19
    return "Anyone can see me\n";                               20
    } // End publicMessage                                      21
                                                                22
private String privateMessage()                                 23
    {                                                           24
    return "I have been accessed from within encapsulationEg\n"; 25
    } // End privateMessage                                     26
                                                                27
protected String protectedMessage()                             28
    {                                                           29
    return "I have been accessed from within this              30
    class or a subclass\n";
    } // End protectedMessage                                   31
                                                                32
public String getThePrivateMessage()                            33
    {                                                           34
    return "String returned from privateMessage\n"             35
    + privateMessage();
    } // End getThePrivateMessage                               36
                                                                37
} // End EncapsulationEg                                         38
                                                                39
class EncapsulationEgSubclass extends EncapsulationEg           40
{                                                               41
                                                                42
public String getTheProtectedMessage()                          43
    {                                                           44
    return "String returned from parent Object:\n"             45
    + protectedMessage();
    } // End getTheProtectedMessage                             46
                                                                47
} // End EncapsulationEgSubclass                                48
```

In the program above, we show how to access three different types of method. (i) protected; (ii) private; and (iii) public.

We create a class definition to hold these methods called EncapsualtionEg. This class contains three methods. publicMessage is publicly accessible so that it can be called from the entryPoint method (line 7) which is in a separate object. privateMessage can only be called from within the object so we use a public method called getThePrivateMessage to call it and return the result (line 8). protectedMessage is treated the same as privateMessage, you cannot access it directly but must go through a method. In the class definition EncapsulationEg there is no method which will access protectedMessage for us. However, in this example, we are using the class EncapsulationEgSubclass to access the method protectedMessage. So, we declare an object of type EncapsulationEgSubclass in line 10. This creates an object which holds an object of type EncapsulationEg-Subclass and EncapsulationEg. We call the getTheProtectedMessage method in this object which in turn will access the protectedMessage method in the object of type EncapsulationEg. Figure 6.8 shows how the output of the above program will look like.

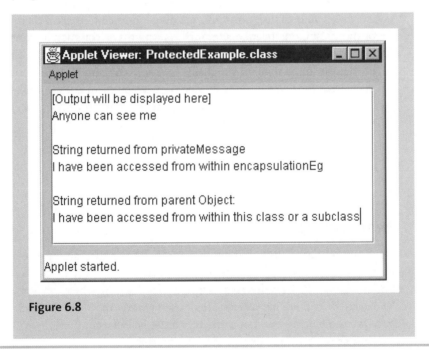

Figure 6.8

6.4 POLYMORPHISM

Polymorphism means many shapes and in the context of a programming language it means that you can use one name to refer to many different methods.

While many methods can have the same name, only one of them can be executed in response to a call and the system makes its decision about which one to execute based on the form of the method call. That decision is based on the number and/or type of actual parameters of the call to the method. So, instead of distinguishing methods by a unique identifier you can tell them apart because of their differing number and/or type of formal parameters. Each method must therefore be unique in the number and/or type of formal parameters it has. Different return types are not considered a valid way of defining different methods and will be rejected by the compiler if used.

6.4.1 Analogy

Imagine an automated call processing system, like a car insurance company. You call one single number and then are asked to choose from a list of numbers to select your service, press 1 to get an operator, press 2 to get quote, press 3 to make a claim, and so on. This is polymorphism, one telephone number is acting as a common starting mechanism for different types of services. The service you want can be deduced from the parameter you supply but the initial number you dial is the same no matter what the service is.

This is what the programming version of polymorphism does as well, it allows you the ease of remembering a single name and decides what to do with the call once it is made.

The two forms of polymorphism we look at are:

1 Overloading
2 Overriding

6.4.2 Overloading

Overloading means declaring another method with the same name as one you have used before. A method which is declared again in this way is said to be 'overloaded'. Both methods can be called with the compiler deciding which one you actually want to be executed. You are not allowed to declare exactly the same method, the method can have the same name but its parameters must be different.

Example of permitted overloading declarations:

```
public void methodName(int Value)
{ // Code for this method, version 1
}
public void methodName(String Name)
{ // Code for this method, version 2
}
```

You can also overload methods to accept a different number of parameters.

```
public void methodName(int Value, int Total)
{ // Code for this method, version 3
}
```

The above methods, all called `methodName`, are regarded as different by the compiler since they all have unique formal parameters. The compiler will decide which method to call based on the context of the call, that is, the number and or type of the actual parameters. For example,

```
methodName(2,3); // would result in version 3 of methodName
                 // being called
methodName(3); // would call version 1
methodName("Tuesday"); // would call version 2
```

If you try to use exactly the same method name and parameters in another declaration, you will get the error message:

```
Duplicate method declaration
```

Example of invalid declarations

```
public void methodName(int Parameter)
public void methodName(int AnotherParameter)
```

There is no way for the compiler to tell the above two methods apart, so it reports an error.

6.4.2.1 Example: why would you want to overload?

The following program provides an example of how overloading can be used. I want to use the name `getValue` to return to me the results for a certain quarter. I want to be flexible as to what I pass the method `getValue`, so I overload the method. In one version of the method (line 13), I can pass in the name of the quarter that I want the result for. In another version of the method (line 27), I can pass in a character a,b,c or d to denote which of the four quarters I want. I use one version of `getValue` in line 8 and another version in line 10. The point of overloading in this case is that I have a consistent name for the method I use to get values, that is, I don't have to create one method for handling strings and one for chars (e.g. `getValueString` and `getValueChar`).

One point to note about this program is the presence of the line `return 0` at the end of each version of `getValue`. These return statements are necessary in the event of the input received matching none of the `if` statements (e.g. if I call `getValue` with the string `"first"`, it will not recognise it since it is in the incorrect case). The compiler demands that a method declaring a return type must always return a value of that type, whether it is the correct value or not. Therefore, a value of 0 is returned to indicate that the parameter passed to the method could not be dealt with properly. The correct way to write the program below would be to test the value returned by `getValue` and if it were 0 to output an error message to indicate that the parameter was incorrect.

```
public class OverloadExample extends TrainingWheels        1
{                                                          2
                                                           3
private int quarterlyAccounts[] = {6,9,3,5};               4
public void entryPoint()                                   5
   {                                                       6
   outputOnScreen("The results for the 'Second' Quarter are");   7
   outputOnScreen(getValue("Second"));                     8
   outputOnScreen("The results for the Quarter 'c' are");   9
   outputOnScreen(getValue('c'));                          10
   } // End entryPoint                                     11
                                                           12
public int getValue(String quarterStringParameter)        13
   {                                                       14
   if(quarterStringParameter.equals("First"))             15
      return quarterlyAccounts[0];                         16
   if(quarterStringParameter.equals("Second"))            17
      return quarterlyAccounts[1];                         18
   if(quarterStringParameter.equals("Third"))             19
      return quarterlyAccounts[2];                         20
   if(quarterStringParameter.equals("Fourth"))            21
      return quarterlyAccounts[3];                         22
                                                           23
   return 0; // Return required at end of int getAccount(String)   24
   } // End getValue(String)                              25
                                                           26
public int getValue(char quarterCharParameter)            27
   {                                                       28
   if(quarterCharParameter = = 'a')                       29
      return quarterlyAccounts[0];                         30
   if(quarterCharParameter = = 'b')                       31
      return quarterlyAccounts[1];                         32
   if(quarterCharParameter = = 'c')                       33
      return quarterlyAccounts[2];                         34
   if(quarterCharParameter = = 'd')                       35
      return quarterlyAccounts[3];                         36
                                                           37
   return 0; // Return required at end of int getAccount(char)   38
   } // End getValue(char)                                39
                                                           40
} // End OverloadExample                                  41
```

The result of the above program is shown in Figure 6.9.

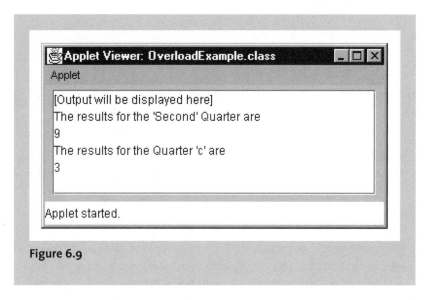

Figure 6.9

6.4.2.2 Overloading and constructors

Another example of overloading is supplying multiple methods as constructors. This will allow you to have flexibility when it comes to setting up an object.

In the example below, we are able to write a definition for a class which has the option of being setup with an initial value for a variable `balance` or without one (if no initial value for `balance` is supplied then the initial `balance` should be set to 0).

We can therefore supply two versions of the constructor method, one which will execute if a parameter is supplied and one if no parameter is received.

```
class Bank
{
private int balance;

// First constructor for the bank class, takes the initial
// balance (int)
public Bank(int firstbalance)
    {
    balance = firstbalance;
    } // End Bank constructor(int)

// Second constructor for the bank class, takes no parameter
public Bank()
```

```
    {
    balance = 0;
    }// End Bank constructor()

// Other methods
} // End Bank class
```

The form of the object declarations will decide which constructor is called:

```
Bank Gus = new Bank(10); // calls first constructor method
Bank Jill = new Bank(); // calls second constructor method
```

6.4.3 Overriding

Overriding a method means replacing a method in an extended class. This differs from overloading in that you are replacing a method entirely and not just writing different versions of the method with different parameters.

Overriding involves writing a method with the same method name and parameters as occured in the parent class (or one of the parent class if there are a number of them). Instead of reporting a duplication error the compiler will simply replace one method definition by another, it replaces the older version of the method by the most recent one.

If a method in your class overrides a method in the class you extend, then your method is executed in preference to that method. Overriding makes it easier to change the methods in parent classes without having to bother rewriting those parent classes. If you do not like what the method in the parent class does, then you can replace it. If you don't override a method, then the method contained in the class you extend is executed.

Why would you want to override? You usually override to maintain a standard method name, this makes it easier for people to use your classes. The method name may be standard but the operations associated with the name may differ from class to class hence the need to rewrite it.

EXAMPLE   In a class `Employee`, I declare a method `computePay`, this works fine for any object of type `Employee` that I create.

```
class Employee
{
private String DOB;
protected int monthlySalary;

public int computePay()// Version 1 of computePay
```

```
        {
        return monthlySalary;
        } // End computePay

    // Other methods would go here

    } // End of class Employee
```

However, I now want to create a new class that will extend the employee class and alter the behaviour of the method `computePay` to reflect a different type of employee whose wages require a different formula to compute.

I want to keep the method name but I need to alter what `computePay` does, so I override `computePay` in my new class definition.

```
    class PartTimeEmployee extends Employee
    {

    private int hoursWorkedThisMonth;
    private int ratePerHour;

    public int computePay()
        {// Version 2 of computePay,replaces version 1 in object
        // of this class
        return(monthlySalary + (hoursWorkedThisMonth * ratePerHour));
        }

    // Other methods would go here

    } // End class PartTimeEmployee
```

We can declare an object of our new class type:

`PartTimeEmployee fred = new PartTimeEmployee();`

We can call the new `computePay` method in the new object:

`fred.computePay();// Version 2 of computePay is executed`

We can also create an object of the original parent class:

`Employee jane = new Employee();`

and call the original `computePay` method:

`jane.computePay();// Version 1 of computePay is executed`

Note that access to the `monthlySalary` variable defined in the `Employee` class was needed in the `PartTimeEmployee` class so this variable was declared as protected to facilitate this.

The following example also shows what happens when a `child` class redeclares a method defined in the `parent` class. A class called `ExampleParentClass` is defined (line 25). It defines two methods `printParentMessage` and `printPurpose`. Any object created from this class can access these methods. Another class called `ExampleChildClass` is declared and this class inherits `ExampleParentClass`. `ExampleChildClass` also declares a method called `printPurpose`. This method replaces the method in the class `ExampleParentClass` in any object of type `ExampleChildClass` which is created. This can be seen in the main program which declares an object of each class type (`ExampleParentClass` and `ExampleChildClass`). It can be seen in line 14 that a call to the method `printPurpose` in the `ExampleChildClass` object will return a message from the `printPurpose` method that overrode the method inherited from `ExampleParentClass`. The other methods inherited from `ExampleParentClass` (`printParentMessage`) can still be used as they have not been overridden.

```
public class OverrideExample extends TrainingWheels          1
{                                                            2
                                                             3
private ExampleParentClass ExampleParentObject;              4
private ExampleChildClass ExampleChildObject;                5
                                                             6
public void entryPoint()                                     7
   {                                                         8
   ExampleParentObject = new ExampleParentClass();           9
   ExampleChildObject = new ExampleChildClass();            10
                                                            11
   outputOnScreen("ExampleParentObject.printPurpose() = "   12
   + ExampleParentObject.printPurpose());
   outputOnScreen("ExampleChildObject.printPurpose() = "    13
   + ExampleChildObject.printPurpose());
                                                            14
   outputOnScreen("ExampleChildObject.print ParentMessage()="  15
   + ExampleChildObject.printParentMessage());
   outputOnScreen("ExampleChildObject.printChildMessage()= "  16
   + ExampleChildObject.printChildMessage());
                                                            17
   } // End entryPoint                                      18
} // End class OverrideExample                              19
                                                            20
class ExampleParentClass                                    21
{                                                           22
                                                            23
```

```
public String printPurpose()                              24
    {                                                     25
    return "printPurpose(from ExampleParentClass)";       26
    } // End printPurpose                                 27
                                                          28
public String printParentMessage()                        29
    {                                                     30
    return "Message from printParentMessage               31
    (ExampleParentClass)";
    } // End printParentMessage                           32
                                                          33
} // End ExampleParentClass                               34
                                                          35
class ExampleChildClass extends ExampleParentClass        36
{                                                         37
                                                          38
public String printPurpose()                              39
    {                                                     40
    return "printPurpose(from ExampleChildClass)";        41
    } // End printPurpose                                 42
                                                          43
public String printChildMessage()                         44
    {                                                     45
    return "Message from                                  46
    printChildMessage(ExampleChildClass)";
    } // End printChildMessage                            47
                                                          48
} // End ExampleChildClass                                49
```

The results of the method calls can be seen in the sample output (Figure 6.10 in p. 250).

6.5 / STATIC

6.5.1 Introduction

A method or variable can also be described as 'static'. This means that it belongs to the class and not to the objects created from the class.

Static elements can be accessed without having to create an object of the class that contains them. This may sound like a contradiction of the fundamental principle that we stated in Chapter 2, that classes are not useful on their own and an object must be created from them in order to use the code defined in the class. Indeed, it is still the

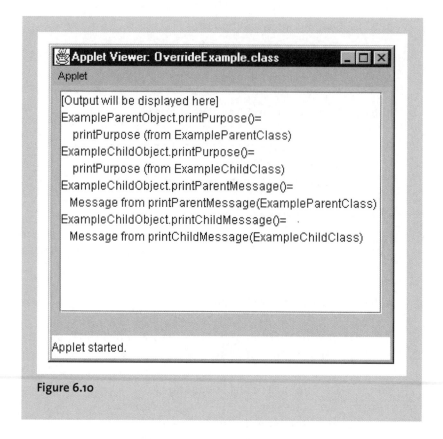

Figure 6.10

case that classes are not very useful unless objects are created from them but there are certain circumstances in which it is desirable to be able to use parts of a class without having to create an object.

Static elements are mainly used for storing and accessing standard values or for performing very basic operations, for example, PI, Square(number). They are also used as a means of starting up programs, an application is started via a static method, called main. Static elements are not meant to replace the creation of an object from a class definition, they merely give you more flexibility when programming.

Static elements belong to the class. This idea is particularly important with regard to static variables. Only one static variable can exist no matter how many objects are created from a class. This single common static variable is accessible from all objects created from that class.

6.5.2 Analogy

Imagine we want to use the jelly mould (the equivalent of a class definition) for something else as well as making jelly (the object). For example, we may wish to use the mould to keep a track of how many jellies it has created.

We can put a counter on it which allows a count to be kept of how many jellies it makes (so we can sterilise the mould after every 20 jellies). Each time a jelly is made, we change the value of the counter on the mould.

Each jelly the mould makes is still distinct but the single counter variable changes for each jelly. There is only one counter no matter how many jellies are made and the counter stays on the jelly mould.

This is like a static variable. A static variable or method is one which is made use of using the class definition, in our example the jelly mould.

Another example of using a static method on the jelly mould will be to write the instructions for creating a jelly on the outside of the mould. People will thus be able to read these instructions without having to create a jelly. Likewise, static methods can be used without having to create an object.

6.5.2.1 Syntax

If you wish to make an element static, you put the word 'static' after the modifier for the element (static elements still obey the public / private / protected rules).

You access a static element by giving the name of the class and the name of the static element seperated by a full stop (as if you were accessing the element in an object). For example,

```
class ExampleStatic
{
public static int vat;

public static int computePrice(int price)
    {
    return (price + ((vat * price) / 100));
    } // End computePrice

} // End ExampleStatic
```

To change the contents stored in variable vat use a statement of the form:

```
ExampleStatic.vat = 20;
```

The above will change the value of the class variable vat. This variable will hold this value of vat as long as the program uses the class ExampleStatic. That is, the value will disappear when the program is finished. If you start up another program while one program is using a static variable that program will have access to a different static variable, that is, the static variables belong to the program which is using them.

To access the static method computePrice use statement of the form:

```
ExampleStatic.computePrice(50);
```

```
public class StaticExample extends TrainingWheels       1
{                                                        2
                                                         3
public void entryPoint()                                 4
   {                                                      5
   outputOnScreen("Markup on all goods is "+StockItem.markup);   6
                                                         7
   StockItem book,table;                                 8
                                                         9
   StockItem.markup = 10;                                10
                                                         11
   outputOnScreen("Markup on all goods is "+StockItem.markup);  12
                                                         13
   book = new StockItem("Book",10);                      14
                                                         15
   table = new StockItem("Table",90);                    16
                                                         17
   outputOnScreen("Markup for " + book.getName() + " = "  18
   + book.getMarkup());
   outputOnScreen("Price for " + book.getName() + " = "   19
   + book.getRetail());
                                                         20
   outputOnScreen("Markup for " + table.getName() + " = " 21
   + table.getMarkup());
   outputOnScreen("Price for " + table.getName() + " = "  22
   + table.getRetail());
                                                         23
   StockItem.markup = 20;                                24
                                                         25
   outputOnScreen("Markup on all goods is " + StockItem.markup);  26
                                                         27
   outputOnScreen("Markup for " + book.getName() + " = "  28
   + book.getMarkup());
   outputOnScreen("Price for " + book.getName() + " = "   29
   + book.getRetail());
                                                         30
   outputOnScreen("Markup for " + table.getName() + " = " 31
   + table.getMarkup());
   outputOnScreen("Price for " + table.getName() + " = "  32
   + table.getRetail());
                                                         33
   } // End entryPoint                                   34
```

```
} // End staticExample                                    35
                                                          36
                                                          37
                                                          38
class StockItem                                           39
{                                                         40
public static int markup;                                41
private int itemPrice;                                    42
private String itemName;                                  43
                                                          44
public StockItem(String description,int price)           45
    {                                                     46
    itemPrice = price;                                    47
    itemName = description;                               48
    } // End StockItem constructor                        49
                                                          50
public int getRetail()                                    51
    {                                                     52
    return itemPrice + computeItemMarkup();               53
    } // End getRetail                                    54
                                                          55
public int getMarkup()                                    56
    {                                                     57
    return markup;                                        58
    } // End getMarkup                                    59
                                                          60
private int computeItemMarkup()                           61
    {                                                     62
    return((itemPrice * markup) / 100);                   63
    } // End computeItemMarkup                            64
                                                          65
public int getPrice()                                     66
    {                                                     67
    return itemPrice;                                     68
    } // End getPrice                                     69
                                                          70
public String getName()                                   71
    {                                                     72
    return itemName;                                      73
    } // End getName                                      74
                                                          75
} // End StockItem                                        76
```

In the example program above, we use a static variable to hold a value that all the objects created from this class will want access to, the price markup percentage. As opposed to setting the markup rate in each individual object (and therefore having to change every object when the markup rate changes) we set variable `markup` to be static (line 41). Note that `markup` is a public variable, if it was declared as private we would have to declare a public static method to access it.

In the main class, we check the value of `markup` in line 6 before we declare any object of that class type. The value returned is 0 indicating that it exists and is accessible even though no objects of this class have been created. We setup the object variables in line 8. In line 10, we set the value of `markup` to be 10 (again remember no object of this class type exists yet). So the value of `markup` for the class is 10. This means that every object created from the class definition `StockItem` will have a value of 10 for `markup`. We check this out in lines 18 and 19. Next we setup two objects and compute their retail price (which involves using the variable `markup`). In line 24, we change the value of `markup` and compute again just to show that the value changes for all objects derived from this class definition, that is, to show that all the objects created from `StockItem` share the one static variable.

Sample output for the program is shown in Figure 6.11.

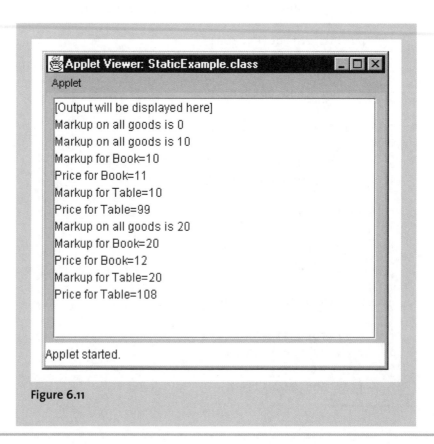

Figure 6.11

6.6 / APPLICATIONS

At this point we look at how Java applications are written and what happens when they are started. Free standing programs (or Applications) use the stand alone Java interpreter (VM). This VM differs to that used for running applets. Applications run outside of a browser, that is, no html file is involved, you simply pass the name of the application class file to the VM.

Users do not have to possess the full Java Development Kit to run applications, just a VM (Sun make one available under the name Java Runtime Environment).

There are two types of application:

1 *Text based* – where input and output happen on a console window (no mouse or icons)

2 *GUI based* – where input and output happen in a graphical window.

At this stage, we look at the text based applications and examine how graphical ones are created in Chapter 7.

6.6.1 Procedure

Every application program starts its execution at the method `main` (the equivalent to `entryPoint`). The method `main` must be declared as `public static void` and must take an array of strings as a parameter.

You usually start an application by typing out the name of the VM and the name of the class file containing your code (do not supply any extension). For example,

```
java MyProgram
```

The word `java` in the above refers to the java VM (full name `java.exe`). The word `MyProgram` refers to the class file `MyProgram.class`, which is located in the current directory. You can supply arguments to the program on the command line. These are placed in an array which is passed as a parameter to `main`.

The important point to fix on here is that `main` is declared as 'static'. This means that `main` can be accessed even if no object of the type that `main` belongs to exists. So, when an application is started no object is created, the VM simply looks for the method `main` and starts to execute the instructions it finds there.

EXAMPLE In the program below, no object of type `ApplicationExample` actually exists. However, the method `main` can be executed. It can even create variables. The way output is printed in an application is to use `System.out.println`. Note that this will only take a `String` as a parameter.

`System.out.println` refers to an object called 'out' which is held as a static parameter of the class `System`. This object `out`, which is of a class type `java.io.PrintStream`, contains a method called `println`. This `out` object is present for all executions and relates to the output on the console.

The output for the program will be:

```
Hello Mr. Black
```

```
public class ApplicationExample
{

public static void main(String parameters[])
    {
    String name = "Mr.Black";
    System.out.println("Hello " + name);
    } // End main

} // End class ApplicationExample
```

EXAMPLE

As mentioned above, you can supply zero or more parameters which are placed in an array and passed to the main method by the VM.

We will call this program with two parameters, a first name and a second name.

```
public class ApplicationExampleParam
{

public static void main(String parameters[])
    { System.out.println("Hello " + parameters[0] +
    " " + parameters[1]);
    } // End main
} // End class ApplicationExampleParam
```

You call the program using a command of the form

```
java ApplicationExampleParam Jill Jack
```

The program will take the two strings following the program name and put them, in the order supplied, into the array the main method takes as a parameter. So, Jill will be placed in parameters[0] and Jack will be placed in parameters[1].

The output will therefore be:

```
Hello Jill Jack
```

EXERCISE

1 See what happens if you execute the above program with one or no parameters (i.e. note the error message generated for future reference).

2 How will you check whether any parameters have been passed to the application before you attempt to access them?

6.6.2 Using main to create an object

In the vast majority of cases you will want to execute the object whose class contains the main method. To do this you must give instructions in the main method to create such an object and to call a method that will start this object (the name of this method is up to you to decide).

EXAMPLE In the following program, I create an object of the class ApplicationObject in the main method and call a method (called message) in that object.

```
public class ApplicationObject
{

private String name = "Ms.White";

public static void main(String parameters[])
    {
    ApplicationObject thisProgram = new ApplicationObject();
    thisProgram.message();
    } // end main

public void message()
    {
    System.out.println("Hello" + name);
    } // End message

} // End Class ApplicationObject
```

After the first line of the main method is executed, an object of class Application-Object is created and its methods can be accessed from main. This object of ApplicationObject will exist as long as it has something to do.

You can transfer control from the main method to any method of the object by simply calling the method. In the following example, control is passed to the start-Program method.

```
public static void main(String parameters[])
{
ApplicationObject thisProgram = new ApplicationObject();
thisProgram.startProgram();
}
```

You can create other objects, not necessarily of the class type as the application. For example, you can create objects such as stockItem, Employee, and so on, and use them.

6.7 IMPLEMENTS – USING AN INTERFACE

An interface is a definition of a set of methods and their parameters. It does not supply the body of the method or variables. An interface is not a class.

What an interface does is force the program that uses (implements) the interface to declare the same method names (with the same parameters and return type) as the interface contains. An interface is a way of making sure a program contains certain agreed methods, this means that you can force users to use consistent method names.

An interface is not inherited (using extends) but 'implemented' (using the word implements). When source code which implements an interface is compiled, it means that the code contained in the interface is matched against the program which implements the interface. The compiler checks to make sure all the methods mentioned in the interface are contained in the program which implements it. If one or more methods are missing or a method's parameters or return types are different, then the compiler will report an error and refuse to compile your program. You will see more of interfaces in Chapter 7 when they are used to make sure that you have included methods that handle input supplied from the user (like pressing a button or a keyboard key).

6.7.1 Syntax

6.7.1.1 Declaration of interface

An interface must be defined in a separate file, rather like a class. The interface must start with the word interface and be followed by the name of the interface.

Interfaces are saved in files with the extension .java. Interfaces contain the names of methods and their parameter(s) and return types but do not contain any statements in these methods, that is, the methods are empty.

EXAMPLE 1

```
interface InterfaceTest
{
public void testMethod();
public int anotherTestMethod(int parameter);
} // End of interface
```

EXAMPLE 2

The interface below is intended to be used by a number of different programmers working on the same team. Each programmer should implement the interface in their code and therefore will be obliged to define the two methods contained in the interface, that is, `printPurpose` and `printContent`. These methods are intended to provide useful information for people using objects of these classes.

```
// Definition of interface 'test'                        1
interface ProgrammerRules                                2
{                                                        3
public String printPurpose();// Print the purpose of the class  4
public String printContents();// Print the variables     5
                            // contained in the class    6
} // End interface ProgrammerRules                       7
                                                         8
```

6.7.1.2 Using the interface

An interface is used by placing the word `implements` and the name of the interface following the declaration of the class name. You can implement one or more interfaces by separating each interface name with a comma and/or combine an interface implementation with an `extends` instruction. If `extends` is used it is placed before the `implements`.

```
class ExampleClass implements InterfaceExample
{
// Class which must contain methods mentioned in InterfaceExample
}

class ExampleClass implements InterfaceExample,
ProgrammersTemplate
{
// Class which must contain methods mentioned in InterfaceExample
// and those contained in ProgrammersTemplate
}

class ExampleClass extends TrainingWheels implements
InterfaceExample
{
// Class which must contain methods mentioned in
// InterfaceExample and which inherits the TrainingWheels class
}
```

6.7.1.3   Programs which use the interface

There follows a program which uses two different classes, UserRecord and Stock-Item, each of which uses the interface defined in Section 6.7.1.3. Both the objects defined, userRecordObject and stockItemObject, can have the methods printPurpose and printContents called. These give information about the classes function and the current contents of the objects' variables.

```
public class UseInterfaceExample extends TrainingWheels    1
{                                                          2
private UserRecord userRecordObject;                       3
private StockItem stockItemObject;                         4
                                                          5
public void entryPoint()                                   6
    {                                                      7
    // Create the object userRecordObject                  8
    userRecordObject = new UserRecord("Jane Smith");       9
                                                          10
    // Call the printPurpose and printContents methods in 11
    // userRecordObject                                    12
    outputOnScreen("UserRecordObject");                   13
    outputOnScreen(userRecordObject.printPurpose());      14
    outputOnScreen(userRecordObject.printContents());     15
                                                          16
    // Create the object StockItemObject                  17
    stockItemObject = new StockItem("Table",99);          18
                                                          19
    // Call the printPurpose and printContents methods in 20
    // stockItemObject                                     21
    outputOnScreen("StockItemObject");                    22
    outputOnScreen(stockItemObject.printPurpose());       23
                                                          24
    outputOnScreen(stockItemObject.printContents());      25
    } // End entryPoint                                    26
                                                          27
} // End UseInterfaceExample                              28
                                                          29
// This class will store peoples names                    30
class UserRecord implements ProgrammerRules               31
{                                                         32
private String name;                                      33
                                                          34
```

```
public UserRecord(String nameParameter)                        35
    {                                                          36
    name = nameParameter;                                      37
    } // End UserRecord constructor                            38
                                                               39
public String printPurpose()                                   40
    {                                                          41
    return "This object holds customer information";           42
    } // End printPurpose                                      43
                                                               44
public String printContents()                                  45
    {                                                          46
    return "The contents are: Name:" + name;                   47
    } // End printConents                                      48
                                                               49
} // End UserRecord                                            50
                                                               51
// This class will store information about stock items         52
class StockItem implements ProgrammerRules                     53
{                                                              54
private String itemName;                                       55
private int price;                                             56
                                                               57
public StockItem(String nameParameter,int priceParameter)      58
    {                                                          59
    itemName = nameParameter;                                  60
    price = priceParameter;                                    61
    } // End StockItem constructor                             62
                                                               63
public String printPurpose()                                   64
    {                                                          65
    return "This object holds stock item information";         66
    } // End printPurpose                                      67
                                                               68
public String printContents()                                  69
    {                                                          70
    return "The contents are: ItemName:" + itemName + " Price "  71
        + price;
    } // End printContents                                     72
                                                               73
} // End StockItem                                             74
```

The result of the above program will be as in Figure 6.12 in p. 262.

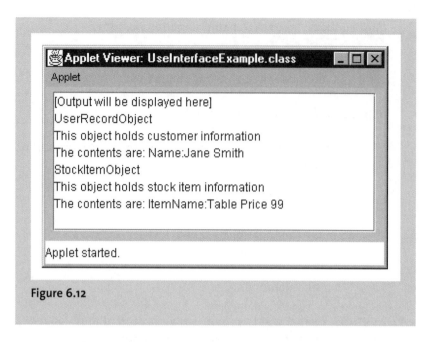

Figure 6.12

6.8 LAYERS (OR TIERS) OF AN APPLICATION

So far the programs we have seen are usually written in a single class or if another class is used its function is merely to store data. Software in the real world normally takes the form of a number of independent classes, like lego blocks, that can be stuck together in whatever form the designer wishes.

Programmers thus write sections or components of a solution and put them together as they go along. Classes (also known as components) can be reused for other problems or even sold as a product in their own right.

This structure, where a solution is made out of connected components, is called a layered or tiered approach. This means that distinct parts of the solution are organised into distinct groups, these groups are then put together to form layers. Different layers are responsible for different aspects of the solution and information is passed between the layers. There are usually three distinct layers: (i) the user interface; (ii) the logic layer; and (iii) the data layer. The user interface layer is intended to contain all the statements necessary to supply information to and obtain information from the user. The user interface layer may not necessarily process the information or store that information, for these functions it can pass the information to an application layer. The application layer, sometimes called the business logic or logic layer, is usually responsible for managing the information and performing operations on it, for example, retrieving information, computing results, applying rules. The data layers' responsibility is to store or retrieve the data on disk, in memory or in a database.

For example, imagine that you are asked to write an Information System for a bank. The structure for a bank is already familiar to you, you meet the teller when you go in the door, they take your particular request and then defer to a manager. The manager then looks up your file to see if you can be granted your request, passes their decision to the teller who will notify you.

To computerise this will require a User Interface to the system that the tellers can use to create new accounts and to lodge and withdraw money from accounts. This User Interface will use another part of the program which will manage accounts. The layer which manages accounts will effectively replace the manager and therefore carries out business logic. Account information can be stored as objects in the data layer. Therefore, we have three distinct sections for our problem: (i) a GUI layer; (ii) a Business Logic layer; and (iii) a Data layer. The functions of these layers are shown in Table 6.5.

Table 6.5

Layer name	Function of this layer
GUI	To provide a graphic environment for the user to interact with
Business Logic/ Application	To provide the algorithms, to carry out the tasks required of the program (create accounts, access accounts, change information)
Data/Database	To store the data for the application

One important aspect of the layering approach is that the layers can be written using different programming languages and can even operate on different computers. For example, in our bank application discussed above a GUI layer could run on each tellers computer while each tellers computer will communicate with the application layer on a central computer. The application layer could then in turn communicate with a database program running on yet another computer.

All the layers can be written in Java and this is one advantage of the Java programming language, that is flexible and applicable in many different areas.

An important point to make about layers is that they do not need to know anything about how the other layers work. All a layer needs to know is that another layer is responsible for a particular problem and how to call the relevant method in the relevant layer.

The different layers communicate using interfaces, an interface is a means of defining communication, that is, an agreed point of communication and protocol. This definition of an interface is different to the idea of an interface as a template, discussed in Section 6.7.

For example, an interface for ordering takeaway could be the phone number of the takeaway and the names or numbers of the relevant menu items. Interfaces are commonly achieved using methods, for example, one object calls a particular method in another object with certain agreed parameters.

Interfaces must be agreed on when writing the layers so that when programmers are writing their various layers they know what methods other layers will contain and what they do (but not how they do it) and can therefore write their code without having to see the completed other layer. They can substitute 'dummy' layers in place of the layers not completed. These dummy layers will give the appearance of working but will actually return only a limited set of test data. Their function is to allow you to try out your layer without waiting for other programmers to finish the layer that your layer needs. More on this in Chapter 8.

Let's look at the layers in our example in more detail and examine their possible functions (Table 6.6).

Table 6.6 Banking application

Layer name	Function of this layer
GUI	To allow the user to input and view information.
	Specifically:
	▶ Create a new account
	▶ Lodge money
	▶ Withdraw money
	▶ Check balance
Business Logic/ Application	To receive requests from the GUI and to pass it back the result of those requests.
	Operations to handle:
	▶ Create a new account: Search for an existing account with the same name, if it exists, deny request. If number of accounts created exceeds a preset limit, deny creation request.
	▶ Lodge money: Search to see if the named account exists, if so add the amount supplied to the balance of the account and return the new balance, return a message otherwise.
	▶ Withdraw money: Search to see if the named account exists, if it does deduct a supplied amount from the account provided, there are sufficient funds to meet the withdrawal and return the new balance, refuse withdrawal otherwise.
Data/Database	Hold account name and balance of that account.
	Operations to handle:
	▶ Create new record
	▶ Get record information
	▶ Store information

SUMMARY

We have seen that object variables do not store objects but rather the address of an object in memory. This address can be copied and passed to a method as a parameter allowing methods to have access to an object created elsewhere in the program.

Classes can be built on top of other classes. When building, you can add extra methods or variables to the original class or you can replace methods you want to change. This combination of classes is known as inheritance.

A third modifier was introduced, the protected modifier lies between the public and private modifiers. Protected is intended to be used to allow objects which inherited the class containing the protected item to use it while preventing other objects from accessing it.

More than one method can have the same name but each can be identified uniquely if they all have different parameters. This is known as overloading a method. Methods can also replace methods of the same name and properties in child classes. This is known as overriding a method. Both of these properties are types of polymorphism. Polymorphism is not strictly necessary but is useful for programmers as they can use consistent names for a variety of different circumstances.

A static method or variable is one which belongs to a class, that is, an object does not have to be created from the class for a static method or variable to be used. Objects created from a class with a static variable all share the same variable. A static method called main is used to start an application. When an application starts no object of the class type is automatically created, unlike an applet.

An interface is a template used by programmers to force them to adhere to a particular standard. Implementing an interface in a class will require the programmer to write methods which were mentioned in the interface. An interface cannot be used as a class as it contains method names only, that is, no code is defined for the methods.

Layers or tiers of classes can be constructed with each layer solving part of a problem. This benefits a programmer since the various layers are usually modular meaning that they can be replaced or rewritten without affecting the other parts of the program.

KEYWORDS

▶ *Constructor* – A method which has the same name as the class which contains it and is always executed whenever an object of that class type is created.
▶ *Hierarchy* – When classes are linked by inheritance this is referred to as a hierarchy of inheritance.
▶ *Inheritance* – The situation where one class can be combined with another class to form a new class more appropriate to the programmers needs.
▶ *Interface* – (1) A class which contains names for methods which will be required in any class which implements an interface; (2) An agreement for exchanging information (e.g. method names and parameters).
▶ *Layer* – A class which uses another class to solve a problem. Layers depend on other classes but are not interested in how they work. They use an agreed system of communication.

▶ *Polymorphism* – The ability to use the same method name and have the compiler decide which of the multiple method you wish to be used.

▶ *Protected* – A modifier used in situations where a class inherits another class and can use the parent classes `private` methods and variables.

▶ *Tier* – Another name for layer.

KEY CONCEPTS

▶ Inheriting a class:

```
class MyClass extends ClassToInherit
```

▶ Implementing an interface:

```
class MyClass implements ProgrammersInterface
```

▶ Creating a static variable:

```
class MyClass
{
public static variableName;
// Don't forget it should be public if it is to be used
// outside the class
} // End MyClass
```

▶ Using a static variable:

```
MyClass.variableName = value;
```

▶ Creating a static method:

```
class MyClass
{
public static void methodName(parameters)
    {
    }
// Don't forget it should be public if it is to be used
// outside the class
} // End MyClass
```

▶ Using a static method:

```
MyClass.methodName()
```

▶ Creating a constructor:

```
class ClassName
{
// constructor
public ClassName(parameters)
    {
    }
}
```

1 This exercise is intended to familiarise you with overloading.

Write a program which will contain information stored about customers in an array of objects of type `Person`. The `Person` class will have the following attributes:

```
Name — String
ID — int
Phone — String
```

An object of the `Person` class can be setup with just the name of the person or the name and phone number of a person, that is,

```
Person personObject=new Person(name);
Person personObject=new Person(name,phone);
```

A separate method called `setID` will be used to place a value for `ID` in an object of type `Person`. This method will be contained in the `Person` object. The ID must be unique therefore you should check all the other `Person` objects to see if they have a similar ID. If one of them does, then the user is required to enter a new ID.

The user can enter the relevant data for any number of persons and the program should create a new object to store that data (up to a limit of 20 objects). If the limit is reached, an error message is output and the user is informed that no more objects can be created.

2 This exercise is intended to familiarise you with a three tiered application.

Using the code developed in exercise 1, divide the program into a three tiered application. The first class should perform GUI only tasks, that is, accept input from the user and pass it to the application object. The application object should be of class type `PersonManager`.

You should incorporate a search feature into the program, the user can type in the name or ID of a person and press a button which passes the information to the application object. The `PersonManager` object will then search in its list of objects for any matching entries and output them. Note that while it is not possible for more than one object to contain the same value for ID it is possible that more than one object can contain the same name (e.g. we could have two John Smiths).

3 This exercise is intended to familiarise you with the idea of overriding.

Write a definition for a `BankAccount` class. This object can be setup with the name of an account holder and the value of their initial balance. If there is no initial balance, then the value of the balance is set to 0. The `BankAccount` class will contain the following methods:

```
public boolean widthDraw(int amount); //Returns true if the
//user can withdraw the requested amount and false otherwise
//(i.e. if there is insufficient funds to cover the withdrawal).
//If the user can withdraw then the amount of the withdrawal is
//deducted from their balance.
```

```
public int getBalance();// Returns the value of balance
```

Write a definition for an `OverDraft` class, this will inherit the `BankAccount` class but will override the methods withdraw and contain a new variable `overdraftAmount`. The `OverDraft` class will be setup with the parameters required for the `BankAccount` class (which will be passed to the `BankAccount` constructor) as well as a value for the overdraft. The user is allowed to withdraw money only if it does not exceed their balance plus their overdraft limit (the balance will be a negative value if they take out an overdraft).

Write the GUI to handle the above classes. The operation to be carried out will be supplied by the user in the form of a command. For example, the commands can be:

▶ `create` – create a new account. This will be followed by the values required for a new account.

▶ `withdraw` – withdraw from an account. This will be followed by information which indicates the account to withdraw from and the amount of the withdrawal.

4 This exercise should make you more familiar with the idea of static.

Write a program holding information about students and their courses.

- A `Student` object will contain information about a student (Name, Address, ID, etc.)
- A Course object will contain information about a course of study (`CourseCode`, `CourseDescription`, etc.)
- Each `Student` object will have a unique ID which will be assigned to it when it is first created (*Hint*: this can be obtained using a static variable)
- Each `Student` object will have an array of the courses they are attending
- Each course will contain an array of the students who are attending it.

Write a program which will create a number of students, and courses and assign students to relevant courses. It should finish by printing out the name of the students who are attending each course.

5 Write a class `Statistics` which will contain the following static methods:

```
public double getAverage(double values[]);// Method takes
a // reference to an array of values and returns the average
public double getMedian(double values[]);// Method takes a reference
// to an array of values and returns the median (middle) value
public double getStdDeviation(double values[]);// Method
// takes a reference to an array of values and returns their
// standard deviation
```

Use this class in an example program and test that your methods are correct (the output from your method can be compared with the output from a spreadsheet or calculator).

Solutions to exercises and interactive exercises can be obtained at:
http://www.palgrave.com/resources

Applets and GUI components

INTRODUCTION

In this chapter, we look at how to setup and use graphical elements and displays. We examine how to build user interfaces for applets, looking more closely at applications in the next chapter. User interfaces can be divided into input and output elements, each of which have their own particular characteristics.

7.1 APPLETS

Applets, as discussed in earlier chapters, are programs which are started using references in HTML pages. This reference is known as a tag and is understood by most Internet browsers. The browser reads the tag, interprets it (figures out what it means), looks for the applet mentioned in it and downloads the applet bytecode. The browser then gives the applet to a VM to execute. Most browsers come with a VM but some must have a VM installed before a Java applet can run. The Java applet runs in the browsers window, that is, the browser will allocate a certain portion of its window for the applet. The HTML tag which caused the browser to load the applet contains other information, principally the size of window which the applet should have to display in.

Our examples have taken the form of applets but the specific details about how an applet works and how the graphical elements of a user interface (such as buttons and text boxes) are managed have been kept from you.

The first item to discuss is the class which is extended to give you an applet. In earlier versions of Java, you would have extended the `Applet` class. In more recent versions of Java an improved applet class has been developed and is named `JApplet`. It is this class that we use to create applets. `JApplet` is part of a library called `Swing` and it is this library of classes that we use to provide us with GUI elements. The older `Applet` class, which can still be used, used a library of classes called AWT (which stood for Abstract Window Toolkit). Therefore, anywhere we refer to an applet in this chapter you can assume that applet is created using the `JApplet` class. So, from now on you no longer extend the `TrainingWheels` class, you should instead extend the `JApplet` class as described below (in fact `JApplet` is the class `TrainingWheels` extended so you are basically cutting out the middle layer).

When you create an applet you are inheriting the methods and variables that form your applet object from the `JApplet` class. The `JApplet` class contains three particularly important methods that you should be familiar with. These methods are executed by the VM when it creates an object from your applet, which occurs when the browser calls its VM with the downloaded applet class. There is a specific order associated with the execution of these methods when the VM starts your applet.

The three important methods are:

1   `init()` – intended to initialise the applet (setup GUI, setup variables, etc.). This method is called only once.

2   `start()` – called when browser wants to start executing the applet, can be called many times. Start will be called again if the browser window is selected after the user selects another window (i.e. start is executed each time the window containing the applet is activated).

3   `paint(Graphics screen)` – called when the browser needs to draw the applet. A graphics object (the applet window) is created automatically by the VM and is passed as a parameter to the `paint` method. Therefore, the `screen` formal parameter of type `Graphics` that the `paint` method gets represents the window that the user sees displayed in the browser. You can draw on this window by accessing various methods in the Graphics object `screen`.

All the methods listed above are contained in the `JApplet` class that you inherit, however they don't do anything much, they are in the `JApplet` class to make sure that the relevant methods are present when the VM looks for them. You could say that these methods are dummies and they exist only to act as backups if you do not replace/override them in your program. To get your own code executed when the applet starts up all you need to do is replace the relevant method with your own version (i.e. you override the methods contained in the parent with your method).

How do we know where to put the instructions that we want to be executed, that is, which are the 'relevant' methods for what we want to achieve? Well, the trick here is to look at when each of the methods are executed and what the methods have access to.

Init and start are the same in terms of what they have access to but differ in terms of when they are executed. Init is executed only once, whereas the start method is executed each time a browser window is deselected and selected. Therefore, if you want to get some one off instructions executed, such as variable initialisation or object creation, then you should put them in the init method. If you want the statements to be executed every time the window is selected, then put them in start. The paint method has access to an object of type Graphics which neither init or start has. The Graphics object is the applet window that is currently being shown to the user, so if you want to draw on that screen, you should put your instructions in the paint method. Note that the paint method will automatically be executed when the applet starts up (following the execution of start and init) but can only be executed again if the method repaint() is called. The repaint method, which is contained in the class JApplet, will clear the screen of all drawings and call the paint method again.

So, if you want to replace any of these methods, you simply write a new method, giving it the existing method's name and making sure that it is public and returns void, for example, public void paint(Graphics screen).

7.1.1 Starting a simple applet – the HTML file

Applets are started from a HTML page. This HTML page can be loaded into a browser or into a VM, such as Suns appletviewer (see Appendix A).

HTML code for applet (this is what the browser sees) is

```
<APPLET CODE = "Welcome.class" WIDTH = 200 HEIGHT = 50>
</APPLET>
```

The tag for the applet is started with <Applet> and finished with </Applet>. What the above tag says is that the applet to be loaded can be found in the same place that the HTML page comes from and has the name "Welcome.class". The tag also says that the browser should give it a window 200 pixels wide by 50 pixels high to display in. A pixel is a Picture Element, one single dot on the screen. Screens have a specific number of pixels available for use, for example, most screens are at least 800 pixels wide × 600 pixels high.

When you call the browser with the above HTML file, you must make sure that the class file is in the same directory as the HTML file, otherwise the class file will not be located and an error will be output. If you are putting the HTML file on a website, then make sure to put the class file in the same directory.

Since Swing is a relatively new addition to Java, some browsers may not be able to deal with Swing. If a browser cannot cope with the applet loaded using the tag defined above, then try the following:

```
<object classid = "clsid:8AD9C840-044E-11D1-B3E9-00805F499D93"
width = "300" height = "500">
<param name = "code" value = "ReplacePaintApplet.class">
</object>
```

If your browser is equipped with the correct Java VM, it will understand this tag as an instruction to execute that VM and pass the Java code named to it. If your browser does not have the correct VM, then make sure that your computer is connected to the Internet and use the following tag:

```
<object classid = "clsid:8AD9C840-044E-11D1-B3E9-00805F499D93"
width = "300" height = "500" codebase = "http://java.sun.com/prod-
ucts/plugin/1.2.2/jinstall-1_2_2-win.cab#Version = 1,2,2,0">
<param name = "code" value = "ReplacePaintApplet.class">
<param name = "type" value = "application/x-java-applet;version =
1.2.2">
No JDK 1.2 support for applet, attempting to download plugin
</object>
```

The above tag will contact Sun Microsystems Java plugin page and attempt to download a plugin for your browser. The purpose of this tag is to give instructions to your browser, what to do if it cannot deal with a Swing applet.

7.1.2 Basic applet code

In the following example, we look at writing an applet. We override no methods and so the executed applet will not display anything or do anything.

```
public class ExampleApplet extends javax.swing.JApplet      1
{                                                            2
                                                             3
} // End ExampleApplet                                       4
```

In line 1 of the above file, you indicate that you are inheriting the JApplet class, but why does the phrase javax.swing. precede it? Well, the classes that we inherited before this are always in the same directory as the program we are writing so the compiler knows where to find them. The class that you are using in this case, JApplet, is not the one we define but the one that comes with the code development environment. In order to use JApplet.class, you need to tell the compiler where it can be found. Each class that is contained in the development environment is part of the Application Programming Interface (API) family for Java. Classes are grouped into packages and packages are grouped into families. Families manage different areas of Java; networking, connecting to databases and so on. Packages are divided up into groups. For example, the API which Swing is a part of is called the Java Foundation Class (JFC). To indicate to the compiler where to find the class file you want to use, you need to tell it what the API and package of that class are. JApplet is in the Swing package and the Swing package is in the javax API. So, if we use a class that is not contained in the current directory or defined later in our source code file, then we must attach to the class name its location in the API. The compiler knows where to find the API as this is built into it, so it locates the API and using our directions it locates the class file. So, line 1 says that `JApplet` is in Swing which is in javax (there is a shortcut for writing this which we will see in Section 7.14).

You can compile and execute (via a html file) the above program and see the result. The VM will find the `start`, `init` and `paint` methods but they will be the default ones contained in the `JApplet` class and therefore will produce no result that you can see.

There is a particular story associated with the javax API. As we discussed, this API holds the set of components called 'swing' which we use for input and output via a graphical interface. The 'x' part of the name indicates that the library is experimental, this is the case in earlier versions of Java where it is offered as an add on to the main Java libraries but for up to date releases javax is a full part of the JDK. Swing's recent emergence sometimes poses problems for older browsers and compilers but these problems are concerned mainly with getting older browsers to display programs written with Swing components. Programs still continue to be written using the old Abstract Window Toolkit (AWT) which you may run across from time to time.

7.1.3 Replacing the paint method

In this example, we replace the `paint` method to see how you can get the VM to do something. In case of the example program provided, the goal is to draw a string on the applets display window.

To draw a string, you need to use the method `drawString` which is in the `Graphics` object that is passed into the `paint` method (the variable called screen in the example). You supply three parameters to the `drawString` method: (i) the string you want to draw on the screen, (ii) the *x* coordinate and (iii) the *y* coordinate you want to draw to start at. For drawing purposes every point (pixel) on the applets screen has a coordinate and if you want something to be drawn (rectangle, circle, string, etc.), you must tell the system where you want the drawing to start from.

The drawing screen starts at coordinate 0,0 (upper left corner). The *x* coordinate is the number of pixels you want to move across the screen (you can remember this by remembering 'across = aX') before drawing the string. The *y* coordinate is the number of pixels you want to move down the screen before drawing the string. A `drawstring` statement will therefore take the following form:

GraphicsObjectName.drawString(StringVariable,Xcoordinate,Y Coordinate);

For example, in Table 7.1, you can see some of the values for *x* and *y* and their relative position. Note that pixels are extremely small, so you usually work in tens of pixels when deciding where to put things. The maximum number of pixels your applet has across and down has been defined in the html file you used to call the applet (this is the size of the window which the applet has to display).

Table 7.1

X Y	0	1	2	3	4
0	$x = 0, y = 0$			$x = 3, y = 0$	
1					
2	$x = 0, y = 2$				
3					
4					$x = 4, y = 4$

So, we come back to the example program shown below. In line 4, we override the paint method which is already present in an object of JApplet which is created when our program executes. In line 6, we use the drawString method of the object screen (of type Graphics) which is passed into our program by the VM to draw the string Welcome to Java on the applet window. As discussed above, the class Graphics belongs to a particular API and so we must give the compiler directions to it. The directions to it are java.awt.

```
public class ReplacePaintApplet extends javax.swing.JApplet      1
{                                                                 2
                                                                  3
public void paint(java.awt.Graphics screen)                       4
   {                                                              5
   screen.drawString("Welcome to Swing",20,20);                   6
   } // End method paint                                          7
                                                                  8
} // End class ReplacePaintApplet                                 9
```

The above program will output a string in the portion of the browser given to the applet. An example of the output is shown in Figure 7.1 in p. 276.

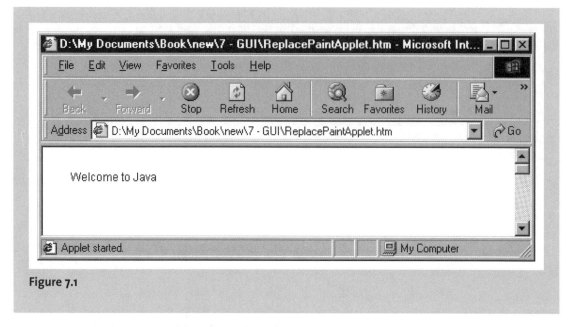

Figure 7.1

7.1.4 Overriding init and paint

In the next example, we override the `paint` method and the `init` method. Before we discuss that, let's look at two instructions in the example program below. The instructions on lines 1 and 2 say:

```
import javax.swing.*;
import java.awt.*;
```

Do you remember `javax.swing` and `java.awt` from the previous two programs? These were the locations of the class files `JApplet` and `Graphics` which we used in the programs. Well, instead of supplying the full name of the location for a class file every time we need to reference it, as we did in the two previous programs, we can tell the compiler at the start of the program where to look for classes it does not recognise. So the two import instructions tell the compiler to search the areas `javax.swing` and `java.awt` if it comes across a class it has no definition for. So, when the compiler sees the class `JApplet` referenced in line 4, it looks in the class definitions contained in `javax.swing` for a class `JApplet`, if it finds this class then it checks to see if it is being used correctly in the program (e.g. methods are called with the correct numbers of parameters and types). A similar situation will arise in line 13, the compiler sees a reference to a class called `Graphics`. The compiler will search the classes in `javax.swing` but no class called `Graphics` will be found. The compiler next searches the classes in `java.awt` and finds a class called `Graphics` which it checks. This is the shortcut we mentioned in Section 7.1.2. By using an `import` statement you can notify the compiler that you may be taking classes from a particular group. Therefore, you need not give the full name for a class if the compiler knows where to look for it. What happens if two groups contain the same class name? Well, then the compiler will report an error and require you to give the full name of the class when you use it in order to avoid confusion.

Let's take a look at what the program is doing. The `init` method is overridden (in line 8) because we want our program to setup a `String` variable which we defined as a global variable in line 6. We assign a value of `Welcome to Java` to this string in line 10. When the applet is run the variable `welcomeMessage` is created. `Init` is then called which puts a value in the `welcomeMessage` string. Next `paint` is called which draws the contents of the string on the screen. We know that `init` must have been executed before `paint` as the contents of the string variable `welcomeMessage` are identical to the assignment in the `init` method.

```
import javax.swing.*; // Tell the compiler to look in javax\swing      1
import java.awt.*;  // Tell the compiler to look in java\awt          2
                                                                       3
public class WelcomeApplet extends JApplet                             4
{                                                                      5
private String welcomeMessage;                                         6
                                                                       7
public void init()                                                     8
   {                                                                   9
   welcomeMessage = "Welcome to Java";                                10
   } // End init                                                      11
                                                                      12
public void paint(Graphics screen)                                    13
   {                                                                  14
   screen.drawString(welcomeMessage,20,20);                           15
   } // End paint                                                    16
} // End class WelcomeApplet                                          17
```

An example of the above program's output is shown in Figure 7.2.

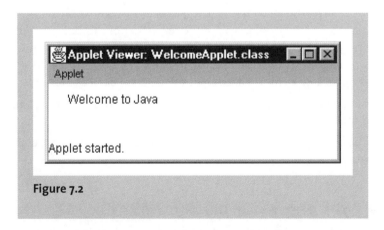

Figure 7.2

7.2   APPLETS AND THE FLOW OF CONTROL

Flow of control has been discussed in Chapter 1, Section 1.4.8, and refers to the sequence of instructions being executed, that is, where does execution start, go next, finish, and so on. The flow of control in applets is that the entry points (or 'main' methods) are the `init`, `start` and `paint` methods. When reading any applet examine these methods, if they are present, in their order of execution, to find out what's happening. Note that each method must finish before the other can execute, for example, you can't call the `paint` method in the `init` method in the above program because that is not the correct sequence of execution.

7.3   IMPORT

As discussed in the above section, the `import` command is used to give the compiler locations to look for if it cannot immediately identify classes referenced in a program. One particular `import` command is added by default to every program, this command is `import java.lang.*`. The `java.lang` group of classes contains classes which the authors of Java believe the users should always have access to.

One of the commonest questions regarding `import` is what happens if there are unnecessary `import` commands? These are discarded. There is no difference in the speed of execution or size of a program which contains only the necessary `import` commands and one containing one hundred unnecessary ones. The program may compile slower if all the unnecessary imports are not removed as the compiler may have to search many more directories than it should for classes referenced in the program. Import is used solely at the programmers discretion to simplify their program (it also allows readers of the program to quickly see what packages the programmer has used in their class). You can even ignore the `import` command entirely and supply the full name of a class anytime you use it (e.g. `java.awt.Graphics`).

As classes are introduced to you in the remainder of this book, the package that the class belongs to is indicated. Therefore you should be on the lookout for any errors which will indicate that you neglected to supply the correct `import` (or misspelled the class or package name). These types of error will be of the form:

```
WelcomeApplet.java:Line 4: Superclass JApplet of class Welcome-
Applet not found.
```

This error occurs because the `import javax.swing.*` command is omitted from the program.

7.4   DRAWING METHODS OF GRAPHICS OBJECT

You can do more than just draw strings on the screen as there are a number of methods in the `Graphics` class which will draw different shapes. Since all the drawing methods are contained in an object of type `Graphics` and an object of this type is passed by the VM to the `paint` method, you can initiate drawing operations usually only from the `paint` method. Remember `paint` is only executed after `start` and `init` are executed. We look at some of the methods used for drawing in this section.

7.4.1 Pen colour

A default pen colour (black) is used to draw all elements (lines, shapes, etc.). You can use `GraphicsObject.setColor(Color.<colorname>)` to change pen colour where `colorname` is a common colour (blue, black, green, etc.). A definition for each colour exists as a static variable in the class `Color`. So, for example, to change the pen colour to blue you should place the following statement at the beginning of `init`:

```
screen.setColor(java.awt.Color.blue);
```

```
public class ChangeColourApplet extends javax.swing.JApplet    1
{                                                               2
                                                                3
public void paint(java.awt.Graphics screen)                    4
    { // Change from default colour to blue                    5
    screen.setColor(java.awt.Color.blue);                      6
                                                                7
    screen.drawString("Welcome to Java",20,20);                8
    } // End method paint                                      9
                                                               10
} // End class ChangeColourApplet                              11
```

Custom colours can be created by specifying the mix of Red, Green and Blue (RGB) in the `setColor` method and creating a new object of type `Color`.

```
GraphicsObject.setColor(new    java.awt.Color(redAmount,greenAmount,
blueAmount));
// where each amount is an integer in the range 0–255
```

The above object will not disappear after it has been created since it is passed to the `setColor` method as a parameter and used in the `Graphics` object. If you want to create a specific colour object and repeatedly use it, then you can setup a `Color` object as follows:

```
Color mySpecialColor = new Color(10,150,25);
GraphicsObject.setColor(mySpecialColor);
```

7.4.2 Setting the background colour

You can change the background colour of an applet by using the `setBackground` method and supplying a reference to a specific colour or passing an object of type `Color` as a parameter.

For example:

```
setBackground(Color.white);
setBackground(mySpecialColor);
```

7.4.3 Drawing a line

To draw a line from one point to another you need to know four coordinates. The *x* and *y* coordinates of the point where the line starts from and the *x* and *y* coordinates where the line ends. The line, which is a single pixel wide, is then drawn as straight as possible between the two coordinates. All the values should be integers since you cannot have a fraction of a pixel.

The statement will take the form:

GraphicsObject.drawLine (startXcoord,startYcoord,endXcoord,endYcoord);

7.4.4 Drawing a rectangle

You need four parameters for a drawRect method. You need the *x* and *y* coordinates from which the drawing will start. You also need the number of pixels wide and the number of pixels high that the rectangle will be. Again all the values are integers.

The relevant statement is:

GraphicsObject.drawRect(startXcoord,startYcoord,width,height);

The VM will draw the rectangle 'down' from the starting point. For example, if your command is:

```
GraphicsObject.drawRect(10,20,30,25);
```

then the rectangle which will be drawn will have its four corners the *x*–*y* values as:

(10,20),(40,20),(10,45),(40,45)

7.4.5 Drawing a filled rectangle

A filled rectangle takes the same parameters as a rectangle but when it is drawn it is shaded with the current pen color. The syntax is:

GraphicsObject.fillRect(startXcoord,startYcoord,width,height);

7.4.6 Drawing a rectangle with rounded edges

Sometimes you may want to draw a rectangle with round edges instead of sharp ones. You can do this by using the method drawRoundRect. This will take the same parameters as the rectangle drawing method plus two values which indicate how round the edges should be. The values indicate how many pixels to move, from where the point should be if a square corner were drawn. These values are used to shape the round edge of the rectangle. The syntax is:

GraphicsObject.drawRoundRect(start x coord, start y coord, width, height, move in x, move in y)

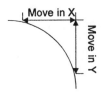

You can draw a rounded rectangle which is shaded using the current pen colour by using the method `fillRoundRect` instead of `drawRoundRect`.

7.4.7 Drawing an oval

To get an oval you need to supply the starting coordinates and how wide and high the oval will be. As with previous shapes the oval is drawn 'down' from the starting coordinates. Note that if your width and height are the same then your oval is a circle.

GraphicsObject.drawOval(start x coord,start y coord, width, height)

You can get a shaded shaped using the method `fillOval` instead.

The example below demonstrates the shapes discussed above. When the VM creates an object of type `ShapesExample` eight integer variables are declared (lines 8 and 9). These variables will hold coordinates and size values for the shapes drawn in the program. The execution of the program starts off with the `init` and `start` methods (no `init` or `start` methods are overridden in the program so the `init` and `start` methods executed are the ones contained in the `JApplet` object created when the program started). The next method which the VM looks for is the `paint` method. The program contains such a method so that it is executed instead of the `paint` method contained in the `JApplet` object part of the program. The `paint` method first executes a `drawString` instruction to write a description string on screen (line 13). Then it starts to call other methods with the parameter `screen`. This is done because the program is written to place the instructions for each shape into special methods. These special methods are `drawALine`, `drawARectangle`, `drawAFullRectangle`, `drawARoundRectangle` and `drawACircle` and `drawAnEgg`. Each of these methods need an object of type `Graphics` so that they can call their respective methods (`drawLine`, etc.). This object (`screen`) is passed to them in the `paint` method. It means that other methods can be called with the `Graphics` object parameter which is passed into `paint` by the VM and these methods can perform their instructions as if they are included as part of the `paint` method. All the formal parameters used in the `shape` methods have the same name `screen` but each has a different scope, that is, they exist only for the life of the method they are declared in and can be seen only in that method.

```
// Locate class for JApplet                                 1
import javax.swing.*;                                       2
// Locate class for Graphics                                3
import java.awt.*;                                          4
                                                            5
public class ShapesExampleApplet extends JApplet            6
{                                                           7
private int startXcoord,startYcoord,endXcoord,endYcoord;    8
private int width,height,moveInX,moveInY;                   9
                                                           10
public void paint(Graphics screen)                         11
    {                                                      12
    screen.drawString("Shapes",10,10);                     13
                                                           14
    // Call a method to draw a line                        15
    // supply the current screen as a parameter            16
    drawALine(screen);                                     17
                                                           18
    // Call a method to draw a rectangle                   19
    // supply the current screen as a parameter            20
    drawARectangle(screen);                                21
                                                           22
    // Call a method to draw a full rectangle              23
    // supply the current screen as a parameter            24
    drawAFullRectangle(screen);                            25
                                                           26
    // Call a method to draw a round rectangle             27
    // supply the current screen as a parameter            28
    drawARoundRectangle(screen);                           29
                                                           30
    // Call a method to draw a circle                      31
    // supply the current screen as a parameter            32
    drawACircle(screen);                                   33
                                                           34
    // Call a method to draw an egg                        35
    // supply the current screen as a parameter            36
    drawAnEgg(screen);                                     37
    } // End paint                                         38
                                                           39
public void drawALine(Graphics screen)                     40
    {                                                      41
    // Write out the description                           42
    screen.drawString("Line",60,30);                       43
                                                           44
```

```
    // Setup the coordinates for the shape           45
    startXcoord = 10;                                46
    startYcoord = 20;                                47
    endXcoord = 30;                                  48
    endYcoord = 40;                                  49
                                                     50
    // Draw the line on the screen using the above coordinates  51
    screen.drawLine (startXcoord,startYcoord,endXcoord,endYcoord);  52
    } // End drawALine                               53
                                                     54
public void drawARectangle(Graphics screen)          55
    {                                                56
    // Write out the description                     57
    screen.drawString("Rectangle",60,60);            58
                                                     59
    // Setup the coordinates for the shape           60
    startXcoord = 10;                                61
    startYcoord = 50;                                62
    width = 20;                                       63
    height = 10;                                      64
                                                     65
    // Draw the rectangle on the screen using the above coordinates  66
    screen.drawRect(startXcoord,startYcoord,width,height);  67
    }// End drawARectangle                           68
                                                     69
public void drawAFullRectangle(Graphics screen)      70
    {                                                71
    // Write out the description                     72
    screen.drawString("Full Rectangle",60,90);       73
                                                     74
    // Setup the coordinates for the shape           75
    startXcoord = 10;                                76
    startYcoord = 80;                                77
    width = 20;                                       78
    height = 10;                                      79
                                                     80
    // Draw the full rectangle on the screen using the  81
    // above coordinates                             82
    screen.fillRect(startXcoord,startYcoord,width,height);  83
    }// End drawAFullRectangle                       84
                                                     85
public void drawARoundRectangle(Graphics screen)     86
    {                                                87
    // Write out the description                     88
    screen.drawString("Round Rectangle",60,120);     89
```

```
    // Setup the coordinates for the shape          90
    startXcoord = 10;                               91
    startYcoord = 100;                              92
    width = 30;                                     93
    height = 20;                                    94
    moveInX = 5;                                    95
    moveInY = 2;                                    96
                                                    97
    // Draw the round rectangle on the screen using the above  98
    // coordinates                                  99
    screen.drawRoundRect(startXcoord,startYcoord,width,  100
    height,moveInX,moveInY);
    } // End drawARoundRectangle                    101
                                                    102
public void drawACircle(Graphics screen)           103
    {                                               104
    // Write out the description                    105
    screen.drawString("Circle",60,150);            106
                                                    107
    // Setup the coordinates for the shape          108
    startXcoord = 20;                               109
    startYcoord = 130;                              110
    width = 20;                                     111
    height = width;                                 112
                                                    113
    // Draw the circle on the screen using the above coordinates  114
    screen.drawOval(startXcoord,startYcoord,width,height);  115
    } // End drawACircle                            116
                                                    117
public void drawAnEgg(Graphics screen)             118
    {                                               119
    // Write out the description                    120
    screen.drawString("Egg",60,180);               121
                                                    122
    // Setup the coordinates for the shape          123
    startXcoord = 20;                               124
    startYcoord = 160;                              125
    width = 10;                                     126
    height = 20;                                    127
                                                    128
    // Draw the egg on the screen using the above coordinates  129
    screen.drawOval(startXcoord,startYcoord,width,height);  130
    } // End drawAnEgg                              131
                                                    132
} // End of ShapesExampleApplet                     133
```

The output of the above program is shown in Figure 7.3.

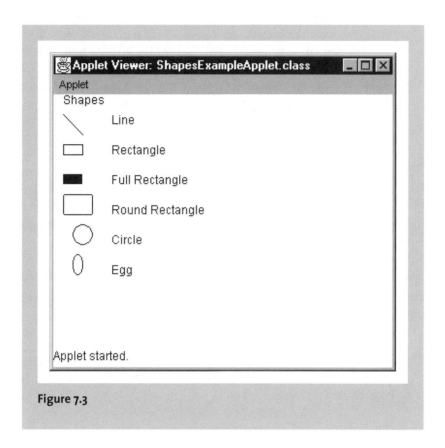

Figure 7.3

7.5 / GUI COMPONENTS

7.5.1 Introduction

Drawing shapes and strings are all very well but how do you interact with the user? Well, you can use GUI components (known as widgets or controls in other programming environments) to get input from the user and display output. Components are placed in a container and the container is shown to the user in the form of a window. The two containers we look at are JApplet and JFrame (which is a GUI class associated with applications, more about this in Chapter 8, Section 8.2.1). When you create your component object you must place it in the container. You do this by using the method add which is contained in an object obtained by calling the getContentPane method of the relevant container object.

We look at two distinct groups, the input elements and the output elements.

7.5.1.1   The input elements

When working with the input elements, the first question to consider is how does the program know when something has been input? Well, the VM will call a certain method whenever the user makes use of an input element. How does the VM know what input element is being used? Well, the Operating System tells it. This way you can write methods which will deal with specific input elements. These methods will be executed when the component is used. You must however tell the VM that you are interested in receiving a notification that something has happened with regard to an input element since even moving a mouse can be grounds for the operating system notifying the VM and the VM calling a method. This system of noting your interest in an input element eliminates a lot of overhead processing notifications that no one is interested in. The situation when something happens regarding an input element is called an 'event'. Each input element has a specific event associated with it, for example, clicking on the input element, moving the mouse, pressing return, and so on. You indicate that you are interested in an event by associating an object with an event, that is, you tell the VM what object will contain methods which will deal with the relevant event. The VM also supplies information about the event itself (what exactly caused it, etc.) in an object which is passed as a parameter to the method called to deal with the event. Some elements can be used for input only, some for input and output.

7.5.1.2   The output elements

The output elements we look at can display text or even HTML formatted pages. Some output elements can also serve as a means of supplying input. Some can cause events to be generated and some cannot.

7.5.2   Output elements

7.5.2.1   Setting up the screen to take components

Components added to an applet or application window are arranged on that window by a part of the VM called a layout manager. A layout manager decides where to put elements so that they do not overlap each other and ensures that the available screen space is used in the most efficient manner. There is a default component manager used for applets and applications but for the moment we do not want to use it (we will take a more detailed look at layout managers in Chapter 8, Section 8.5). We can change the layout manager for the container by putting the following statement in the init method:

```
getContentPane().setLayout(new FlowLayout());
```

The new layout manager used is an object of a class called FlowLayout. In a flow layout, the order the elements are placed on the screen is the order they are added to the screen in the program. For instance, if you add two buttons, a text area and a text field then the screen will show two buttons, followed by a text area followed by a text field.

The first element added will appear on the left hand side of the screen with subsequent elements appearing to the right of the previous ones.

A flow layout will arrange the elements to 'fit' on the screen, that is, you cannot decide to move an element to the next line as you have no direct say as to where they are positioned. The `FlowLayout` object will place them in a single line if it can and will only move onto a new line when it runs of space on the screen. The only way to alter where the elements are placed is to change the width of the applet using the WIDTH tag. This will change the number of elements that flow layout can fit in a line and therefore can help to customize the position of elements.

The instruction `new FlowLayout` will return a reference to an object of type `FlowLayout` which is all that the `setLayout` method needs. You can if you wish declare a separate `FlowLayout` object and pass its address to the `setLayout` method, that is,

```
FlowLayout layoutObject=new FlowLayout();
getContentPane().setLayout(layoutObject);
```

7.5.2.2 Procedure for setting up and placing output components on the screen

Step 1: Declare an object variable of an output component class. These objects are usually declared outside any method, that is, as global (class) variables.

Step 2: Create this object (remembering to supply any relevant parameters).

Step 3: Add the output object to screen. This step is usually done in the `init` method or can be delayed until later in the program if you want to add and remove elements at different points in the program to change the user interface. Adding an output element object to the screen involves adding it to the container that is being displayed. This is usually done using a command of the form:

```
getContentPane().add(outputObject);
```

Note that `getContentPane` is a call to a method which will return an object.

The `add` method essentially tells the VM that a particular object is to be associated with the screen. The memory address for the object is then added to the object which represents the screen. This screen object will get the details of the element added and draw its representation on the screen.

REMEMBER

- If you forget to 'add' an element it will not appear on the screen even if you have created the object.
- If you 'add' an element before an object has been created you will get an error message since you are trying to add a 'null' reference (i.e. an empty object) to the screen.

Step 4: Use the output object. This can be done anywhere in the program once the creation of the output object has been carried out. Objects can be used before they are added to the screen.

7.5.2.3 Text fields

The first element we look at is called a text field, this can also be used as an input element and we shall see how in the relevant section. A text field object can be created using the class JTextField and is defined as a box which can hold a single line of text. When you create your JTextField object, you indicate how many characters of the string it contains are displayed. The constructor has been overloaded, so if you wish you can also supply an initial string that will appear in the text field when it is added to the screen. Later on in the program, you can place a different message in the text field by using the setText method in the JTextField object you have created. Note that any message to be displayed in a text field must be in the form of a string, so if you have an integer or other variable, concatenate (i.e. use +) with a string before trying to place it in a text field. If you want the option of creating a text field object which displays a particular string when it appears, then use the command:

JTextField textfieldObject = new JTextField(MessageString, width in characters);

or you can create an empty text field.

JTextField textfieldObject = new JTextField(width in characters);

You can erase the text currently in the text field window and replace it with a string you supply using the setText method contained in the object of JTextField. For example,

```
textfieldObject.setText("This is a new string");
```

```
import javax.swing.*;                                         1
                                                             2
public class JTextFieldExample extends JApplet               3
{                                                            4
                                                             5
private JTextField predefinedMessage;                        6
                                                             7
public void init()                                           8
    {                                                        9
    // Create the JTextField object (which will show 20 chars) 10
    predefinedMessage = new JTextField("This message is     11
    predefined",20);

                                                            12
    // Add the JTextField to the container                  13
    getContentPane().add(predefinedMessage);                14
                                                            15
    } // End method init                                    16
                                                            17
} // End class JTextFieldExample                            18
```

The above program shows a `JTextField` object being created and used. In line 1 the compiler is notified of the location of the `JTextField` and `JApplet` classes which are used in the program. There is no need to notify the compiler about any other locations since we are not using other classes. For example, we do not place an `import java.awt.*;` instruction at the start of the program since we are not using the `paint` method whose parameter, class type `Graphics`, needs this location. This example shows that you can tailor your `import` commands to fit the classes you need and not simply import everything you think you need. There is no penalty for importing elements you do not need, it just makes for neater programming to confine imports to a minimum. When a reader of your program examines the list of imports, they can begin to form an impression of what is in the program. If that list contains imports that are never used it may mislead the reader.

We can see the result of the above program in Figure 7.4. You can click on the text field with the mouse pointer to select it and type in extra text or erase existing text. The text field is large because the default layout manager will 'stretch' elements to fill the available screen, when we change layout to a flow layout manager we will not see such an effect.

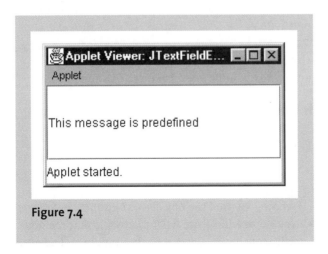

Figure 7.4

In the following program, we use more than one text field. In order to display the two text fields correctly, we change the layout manager in line 13. We must also `import java.awt.*` in line 2 because the `FlowLayout` class mentioned in line 13 is contained in the `java.awt`.

```
import javax.swing.*;                                    1
import java.awt.*;                                       2
                                                         3
public class JTextFieldsExample extends JApplet          4
{                                                        5
                                                         6
private JTextField messageBox;                           7
```

```
    private JTextField predefinedMessage;                        8
                                                                 9
    public void init()                                          10
      {                                                         11
      // Change the way components are laid out on the screen   12
      getContentPane().setLayout(new FlowLayout());             13
                                                                14
      // Create the JTextField object (which will hold 20 chars) 15
      messageBox = new JTextField(20);                          16
                                                                17
      // Insert a string into the JTextField object            18
      messageBox.setText("Hello from JTextField");              19
                                                                20
      // Add the JTextField to the container                   21
      getContentPane().add(messageBox);                        22
                                                                23
      // Create the JTextField object (which will hold 25 chars) 24
      predefinedMessage = new JTextField("This message is      25
      predefined",25);
                                                                26
      // Add the JTextField to the container                   27
      getContentPane().add(predefinedMessage);                 28
                                                                29
      } // End method init                                     30
                                                                31
    } // End class JTextFieldsExample                          32
```

Note that in line 19 above, we used the object messageBox before we added it to the container. This is a valid operation since what matters is that the object messageBox exists before you use it, not that it is added to the container. The purpose of the container is to display what is in the object, so that any text you place in a component will not be visible to the user until the element is added to the screen.

We can see the result of the above program in Figure 7.5 in p. 291.

7.5.2.4 Text area

The next element we look at is called a text area. A text area is a box in which text can be typed. This box usually shows a fixed number of characters wide and a fixed number deep (high). If the size and width of text input exceed the limits supplied to the constructor, then the text area box will expand to fit the text. Text areas are objects of type JTextArea. As you did with a text field you can put text into the text area using the setText method of the JTextArea object. You can add to or 'append' the contents of a text area using the append method. Since you have more than one line of a display, you can spread your text message over several lines by putting a '\n'

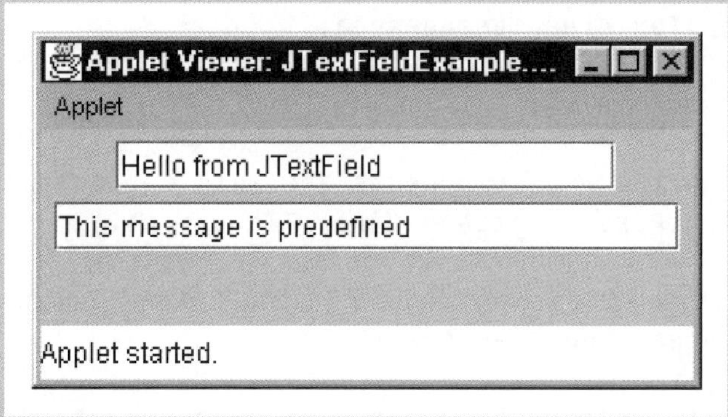

Figure 7.5

in your output string every time you want to start a new line. You can also use the '\t' character to move the text in a few spaces from the start of the line (called a 'tab'). If you want to erase the contents of a text field or text area, you can call the setText method with an empty string, for example, `TextAreaObject.setText("");`
   The syntax is:

JTextArea TextAreaObject = new JTextArea(height, width);

or

JTextArea TextAreaObject = new JTextArea("Contents",height, width);

where height and width are integers.
   Replace the contents of a text area with a string by calling the setText method

TextAreaObject.setText(string);

Add a string to the contents presently being displayed in the text area using append. The new string will be placed after the string currently being displayed (i.e. at the end).

TextAreaObject.append(string);

The following example will create a JTextArea object with 20 characters in width and five characters in height (line 15). A string is placed in the text area in line 18, which replaces any message currently in the text area. A string is appended to the existing contents of the text area in line 20.

```
import javax.swing.*;                                    1
import java.awt.*;                                       2
                                                         3
public class JTextAreaExample extends JApplet            4
{                                                        5
```

```
private JTextArea messageArea;                              6
                                                            7
                                                            8
public void init()                                          9
{                                                           10
// Change the way components are laid out on the screen     11
getContentPane().setLayout(new FlowLayout());               12
                                                            13
// Create the JTextArea object (5 chars deep×20 chars wide) 14
messageArea = new JTextArea(5,20);                          15
                                                            16
// Insert a string into the JTextArea object                17
messageArea.setText("You can use\nmore than one line\n");   18
                                                            19
messageArea.append("You can also append text");             20
                                                            21
// Add the TextArea to the screen                           22
getContentPane().add(messageArea);                          23
} // End method init                                        24
                                                            25
} // End class JTextAreaExample                             26
```

The above code will result in an output similar to Figure 7.6 which shows the text added with setText and the text appended to the contents using append.

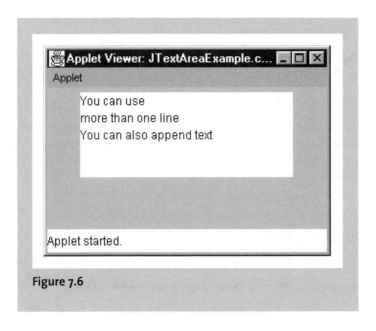

Figure 7.6

7.5.2.5 JLabel

JLabel is not an input or output element. It is intended to act as a means of describing a component being displayed. You setup a label with a specific string and you add the label to the screen just like any other component, the string contents of the label are then placed on the screen. JLabel is therefore like drawString in its result but it is treated as a component which is manged by the layout manager. That is you don't get to control where your JLabel goes using *x* and *y* coordinates. JLabel objects are therefore added to the screen before the input or output component they describe. The description depends on the component, for example, input name, input price and so on. The syntax is:

JLabel TextAreaFunction = new JLabel("String");

In the following program a JLabel is created (line 16) and added to the screen (line 19) to provide a guide to the user as to what to do with the text field following the label.

```
import javax.swing.*;                                          1
import java.awt.*;                                             2
                                                              3
public class JLabelExample extends JApplet                    4
{                                                             5
                                                              6
private JTextField messageBox;                                7
private JLabel instructions;                                  8
                                                              9
public void init()                                           10
   {                                                         11
   // Change the way components are laid out on the screen   12
   getContentPane().setLayout(new FlowLayout());             13
                                                             14
   // Create the JLabel object                               15
   instructions = new JLabel("Enter details");               16
                                                             17
   // Add the JLabel to the container                        18
   getContentPane().add(instructions);                       19
                                                             20
   // Create the JTextField object (which will hold 20 chars) 21
   messageBox = new JTextField(10);                          22
                                                             23
   // Add the JTextField to the container                    24
   getContentPane().add(messageBox);                         25
                                                             26
   } // End method init                                      27
                                                             28
} // End class JLabelExample                                 29
```

Figure 7.7 shows the label and its associated text field. If the text field is too wide for the available width of the screen, it will be placed on the next line. In such a circumstance you can change the 'width' tag in the HTML page to allow the elements to appear on the same line.

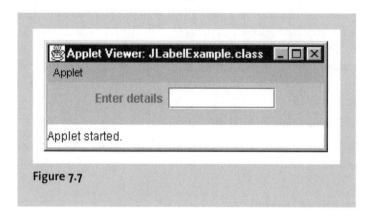

Figure 7.7

7.5.3 Input elements

7.5.3.1 Actions or events

How can you write a program which will respond when the user clicks a button or moves the mouse? Well, certain graphical elements, such as buttons, can cause events. An event is when a situation arises which needs to be dealt with. An event is caused by some sort of action on the part of the user, for example:

▶ User clicks mouse button

▶ User moves mouse

▶ User presses key

All of the above are actions which can cause events. An event is a signal from the operating system to the VM that some action has occurred. The VM must then decide if it supposed to do anything about the event (events can be ignored).

In Java you define a specific method to handle events. This method is known as an event handler. The VM will then call this method in order to deal with a particular type of event. It deals with the event by executing the instructions you have defined when you were writing the program and which you placed in the event handler.

For example, if a user moves the mouse and the program expresses an interest in being notified about this movement, then the Java VM calls a method called `mouse-Move` to deal with this action. The method can carry out any instructions it wishes, for example, the image on the screen may be changed, or a line drawn at the point where the mouse is moved to.

Event handlers have to be written and associated in some way with the elements likely to cause events. Event handlers must have specific names (just as the VM looked for methods called `init` and `paint`, it also looks for specific methods when the events associated with those methods occur). For example, you can write an event handler to draw a line in response to a movement from the mouse. To get this method executed you must tell the Java VM to listen to the mouse. If the mouse moves, then the VM will call the event handler you have written. This process is known as associating a listener with an event handler. If you do not tell the VM to listen for an event, then the VM will ignore that event when it happens.

7.5.3.2 Procedure for setting up input elements

Input elements are similar to output elements in that they are created from class definitions and added to the container (screen). Where they differ to output elements is that once you have added the input element to the screen, you must give an instruction that indicates you are interested in events related to that element. That instruction should contain the name of an object that will deal with any event relating to that input element. The object that deals with the input element event must contain one or more methods with particular names which will handle the various types of events generated by input elements.

So, in summary the steps are:

1   Create an input element object and add it to screen.

2   Set up a listener object for that input element and associate the listener object with the input element object (i.e. the OS listens to that element and if anything happens, it notifies the VM which contacts an agreed method in that object). The name of the agreed method to contact will depend on the type of input element involved. The object which is contacted will contain the event handler, that is, it will handle the event listened for (button click, mouse movement, key pressed, etc.) which occurs in the window.

3   Write the definition for the listener class. If the listener object is going to be the same program as that which added the input element to the screen then write the relevant methods to deal with any event associated with the input element.

We now look at some example input elements. These input elements all call the same method, called `actionPerformed`, if an event related to them occurs. If you forget to write the `actionPerformed` method, you get an error from the compiler which says:

```
class must be declared abstract. It does not define void action-
Performed(java.awt.event.ActionEvent) from interface java.awt.event.
ActionListener.
```

Another point to make is that any class which intends acting as an event handler object must implement an interface associated with the input element (see Chapter 6 for a discussion of interfaces). This is to ensure that the class will contain the method necessary (e.g. `actionPerformed`) to handle the event. You must also import the `java.awt.event` package as you may use some of its classes.

We look at the `JButton` and `JTextField` input elements first.

7.5.3.3 JButton

Let's look at the `JButton` input element first and see how that is created, listened to and handled.

The steps for creating a button are to first create an object variable which holds a reference to an object of type `JButton`.

```
JButton PressForMessage;
```

Next create the `JButton` object and put its reference into your variable. The constructor for `JButton` will take a string as a parameter and this string will be displayed on the button when it is shown on the window (once the element is added to the window of course).

```
PressForMessage=new JButton("Press this button for a message");
```

That completes the creation part.

The next step is to deal with the button being pressed. For that we need to decide what object will deal with a button event. You can either indicate that the applet object which created the button also deals with its events or you can setup a new object to do this.

Let's assume that we use the applet object to handle a button event. To mark the applet as handling an event generated by a `JButton` object, we place the phrase `implements ActionListener` after the declaration for the applet class. The `ActionListener` interface is contained in the `java.awt.event` library so be sure to import that at the start of the program.

The phrase `implements ActionListener` does two things. First, it marks the class definition which follows as implementing an action listener, so an object of the class will be accepted as a parameter for event handlers (when an event handler is setup you must tell it what object will handle its event). Second, it forces the compiler to check that a method called `actionPerformed` is present in the applet class. `ActionListener` is actually not a class but an interface. An interface contains method descriptions (names, parameters, return types) but has no code for those methods. Interfaces are intended to act as checklists for classes which implement them. When a compiler sees that your program has implemented a certain interface, it will seek out the methods defined in that interface and check to see that the same methods are defined in the class it is compiling.

The last step is to associate our button with the object which deals with it. The instruction

```
PressForMessage.addActionListener(ObjectWhichDealsWithButton);
```

will tell the system that if the button `PressForMessage` is clicked by the user, then the `actionPerformed` method in the object supplied (`ObjectWhichDealsWithButton`) should be executed. So `ObjectWhichDealsWithButton` is an address. The address supplied can be that of the current object, that is, the applet executing. How do we write an instruction which contains an address that we do not know in advance of the execution? The address of the applet is only decided when the applet is created by the VM. Therefore, we have no way of knowing what address the applet will have when the program is run and an object of the applet is created by the VM. Fortunately, there is a word which can be used to indicate this address, that word is `this`. When the compiler sees the word `this`, it knows that you refer to the address the object which contains the word `this` will have when executed. When the program is run and the applet object is created, the word this will be replaced by the address of the object and so the statement will be complete. So, to get the button listened to by the applet, we give the instruction:

```
PressForMessage.addActionListener(this);
```

You then need to write the instructions which will be executed when the button is pressed and put these instructions in the method actionPerformed. Action-Performed will take a single parameter of type ActionEvent. This parameter will be an object which contains relevant information about the event which has occurred. For example what caused it, that is, which specific object the user used (you may have created and displayed several buttons). You can do anything you like in the action-Performed method, call repaint, output information, create objects, and so on.

You can see all the steps discussed laid out in the program below. This program will create a button and a text area and place them on the screen. Each time the button is pressed a message is added to the text area. In line 8, the interface ActionListener is referred to. The compiler will check to see if there is a method in the class JButtonExample which is called actionPerformed and takes as its parameter an object of type ActionEvent. It finds the method in line 37. In line 11, we declare a button, called printMessage. In line 12, we declare a text area which will hold messages printed out when the button is pressed.

In line 33, we instruct the system to handle any event relating to the button in this object, that is, in the applet JButtonExample. The method actionPerformed (line 37) is therefore called anytime the button is pressed and it prints out a string in the text area. After this method has executed, the VM goes back to listening to the button and acting if the button is pressed, and so on until the program is stopped.

Sequence of events

1 VM creates object from JButtonExample class definition

2 VM starts init

3 init sets up button object, adds button to applet window and tells VM to listen out for button. It also says that VM button will be processed in this object (as opposed to being sent to another object)

4 VM listens for button being pressed

5 When VM hears button pressed it calls actionPerformed with information about the event (contents of button, etc.)

6 actionPerformed sets the contents of output text area (i.e. it calls setText with a string)

7 Go back to step 4.

```
// Locate classes for JApplet,JButton          1
import javax.swing.*;                           2
// Locate classes for FlowLayout                3
import java.awt.*;                              4
```

```
// Locate classes for ActionEvent,ActionListener          5
import java.awt.event.*;                                   6
                                                           7
public class JButtonExample extends JApplet implements     8
ActionListener
{                                                          9
                                                          10
private JButton printMessage;                             11
private JTextArea output;                                 12
                                                          13
public void init()                                        14
   {                                                      15
   // Setup the layout manager                            16
   getContentPane().setLayout(new FlowLayout());          17
                                                          18
   // Setup the button                                    19
   printMessage = new JButton("Press for message");       20
                                                          21
   // Add the button to the window                        22
   getContentPane().add(printMessage);                    23
                                                          24
   // Setup the Text Area (5 chars deep × 10 chars wide)  25
   output = new JTextArea(5,10);                          26
                                                          27
   // Add the Text Area to the window                     28
   getContentPane().add(output);                          29
                                                          30
   // Tell the button which object will be dealing        31
   // with events it generates                            32
   printMessage.addActionListener(this);                  33
                                                          34
   }// End of init                                        35
                                                          36
   public void actionPerformed(ActionEvent eventInfo)     37
   {                                                      38
   // Add text to Text Area created in applet             39
   output.append("The Button has been pressed\n");        40
   } // End actionPerformed                               41
                                                          42
} // End of JButtonExample                                43
```

Figure 7.8 shows what the button and the text area look like when the program is started.

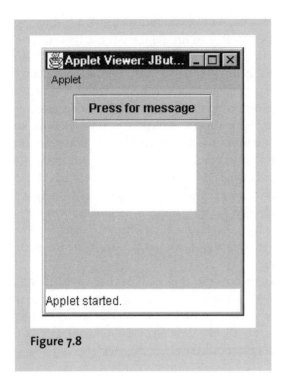

Figure 7.8

Figure 7.9 shows the output that results from the user pressing the button once.

Figure 7.9

In the next example dealing with creating and using a button, we indicate that a separate object from the applet is to handle the button, that is, we define a specific class which will deal with events associated with the button. This class, `Handle-ButtonClass`, is defined in line 44 of the program and it contains two methods, a `constructor` and the `actionPerformed` method which is executed when the button is pressed. The program will increase the value of an integer variable, called `numberOfTimesPressed`, each time the button is pressed. The current value of `numberOfTimesPressed` will also be output when the user presses the button.

The constructor in `HandleButtonClass` is passed the reference to an object of type `JTextArea` (called output), which is created in the `init` method of the applet. This is the object that the `HandleButtonClass` object needs to output the contents of the `numberOfTimesPressed` variable, which is keeping track of how many times the button is pressed. Therefore, we have a situation where the text area object (output) created in the applet is shared with the object which is handling the button event (called `handleButtonObject`).

The process works like this, in the applet, `JButtonExampleClass`, we define an object variable which holds an address of an object of type `HandleButtonClass` (line 12). We setup our button and text area objects as usual but also setup an object of type `HandleButtonClass` (line 34). The `handleButtonObject` object is passed the address of the object called output, which is the text area we have created in line 27.

In line 38, we tell the VM that any event relating to the button will be handled in the object `handleButtonObject`. When the user presses the button the `action-Performed` method in the `handleButtonObject` is executed.

```
// Locate classes for JApplet,JButton            1
import javax.swing.*;                             2
// Locate classes for FlowLayout                  3
import java.awt.*;                                 4
// Locate classes for ActionEvent,ActionListener  5
import java.awt.event.*;                           6
                                                  7
public class JButtonExampleClass extends JApplet  8
{                                                 9
                                                  10
private JButton printMessage;                     11
private HandleButtonClass handleButtonObject;     12
private JTextArea output;                         13
                                                  14
public void init()                                15
   {                                              16
   // Setup the layout manager                    17
   getContentPane().setLayout(new FlowLayout());  18
                                                  19
```

```
    // Setup the button                                        20
    printMessage = new JButton("Press for message");           21
                                                               22
    // Add the button to the window                            23
    getContentPane().add(printMessage);                        24
                                                               25
    // Setup the Text Area (5 chars deep × 10 chars wide)      26
    output = new JTextArea(5,10);                              27
                                                               28
    // Add the Text Area to the window                         29
    getContentPane().add(output);                              30
                                                               31
    // Setup the object which will handle events               32
    // relating to the JButton                                 33
    handleButtonObject = new HandleButtonClass(output);        34
                                                               35
    // Tell the button which object will be dealing            36
    // with events it generates                                37
    printMessage.addActionListener(handleButtonObject);        38
    }// End of init                                            39
                                                               40
} // End of JButtonExampleClass                                41
                                                               42
                                                               43
class HandleButtonClass implements ActionListener              44
{                                                              45
                                                               46
private JTextArea outputArea;                                  47
private int nrOfTimesPressed;                                  48
                                                               49
public HandleButtonClass(JTextArea outputParameter)            50
    {// Parameter is used to display output                    51
    outputArea = outputParameter;                              52
    nrOfTimesPressed = 0; // Initialise the counter            53
    }// End HandleButtonClass constructor                      54
                                                               55
public void actionPerformed(ActionEvent eventInfo)             56
    {// Add text to Text Area created in applet                57
    nrOfTimesPressed ++ ;                                      58
    outputArea.append("Button pressed " + nrOfTimesPressed +   59
    "times\n");
    } // End actionPerformed                                   60
                                                               61
} // End HandleButtonClass                                     62
```

Some sample output from the above program is shown in Figure 7.10.

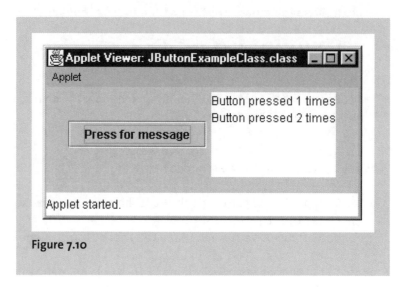

Figure 7.10

7.5.3.4 TextField

We have seen earlier in Section 7.5.2.3 that we can use the text field object to display a single line of characters. Well, like the button component, it is possible for a text field object to generate an event and cause the VM to execute the method `action-Performed`. To generate an event in a text field, the user must press the return key. This causes the VM to look for a method to process this event (provided, of course, that the VM has been told to listen to the text field).

You can extract the string that is contained in the text field by calling the method `getText` in the text field object. The `getText` method will return a string which consists of the current contents of the text field.

In the following program, we setup a text field (line 20) and a text area object (line 26). We tell the VM that we want it to listen to the text field and to call `this` object if any event occurs (line 32). In the `actionPerformed` method (line 35), we take the contents of the text field and append them to the contents of the text area (line 39). We then erase the contents of the text field ready for the next input by setting the contents of the text field to the empty string `" "` (line 42).

```
// Locate classes for JApplet,JButton              1
import javax.swing.*;                              2
// Locate classes for FlowLayout                   3
import java.awt.*;                                 4
// Locate classes for ActionEvent,ActionListener   5
import java.awt.event.*;                           6
                                                   7
```

```
public class JTextFieldInputExample extends JApplet      8
implements ActionListener
{                                                        9
                                                        10
private JTextField inputMessage;                        11
private JTextArea output;                               12
                                                        13
public void init()                                      14
    {                                                   15
    // Setup the layout manager                         16
    getContentPane().setLayout(new FlowLayout());       17
                                                        18
    // Setup the textfield                              19
    inputMessage = new JTextField(15);                  20
                                                        21
    // Add the textfield to the window                  22
    getContentPane().add(inputMessage);                 23
                                                        24
    // Setup the Text Area (5 chars deep × 10 chars wide) 25
    output = new JTextArea(5,10);                        26
                                                        27
    // Add the Text Area to the window                  28
    getContentPane().add(output);                       29
    // Tell the textfield which object will be dealing  30
    // with events it generates                         31
    inputMessage.addActionListener(this);               32
    }// End of init                                     33
                                                        34
public void actionPerformed(ActionEvent eventInfo)      35
    {                                                   36
    // Add the text in the Text Field to the Text Area object 37
    // created in applet                                38
    output.append("\nMessage " + inputMessage.getText()); 39
                                                        40
    // Set the TextField to blank                       41
    inputMessage.setText("");                           42
    } // End actionPerformed                            43
                                                        44
} // End of JTextFieldInputExample                      45
```

Figure 7.11 in p. 304 shows the output of the above program when it starts up. Select the text field using your mouse pointer, type in a string and press return.

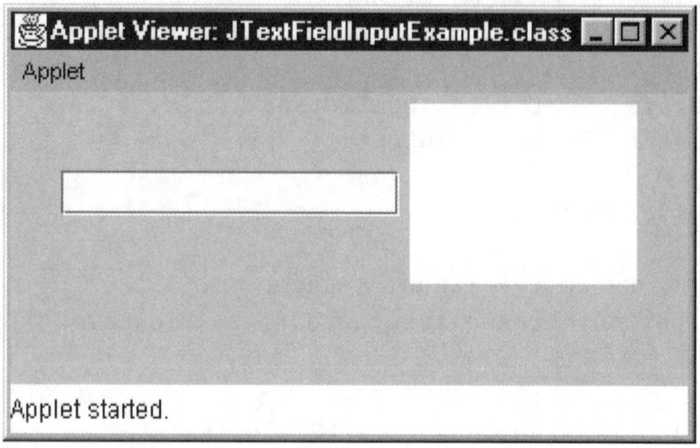

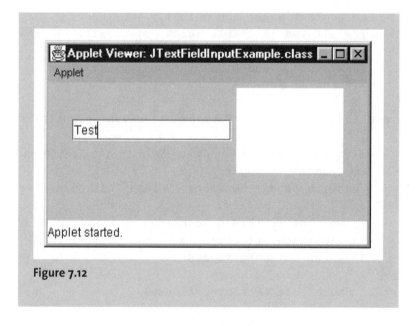

Figure 7.11

Figure 7.12 shows the scene after the user types in the word 'Test' but before they press return.

Figure 7.12

Figure 7.13 shows what happens just after the user presses return after typing in a string. The `actionPerformed` method is called and it takes the contents of the text field and places it in the text area. Instructions in the `actionPerformed` method also clear the text field ready for the next input.

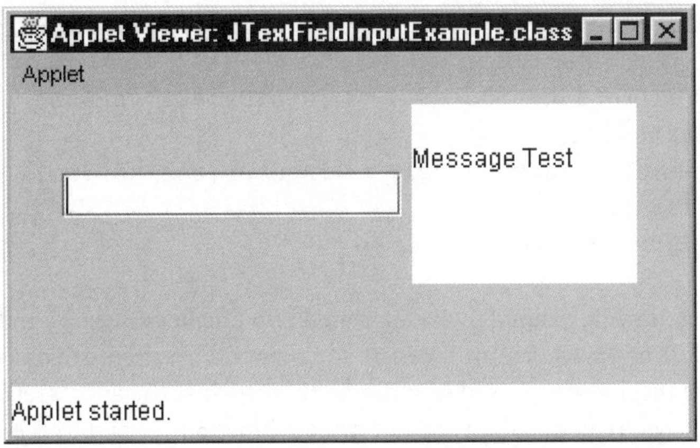

Figure 7.13

7.5.3.5 Finding out what caused an event: getSource

You may add several input components (buttons, textfields, etc.) to the screen and tell the VM to listen to them all. The `actionPerformed` method is then called whenever an action is generated by any of those components. What happens if you have more than one component and you want a different group of statements executed in response to each particular component, that is, how do you tell which button of the three being listened to was pressed when the `actionPerformed` method is called? You have two options, one option involves creating each component which can generate an event with seperate objects, each of which contains an event handler. If the user presses one button, the `actionPerformed` method in the object associated with that button will be executed. If another button is pressed, a different object will be used, and so on. This way you can tailor the class definition of the objects to carry out the instructions that you wish.

The other, more common option is to use the fact that the `ActionEvent` object passed to `actionPerformed` by the VM will contain as one of its variables the memory address of the object which caused the event, that is, that caused the method `actionPerformed` to be executed. So, for example, if the user presses one of several available buttons then the address of the specific button object they pressed will be contained in the `ActionEvent` object. You use this address by extracting the objects address from the `ActionEvent` object using the `getSource` method and comparing this address with the addresses of the components you created. So, in effect, what you are doing is going through the list of input objects you created and setup a listener for in order to try and match each object you created with the object address which caused the event (a sort of identity parade for events).

The common form of this test is as follows:

```
public void actionPerformed(ActionEvent eventInfo)
{
if(eventInfo.getSource() = = inputObjectTypeOne)
    statement;
if(eventInfo.getSource() = = inputObjectTypeTwo)
    statement;
} // End actionPerformed
```

In the following example, I have created two buttons (lines 21 and 31) and a text field (line 36) and have set up listeners for them all. In the `actionPerformed` method, I check the address passed into the method against the addresses of the objects which could have triggered `actionPerformed` (lines 55, 57 and 59). A different message is output depending on the result.

```
// Locate classes for JApplet,JButton                    1
import javax.swing.*;                                     2
// Locate classes for FlowLayout                         3
import java.awt.*;                                        4
// Locate classes for ActionEvent,ActionListener         5
import java.awt.event.*;                                  6
                                                         7
public class GetSourceExample extends JApplet implements 8
ActionListener
{                                                        9
                                                         10
private JButton buttonObjectOne,buttonObjectTwo;         11
private JTextField textFieldObject;                      12
private JTextArea output;                                13
                                                         14
public void init()                                       15
   {                                                     16
   // Setup the layout manager                           17
   getContentPane().setLayout(new FlowLayout());         18
                                                         19
   // Setup the button                                   20
   buttonObjectOne = new JButton("Button 1");            21
                                                         22
   // Add the button to the window                       23
   getContentPane().add(buttonObjectOne);                24
                                                         25
```

```
    // Tell the button which object will be dealing      26
     // with events it generates                         27
    buttonObjectOne.addActionListener(this);             28
                                                          29
    // Do the same for the second button                 30
    buttonObjectTwo = new JButton("Button 2");           31
    getContentPane().add(buttonObjectTwo);               32
    buttonObjectTwo.addActionListener(this);             33
                                                          34
    // Setup the text field                              35
    textFieldObject = new JTextField(10);                36
                                                          37
    // Add the text field to the window                  38
    getContentPane().add(textFieldObject);               39
                                                          40
    // Tell the text field which object will be dealing  41
    // with events it generates                          42
    textFieldObject.addActionListener(this);             43
                                                          44
    // Setup the Text Area (5 chars deep × 10 chars wide) 45
    output = new JTextArea(5,10);                        46
                                                          47
    // Add the Text Area to the window                   48
    getContentPane().add(output);                        49
                                                          50
    }// End of init                                      51
                                                          52
  public void actionPerformed(ActionEvent eventInfo)     53
     {                                                    54
     if(eventInfo.getSource() == buttonObjectOne)        55
        output.append("You pressed button 1\n");         56
     if(eventInfo.getSource() == buttonObjectTwo)        57
        output.append("You pressed button 2\n");         58
     if(eventInfo.getSource() == textFieldObject)        59
        output.append("You pressed return in the textfield\n"); 60
     } // End actionPerformed                            61
                                                          62
  } // End of GetSourceExample                           63
```

The display when the above program starts is shown in Figure 7.14 in p. 308.

If the user presses Button 1 then the output will be as shown in Figure 7.15 (i.e. the statement eventInfo.getSource()==ButtonObjectOne evaluates to true).

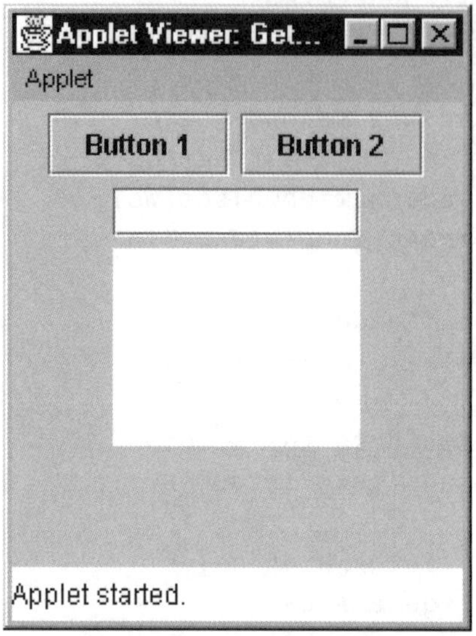

Figure 7.14

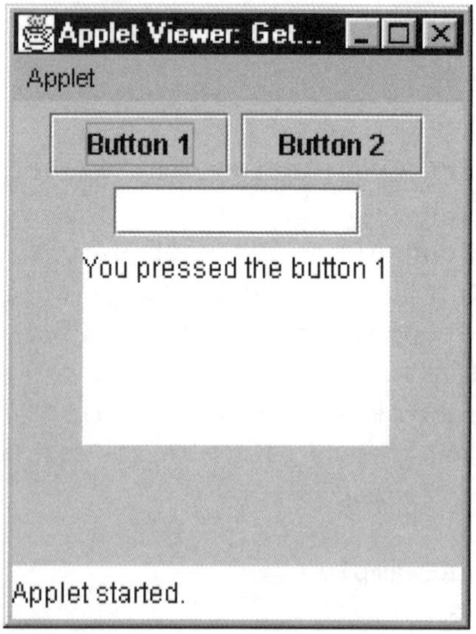

Figure 7. 15

If the user then presses `Button 2`, then the output will be as shown in Figure 7.16 (i.e. the statement `eventInfo.getSource()==ButtonObjectTwo` evaluates to true).

Figure 7.16

Finally, you can see in Figure 7.17, the result of the user next pressing return whilst in the text field box (`eventInfo.getSource()==TextFieldObject` is true).

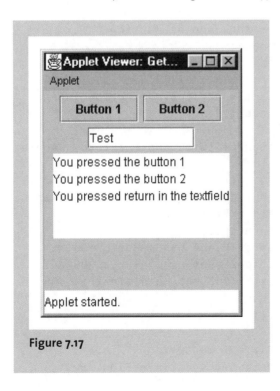

Figure 7.17

Remember what you are doing is comparing the addresses of the objects you created with the address of the object which cause the event handler to be executed.

7.5.3.6   Example: using different objects to handle events

The next example program shows the alternative to using getSource. Different classes are written to cope with the three different components. Objects of these classes are then associated with the relevant components and the program will call those objects when the relevant component generates an event. The three classes which will deal with the elements are HandleButton1Event, HandleButton2Event and HandleTextFieldEvent. The program performs the same functions as the one seen in the previous section but as opposed to handling all the events in the same object it passes responsibility for handling events to three different objects, each of which is associated with only one of the components. Each of the three objects is setup with a reference to the text area object defined in the applet. This is done so that the event handling objects can have access to an output area without having to setup their own user interface. The button buttonObjectOne has handleButton1Object, the textfield textFieldObject has handleTextFieldObject, and so on. As discussed in p. 300, all three objects use a common object to output information which is created in the applet (line 40) and passed as a parameter to each of the event handler objects constructors. So, for example, when the button buttonObjectTwo is pressed the actionPerformed method defined in handleButton2Event is called (line 88). This will use the text area object called output to display a string.

```
// Locate classes for JApplet,JButton                      1
import javax.swing.*;                                       2
// Locate classes for FlowLayout                           3
import java.awt.*;                                          4
// Locate classes for ActionEvent,ActionListener           5
import java.awt.event.*;                                    6
                                                            7
public class GetSourceClassExample extends JApplet         8
{                                                           9
                                                           10
private JButton buttonObjectOne,buttonObjectTwo;           11
private JTextField textFieldObject;                        12
private JTextArea output;                                  13
private HandleButton1Event handleButton1Object;           14
private HandleButton2Event handleButton2Object;           15
private HandleTextFieldEvent handleTextFieldObject;       16
                                                           17
public void init()                                         18
   {                                                       19
   // Setup the layout manager                             20
   getContentPane().setLayout(new FlowLayout());           21
```

```
                                                              22
    // Setup the button                                      23
    buttonObjectOne = new JButton("Button 1");               24
                                                              25
    // Add the button to the window                          26
    getContentPane().add(buttonObjectOne);                   27
                                                              28
    // Do the same for the second button                     29
    buttonObjectTwo = new JButton("Button 2");               30
    getContentPane().add(buttonObjectTwo);                   31
                                                              32
    // Setup the text field                                  33
    textFieldObject = new JTextField(10);                    34
                                                              35
    // Add the text field to the window                      36
    getContentPane().add(textFieldObject);                   37
                                                              38
    // Setup the Text Area (5 chars deep × 10 chars wide)    39
    output = new JTextArea(5,10);                            40
                                                              41
    // Add the Text Area to the window                       42
    getContentPane().add(output);                            43
                                                              44
    // Setup the handlers for the events                     45
    handleButton1Object = new HandleButton1Event(output);    46
    handleButton2Object = new HandleButton2Event(output);    47
    handleTextFieldObject = new HandleTextFieldEvent(output);48
                                                              49
    // Tell the buttons which object will be dealing         50
    // with events they generate                             51
    buttonObjectOne.addActionListener(handleButton1Object);  52
    buttonObjectTwo.addActionListener(handleButton2Object);  53
                                                              54
    // Tell the text field which object will be dealing      55
    // with events it generates                              56
    textFieldObject.addActionListener(handleTextFieldObject);57
                                                              58
    }// End of init                                          59
                                                              60
} // End of GetSourceClassExample                            61
                                                              62
class HandleButton1Event implements ActionListener           63
{                                                            64
private JTextArea outputReference;                           65
                                                              66
```

```
public HandleButton1Event(JTextArea outputSupplied)          67
  {                                                          68
  outputReference = outputSupplied;                          69
  } // End HandleButton1Event constructor                    70
                                                             71
public void actionPerformed(ActionEvent eventInfo)           72
  {                                                          73
  outputReference.append("You pressed button 1\n");          74
  } // End actionPerformed                                   75
                                                             76
} // End HandleButton1Event                                  77
                                                             78
class HandleButton2Event implements ActionListener           79
{                                                            80
private JTextArea outputReference;                           81
                                                             82
public HandleButton2Event(JTextArea outputSupplied)          83
  {                                                          84
  outputReference = outputSupplied;                          85
  } // End HandleButton2Event constructor                    86
                                                             87
public void actionPerformed(ActionEvent eventInfo)           88
  {                                                          89
  outputReference.append("You pressed button 2\n");          90
  } // End actionPerformed                                   91
                                                             92
} // End HandleButton2Event                                  93
                                                             94
class HandleTextFieldEvent implements ActionListener         95
{                                                            96
private JTextArea outputReference;                           97
                                                             98
public HandleTextFieldEvent(JTextArea outputSupplied)        99
  {                                                          100
  outputReference = outputSupplied;                          101
  } // End HandleTextFieldEvent constructor                  102
                                                             103
public void actionPerformed(ActionEvent eventInfo)           104
  {                                                          105
  outputReference.append("You pressed return in the          106
  TextField\n");
  } // End actionPerformed                                   107
                                                             108
} // End HandleTextFieldEvent                                109
```

The output of the program is the same as the previous example. In the actionPerformed methods in the above classes, there is no need to use the getSource
method to determine the source of the events since each event has its own unique
object which will not be called if any other event occurs.

7.5.3.7   TextArea

We mentioned earlier in Section 7.5.2.4 that a JTextArea object can be used for
input. Input can be placed in the JTextArea object and extracted from the object
using a method called getText. A JTextArea object does not have any listener
associated with it, however so any action that occurs within a text area will not
result in a method being called. If you want to receive a signal to indicate when the
contents of a JTextArea object can be processed, you need to use some other input
element which can be listened to, for example, a JButton. The reason there is no
listener is that the actions which generate events (clicking a mouse button, moving
the mouse, pressing return, etc.) are used for editing purposes within the text area
object.

Two more methods that should be mentioned are setEditable and get-
SelectedText. The setEditable method will take a boolean parameter, if the
parameter is false, then the user will not be permitted to edit the contents of a text
area. If the parameter is true, then they can edit the text area. This method is contained in an object of type JTextField.

The getSelectedText() method takes no parameter but returns a value of type
String. The string it returns is one which has been highlighted (or selected) by the
user using the mouse.

The example program below shows the two methods in use.

```
import java.awt.*;                                                    1
import javax.swing.*;                                                 2
import java.awt.event.*;                                              3
                                                                     4
// This applet shows how text which is selected in one textarea      5
// can be copied into another                                        6
                                                                     7
public class CopySelectedText extends JApplet implements             8
ActionListener
{                                                                    9
private JTextArea mainTextArea; // Declare main text area           10
private JTextArea copyTextArea; // Declare text area where          11
// copy is placed                                                   12
private JButton makeCopy; // Button which is pushed to              13
// cause a copy of a section of text to be made                     14
                                                                    15
```

```
public void init()                                          16
   {                                                        17
   getContentPane().setLayout(new FlowLayout());            18
                                                            19
   // Set up variables                                      20
   mainTextArea=new JTextArea("Example default text",5,20); 21
   copyTextArea = new JTextArea(5,20);                      22
   makeCopy = new JButton("Copy selected text");            23
                                                            24
   // add components to applet window                       25
   getContentPane().add(mainTextArea);                      26
   getContentPane().add(copyTextArea);                      27
   getContentPane().add(makeCopy);                          28
                                                            29
   // associate button with event handler                   30
   makeCopy.addActionListener(this);                        31
                                                            32
   // Stop the user from editing the copyTextArea           33
   copyTextArea.setEditable(false);                         34
   } // End init                                            35
                                                            36
public void actionPerformed(ActionEvent event)             37
{                                                           38
// Copy the selected text and place it in the other text area 39
copyTextArea.setText(mainTextArea.getSelectedText());      40
} // End actionPerformed                                    41
                                                            42
} // End class CopySelectedText                             43
```

The output of the example is shown in Figure 7.18 in p. 315 which shows how the highlighted piece of text is copied into the other text area.

Another point to make about **JTextArea** as an input mechanism is that, by default, a **JTextArea** object will expand when extra text is typed in. It may even expand beyond the bounds of the screen making some of the text no longer visible. If you want to stop your **JTextArea** object expanding horizontally, then call the **setLine-Wrap** method in your **JTextArea** object with a parameter of true. This causes the VM to move onto a new line when you have exceeded the width of the **JTextArea** you are entering input into. Your **JTextArea** object can still expand vertically though. For example,

```
messageArea.setLineWrap(true);
```

Another solution to the problem of the expanding text area is to use a component called **JScrollPane** to manage a view of a text area. **JScrollPane** will contain a **JTextArea** within its preset boundary and will add horizontal and vertical scroll bars

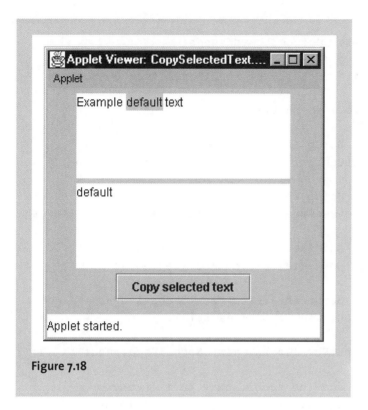

Figure 7.18

to the screen if the text in the box exceeds the limits set for the text area. `JScroll-Pane` is created like any other GUI component. If you want to place a component, such as text area in a scroll pane object, you add that component to the scroll pane object instead of to the screen. This is because `JScrollPane` will contain the component and manage its display to stop the element exceeding its originally allotted section of the screen. The `JScrollPane` component is then added to the screen.

The following program creates two `JTextArea` objects. These objects are added to two `JScrollPane` objects (called `inputScrollArea` and `outputScrollArea`). A button is added and a listener is associated with the button. When the user presses the button, the `actionPerformed` method in the applet is executed and places the entire contents of one of the text areas (input) into the other (output) (line 51).

```
// Locate classes for JApplet,JButton                   1
import javax.swing.*;                                    2
// Locate classes for FlowLayout                         3
import java.awt.*;                                        4
// Locate classes for ActionEvent,ActionListener         5
import java.awt.event.*;                                  6
                                                         7
public class JTextAreaInputExample extends JApplet        8
implements ActionListener
                                                         9
```

```
{                                                          10
private JButton copyMessage;                               11
private JTextArea input,output;                            12
private JScrollPane inputScrollArea,outputScrollArea;      13
                                                           14
public void init()                                         15
    {                                                      16
    // Setup the layout manager                            17
    getContentPane().setLayout(new FlowLayout());          18
                                                           19
    // Setup the button                                    20
    copyMessage = new JButton("Press to copy message");    21
                                                           22
    // Add the button to the window                        23
    getContentPane().add(copyMessage);                     24
                                                           25
    // Setup the Text Area (5 chars deep × 10 chars wide)  26
    input = new JTextArea(5,10);                           27
                                                           28
    inputScrollArea = new JScrollPane(input);              29
                                                           30
    // Add the scroll pane to the window                   31
    getContentPane().add(inputScrollArea);                 32
                                                           33
    // Setup the Text Area (5 chars deep × 10 chars wide)  34
    output = new JTextArea(5,10);                          35
                                                           36
    // Create the scrollpane,supplying the textarea        37
    // object it will contain                              38
    outputScrollArea = new JScrollPane(output);            39
                                                           40
    // Add the Text Area to the window                     41
    getContentPane().add(outputScrollArea);                42
                                                           43
    // Tell the button which object will be dealing        44
    // with events it generates                            45
    copyMessage.addActionListener(this);                   46
    }// End of init                                        47
                                                           48
public void actionPerformed(ActionEvent eventInfo)         49
    {// Copy the contents of one TextArea to the other     50
    output.setText(input.getText());                       51
    } // End actionPerformed                               52
} // End of JTextAreaInputExample                           53
```

Figure 7.19 shows how the output of the program looks when first run. Neither text area contains scroll bars as there is no text in them to scroll through.

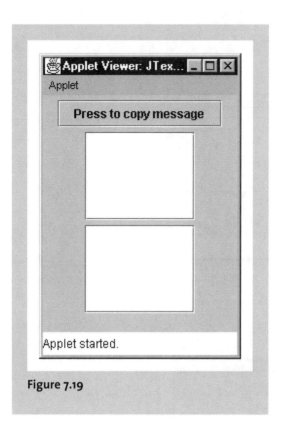

Figure 7.19

Figure 7.20 in p. 318 shows what happens when the string This is a message written in a text area is typed in. This message exceeds the horizontal limit set for the text area and so the JScrollPane object adds scroll bars to allow the user to view all the message.

After pressing the button the message in one text area is copied into the other. Since the message in one text area exceeds the viewable limit of the other, scroll bars are added to the second text area (see Figure 7.21).

The first area remains untouched after the copying but you can clear it by calling setText with an empty string (""). Make sure if you do this that you put the instruction which clears the area after any instruction which uses the contents of the area (getText), otherwise the area will be empty by the time you read its contents.

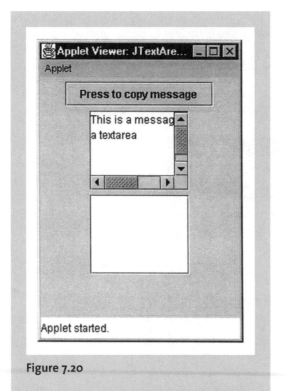

Figure 7.20

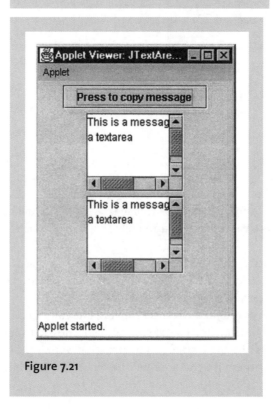

Figure 7.21

7.5.3.8 Help messages

It would be useful to have some quick way of reminding a user the purpose of various buttons and text areas (e.g. input name, input address, display result, press for calculation, etc.). We have seen that you can place labels beside these elements but a detailed enough explanation may not fit into a label. A method called setToolTip-Text is present in all the component objects that you have seen and can be used to setup a message which appears when the user places their mouse pointer over a component (they do not have to press the mouse button to get the message, instead the message will appear automatically and disappear when the mouse is moved). Placing a mouse button over an element is known as 'hovering'.

The following program will create some components and setup some tool tip text messages for them. It does nothing if the elements are used since the elements are not listened to.

```
// Locate classes for JApplet,JButton                      1
import javax.swing.*;                                        2
// Locate classes for FlowLayout                            3
import java.awt.*;                                           4
                                                             5
public class ToolTipTextExample extends JApplet             6
{                                                            7
                                                             8
private JButton displayInstructions;                         9
private JTextField usersName;                               10
                                                            11
public void init()                                          12
    {                                                       13
    // Setup the layout manager                             14
    getContentPane().setLayout(new FlowLayout());           15
                                                            16
    // Setup the button                                     17
    displayInstructions = new JButton("Calculate Result");  18
                                                            19
    // Add the button to the window                         20
    getContentPane().add(displayInstructions);              21
                                                            22
    // Setup the textfield                                  23
    usersName = new JTextField(10);                         24
                                                            25
    // Add the textfield to the window                      26
    getContentPane().add(usersName);                        27
                                                            28
    // Setup the tool tip text for both input objects       29
    displayInstructions.setToolTipText("Click on this       30
```

```
        button to calculate the result");
        usersName.setToolTipText("Click on this box, Type in your      31
        price and press return");

                                                                       32
        } // End init                                                  33

                                                                       34
} // End ToolTipTextExample                                            35
```

Figure 7.22 shows what is displayed when the program starts up.

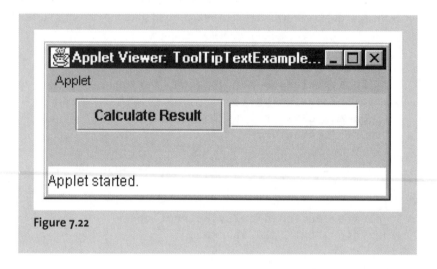

Figure 7.22

If the user places the mouse pointer over the Calculate Result button, then the tool tip text message associated with that button will appear, as shown in Figure 7.23.

When the user moves the mouse pointer to the text field, the relevant message is displayed. Note that the message previously displayed has disappeared (see Figure 7.24).

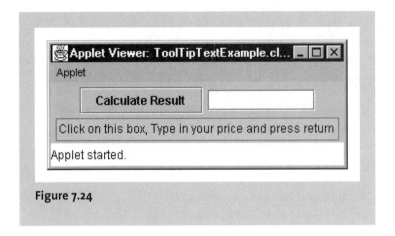

Figure 7.24

7.5.3.9 Checkboxes

A checkbox is an element which consists of a small square that can be empty or contain a tick. You use a checkbox to indicate one of two possible values, for example, yes or no, on or off. You can deal with input via a checkbox in two ways. You can listen to each checkbox element and execute a method in response to the selection of a text box. Alternatively you can choose not to listen to the checkboxes and use another component (like a button) to trigger an event handler. In the event handler method you can check the state of the checkboxes (i.e. whether they are checked or unchecked). The event handler method called if a checkbox is listened to is named `itemStateChanged` and is passed a parameter of type `ItemEvent` by the VM. Any class which wants to listen to a checkbox (i.e. to contain the method `itemState-Changed`) also needs to implement the interface `ItemListener`.

The checkbox class is called `JCheckBox`. When you declare an object of type `JCheckBox`, you can supply a string to its constructor. This string will be placed before the checkbox on the screen so that the user has some explanation of what the checkbox is for (you can also provide extra information via `setToolTipText`).

In the following program, two checkboxes are created (lines 15 and 21) and added to the screen. A tool tip text message is setup for each checkbox (lines 16 and 22). Finally a listener is associated with both text boxes (lines 19 and 25).

When one of the text boxes is clicked, this will reverse the state of the checkbox (i.e. if the checkbox was on, it is now off) and will result in the `itemStateChanged` method (line 31) being called. In the `itemStateChanged` method below, we check to see which checkbox caused the method to be executed (i.e. which one did the user click on) using `getSource`. A checkboxes' state can be determined at any point in the program by calling the method `isSelected()` contained in the checkbox object. The method `isSelected()` will return true if the checkbox object question is on (ticked) and false if it is off.

```
import javax.swing.*;                                          1
import java.awt.event.*;                                       2
import java.awt.*;                                             3
                                                               4
public class CheckBoxExample extends JApplet implements        5
ItemListener
   {                                                           6
   private JCheckBox checkBoxOne,checkBoxTwo;                  7
   private JTextArea output;                                   8
                                                               9
   public void init()                                          10
   {                                                           11
   // Setup the layout manager                                 12
   getContentPane().setLayout(new FlowLayout());               13
                                                               14
   checkBoxOne = new JCheckBox("Check Box 1");                 15
   checkBoxOne.setToolTipText("Press to switch on/off");       16
                                                               17
   getContentPane().add(checkBoxOne);                          18
   checkBoxOne.addItemListener(this);                          19
                                                               20
   checkBoxTwo = new JCheckBox("Check Box 2");                 21
   checkBoxTwo.setToolTipText("Press to switch on/off");       22
                                                               23
   getContentPane().add(checkBoxTwo);                          24
   checkBoxTwo.addItemListener(this);                          25
                                                               26
   output = new JTextArea(8,20);                               27
   getContentPane().add(output);                               28
   } // End init                                               29
                                                               30
public void itemStateChanged(ItemEvent eventInfo)             31
   {                                                           32
   output.setText(""); // Clear the text area                 33
                                                               34
   if(eventInfo.getSource() == checkBoxOne)                    35
      output.append("Check Box One pressed\n");                36
   if(eventInfo.getSource() == checkBoxTwo)                    37
      output.append("Check Box Two pressed\n");                38
                                                               39
   if(checkBoxOne.isSelected())                                40
      output.append("Check Box One Switched on\n");            41
   else                                                        42
      output.append("Check Box One Switched off\n");           43
```

```
                                                                 44
    if(checkBoxTwo.isSelected())                                 45
        output.append("Check Box Two Switched on\n");            46
    else                                                         47
        output.append("Check Box Two Switched off\n");           48
    } // End itemStateChanged                                    49
                                                                 50
} // End CheckBoxExample                                         51
```

Figure 7.25 shows the display when the program is started. The user has placed the mouse pointer over one of the checkboxes thus displaying the message setup using the setToolTipText method.

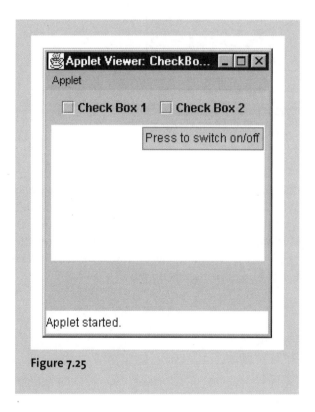

Figure 7.25

Figure 7.26 shows what happens after the user has clicked on the box beside the description Check Box 2. A tick mark appears in the box and the itemStateChanged method has been called resulting in a message being placed in the text area.

In the second example, we have chosen not to listen to actions involving the individual checkbox objects but instead listen to a button. When the user presses the button, the actionPerformed method is called and we place statements in it which examine the state of the checkboxes. We perform tests on the checkboxes state in the

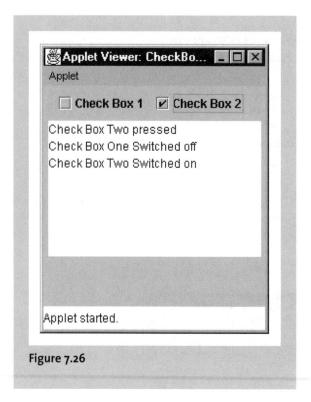

Figure 7.26

method `actionPerformed` which is the method called in response to a button click (lines 42 and 47). We can also switch a checkbox on at any point in the program by calling the `setSelected` method in the checkbox object with the value true, calling it with false will set it off. One of the checkboxes is switched on (ticked) using the `setSelected` method called with a value of true (line 21). Checkboxes can be switched on and off at any point using this method.

```
import javax.swing.*;                                    1
import java.awt.event.*;                                 2
import java.awt.*;                                       3
                                                         4
                                                         5
public class CheckBoxStateExample extends JApplet        6
implements ActionListener
{                                                        7
public JCheckBox testCheckBoxOne,testCheckBoxTwo;        8
public JTextArea output;                                 9
public JButton checkStates;                              10
                                                         11
public void init()                                       12
```

```
   {                                                        13
   // Setup the layout manager                             14
   getContentPane().setLayout(new FlowLayout());           15
                                                            16
   testCheckBoxOne = new JCheckBox("Test Check Box 1");    17
   testCheckBoxOne.setToolTipText("Press to switch on/off"); 18
                                                            19
   getContentPane().add(testCheckBoxOne);                  20
   testCheckBoxOne.setSelected(true); // Set the box to ticked 21
                                                            22
   testCheckBoxTwo = new JCheckBox("Test Check Box 2");    23
   testCheckBoxTwo.setToolTipText("Press to switch on/off"); 24
                                                            25
   getContentPane().add(testCheckBoxTwo);                  26
                                                            27
   output = new JTextArea(5,15);                           28
   getContentPane().add(output);                           29
                                                            30
   checkStates = new JButton("Check States");              31
   checkStates.setToolTipText("Press to show the states of 32
   the checkboxes");
                                                            33
   getContentPane().add(checkStates);                      34
   checkStates.addActionListener(this);                    35
   } // End init                                           36
                                                            37
public void actionPerformed(ActionEvent eventInfo)         38
   {                                                        39
   output.setText("");                                     40
                                                            41
   if(testCheckBoxOne.isSelected())                        42
      output.append("TestCheckBoxOne is selected\n");      43
   else                                                     44
      output.append("TestCheckBoxOne is not selected\n");  45
                                                            46
   if(testCheckBoxTwo.isSelected())                        47
      output.append("TestCheckBoxTwo is selected\n");      48
   else                                                     49
      output.append("TestCheckBoxTwo is not selected\n");  50
                                                            51
   output.append(" ==============\n");                     52
   } // End actionPerformed                                53
                                                            54
} // End CheckBoxStateExample                              55
```

When the program is started, the first checkbox has been switched on and so a tick appears in it (see Figure 7.27). Clicking on either checkbox will have no effect as they are not being listened to.

When the user presses the button (which is being listened to), the states of the two checkboxes are tested in `actionPerformed` and the results are printed out in the text area (see Figure 7.28 in p. 327).

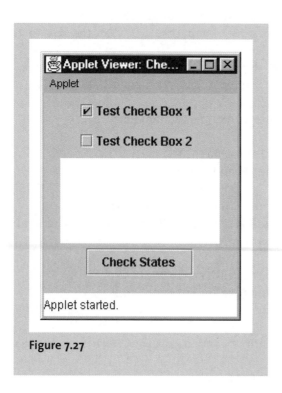

Figure 7.27

7.5.3.10　Radio button group

The next input component we look at are radio buttons. These buttons, named after radio station selection buttons, are intended to be used in a group. The rule is that only one button in the group can be switched on at a time (as you can only listen to one radio station at a time).

We create and add the radio buttons individually (they are objects of type `JRadioButton`) and then we have to add them to a group of type `ButtonGroup` in order to guarantee that only one radio button in the group will be switched on at any time. Note that the `ButtonGroup` object is not an input element and therefore is not added to the screen or listened to.

Like checkboxes you have a choice as to how you handle radio buttons, you can either listen to each one, causing the method `actionPerformed` to be executed when one is clicked, or you may not listen to any of them and use another component, such as a button, to call an event handler which will check the state of all the radio buttons. The

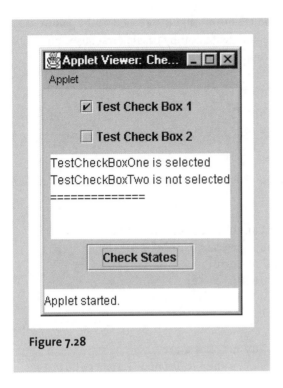

Figure 7.28

program below uses three radio buttons and adds them to the one `ButtonGroup` object (lines 26–28) and following that, to the screen (lines 31–33). The user can select whatever radio button they want and press a `JButton` when they are finished. The method `actionPerformed` is then called and the radio button states are checked. We have nested the tests for the radio buttons because we want to make sure that if no button is selected then an error message is output. The decision tree implemented in the program is shown in Figure 7.29.

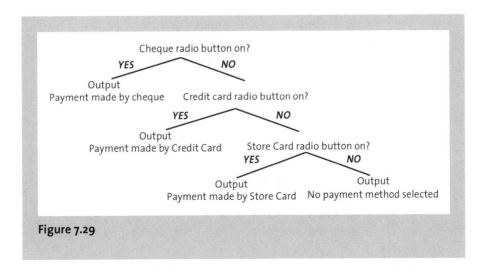

Figure 7.29

As with a checkbox, a radio button can be switched on by calling the `setSelected` method with a true value and switch off by passing it a false value. The default is that all the buttons in each group are off.

```java
import javax.swing.*;                                              1
import java.awt.event.*;                                          2
import java.awt.*;                                                3
                                                                  4
public class ButtonGroupExample extends JApplet implements        5
ActionListener
{                                                                 6
public JRadioButton cheque,creditCard,storeCard;                  7
public ButtonGroup paymentOptions;                               8
public JTextArea output;                                         9
public JButton checkStates;                                      10
                                                                 11
public void init()                                               12
   {                                                             13
   // Setup the layout manager                                  14
   getContentPane().setLayout(new FlowLayout());                15
                                                                 16
   // Create radio buttons                                      17
   cheque = new JRadioButton("Cheque");                         18
   creditCard = new JRadioButton("Credit Card");                19
   storeCard = new JRadioButton("Debit Card");                  20
                                                                 21
   // Create group object to hold radio buttons                 22
   paymentOptions = new ButtonGroup();                          23
                                                                 24
   // Add radio button objects to group                        25
   paymentOptions.add(cheque);                                  26
   paymentOptions.add(creditCard);                              27
   paymentOptions.add(storeCard);                               28
                                                                 29
   // Add radio buttons to screen                              30
   getContentPane().add(cheque);                                31
   getContentPane().add(creditCard);                            32
   getContentPane().add(storeCard);                             33
                                                                 34
   // Setup help messages for radio buttons                    35
   cheque.setToolTipText("Click to pay by cheque");             36
   creditCard.setToolTipText("Click to pay by Credit Card");    37
   storeCard.setToolTipText("Click to pay by Store Card");      38
                                                                 39
```

```
// Create and add area to display results            40
output = new JTextArea(5,15);                        41
getContentPane().add(output);                        42
                                                     43
// Create and add button which is pressed to process 44
// radio buttons                                     45
checkStates = new JButton("Process payment");        46
checkStates.setToolTipText("Press to show process the 47
payment");
                                                     48
getContentPane().add(checkStates);                   49
checkStates.addActionListener(this);                 50
} // End init                                        51
                                                     52
public void actionPerformed(ActionEvent eventInfo)   53
{                                                    54
if(cheque.isSelected())                              55
    output.append("Payment made by cheque\n");       56
else                                                 57
    {                                                58
    if(creditCard.isSelected())                      59
        output.append("Payment made by Credit Card\n"); 60
    else                                             61
        {                                            62
        if(storeCard.isSelected())                   63
            output.append("Payment made by Store Card\n"); 64
        else                                         65
            output.append("No payment method selected"); 66
        }                                            67
    } // end of else for if(CreditCard.isSelected()) 68
                                                     69
output.append(" =============\n");    // Put formatting 70
                                      // between output 71
} // End actionPerformed                             72
                                                     73
} // End ButtonGroupExample                          74
```

So, the applet starts off by displaying the radio buttons (none of which are selected) as shown in Figure 7.30 in p. 330.

Going back to the example a radio button is selected (see Figure 7.31), since the radio button is not being listened to, nothing happens if this button is selected. If you want to listen to a radio button you will have to call the `addActionListener` method in the button and set the object which will handle the event. The event will be processed in the `actionPerformed` method.

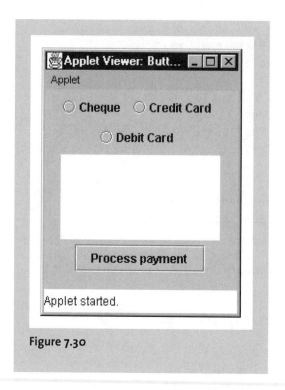

Figure 7.30

In Figure 7.31, the radio button Credit Card is now shown to be on.

Figure 7.31

The next step is to press the Process Payment button. Figure 7.32 shows the consequences of this. The actionPerformed method is called and the status of each radio button is examined. The Credit Card button is detected as being on and so the relevant output is placed in the text area.

Figure 7.32

7.5.3.11 JOptionPane

Sometimes it might be useful to open up another window to give the user a simple message. You can do this using a JOptionPane object. There are a number of different option pane types, some of which are shown in the program below.

The procedure is that first you create an object of type JOptionPane. Next, you call one of two methods in this object, either of which will result in a small window being created and the user being asked to press a button. The methods can create two types of window, one window simply presents the user with one button which the user clicks to confirm that they have seen the message. When they do this, the window closes. The method called to get this window is showMessageDialog. The method called showConfirmDialog and will open up a window which requires the user to select from a number of answers, for example, the user can select a yes or a no answer. On selecting an answer, the window is closed and an integer which corresponds to the answer is passed back to the program. The method showConfirmDialog will therefore evaluate to an integer. If the integer result is 0, then this indicates the user pressed the Yes button, if it is 1, the user pressed No. Some versions of this window also allow the user to press a button labelled Cancel which will return a value of 2.

There are four parameters required for these methods. They are (in order):

- ▶ The object which is the parent window (usually left as the value null)
- ▶ The object to display (usually a string)
- ▶ The title of the window which will be opened (a string)
- ▶ The type of message. The message type is actually represented by an integer value which indicates what sort of window to display. You can use static variables contained in the JOptionPane class to obtain the integer values for each relevant window type. The static variables we use are JOptionPane.INFORMATION_MESSAGE, JOptionPane.ERROR_MESSAGE (neither of which will return a result) and JOptionPane.YES_NO_OPTION, JOptionPane.YES_NO_CANCEL_OPTION (both of which will return an integer value).

In the following program, we use a radio button group to select the window that we want to display. There are four buttons and the four windows discussed above will appear if any of these buttons are pressed. All radio buttons are listened to (lines 33–36) and the actionPerformed method is called if a radio button is selected. We create a JOptionPane object in line 54 and use it depending on which the radio button has been selected.

The actual window opened depends on the radio button selected, two windows simply output a message and require confirmation that the user has read the message before closing the window. One of these is an information window, used to let the user know what is happening (line 64), one outputs an error message (line 59). The other two windows require the user to choose an answer, the integer which represents this answer is then returned when the window is closed, for example, line 69.

```
import javax.swing.*;                                          1
import java.awt.event.*;                                       2
import java.awt.*;                                             3
                                                               4
public class OptionGroupExample extends JApplet implements     5
ActionListener
{                                                              6
private JRadioButton errorMessage,                             7
informationMessage,yesNo,yesNoCancel;                          8
private ButtonGroup optionPaneOptions;                         9
private JTextArea output;                                     10
                                                              11
public void init()                                           12
    {                                                        13
    // Setup the layout manager                              14
```

```
getContentPane().setLayout(new FlowLayout());              15
                                                          16
// Create each radio button                               17
errorMessage = new JRadioButton("Error Message");         18
informationMessage = new JRadioButton("Information        19
Message");
yesNo = new JRadioButton("Yes/No");                       20
yesNoCancel = new JRadioButton("Yes/No/Cancel");          21
                                                          22
// Create the radio button group                          23
optionPaneOptions = new ButtonGroup();                    24
                                                          25
// Add the radio buttons to the group                     26
optionPaneOptions.add(errorMessage);                      27
optionPaneOptions.add(informationMessage);                28
optionPaneOptions.add(yesNo);                             29
optionPaneOptions.add(yesNoCancel);                       30
                                                          31
// Add the radio buttons to the screen                    32
getContentPane().add(errorMessage);                       33
getContentPane().add(informationMessage);                 34
getContentPane().add(yesNo);                              35
getContentPane().add(yesNoCancel);                        36
                                                          37
// Listen to the radio buttons                            38
errorMessage.addActionListener(this);                     39
informationMessage.addActionListener(this);               40
yesNo.addActionListener(this);                            41
yesNoCancel.addActionListener(this);                      42
                                                          43
// Create a text area to display output and add it to     44
// the screen                                             45
output = new JTextArea(5,15);                             46
getContentPane().add(output);                             47
                                                          48
} // End init                                             49
                                                          50
public void actionPerformed(ActionEvent eventInfo)        51
   {                                                       52
JOptionPane messagePane;                                  53
messagePane = new JOptionPane();                          54
output.setText(""); // Clear the output window            55
                                                          56
if(eventInfo.getSource() == errorMessage)                 57
```

```
                                                             58
        messagePane.showMessageDialog(null, "Error found!",    59
        "Error", JOptionPane.ERROR_MESSAGE);
        }                                                    60
                                                             61
    if(eventInfo.getSource() == informationMessage)          62
        {                                                    63
        messagePane.showMessageDialog(null,"Your program is   64
        working","Status",JOptionPane.INFORMATION_MESSAGE);
        }                                                    65
                                                             66
    if(eventInfo.getSource() == yesNo)                       67
        {                                                    68
        int answer=messagePane.showConfirmDialog(null,"What   69
        is your answer","Question",JOptionPane.YES_NO_OPTION);
                                                             70
        if(answer == 0)                                      71
           output.append("The answer is Yes\n");             72
        else                                                 73
           output.append("The answer is No\n");              74
        }                                                    75
                                                             76
    if(eventInfo.getSource() == yesNoCancel)                 77
        {                                                    78
        int answer = messagePane.showConfirmDialog(null,     79
        "What is your answer","Question",
        JOptionPane.YES_NO_CANCEL_OPTION);
                                                             80
        if(answer == 0)                                      81
           output.append("The answer is Yes\n");             82
        if(answer == 1)                                      83
           output.append("The answer is No\n");              84
        if(answer == 2)                                      85
           output.append("The window was cancelled\n");      86
        }                                                    87
                                                             88
    output.append("============== \n");                     89
    } // End actionPerformed                                 90
                                                             91
} // End OptionGroupExample                                  92
```

Figure 7.33 shows the applet on startup. No radio buttons have been selected.

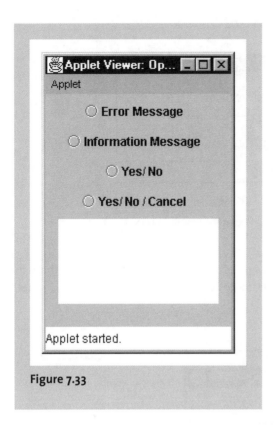

Figure 7.33

When the `Error Message` radio button is selected, `actionPerformed` is executed and the following window is opened (Figure 7.34). It outputs its message and waits for the user to dismiss it by clicking on the OK button.

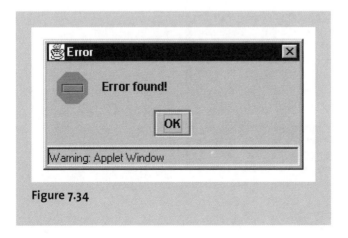

Figure 7.34

When the `Yes/No/Cancel` radio button is selected, the window is displayed, as in Figure 7.35 in p. 336. The user presses one of the three buttons and an integer value is then passed back to the program.

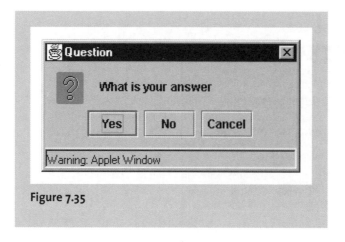

Figure 7.35

Figure 7.36 shows the result of selecting the Yes button in the window shown in Figure 7.35. The value passed back from the window is tested and relevant output is placed in the text area.

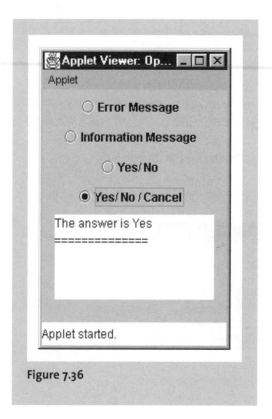

Figure 7.36

7.5.3.12   JComboBox

The JComboBox component allows the programmer to create a drop down menu of options for the user. If the component is being listened to then the selection of a menu item from the list shown will cause the `actionPerformed` method to be executed. The item which has been selected can be determined by calling the `get-SelectedItem` method in the relevant `JComboBox` object. This method will return the string which is part of the menu of options and which is selected by the user. An alternative to this method is the `getSelectedIndex` method, also contained in the `JComboBox` object, which returns an integer which indicates the position of the item in the list of options. For example, if the item selected from the menu is the first option displayed then the number returned by `getSelectedIndex` will be 0, if the item is the third then the number will be 2, and so on. This method is very useful if you want to use the option box component to select an item from an array of elements. You can simply take the number returned by `getSelectedIndex` and use it as an index for an array.

JComboBox objects are created in the usual way:

JComboBox MenuOfOptions = new JComboBox();

You can then add the menu items using the `addItem` method. `addItem` will take a string as a parameter.

MenuOfOptions.addItem("First Option");
MenuOfOptions.addItem("Second Option");

In the following program, three menu options are added to a `JComboBox` object called `PaymentMethod` (lines 19–21). This object is then added to the window. A listener is then associated with the combo box object (lines 28) and an output area is added to show the result of a selection from the menu (lines 30 and 31). In the `action-Performed` method, both the string selected from the menu by the user (obtained using the `getSelectedItem` method, line 36) and the position of that item in the menu of the combo box (obtained using the `getSelectedIndex` method, line 37) are printed out.

```
import javax.swing.*;                                            1
import java.awt.event.*;                                         2
import java.awt.*;                                               3
                                                                 4
public class JComboBoxExample extends JApplet implements         5
ActionListener
{                                                                6
private JComboBox paymentMenu;                                   7
private JTextArea output;                                        8
                                                                 9
public void init()                                              10
    {                                                           11
    // Setup the layout manager                                 12
```

```
getContentPane().setLayout(new FlowLayout());          13
                                                       14
// Create the combo box object                         15
paymentMenu = new JComboBox();                          16
                                                       17
// Add options to the combo box menu                   18
paymentMenu.addItem("Cheque");                          19
paymentMenu.addItem("Credit Card");                    20
paymentMenu.addItem("Debit Card");                     21
                                                       22
// Add the combo box object to the screen              23
getContentPane().add(paymentMenu);                     24
                                                       25
                                                       26
// Listen to the combo box                             27
paymentMenu.addActionListener(this);                   28
// Setup and add the output text area                  29
output = new JTextArea(5,15);                           30
getContentPane().add(output);                          31
} // End init                                          32
                                                       33
public void actionPerformed(ActionEvent eventInfo)     34
    {                                                  35
    output.append("\nItem selected:"                   36
    + paymentMenu.getSelectedItem());
    output.append("\nItem number item selected:"       37
    + paymentMenu.getSelectedIndex());
                                                       38
    output.append("\n==============");                 39
    } // End actionPerformed                           40
                                                       41
} // End JComboBoxExample                              42
```

The program starts off with the first option in the combobox box menu as shown in Figure 7.37.

When the user clicks the mouse pointer on the combo box object, it reveals the other menu options. The user can scroll down the options and select the one they wish, in Figure 7.38 this is the Credit Card option.

After the user clicks on the option to indicate they wish to select it, the action-Performed method is executed and that outputs the name of the option selected (Credit Card) and the number that option was on the list of choices (Credit Card was number 1, number 0 being the Cheque option). This result is shown in Figure 7.39 in p. 340.

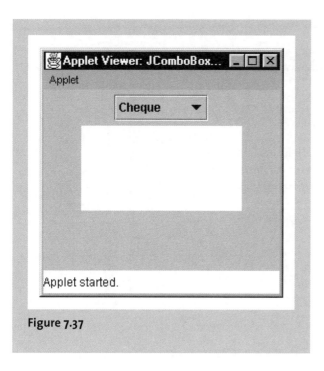

Figure 7.37

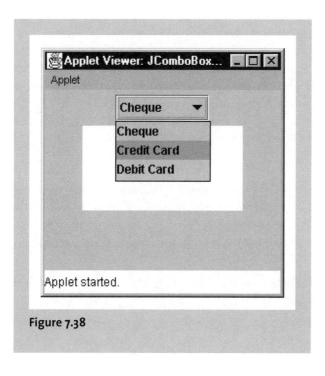

Figure 7.38

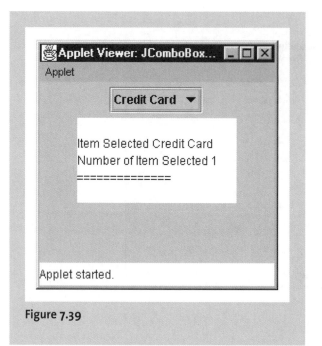

Figure 7.39

SUMMARY

An applet is a class which extends the `JApplet` class. An applet needs a specific VM which usually uses a browser window to display. When a VM loads an applet class, it automatically creates an object and executes the methods called `start`, `init` and `paint`. You should override these methods in order to customise an applet.

There are two types of graphical component object, an input element and an output element. Ouput element objects are created and added to the screen. Input elements are also created and added to the screen but they must also be associated with an object which 'listens' to them. This object will contain a method, which will be executed when an event relating to an input element occurs (e.g. when a user presses a button). This method is called an event handler.

KEYWORDS

▶ *Action* – The process that causes an event (e.g. the user pressing a button).

▶ *Component* – A class which will form part of a graphical user interface, for example, a button, text field.

▶ *Container* – The object which will hold the display that is being shown to the user, that is, the applet screen.

▶ *Event* – An occurance of user interaction with your graphical user interface (e.g. when a user presses a button).

> ▶ *Event Handler* – A method which will deal with an event, different types of event will execute different methods.
>
> ▶ *Graphical User Interface* – The screen as viewed by the user. A graphical user interface is used to show information to the user and to receive input from the user.

KEY CONCEPTS

Component name	Input/Output	Declaring	Event handler	Interface
JButton	Input	`JButton button=new JButton("label");`	`actionPerformed (ActionEvent)`	Action Listener
JTextField	Both	`JTextField text=new JTextField("contents", size); or JTextField text=new JTextField(size);`	`actionPerformed (ActionEvent)`	Action Listener
JTextArea	Output	`JTextArea output=new JTextArea("contents", height,width); or JTextArea output=new JTextArea(height, width);`	na	na
JCheckBox	Input	`JCheckBox box=new JCheckBox("label");`	`itemStateChanged (ItemEvent)`	Item Listener
JRadio Button	Input	`JRadioButton button1=new JRadioButton("label"); ButtonGroup group=new ButtonGroup();`	`actionPerformed (ActionEvent)`	Action Listener
JComboBox	Input	`JComboBox box=new JComboBox(); box.addItem ("MenuItem");`	`actionPerformed (ActionEvent)`	Action Listener

To add components to the applet window use:

getContentPane().add(componentObject);

PROJECTS

1 Write an applet which will encrypt (or disguise) a sentence so that it cannot be understood by an unauthorised reader. Your applet should also allow for the reversal of this encryption.

Your applet will contain two text fields (Uncoded and Encoded). If the user is in the Uncoded text field and presses return, then the string in that text field will be encoded and printed out in the other text field. If the user is in the Encoded text field and presses return, then the string in that text field will be decoded and printed out in the other text field.

The encryption algorithm you should use will reverse every second character in your sentence, for example, the sentence 'MY NAME IS COLIN' will become 'YMN MA ESIC LONI'.

Hints:

▶ Use `StringObject.charAt(int)` to pick out individual characters.
▶ If a string has an odd number of characters, you can add a space to make it even.

2 Write an applet which will allow two people to play the paper–rock–scissors game. In this game, two people choose from paper, rock or scissors. The rules for who wins are the following:

- Paper beats rock
- Rock beats scissors
- Scissors beats paper
- Any other situation is a draw.

The applet will display three buttons and print out whose turn it is. When player 1 presses the choice, the applet indicates that it is player 2's turn and waits for them to press the button. When both players have taken their turn, the applet prints out the winner. The turn that each player takes is not printed out until the program outputs the winner so as not to spoil the game.

3 Write a calculator applet which will perform addition, subtraction, multiplication and division on two integer values. The user will have a text field in which to enter the operator (+,–,/, *) and then the two numbers to be operated on.
Note that

▶ Your program must not allow division by zero (output an error message if the user tries this)
▶ Your program must report an error message if the user enters a non-integer (a string) instead of a number when the program expects a number
▶ Your program must report an error if the user enters a non-valid operator (e.g. %).

Hint: You will need to use the `TrainingWheels` class for this program.

4 You are required to produce an applet which has two buttons. One 'compresses' and one 'uncompresses' a sentence typed into a text area. The program replaces the following phrases with the given numbers:

▶ the = 0
▶ and = 1
▶ program = 2

So, the sentence 'The name of the program is BestBuy' would be replaced by the compressed sentence: 0 name of 0 2 is BestBuy.

Pressing the uncompress button with the above sentence will produce the original.

The user should not enter any numerals as part of their message as this will affect the uncompression part, if they do, it will output an error message.

Hint: Remember `String.indexOf(substring)` returns the position of a substring and `charAt(index)` returns the character at the given index.

5 Write an applet which will check for a username–password combination. The applet will return the following messages in a status window.

Circumstance	Error message
Username is not in the list	Error: User not found
Password is incorrect	Error: Incorrect Password
Username and Password are correct	Access granted
Username omitted	Error: No user name supplied
Password omitted	Error: No password supplied

Example Password/Name set to be used:

Username	Password
Sue	abc
Joe	xyz

Warning: watch your capitalisation when testing.

6 Write an applet that will take integer values as input and will draw a graph of those values. Each time a value is input, the next part of the graph is drawn. If the value input is less than the last value input, then the colour of the line is red; if it is greater, then the line is green; if it's equal, then the line colour is black.

Solutions to exercises and interactive exercises can be obtained at:
http://www.palgrave.com/resources

Chapter

8

Applications

INTRODUCTION

This chapter is a continuation of the user interface discussion of Chapter 7. It contains an introduction to applications and discusses how to create a GUI for applications. It also explains some advanced GUI component material. Remember that the material presented in these chapters is a subset of the available resources that Java has to offer. For more advanced textbooks see the bibliography at the end of this book.

Finally, the `TrainingWheels` class used in the earlier chapters is discussed.

8.1   APPLICATIONS AND APPLETS

In this chapter, we discuss how to create a GUI for an application. Applications, as you have seen, are distinctly different to applets in the way they start up and are used. Applications also have some differences as regards setting up the window which will hold the components you were introduced to in Chapter 7 and this chapter.

8.2   CREATING APPLICATIONS: FRAME

In Chapter 7, we discussed how to write an application that is non-graphical, that is, it just output results to the console window.

Applications are slightly different to applets in the way they are written. Applets have some of the necessary work done for them by the VM and the OS, for example, they are provided with a window to display in. Another facility offered to applets is that an object is automatically created from an applet class definition by the VM and certain specific methods (`init`, `start`, `paint`) are then called by the VM. This gives entry points (methods where execution starts) for the applet. Applications do not have these niceties and so you have to define your own window and call your own entry point methods.

About the only thing the VM will do for an application class is to call the static method `main`. It will not automatically create an object of the application class and it will not create a window for the elements to be added to. You must do that using instructions in the application. We can place these instructions in the `main` method or we can use the `main` method to cause these instructions to be executed. The second approach is the more common for large programs, since if you put all your instructions in the `main` method, your program becomes difficult to read. The first thing we need to do to use a method other than `main` is to create an object of an application class. Methods other than `main` can then be called and global variables can be used. Remember when the VM starts executing the `main` method in the class, no other methods are accessible (unless they are declared as static, which should never be done unless there is a convincing reason for doing so). For example, to access the other methods defined in the class below (`setupUI`, `displayResults`), an object of the class `ApplicationClass` must be created so that these methods 'exist' and can be executed.

```
public class ApplicationClass                               1
{                                                           2
                                                            3
public void setupUI()                                       4
    {                                                       5
    //Code for setupUI                                      6
    displayResults();                                       7
    }                                                       8
                                                            9
public void displayResults()                               10
    {                                                       11
    // Code for displayResults                              12
    }                                                       13
                                                           14
public static void main(String parameterArray[])           15
    {                                                       16
    ApplicationClass applicationObject=new ApplicationClass();  17
    applicationObject.setupUI();                            18
    } // End main                                           19
                                                           20
} // End ApplicationClass                                  21
```

You can see in the above example that the only instruction in the main method causes an object to be declared and created. That object is of type Application-Class, the class which contains the main method which is creating the object. You may think this is a strange thing to do but think about it for a moment. You know that the only method called in the ApplicationClass when it is started is main. You know that to get an object of the class type created, you must declare and create it in the main method as there is no other part of the program executed. Once the object is created, you can then call methods in it or you can attach it to the VM via a window. So, for example, in the above program once the object of type application class has been created, the method setupUI (line 18) can be called which in turn calls displayResults.

8.2.1 JFrame

The next step is to create a window to display elements setup in the application. A window in an application is an object of type JFrame. So, somewhere we must create an object of type JFrame. We can either create it in the main method or, since we are already creating an object in the main method, we can create it in the constructor for that object. In the example below, the window is created in the constructor for that object.

```
import javax.swing.*;                                          1
                                                               2
public class ApplicationClass                                  3
{                                                              4
                                                               5
private JFrame window;                                         6
                                                               7
public ApplicationClass()                                      8
    {                                                          9
    window = new JFrame();                                     10
    } // End applicationClass constructor                     11
                                                               12
public static void main(String parameterArray[])              13
    {                                                          14
    ApplicationClass applicationObject = new ApplicationClass();  15
    } // End main                                             16
                                                               17
} // End ApplicationClass                                      18
```

Hint: Always pay careful attention to the object being created in the main method. The system doesn't care what object it creates, so sometimes if you copy code and reuse it but forget to change the name of the class used to create the object, you may setup an object which has no relevance at all to the program. This can result in much confusion.

EXAMPLE   The following program is an example of an incorrect alteration of the class just discussed. The code will compile just fine as it contains no syntax errors. It does however contain a logical error in the statement at line 14. This statement creates an object from a class called ApplicationClass, not the class called ApplicationClassVersion2 which it should have declared. Every time the user runs this program, it will therefore start up another program the object of which it has obtained from the definition of ApplicationClass.

```
import javax.swing.*;                                          1
                                                               2
public class ApplicationClassVersion2                          3
{                                                              4
private JFrame window;                                         5
```

```
                                                                6
    public ApplicationClassVersion2()                            7
        {                                                        8
        window = new JFrame();                                   9
        } // End applicationClassVersion2 constructor           10
                                                                11
    public static void main(String parameterArray[])            12
        {                                                       13
        ApplicationClass applicationObject = new ApplicationClass();  14
        } // End main                                           15
                                                                16
    } // End ApplicationClassVersion2                           17
```

Applications continued

The ApplicationClass example discussed prior to the program above will create the window object, but if you type in the program and run it, you will not see any window. The reason for this is that to display a window in an application you need to tell the VM to show the window. One way to do this is by calling the show method in the window object. So, the complete version of the constructor will be:

```
public ApplicationClass()
{
window=new JFrame();
window.show();
}
```

If you change your ApplicationClass program constructor to the above, you will see a window. We are not quite done yet as the window shown will be extremely small. This is because no size has been set for the window. So, again you need to call a method in the window object. This method is called setSize and will take the *x* and *y* dimensions of the window (in pixels).

```
public ApplicationClass()
{
window = new JFrame();
// Make the window 200 pixels wide and 100 pixels high
window.setSize(200,100);
window.show();
}
```

Now you will see an empty window displayed. You can set the title of the window by using the JFrame constructor and supplying a string, for example,

```
window=new JFrame("My Program");
```

This will set the window title to be the string "My Program" as shown in Figure 8.1.

Figure 8.1

You could have put the JFrame window setup statements into a different method but it is common to see them in the constructor.

8.2.1.1   Adding components to a JFrame

Next let's look at an example where we add some input and output elements to the frame just created. As with an applet we need to change the flow layout for the display area (the object called window in the example below), but unlike an applet, we use the name of the JFrame object (called window in the example program below) anytime we want to refer to the display the user sees (setSize, adding elements, etc.). In the following example, we add a button and a textfield to a display area. We use an object of type HandleButtonClass to process any events relating to the button (i.e. someone pressing it). An object of class HandleButtonClass will be created with the text field object passed as a parameter, so the program object and the Handle-ButtonClass object will share the same text field, called output. The object of type HandleButtonClass will use this text field object to output the current value of a counter variable which is increased each time someone presses a button.

Notice that in line 30, the call to the show method is at the very end of the method. This is because we want to wait until all the elements are added to the screen before we make it appear. To make any elements added after show is called visible to the user, you should call the validate method (window.validate();). If you call the show or validate methods before you have finished adding the elements they may not appear on the window displayed to the user.

The function of the following program is to create a frame, add a button and a text field to it and setup an object to handle the button being pressed. This event handler object will be passed the reference to the text field so it has somewhere to display its result (which is the number of times the button has been pressed).

```
import javax.swing.*;                                          1
import java.awt.*;                                             2
import java.awt.event.*;                                       3
                                                              4
public class ApplicationInputExample                          5
{                                                             6
                                                              7
private JFrame window;                                        8
private HandleButtonClass handleButtonObject;                 9
private JTextField output;                                   10
private JButton pressMe;                                     11
                                                             12
public ApplicationInputExample()                             13
   {                                                         14
   window = new JFrame("My Program");                        15
   // Make the window 100 pixels wide and 200 pixels high    16
   window.setSize(200,200);                                  17
                                                             18
   window.getContentPane().setLayout(new FlowLayout());      19
                                                             20
   output = new JTextField(15);                              21
   window.getContentPane().add(output);                      22
                                                             23
   pressMe = new JButton("Press Me");                        24
   window.getContentPane().add(pressMe);                     25
                                                             26
   handleButtonObject = new HandleButtonClass(output);       27
   pressMe.addActionListener(handleButtonObject);            28
                                                             29
   window.show();// Dont forget to put this at the end       30
   } // End applicationInputExample constructor              31
                                                             32
public static void main(String parameterArray[])             33
   {                                                         34
   ApplicationInputExample applicationInputExampleObject=new  35
   ApplicationInputExample();
   } // End main                                             36
} // End ApplicationInputExample                             37
                                                             38
                                                             39
class HandleButtonClass implements ActionListener            40
{                                                            41
private int timesPressed;                                    42
```

```
   private JTextField output;                                 43
                                                              44
   public HandleButtonClass(JTextField outputSupplied)        45
      {                                                       46
      output = outputSupplied;                                47
      timesPressed = 0;                                       48
      } // End handleTextFieldClass                           49
                                                              50
   public void actionPerformed(ActionEvent eventObject)       51
      {                                                       52
      timesPressed++ ;                                        53
      output.setText("Button pressed "+timesPressed+" times");  54
      } // End actionPerformed                                55
                                                              56
   } // End HandleButtonClass                                 57
```

So, when you run the above application, the window will appear as shown in Figure 8.2 with the title My Program.

Figure 8.2

After you press the button, the event handler object will output in the text field how many times the button has been pressed (see Figure 8.3 in p.352).

8.2.2 Window listeners

Since we have created a new window, we should listen to this window and deal with any relevant events. In an applet, this is done for us since a window is usually inside a browser

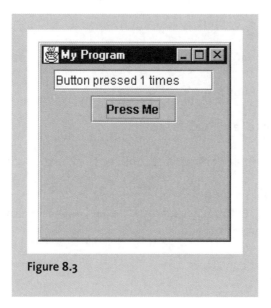

Figure 8.3

but for an application we need to associate any window we create with an object which will contain methods to process window related events, such as the user closing the window, the window being minimised, moved, and so on. If you do not put in place code to process window events, then nothing will be done in response to window events. For example, clicking on the windows close button will not close the window. To close a window and terminate a program, you use the instruction `System.exit(0)`. This instruction tells the VM to terminate all parts of the program it is currently executing which results in the window closing. If you do not want to stop the program but want the window to disappear, then use the `setVisible` method, discussed later in Section 8.3.1.

There follows two examples of programs which deal with window closing events. One example uses a separate class to process the window events. The other example simply implements the window closing interface, called `WindowListener`, in the main application.

Note that in both examples there are several methods without any contents in their body, for example, `windowClosed`. They are left without code because we do not want to do anything in response to these events. Why then are these methods there at all? Well, the interface `WindowListener` states that these methods must be in any class which implements the interface `WindowListener`, so the compiler needs to see them. Whether they contain any code or not is of no importance, they must be present so that the code is in agreement with the interface used.

The command used to listen to a particular frame is:

JFrameObject.addWindowListener(ObjectWhichImplements WindowListener);

The following program is an example of using a separate class to handle window events.

```java
import javax.swing.*;                                              1
import java.awt.*;                                                 2
import java.awt.event.*;                                           3
                                                                   4
public class WindowClosingClassExample                            5
{                                                                  6
private JFrame window;                                             7
private WindowListenerClass windowListenerObject;                 8
                                                                   9
public WindowClosingClassExample()                               10
    {                                                             11
    window = new JFrame("My Program");                           12
    // Make the window 100 pixels wide and 200 pixels high       13
    window.setSize(100,200);                                     14
    window.show();                                               15
                                                                 16
    // Setup an object which handles the window event           17
    windowListenerObject = new WindowListenerClass();            18
                                                                 19
    // Associate the frame with the window listener object      20
    window.addWindowListener(windowListenerObject);             21
    } // End WindowClosingClassExample constructor              22
                                                                 23
public static void main(String parameterArray[])                24
    {                                                             25
    WindowClosingClassExample applicationObject = new           26
    WindowClosingClassExample();
    } // End main                                               27
                                                                 28
} // End WindowClosingClassExample                              29
                                                                 30
class WindowListenerClass implements WindowListener             31
{                                                                 32
// Stop the program if the window is closed                     33
public void windowClosing(WindowEvent e) {System.exit(0);}     34
public void windowClosed(WindowEvent e) {}                     35
public void windowOpened(WindowEvent e) {}                     36
public void windowIconified(WindowEvent e) {}                  37
public void windowDeiconified(WindowEvent e) {}               38
public void windowActivated(WindowEvent e) {}                 39
public void windowDeactivated(WindowEvent e) {}              40
                                                                 41
} // End WindowListenerClass                                    42
```

The following program is an example of handling the window events in the same class as the program.

```
import javax.swing.*;                                               1
import java.awt.*;                                                  2
import java.awt.event.*;                                            3
                                                                    4
public class WindowClosingExample implements WindowListener         5
{                                                                   6
                                                                    7
private JFrame window;                                              8
                                                                    9
public WindowClosingExample()                                      10
   {                                                               11
   window = new JFrame("My Program");                              12
   // Make the window 100 pixels wide and 200 pixels high          13
   window.setSize(100,200);                                        14
   window.show();                                                  15
                                                                   16
   window.addWindowListener(this);                                 17
   } // End WindowClosingExample constructor                       18
                                                                   19
public static void main(String parameterArray[])                   20
   {                                                               21
   WindowClosingExample applicationObject = new                    22
   WindowClosingExample();
   } // End main                                                   23
                                                                   24
public void windowClosing(WindowEvent e) {System.exit(0);}         25
public void windowClosed(WindowEvent e) {}                         26
public void windowOpened(WindowEvent e) {}                         27
public void windowIconified(WindowEvent e) {}                      28
public void windowDeiconified(WindowEvent e) {}                    29
public void windowActivated(WindowEvent e) {}                      30
public void windowDeactivated(WindowEvent e) {}                    31
                                                                   32
} // End WindowClosingExample                                      33
```

8.3 CHANGING THE USER INTERFACE

Sometimes you may wish to add and remove elements to and from the screen. You can add and remove elements at will by using the setVisible method which is contained in most GUI objects. By calling the setVisible method of any component with a boolean value of true, you are indicating that that element should be displayed on the screen; by supplying the parameter false, you are indicating that the element should be hidden from view. If an element is hidden, the object will still exist so you can put information into it (e.g. `setText` for a text field or a text area), you just cannot see it, or its contents, on the screen.

8.3.1 Applet example

In the applet example below, you can choose between two user interfaces using a button. One user interface consists of a text area (declared in line 32), the other user interface shows two text fields (lines 35 and 36). The applet starts off displaying both user interfaces. When the user presses the relevant button, one user interface appears and the other disappears. This is accomplished using the `setVisible` method in the elements which belong to each user interface. Two methods, `displayUIOne` (line 66) and `displayUITwo` (line 86) are called with the state of their relevant user interface, that is, when user interface one is required, `displayUIOne` is called with a value of true (which makes its elements visible) and `displayUITwo` is called with a value of false (which hides its elements).

```
import javax.swing.*;                                            1
import java.awt.event.*;                                         2
import java.awt.*;                                               3
                                                                 4
                                                                 5
public class AppletChangeUI extends JApplet implements          6
ActionListener
{                                                                7
private JButton chooseUIOne,chooseUITwo;                         8
                                                                 9
private JTextArea textAreaUIOne;                                10
private JTextField textFieldOneUITwo,textFieldTwoUITwo;         11
private JOptionPane messagePane;                                12
                                                                13
public void init()                                              14
    {                                                           15
    getContentPane().setLayout(new FlowLayout());               16
                                                                17
    // Setup the buttons used to select each user interface    18
    chooseUIOne = new JButton("Select UI One");                 19
    chooseUITwo = new JButton("Select UI Two");                 20
                                                                21
    // Add button objects to screen                            22
    getContentPane().add(chooseUIOne);                          23
    getContentPane().add(chooseUITwo);                          24
```

```
                                                                    25
    // Listen to button objects                                     26
    chooseUIOne.addActionListener(this);                            27
    chooseUITwo.addActionListener(this);                            28
                                                                    29
    // Setup elements of user interface one (one textarea)          30
    textAreaUIOne = new JTextArea("",5,15);                         31
                                                                    32
    // Setup elements of user interface two (two textfields)        33
    textFieldOneUITwo = new JTextField("",10);                      34
    textFieldTwoUITwo = new JTextField("",10);                      35
                                                                    36
    // Add all the elements of both user interfaces to the screen   37
    getContentPane().add(textFieldOneUITwo);                        38
    getContentPane().add(textFieldTwoUITwo);                        39
    getContentPane().add(textAreaUIOne);                            40
                                                                    41
    // Create a JOptionPane object to tell the user what is happening 42
    messagePane = new JOptionPane();                                43
    } // End init                                                   44
                                                                    45
public void actionPerformed(ActionEvent eventInfo)                  46
    {                                                               47
    // If the button pressed indicates user interface one then call 48
    // the relevant methods                                         49
    if(eventInfo.getSource() == chooseUIOne)                        50
        {                                                           51
        displayUIOne(true);                                        52
        displayUITwo(false);                                       53
        }                                                           54
                                                                    55
    if(eventInfo.getSource() == chooseUITwo)                        56
        {                                                           57
        displayUIOne(false);                                       58
        displayUITwo(true);                                        59
        }                                                           60
                                                                    61
    } // End actionPerformed                                       62
                                                                    63
// This method will show or hide the elements of user interface one 64
// depending on the value of state                                  65
public void displayUIOne(boolean state)                             66
    {                                                               67
    String messageToDisplay;                                        68
                                                                    69
```

```
   if(state)                                          70
      messageToDisplay="UI One selected";             71
   else                                               72
      messageToDisplay="UI One not selected";         73
                                                      74
   displayMessageWindow(messageToDisplay);            75
                                                      76
   // Show or hide the element                        77
   textAreaUIOne.setVisible(state);                   78
                                                      79
   // Refresh the window                              80
   validate();                                        81
   } // End displayUIOne                              82
                                                      83
// This method will show or hide the elements of user interface two   84
// depending on the value of state                    85
public void displayUITwo(boolean state)               86
   {                                                  87
   String messageToDisplay;                           88
                                                      89
   if(state)                                          90
      messageToDisplay="UI Two selected";             91
   else                                               92
      messageToDisplay="UI Two not selected";         93
                                                      94
   // Tell the user whats happening                   95
   displayMessageWindow(messageToDisplay);            96
                                                      97
   // Show or hide the elements                       98
   textFieldOneUITwo.setVisible(state);               99
   textFieldTwoUITwo.setVisible(state);               100
                                                      101
   // Refresh the window                              102
   validate();                                        103
   } // End displayUITwo                              104
                                                      105
public void displayMessageWindow(String messageToDisplay)  106
   {// Open a message window and output the string supplied  107
   messagePane.showMessageDialog(null,messageToDisplay,  108
   "Status",JOptionPane.INFORMATION_MESSAGE);
   } // End displayMessageWindow                      109
                                                      110
} // End AppletChangeUI                                111
                                                      112
```

You can see how the applet executes by examining the screenshots below.

In Figure 8.4, you see what appears when the applet is first run. All the elements are displayed on the screen. This is because when you create an element, it is visible by default. You could have hidden the elements by setting their visibility state to false in the `init` method (i.e. call their `setVisible` method with false as a parameter).

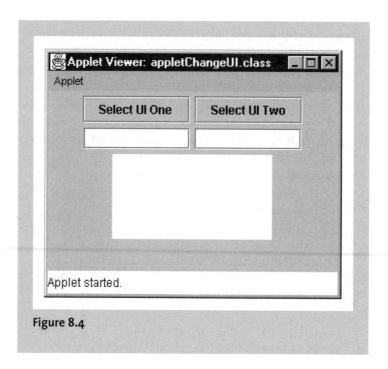

Figure 8.4

When the user presses the `Select UI One` button, the `actionPerformed` method is called. Since the `getSource` test will match the cause of the event with the `Select UI One` button, the method `displayUIOne` will be called with a true value which causes all the elements in UI one (the text area) to have their visible state set to true (which is already is). The method `displayUITwo` is called with a false value which causes all the elements in UI two (the two text fields) to have their visible state set to false, so they disappear. The call to the `validate` method at the end of both of these methods causes the screen to refresh so that any elements which have been switched off will be removed from view. You should always call the `validate` method after changing the user interface.

A message window is also opened in each `displayUI` method to inform the user what is happening. The message windows are shown in Figures 8.5 and 8.6.

After these message windows are closed, the applet shows the result of the selection of one user interface (Figure 8.7).

To remove the text area element, you just need to hit the `Select UI Two` button and the two text fields will replace the text area as shown in Figure 8.8 in p. 360.

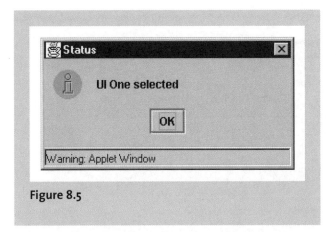

Figure 8.5

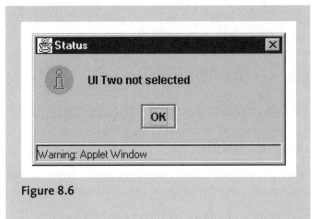

Figure 8.6

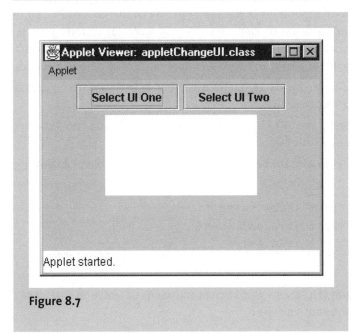

Figure 8.7

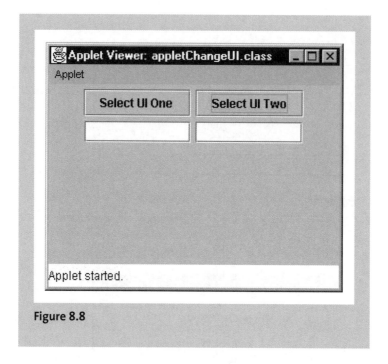

Figure 8.8

8.3.2 Application example

Next, we look at a program which produces much the same output as the one above but is in application form. To change an applet to application form, we do the following:

1 Replace `extends JApplet` with `extends JFrame` (line 6). When an object of your application is created in the `main` method a `JFrame` object will also be created since your class inherits a `JFrame`. Therefore, your program object will be associated with a `JFrame` object, and the `JFrame` object methods can be used without having to reference a specific `JFrame` object (e.g. lines 16, 17 and 41).

2 Change the `init` method so that it becomes a constructor for the application object (line 14).

3 Setup the `JFrame` object (lines 16 and 17) and show the window (line 41) in the `constructor` method.

4 Put in a `main` method and have it create an object of the program class (line 44).

```
import javax.swing.*;                                          1
import java.awt.event.*;                                       2
import java.awt.*;                                             3
                                                               4
                                                               5
public class ApplicationChangeUI extends JFrame implements     6
ActionListener
```

```
{                                                              7
private JButton chooseUIOne,chooseUITwo;                       8
                                                               9
private JTextArea textAreaUIOne;                              10
private JTextField textFieldOneUITwo,textFieldTwoUITwo;       11
private JOptionPane messagePane;                             12
                                                              13
public ApplicationChangeUI()                                  14
    {                                                         15
    super("Change UI"); // Setup the JFrame object inherited  16
    setSize(200,300);                                         17
                                                              18
    getContentPane().setLayout(new FlowLayout());             19
                                                              20
    chooseUIOne = new JButton("Select UI One");               21
    chooseUITwo = new JButton("Select UI Two");               22
                                                              23
    getContentPane().add(chooseUIOne);                        24
    getContentPane().add(chooseUITwo);                        25
                                                              26
    chooseUIOne.addActionListener(this);                      27
    chooseUITwo.addActionListener(this);                      28
                                                              29
    textFieldOneUITwo = new JTextField(10);                   30
    textFieldTwoUITwo = new JTextField(10);                   31
                                                              32
    textAreaUIOne = new JTextArea(5,15);                      33
                                                              34
    getContentPane().add(textFieldOneUITwo);                  35
    getContentPane().add(textFieldTwoUITwo);                  36
    getContentPane().add(textAreaUIOne);                      37
                                                              38
    messagePane = new JOptionPane();                          39
                                                              40
    show();// Show the window                                 41
    } // End applicationChangeUI constructor                  42
                                                              43
public static void main(String parameterArray[])              44
    { // Create an object of the application                  45
    Application ChangeUI application=new ApplicationChangeUI();46
    } // End main                                             47
                                                              48
public void actionPerformed(ActionEvent eventInfo)            49
    {                                                         50
```

```
        if(eventInfo.getSource()==chooseUIOne)          51
           {                                            52
           displayUIOne(true);                          53
           displayUITwo(false);                         54
           }                                            55
                                                        56
        if(eventInfo.getSource()==chooseUITwo)          57
           {                                            58
           displayUIOne(false);                         59
           displayUITwo(true);                          60
           }                                            61
                                                        62
        } // End actionPerformed                        63
                                                        64
    public void displayUIOne(boolean state)             65
       {                                                66
       String messageToDisplay;                         67
                                                        68
       if(state)                                         69
          messageToDisplay="UI One selected";           70
       else                                              71
          messageToDisplay = "UI One not selected";     72
                                                        73
       displayMessageWindow(messageToDisplay);          74
                                                        75
       textAreaUIOne.setVisible(state);                 76
                                                        77
       validate();                                       78
       } // End displayUIOne                            79
                                                        80
    public void displayUITwo(boolean state)             81
       {                                                82
       String messageToDisplay;                         83
                                                        84
       if(state)                                         85
          messageToDisplay = "UI Two selected";         86
       else                                              87
          messageToDisplay = "UI Two not selected";     88
                                                        89
       displayMessageWindow(messageToDisplay);          90
                                                        91
       textFieldOneUITwo.setVisible(state);             92
       textFieldTwoUITwo.setVisible(state);             93
                                                        94
```

```
          validate();                                           95
       } // End displayUITwo                                    96
                                                                97
   public void displayMessageWindow(String messageToDisplay)    98
       {                                                        99
       messagePane.showMessageDialog(null,messageToDisplay,     100
       "Status",JOptionPane.INFORMATION_MESSAGE);
       } // displayMessageWindow                                101
                                                                102
   } // End ApplicationChangeUI                                 103
```

8.3.3 Multiple frames

In an application, we can have multiple frames instead of just one. We rewrite the above program to use three different frames, one frame to hold the buttons and two user interface frames which will be displayed if the user selects them via the buttons. One frame is inherited in the program class (`ApplicationChangeFrame`) itself and the other two are declared in the program. We can now add the user interface elements to their appropriate frames. The main program's frame has the buttons added to it (this is the frame which the main program forms a part of) in lines 23 and 24. The other two frames (`frameOne` and `frameTwo`) are created in the constructor but are not displayed (lines 29 and 30), that is, their show methods are not called. The parts of each user interface are added to their respective frames. When a user interface is selected via clicking a button, the frame itself has its visibility state changed using the `displayUI` methods. Changing the visibility of the frame to true will automatically show the frame, that is, there is no need to call the `show` method in the two user interface frames. This example, when the frames which contain all the elements are hidden and shown, differs to the previous examples where each element's visibility has been changed. It makes it easier to handle groups of elements in a single component, like a frame, rather than have to deal with multiple single elements.

Notice in lines 35 and 36 that we need to change the layout manager in the two frame objects that we created. We do this by putting the name of the frame object before the `getContentPane().setLayout(new FlowLayout())` instruction. This calls the `getContentPane` method in each of the relevant frames and changes that frame's layout manager.

```
   import javax.swing.*;                                        1
   import java.awt.event.*;                                     2
   import java.awt.*;                                           3
                                                                4
   public class ApplicationChangeFrame extends JFrame           5
   implements ActionListener
```

```
{                                                              6
private JButton chooseUIOne,chooseUITwo;                       7
private JTextArea textAreaUIOne;                               8
private JTextField textFieldOneUITwo,textFieldTwoUITwo;        9
private JoptionPane messagePane;                              10
private JFrame frameOne,frameTwo;                             11
                                                             12
public ApplicationChangeFrame()                              13
   {                                                         14
   super("Change UI");                                       15
   setSize(200,100);                                         16
                                                             17
   getContentPane().setLayout(new FlowLayout());             18
                                                             19
   chooseUIOne = new JButton("Select UI One");               20
   chooseUITwo = new JButton("Select UI Two");               21
                                                             22
   getContentPane().add(chooseUIOne);                        23
   getContentPane().add(chooseUITwo);                        24
                                                             25
   chooseUIOne.addActionListener(this);                      26
   chooseUITwo.addActionListener(this);                      27
                                                             28
   frameOne = new JFrame("User interface one");              29
   frameTwo = new JFrame("User interface two");              30
                                                             31
   frameOne.setSize(200,200);                                32
   frameTwo.setSize(200,200);                                33
                                                             34
   frameOne.getContentPane().setLayout(new FlowLayout());    35
   frameTwo.getContentPane().setLayout(new FlowLayout());    36
                                                             37
   textFieldOneUITwo = new JTextField(10);                   38
   textFieldTwoUITwo = new JTextField(10);                   39
                                                             40
   textAreaUIOne = new JTextArea(5,15);                      41
                                                             42
   frameTwo.getContentPane().add(textFieldOneUITwo);         43
   frameTwo.getContentPane().add(textFieldTwoUITwo);         44
   frameOne.getContentPane().add(textAreaUIOne);             45
                                                             46
   messagePane = new JOptionPane();                          47
   show();                                                   48
   } // End ApplicationChangeFrame constructor               49
```

```
public static void main(String parameterArray[])           50
    {                                                      51
    ApplicationChangeFrame application = new               52
    ApplicationChangeFrame();
    } // End main                                          53
                                                           54
public void actionPerformed(ActionEvent eventInfo)         55
    {                                                      56
    if(eventInfo.getSource() == chooseUIOne)               57
        {                                                  58
        displayUIOne(true);                                59
        displayUITwo(false);                               60
        }                                                  61
                                                           62
    if(eventInfo.getSource() == chooseUITwo)               63
        {                                                  64
        displayUIOne(false);                               65
        displayUITwo(true);                                66
        }                                                  67
                                                           68
    } // End actionPerformed                               69
                                                           70
public void displayUIOne(boolean state)                    71
    {                                                      72
    String messageToDisplay;                               73
                                                           74
    if(state)                                              75
        messageToDisplay = "UI One selected";              76
    else                                                   77
        messageToDisplay = "UI One not selected";          78
                                                           79
    displayMessageWindow(messageToDisplay);                80
                                                           81
    frameOne.setVisible(state);                            82
    } // End displayUIOne                                  83
                                                           84
public void displayUITwo(boolean state)                    85
    {                                                      86
    String messageToDisplay;                               87
                                                           88
    if(state)                                              89
        messageToDisplay = "UI Two selected";              90
    else                                                   91
        messageToDisplay = "UI Two not selected";          92
```

```
        displayMessageWindow(messageToDisplay);              93
                                                             94
        frameTwo.setVisible(state);                          95
        } // End displayUITwo                                96
                                                             97
    public void displayMessageWindow(String messageToDisplay)  98
        {                                                    99
        messagePane.showMessageDialog(null,messageToDisplay,  100
        "Status",JOptionPane.INFORMATION_MESSAGE);
        } // displayMessageWindow                            101
                                                             102
    } // End ApplicationChangeFrame                          103
```

8.4   PANELS

In the above example, we are able to group GUI components into a frame and then hide and show that frame. Frames are not always suitable for all circumstances but it will be handy to have a mechanism for grouping GUI components into one single component which can be manipulated. Panels are another way of grouping GUI input and output components. A JPanel object is created and various GUI objects are added to the panel. These GUI objects are now grouped together in the panel so they do not need to be added individually to the screen. You need only to add the panel that contains these elements. The example applet below uses two panel objects (UIOne and UITwo) to contain the objects associated with user interfaces one and two. These panels are then hidden or shown in response to the setVisible method in the panel being called with true or false.

Syntax for panels:

Create a panel

JPanel panelObject = new JPanel();

Add a GUI input/output object to a panel

panelObject.add(GUIObject);

You can listen to the GUI objects that have been added to the panel and the mechanism for listening remains the same. The purpose of the panel is simply to provide a facility to store references to GUI objects in a common object to simplify the process of showing and hiding the elements.

```
    import javax.swing.*;                                    1
    import java.awt.event.*;                                 2
    import java.awt.*;                                       3
```

```
                                                                    4
public class AppletPanelExample extends JApplet implements          5
ActionListener
    {                                                               6
    private JButton chooseUIOne,chooseUITwo;                        7
    private JButton buttonUIOne;                                    8
    private JTextArea textAreaUIOne;                                9
    private JTextField textFieldOneUITwo,textFieldTwoUITwo;        10
    private JPanel UIOne,UITwo;                                    11
                                                                   12
public void init()                                                 13
    {                                                              14
    getContentPane().setLayout(new FlowLayout());                 15
                                                                   16
    chooseUIOne = new JButton("Select UI One");                   17
    chooseUITwo = new JButton("Select UI Two");                   18
                                                                   19
    getContentPane().add(chooseUIOne);                            20
    getContentPane().add(chooseUITwo);                            21
                                                                   22
    chooseUIOne.addActionListener(this);                          23
    chooseUITwo.addActionListener(this);                          24
                                                                   25
    textFieldOneUITwo = new JTextField(10);                       26
    textFieldTwoUITwo = new JTextField(10);                       27
                                                                   28
    textAreaUIOne = new JTextArea(5,15);                          29
    buttonUIOne = new JButton("Dummy button");                    30
                                                                   31
    UIOne = new JPanel();                                         32
    UITwo = new JPanel();                                         33
                                                                   34
    UIOne.add(textAreaUIOne);                                     35
    UIOne.add(buttonUIOne);                                       36
                                                                   37
    UITwo.add(textFieldOneUITwo);                                 38
    UITwo.add(textFieldTwoUITwo);                                 39
                                                                   40
    UIOne.setVisible(false);                                      41
    UITwo.setVisible(false);                                      42
                                                                   43
    getContentPane().add(UIOne);                                 44
    getContentPane().add(UITwo);                                 45
    } // End init                                                 46
```

```
public void actionPerformed(ActionEvent eventInfo)    47
                                                       48
  {                                                    49
  if(eventInfo.getSource() == chooseUIOne)             50
    {                                                  51
    UIOne.setVisible(true);                            52
    UITwo.setVisible(false);                           53
    }                                                  54
                                                       55
  if(eventInfo.getSource() ==chooseUITwo)              56
    {                                                  57
    UIOne.setVisible(false);                           58
    UITwo.setVisible(true);                            59
    }                                                  60
                                                       61
  validate();                                          62
  } // End actionPerformed                             63
                                                       64
} // End AppletPanelExample                            65
```

8.5 LAYOUT MANAGERS

We have briefly discussed the idea of a layout manager. A layout manager is an object which is responsible for arranging GUI components on the screen. We have used the FlowLayout object up to this point which arranges elements from left to right filling all available space on a 'line' before moving to the next 'line' on the screen. Now we take a look at two other layout managers that have a different system of arranging components on the screen. The managers that we look at are BorderLayout and GridLayout. There are other layout managers available but these are not discussed in this book.

8.5.1 Border layout

A border layout manager allows you to place your elements in one of five distinct areas of the screen:

1 North (top of screen)

2 South

3 East

4 West

5 Center (surrounded by the n,s,e and w elements)

`BorderLayout` is the default layout manager used in `JApplet` and `JFrame` and we changed from this layout manager to the `FlowLayout` manager in our examples. If you change the layout manager from `BorderLayout` (which is the default) and need to change back, the syntax is:

setContentPane().setLayout(new BorderLayout());

If a frame is involved, call the `setContentPane` method in the relevant frame object.

So, if we want to add five buttons, we need to place them in the five available areas in the screen.

First we create the buttons:

```
JButton northButton=new JButton("North");
JButton southButton=new JButton("South");
JButton eastButton=new JButton("East");
JButton westButton=new JButton("West");
JButton centerButton=new JButton("Center");
```

Next we add the elements to the screen. We must specify where the element is to be added, that is,

getContentPane().add(GUIObject, "position");

where position is one of the strings: North, South, East, West and Center (don't forget to capitalise).

To add the buttons defined above:

```
getContentPane().add(northButton,"North");
getContentPane().add(southButton,"South");
getContentPane().add(eastButton,"East");
getContentPane().add(westButton,"West");
getContentPane().add(centerButton,"Center");
```

The `BorderLayout` will expand each element to fill the available space allocated to it. So, the window with the buttons added in will look like Figure 8.9.

To make elements assume a more 'normal' size, you can add each of the elements to a panel and then add the panel to the screen.

`BorderLayout` can only accommodate one element in each position. If you add an element to a position that has had an element added to it, then it will replace the existing element. To place more than one element at a position, add the elements to a panel then add the panel as the 'single' element in the relevant position.

The program below adds five elements, one text area, two text fields and two buttons to the screen. As you can see the layout is not changed in the `init` method as the layout used, `BorderLayout`, is the default layout manager.

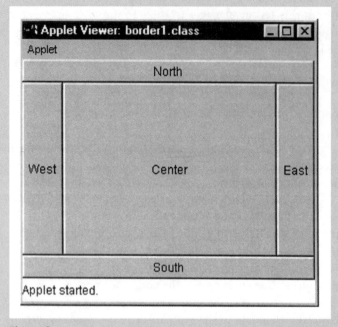

Figure 8.9

```
import javax.swing.*;                                           1
import java.awt.event.*;                                        2
import java.awt.*;                                              3
                                                                4
public class AppletBorderExample extends JApplet               5
{                                                               6
private JButton buttonOne,buttonTwo;                            7
                                                                8
private JTextArea textArea;                                     9
private JTextField textFieldOne,textFieldTwo;                   10
                                                                11
public void init()                                             12
    {                                                          13
    buttonOne = new JButton("North");                         14
    buttonTwo = new JButton("South");                         15
                                                               16
    getContentPane().add(buttonOne,"North");                  17
    getContentPane().add(buttonTwo,"South");                  18
                                                               19
    textArea = new JTextArea("Center",5,20);                  20
```

```
        getContentPane().add(textArea,"Center");        21
                                                        22
        textFieldOne = new JTextField("East");          23
        textFieldTwo = new JTextField("West");          24
                                                        25
        getContentPane().add(textFieldOne,"East");      26
        getContentPane().add(textFieldTwo,"West");      27
    } // End init                                       28
                                                        29
} // End AppletBorderExample                            30
```

Figure 8.10 shows the output of the above program. The elements are stretched to fit the available space.

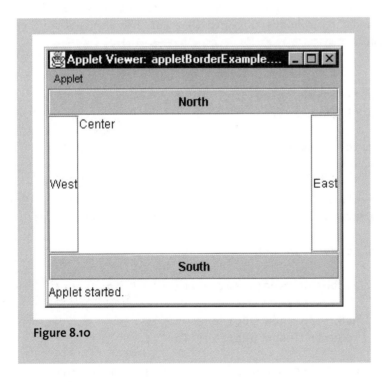

Figure 8.10

8.5.2 Grid layout

The other layout that we look at is `GridLayout`. In this layout manager, you can create a grid with specific dimensions (rows and columns). Elements added to the screen are then placed in the various cells of the grid.

You can have two forms of a declaration of a `GridLayout` object:

new GridLayout(int rows, int columns);

which creates a grid with no spaces between the elements, or

new GridLayout(int rows, int columns,
int <horizontal space between components(in pixels)>,
int <vertical space between components(in pixels)>);

which places a predefined amount of space between each cell in the grid. So, to change from the current layout to the `GridLayout` use:

setLayout(new GridLayout(<parameters>));

The GUI elements are placed in the grid (and therefore on the screen) in the order they are added to the screen. Each column in a specific row is filled first then the layout manager moves on to the next row and fills all the columns in that row. Again, like `BorderLayout`, the elements will expand to fill any free space unless they are added in the form of panels.

The following program will create four buttons and two text fields. A grid of two rows and three columns is created (line 12). The elements are then added to the screen.

```
import javax.swing.*;                                          1
import java.awt.*;                                             2
                                                               3
public class AppletGridExample extends JApplet                4
{                                                              5
                                                               6
private JButton oneButton,twoButton,fiveButton,sixButton;     7
private JTextField threeTextField,fourTextField;              8
                                                               9
public void init()                                            10
    {                                                         11
    getContentPane().setLayout(new GridLayout(2,3));          12
                                                              13
    oneButton = new JButton("One");                           14
    twoButton = new JButton("Two");                           15
                                                              16
    threeTextField = new JTextField("Three",10);              17
    fourTextField = new JTextField("Four",10);                18
                                                              19
    fiveButton = new JButton("Five");                         20
    sixButton = new JButton("Six");                           21
                                                              22
    getContentPane().add(oneButton);                          23
```

```
getContentPane().add(twoButton);                    24
getContentPane().add(threeTextField);               25
getContentPane().add(fourTextField);                26
getContentPane().add(fiveButton);                   27
getContentPane().add(sixButton);                    28
} // End init                                       29
                                                    30
} // End AppletGridExample                          31
```

Figure 8.11 shows the output of the above program. You can match the elements added to the screen in the program with the position that they are placed in on the grid.

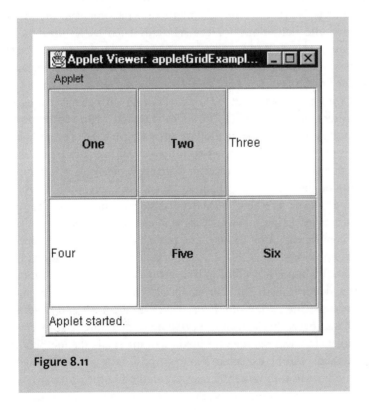

Figure 8.11

As with BorderLayout, you should add elements to a panel and add the panel to the window if you want the elements to have their usual size.

EXERCISE Write a program which allows the user to choose between three different layouts. When they select a layout, the program will change the current layout. Will this work as expected or will some layouts cause problems?

8.6 THE BASE CLASS USED SO FAR: TRAININGWHEELS

In this section, we examine in more detail the class that you relied on in previous chapters.

The code for the class which you inherited in your earlier programs is shown below. Its main goal is to provide basic input and output facilities, you can see this in the declarations (lines 8–10) where a button, a text area and a text field are declared. The init method will setup the output text area and attempt to run a method called entryPoint. If you inherit this class, then you will have to define this method, so the init method in the code below will call the entryPoint method you have written (since it will override the method contained in the parent class). If you do not define an entryPoint method then init will call the entryPoint method as defined in the class TrainingWheels. This entryPoint method will output a message to the effect that you forgot to override it in your class.

After the init method, comes the methods which manage the input and output. You will find the definitions for the methods such as, addButton, addInput-Element, outputOnScreen, and so on. You should note that outputOnScreen is overloaded so that it can cope with integer, double, string and boolean values passed to the method outputOnScreen.

The actionPerformed method (line 51) deals with the user pressing the button or hitting return in the text field. It calls the method ifButtonPressed if the user clicks the button added or the method processInput if the event is hit return while the cursor is in the textfield. Notice that it does a test in the case of a text field event to see if the value supplied is an integer or a string. It does this by attempting to convert the contents of the text field (which are always a string) into an integer using the Integer.parseInt method. If this conversion is successful, the processInput method which takes an integer value as a parameter will be called. If not, then an attempt is made to convert the input into a value of type double. If this attempt is successful, a processInput method is called with a double parameter. If the attempt at conversion fails, then the input is deemed to be a string and the processInput method which takes a string will be called. This conversion process will be looked at in Chapter 9.

Finally, you get the backup methods. These methods should never be executed as the user should override them in the program which inherits this class. However, if the user forgets to write the relevant method or misspells the method name, then one of these methods will be executed. Their purpose is to put a message in the output area to remind the user to write the relevant method in the program. All of the backup methods will call the method missingMethodMessage which outputs a standard error message and the specific method name which caused the problem (passed to it by the method which called it).

At this point we bid farewell to the TrainingWheels class, for the remainder of the book it will no longer be used in example programs. TrainingWheels should have demonstrated to you that you can hide some of the unnecessary detail of programming in order to concentrate on the important details. The concept of having a helper class which is general enough to be of use in many situations should encourage you to make use of classes similar to TrainingWheels in your programming career.

```
import java.awt.*;                                           1
import java.awt.event.*;                                     2
import javax.swing.*;                                        3
                                                             4
public class TrainingWheels extends JApplet implements      5
ActionListener
{                                                            6
                                                             7
private JButton inputButton;                                8
private JTextArea outputArea;                               9
private JTextField inputTextField;                          10
private JScrollPane outputPane;                             11
                                                             12
public void init()                                          13
   {                                                         14
   getContentPane().setLayout(new FlowLayout());            15
   outputArea = new JTextArea("[Output will be displayed    16
   here]\n",10,30);
   outputPane = new JScrollPane(outputArea);                17
                                                             18
   getContentPane().add(outputPane) ;                       19
   entryPoint();                                            20
   } // End init                                            21
                                                             22
// Methods which manage input and output                    23
// The methods below are used for adding and processing     24
// input elements                                           25
public void addButton(String ButtonLabel)                   26
   {                                                         27
   inputButton = new JButton(ButtonLabel);                  28
   getContentPane().add(inputButton);                       29
   inputButton.addActionListener(this);                     30
   validate();                                              31
   } // End addButton                                       32
                                                             33
// Add a textfield to the screen and place the string       34
// supplied before it                                       35
public void addInputElement(String InputLabel)              36
   {                                                         37
   // Add the label                                          38
   JLabel Description = new JLabel(InputLabel);             39
   getContentPane().add(Description);                       40
                                                             41
```

```
        // Add the text field                                        42
        inputTextField = new JTextField(10);                         43
        getContentPane().add(inputTextField);                        44
        inputTextField.addActionListener(this);                      45
        validate();                                                  46
        } // End addInputElement                                     47
                                                                     48
// Called if the user presses the button or presses return          49
// in the textfield                                                  50
public void actionPerformed(ActionEvent event)                       51
    {                                                                52
    // If the user pressed the button then call the method           53
    //  ifButtonPressed                                              54
        if(event.getSource() == inputButton)                         55
            ifButtonPressed();                                       56
                                                                     57
    // If the user pressed enter in the textfield try and figure out the  58
    // contents of the textfield and call the relevant methods       59
    if(event.getSource() == inputTextField)                          60
        try {                                                        61
        // Try to convert input to integer form                      62
        processInput(Integer.parseInt(inputTextField.getText()));    63
        }                                                            64
        catch(NumberFormatException nfeInteger)                      65
        {                                                            66
            try                                                      67
                {                                                    68
                // Try to convert input to double                    69
                processInput(Double.parseDouble(inputTextField.getText()));  70
                }                                                    71
            catch(NumberFormatException nfeDouble)                   72
                {                                                    73
                // If conversion processes fail, treat input as a string  74
                processInput(inputTextField.getText());             75
                }                                                    76
        }                                                            77
    } // End actionPerformed                                         78
                                                                     79
// Clear the output area of its current contents                     80
public void clearScreen()                                            81
    {                                                                82
    outputArea.setText("");                                          83
    } // End clearScreen                                             84
                                                                     85
```

```
// Method executed if outputOnScreen is called with a string    86
// actual parameter                                             87
public void outputOnScreen(String stringToOutput)               88
    {                                                           89
    outputArea.append(stringToOutput + "\n");                   90
    } // End outputOnScreen(string)                             91
                                                                92
// Method executed if outputOnScreen is called with an int      93
// actual parameter                                             94
public void outputOnScreen(int intToOutput)                     95
    {                                                           96
    outputArea.append(intToOutput + "\n");                      97
    } // End outputOnScreen(int)                                98
                                                                99
// Method executed if outputOnScreen is called with a double   100
// actual parameter                                            101
public void outputOnScreen(double doubleToOutput)              102
    {                                                          103
    outputArea.append(doubleToOutput + "\n");                  104
    } // End outputOnScreen(double)                            105
                                                               106
// Method executed if outputOnScreen is called with a         107
// boolean actual parameter                                   108
public void outputOnScreen(boolean booleanToOutput)           109
    {                                                          110
    outputArea.append(booleanToOutput + "\n");                 111
    } // End outputOnScreen(boolean)                           112
                                                               113
// Backup methods                                             114
// The methods below are likely to be used in your program    115
// (i.e. they are overridden in your program)                 116
//  if you do not declare them in your program then the       117
//  virtual machine will execute the ones below, the purpose  118
//  of these is to tell you that you need                     119
//  to put in the relevant methods.                           120
public void entryPoint()                                      121
    {                                                          122
    missingMethodMessage("public void entryPoint()");          123
    } // End entryPoint                                        124
                                                               125
public void ifButtonPressed()                                 126
    {                                                          127
    missingMethodMessage("public void ifButtonPressed()");     128
    } // End ifButtonPressed                                   129
```

```
public void processInput(String inputSupplied)          130
  {                                                     131
  missingMethodMessage("public void processInput(String  132
  inputSupplied)");
  } // End processInput(string)                         133
                                                        134
public void processInput(int inputSupplied)             135
  {                                                     136
  missingMethodMessage("public void processInput(int    137
  inputSupplied)\n");
  } // End processInput(int)                            138
                                                        139
public void processInput(double inputSupplied)          140
  {                                                     141
  missingMethodMessage("public void processInput(double 142
  inputSupplied)\n");
  } // End processInput(double)                         143
                                                        144
public void missingMethodMessage(String message)        145
  {                                                     146
  message = "You have not written a method              147
  called:\n" + message + "\n";
  message+ = "This means your program won't work properly\n";  148
  message+ = "Please write this method, compile your program  149
  again \n and execute it.";
                                                        150
  JOptionPane messagePane = new JOptionPane();          151
  messagePane.showMessageDialog(null,message,"Status",  152
  JOptionPane.INFORMATION_MESSAGE);
                                                        153
  } // End missingMethodMessage                         154
                                                        155
} // End TrainingWheels                                 156
```

SUMMARY

This chapter introduced the JFrame class. An application must deal with an object of type JFrame if it wants a GUI. More than one JFrame object can be created and displayed. Components can be added and removed from a JFrame object. Like components, JFrames must be listened to if you want to deal with events such as closing a window. If a JFrame is not listened to, then the only way to close a window is by stopping the VM.

Panels are a way of grouping components. Panels can be added and removed from a screen, if the programmer wishes to alter the GUI.

Layout managers are used by the VM to decide where to place elements on the screen shown to the user. The default layout manager is BorderLayout, but this is usually changed. A layout manager called `GridLayout` was introduced. This allows the programmer to arrange elements in a table like display.

The `TrainingWheels` class has been shown and briefly discussed. This class allowed you to take shortcuts by handling input and output operations for you.

KEYWORD

▶ *Layout Manager* – An object which decides where graphical components are displayed on a screen.

KEY CONCEPTS

▶ Creating an application window (Frame)

```
JFrame myFrame = new JFrame();
myFrame.setSize(xDimension,yDimension);
myFrame.show();
```

▶ Adding components to the frame

```
myFrame.getContentPane().add(component Object);
```

EXERCISES

1 Write an application which will act as a shop front and a shopping basket. Users can move through the catalogue of descriptions for goods and select if they want to buy a product, the product name is then added to their shopping list and its price is added to the total purchases. If a user decides that they want to remove a product from their basket, then they highlight the product with the mouse and press a button to remove it from the shopping list. When they finish browsing, they can fill in the details necessary to purchase the items.

The application consists of two user interfaces.

Screen1 displays the description of the goods on offer and allows the user to make their selection. The program begins execution by displaying this screen.

Screen2 appears when the user indicates that they wish to make a purchase. The user puts in their credit card details and address and presses a button to make their purchase. The application reports an error if the user fails to supply either of these items of data.

2 Write a program which will store details about users and their sales transactions. The objects that will be stored are: Customer, which contains the customers name, address and phone; Account, which contains the billing address, the amount owed on the account, a unique account number and a reference to the Customer object who owns the account. Finally, an Order object will contain the details of the items ordered as well as the total value of the order and references to the Account object and Customer object associated with these orders.

Write an application which will start off by displaying a screen with five buttons. The buttons are:

- Enter customer details – Used to enter new customer details
- Enter account details – Used to enter new account details
- Enter order details – Used to enter new order details
- View customer debts – Computes the amount that each customer owes
- View orders – Prints out the orders which have been recorded .

These buttons will open other frames which contain the necessary graphical components.

Solutions to exercises and interactive exercises can be obtained at: http://www.palgrave.com/resources

Data storage and manipulation

INTRODUCTION

This chapter discusses how data can be manipulated and stored. We look at how data contained in a program can be formatted for display to the user and examine how data supplied by the user can be transformed into a more useful format. Converting data from one type to another is also often necessary and this too is examined. The class type Date and related classes which format and alter it are discussed. Finally, we look at how data is stored and retrieved from disk.

9.1 NUMBER FORMATTING

So far in this book, we have been using the integer data type in situations where a type of double might have been more appropriate. The main reason for this is to keep things simple, so you can get familiar with the programming side before you get to grips with individual details. Another reason is that numbers declared as type double display in their own particular format which can sometimes cause confusion. Essentially double numbers are displayed with all their floating point digits whether they are relevant or not. This means, for example, that we could have .0021 of a penny represented.

To control how much of a double value is actually displayed, we use another object to format it. This object is of class type `DecimalFormat` and is declared with a parameter passed to the constructor which indicates how doubles passed to the `Decimal-Format` object will be returned. The string given to the constructor usually contains the characters 0 or #. A 0 to the right of a decimal point indicates 'insert a number' (a 0 is placed in the output if no number is present in the result), a # character means insert a number only if there is one to insert. The number of characters to the right of the decimal point denote the accuracy of the display, for example, .00 means the number output will be always formatted to two decimal places. Formatting is done on a 'roundup' basis, that is, any fraction which is greater than or equal to .5 means that a 1 is added to the integer result, otherwise no number is added to the integer (e.g. 3.45 will be 3, 9.51 will be 10). An example of a format object creation is:

```
DecimalFormat formatNumber=new DecimalFormat(".00");
```

The method named `format` in the `DecimalFormat` object is called with the number of type double to format as a parameter, it returns a string which contains the number in the appropriate format.

You must import the `java.text` package to use the `DecimalFormat` class.

The following program shows the result of the application of a number formatting object (created in line 24 and applied in line 25).

```
import javax.swing.*;                                          1
import java.text.*;                                            2
                                                               3
public class NumberFormatExample extends JApplet              4
{                                                              5
private JTextArea output;                                      6
                                                               7
public void init()                                            8
    {                                                          9
    output = new JTextArea(20,10);                            10
    getContentPane().add(output);                             11
                                                              12
    double itemPrice = 12.95;                                 13
    int vatRate = 21;                                         14
                                                              15
    output.append("Unformatted itemPrice is "+itemPrice+"\n");  16
                                                              17
    itemPrice += (itemPrice * vatRate) /100;                  18
                                                              19
    output.append("Unformatted itemPrice is "+itemPrice+"\n");  20
                                                              21
    output.append("\nFormatted itemPrice is");                22
                                                              23
    DecimalFormat formatNumber = new DecimalFormat(".00");    24
    output.append(formatNumber.format(itemPrice) + "\n");     25
    } // End init                                             26
                                                              27
} // End NumberFormatExample                                  28
```

The above program produces the output as shown in Figure 9.1.

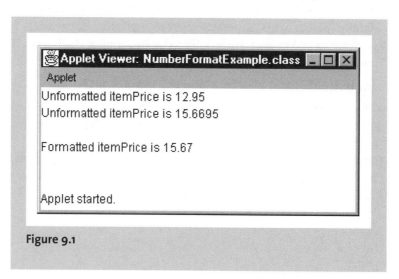

Figure 9.1

9.2   CONVERTING STRINGS INTO NUMBERS

In Chapter 8, we saw how to retrieve a string from a `TextField`. What if that string contains a number that we wish to add to another number? Well, to extract a number from a string we must 'parse' or convert it. This can be done by using a static method in the class type which corresponds to the number type we want to extract.

9.2.1 Integer.parseInt

If you want to convert a string into an integer, then you call the `parseInt` method in the class `Integer`. This method is called with a string (which contains only the number) as a parameter and returns an integer value as its result (provided the string is successfully converted into a number). If the string does not represent an integer, then an exception is generated (see Section 9.4 to handle exceptions) and an error message is printed out. An example of a conversion is:

```
String stringObjectName = "29";
int integerVariableName = Integer.parseInt(stringObjectName);
```

9.2.2 Double.parseDouble

If you want to convert a string into a number of type double, then use the `parseDouble` method which is a static method contained in the class `Double`. For example,

```
String stringObjectName = "12.09";
double doubleVariableName = Double.parseDouble(stringObjectName);
```

9.2.3 Parsing example program

The following program allows the user to input a number in the form of a string. This string is entered into a text field and the user presses return to have it processed. The program uses two states, in one state the string in the text field is converted into an integer and in the other state the string is converted into a double. The result of this conversion is then output. The program begins in a state which will expect the first input to be a string containing an integer (set in line 11). When an integer is entered, it is converted (line 34) and the state changed to expect a double to be contained in the next string (line 35). The program changes from state to state converting and outputting the numbers received.

```
import javax.swing.*;                                      1
import java.awt.event.*;                                   2
import java.awt.*;                                         3
                                                           4
                                                           5
public class ParseExample extends JApplet implements      6
ActionListener
{                                                          7
                                                           8
private JTextField input;                                  9
private JTextArea output;                                  10
private boolean stateIntegerExpected = true;               11
                                                           12
public void init()                                         13
    {                                                      14
    getContentPane().setLayout(new FlowLayout());          15
                                                           16
    input = new JTextField(20);                            17
    output = new JTextArea(5,20);                          18
                                                           19
    getContentPane().add(input);                           20
    input.addActionListener(this);                         21
    getContentPane().add(output);                          22
                                                           23
    output.setText("Enter integer\n");                     24
                                                           25
    } // End init                                          26
                                                           27
public void actionPerformed(ActionEvent eventInfo)         28
```

```
{                                                         29
    String inputString = input.getText();                30
                                                          31
    if(stateIntegerExpected)                             32
        {                                                33
        int integerValue = Integer.parseInt(inputString);  34
        stateIntegerExpected = false;                    35
        integerValue *= 2;                               36
        output.append("Value entered × 2 is "+integerValue +"\n");  37
        output.append("Enter double\n");                 38
        }                                                39
    else                                                 40
        {                                                41
        double doubleValue=Double.parseDouble(inputString);  42
        stateIntegerExpected = true;                     43
        doubleValue /= 2;                                44
        output.append("Value entered / 2 is "+doubleValue+"\n");  45
        output.append("Enter integer\n");               46
        }                                                47
                                                          48
    } // End actionPerformed                             49
                                                          50
} // End ParseExample                                    51
```

Figures 9.2–9.4 show the program operating. When the program starts up it is in the state which expects an integer to be entered (Figure 9.2).

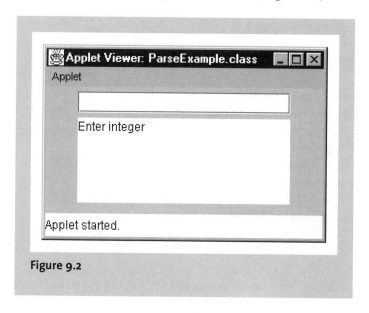

Figure 9.2

When the user enters the integer and presses return the program converts it, outputs the number doubled and enters the state which expects a double to be typed in (Figure 9.3).

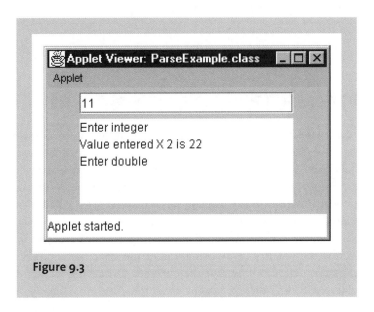

Figure 9.3

When a double value is entered it is converted, halved and its result is output as shown in Figure 9.4.

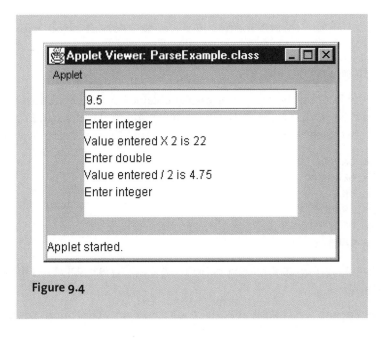

Figure 9.4

EXERCISE See what happens when a non number is entered. Does a message appear on the window to inform the user they made a mistake? Does the program stop working? Are any of the instructions ignored? How will you rewrite the program to handle such an error? (i.e. figure out that an error had occurred).

9.3 CURRENCY FORMATTING

Different currencies have different formatting (and different symbols) associated with them. Java has a class called `NumberFormat` which contains a method called `format` which, if supplied with a value of type double, will return a string which contains a relevant currency symbol and format. In order to output the desired currency symbol and format you must setup the `NumberFormat` object with what is called a `Locale`, that is, a description of the relevant country. `Locale` is a class type and the Locale for a particular country can be obtained by creating a `Locale` object with parameters which describe the country or by using one of the few static `Locales` stored in the `Locale` class. You should note that the currency formatting feature of the `Number-Format` object will not convert currencies as there are no exchange rates built into Java, for this you must use a mathematical expression, the `NumberFormat` object merely displays the relevant symbols (£, $, €, etc.) and numbering conventions.

To use a `NumberFormat` class you must import the `java.text` package.

Setting up a `NumberFormat` object for currency representation:

```
NumberFormat objectName = NumberFormat.getCurrencyInstance(LocaleObject);
```

You then call the `format` method in the `NumberFormat` object with the value you wish to convert and it will return the relevant string:

```
objectName.format(12.91)
```

Locale objects can be created or can be obtained from the static list stored in the `Locale` class. To use a `Locale` class you must import the `java.util` package.

Some of the `Locales` for which objects are stored as static variables are:

```
Locale.CANADA
Locale.GERMANY
Locale.UK
Locale.FRANCE
Locale.US
Locale.JAPAN
```

For example, to setup a `NumberFormat` object to format dates in Japanese currency format:

```
NumberFormat yen = NumberFormat.getCurrencyInstance(Locale.JAPAN);
```

Other countries must have Locale objects created for them, details of countries and the codes associated with them can be found on the Java Internationalization page at: http://java.sun.com/j2se/1.3/docs/guide/intl/

Two examples are shown below, that of the Euro and the Swedish Krona. The Euro is currently associated with each participating European country, for example, the Euro locale is associated with Ireland. A Locale object can be created with two parameters for its constructor, a two letter abbreviation indicating the language of the country and a country code.

Example of a Locale object for the euro:

```
Locale euroLocale = new Locale("en","IE_EURO");
```

Example of a Locale object for the krona:

```
Locale swedishLocale = new Locale("sv","SE");
```

Setting up the NumberFormat objects which use these locales.

```
NumberFormat euro = NumberFormat.getCurrencyInstance(euroLocale);
NumberFormat krona = NumberFormat.getCurrencyInstance(swedishLocale);
```

The following program illustrates the creation of a variety of NumberFormat objects and the output of the relevant currency formats.

```
import javax.swing.*;                                            1
import java.awt.event.*;                                         2
import java.awt.*;                                               3
import java.text.*; // Needed for NumberFormat                   4
import java.util.*; // Needed for Locale                         5
                                                                 6
public class CurrencyFormatExample extends JApplet implements    7
ActionListener
{                                                                8
private JTextArea output;                                        9
private JTextField input;                                        10
                                                                 11
public void init()                                               12
    {                                                            13
    getContentPane().setLayout(new FlowLayout());                14
                                                                 15
    output = new JTextArea(7, 25);                               16
    getContentPane().add(output);                                17
                                                                 18
    getContentPane().add(new JLabel("Input value for            19
    conversion"));
    input = new JTextField(10);                                  20
```

```
        getContentPane().add(input);                              21
        input.addActionListener(this);                            22
        } // End init                                             23
                                                                  24
    public void actionPerformed(ActionEvent eventObject)          25
        {                                                         26
        output.setText("");                                       27
                                                                  28
        try                                                       29
            {                                                     30
            double inputValue = Double.parseDouble(input.getText());  31
            convert(inputValue);                                  32
            }                                                     33
        catch(NumberFormatException exceptionObject)              34
            {                                                     35
            output.append("Error,invalid input");                 36
            }                                                     37
                                                                  38
        } // End actionPerformed                                  39
                                                                  40
    public void convert(double value)                             41
        {                                                         42
        Locale swedishLocale = new Locale("sv","SE");             43
        Locale euroLocale = new Locale("en","IE_EURO");           44
                                                                  45
        NumberFormat euro = NumberFormat.getCurrencyInstance      46
        (euroLocale);
        NumberFormat sterling =                                   47
        NumberFormat.getCurrencyInstance(Locale.UK);
        NumberFormat krona =                                      48
        NumberFormat.getCurrencyInstance(swedishLocale);
        NumberFormat dollar =                                     49
        NumberFormat.getCurrencyInstance(Locale.US);
        NumberFormat lire =                                       50
        NumberFormat.getCurrencyInstance(Locale.ITALY);
        output.append("\n euro " + euro.format(value));           51
        output.append("\n sterling " + sterling.format(value));   52
        output.append("\n krona " + krona.format(value));         53
        output.append("\n dollar " + dollar.format(value));       54
        output.append("\n lire " + lire.format(value));           55
        } // End convert                                          56
                                                                  57
    } // End CurrencyFormatExample                                58
```

Note that if the currency value to be represented cannot accommodate all the decimal places presented in the number to be converted, then the number will be rounded up if greater or equal to five and rounded down otherwise. This can be observed in the screenshot (Figure 9.5) of the program above which shows that the number of lira present has been rounded down to the nearest integer (since there are no fractions of a lira).

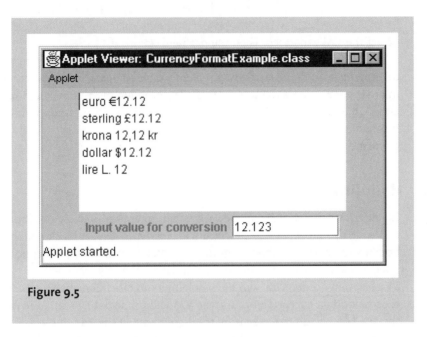

Figure 9.5

EXERCISE Extend the above program so that it also performs a currency value conversion into the relevant currencies. Assume that the number input is in American Dollars and output the relevant quantities in their respective currency formats.

9.4 EXCEPTIONS

An exception is defined as an error event, that is, file not found, URL not responding, incorrect input format, and so on. Certain statements can cause exceptions if they do not execute properly. These statements need to have code written to handle the exceptions which they may generate (e.g. when a file which is being read develops a problem, such as the disk which contains it being removed), other exceptions can be ignored (e.g. input format error). If a statement requires exception handling code and it has been omitted by the programmer, a compiler error message is generated as the program is compiled and the programmer must edit the source code and enter the statements which will handle the exception (even if the statements do not do anything, there must be statements present to handle the exception), otherwise the program will never be compiled.

If an exception occurs while a statement is being executed, an object is created of the appropriate exception class and is passed to the section of the program defined as dealing with the exception. The contents of this object can be accessed. Indeed, it is the generation of this exception object which tells the system which piece of code to execute as exception handling blocks are defined as taking these objects as parameters. So, when an exception of a particular type is generated, the system merely looks for the nearest block whose parameter matches the class type of exception object the VM generated when the problem occurred.

In other programming languages exception handling is solely up to the user. When developing Java, the decision was made to force the user to handle certain exceptions in order to encourage the user to make the program more robust and user friendly. So although exception handling may seem like a waste of time when writing the program it should be done to the best of your ability as it affects the users ability to use the program and consequentially their opinion of the programmer.

9.4.1 Handling exceptions

If you are writing a piece of code where an exception is likely to occur, then you put that code in a block which is started with the word `try`. A block denoted by the word `catch` will be defined following the `try` block to handle any exception. This naming system conveys that the code contained within the `try` block will be 'tried out' and if an exception occurs, this will be handled by `catch` statement(s) associated with that exception. If an exception occurs, the VM will immediately stop executing the code in the `try` block and start executing the statements in the `catch` block.

Visualise the `try` and `catch` blocks as if they are methods. The `try` method is always executed by the VM until some statement causes it to stop, leave the `try` block, and start executing the `catch` block. If no exception is generated, then the VM finishes the statements in the `try` block, ignores the statements in the `catch` block, and carries on with the rest of the program. Therefore, it is important to remember that any statement you place after a statement which can cause a `try` block to be prematurely ended, will never be executed when an exception occurs. For example,

```
ordinary statements;
try
      {
      statement which may cause exception;
      statements which rely on the above statement and which are;
      ignored if it develops a problem;
      }
catch(ExceptionType exceptionObject)
      {
      statements executed when exception occurs(error message,ask for reinput,etc.)
      }
ordinary statements;
```

9.4.2 Example: NumberFormatException

In the last section, we looked at converting strings to numbers. What happens if the VM cannot convert a string to a number, for example, what happened if the system comes across an instruction like:

```
Integer.parseInt("My name is");
```

In this case, the system cannot convert the string to a number because the string is not in the form of a number. Therefore, it generates an exception to notify the program that something has gone wrong. The compiler does not force the programmer to deal with this exception (the parsing example program discussed earlier in Section 9.2.3 functioned without it) but we can write code to 'catch' this exception.

To write the code we need to know what type of object the VM will return to the program if an exception occurs while processing the parseInt method. The class type of the exception will be NumberFormatException. So the code for exception handling a parseInt statement would be:

```
try
    {
    int result = Integer.parseInt("My name is");
    result * = 2;//If the above doesn't work this will not be
    //executed
    }
catch(NumberFormatException exceptionObject)
    {
    System.out.println("Sorry, you did not enter an integer");
    }
```

If you are unsure about the class type of the exception generated, you can use the generic exception class Exception. You should be reluctant to do this as it may cause more exceptions than you expect to be caught by your try-catch block. Therefore only use the Exception class in situations where you wish to experiment, for a final program look up the documentation to ascertain the correct exception for the relevant statement. For example,

```
try
    {
    Statement which generates unknown exception type;
    }
catch(Exception exceptionObject)
    {
    Statement which tells user exception has been caught;
    }
```

In the following example, the number parsing program has been rewritten to handle situations where the user inputs a string in the wrong format. In line 33, the try block for the integer parsing statement is defined. Line 39 marks the start of the definition of the catch block which handles the situation where the statement in line 36 (the parseInt) causes the try block to stop executing and the catch block to start. The catch block executes two statements, one tells the user that an error has occurred and the other outputs the contents of the exception object passed to the catch block (exceptionObject.toString()). Calling the toString method in certain objects will output their contents in the form of a string.

Note that when an exception occurs in the try block execution is abandoned at that point therefore any variables declared within the try block will be lost. Therefore, if an exception occurs in line 35 then lines 36 and 37 are ignored which means the program does not change state. This means that the user gets another chance to enter the data again.

```
import javax.swing.*;                                            1
import java.awt.event.*;                                         2
import java.awt.*;                                               3
                                                                 4
                                                                 5
public class ParseExampleCatch extends JApplet implements       6
ActionListener
{                                                                7
                                                                 8
private JTextField input;                                        9
private JTextArea output;                                        10
private boolean stateInputInt = true;                            11
                                                                 12
public void init()                                               13
    {                                                            14
    getContentPane().setLayout(new FlowLayout());               15
                                                                 16
    input = new JTextField(20);                                  17
    output = new JTextArea(5,20);                                18
                                                                 19
    getContentPane().add(input);                                 20
    input.addActionListener(this);                               21
    getContentPane().add(output);                                22
                                                                 23
    output.setText("Enter integer:\n");                         24
    } // End init                                                25
                                                                 26
```

```
public void actionPerformed(ActionEvent eventInfo)          27
   {                                                         28
   String inputString = input.getText( );                   29
                                                             30
   if(stateInputInt)                                         31
      {                                                      32
      try                                                    33
         {                                                   34
         int value = Integer.parseInt(inputString);          35
         output.append("Value entered is" + value + "\n");   36
         changeState();                                      37
         }                                                   38
      catch(NumberFormatException exceptionObject)            39
         {                                                   40
         output.append("\nERROR: wrong format, must be int\n"); 41
                                                             42
         output.append(exceptionObject.toString());          43
         }                                                   44
      }                                                      45
   else                                                      46
      {                                                      47
      try                                                    48
         {                                                   49
         double value = Double.parseDouble(inputString);     50
         output.append("Value entered is" + value + "\n");   51
         changeState();                                      52
         }                                                   53
      catch(NumberFormatException exceptionObject)            54
         {                                                   55
         output.append("\nERROR: wrong format, must be        56
         double\n");
         output.append(exceptionObject.toString());          57
         }                                                   58
      }                                                      59
                                                             60
   } // End actionPerformed                                 61
                                                             62
private void changeState()                                   63
   {                                                         64
   if(stateInputInt)                                         65
      output.append("Enter double\n");                       66
   else                                                      67
      output.append("Enter integer\n");                      68
                                                             69
```

```
        stateInputInt = !stateInputInt;   // Reverse the value   70
                                          // of stateInputInt    71
    } // End changeState                                          72
                                                                 73
} // End ParseExampleCatch                                       74
```

Figure 9.6 shows the result of the user supplying an incorrect string when the system expects an integer. Notice as expected that line 36 (which outputs the contents of the converted integer) is never executed because this line and the line following it are skipped as a result of the exception. The state of the program does not change so the user has a chance to re-enter the number.

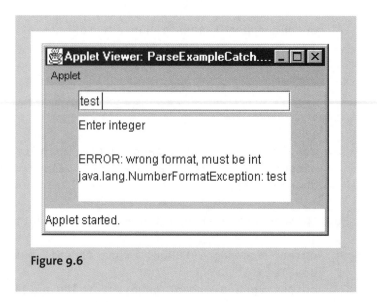

Figure 9.6

EXERCISE   Is an exception generated if the user inputs a double instead of an integer and vice versa?

9.4.3 Using exceptions

As stated above, it is possible to leave the `catch` block empty so that the compiler is happy but nothing is done in response to an exception. This practice should be avoided, as the whole purpose of forcing the program to handle exceptions is to make life easier for the user. If the user is not aware of an exception result from their action, they can keep on repeating the action. Worse, the program could continue and use variables that have not been setup correctly because of an exception. Therefore, you should always respect the spirit of exception handling, and write code to notify the user of what is happening (even if its not the user's fault) and build in some mechanism for rectifying the error (such as remaining in the same state and asking the user to re-enter the data in the correct format).

In some instances, you can use an exception as a decision making mechanism, for example, look back at a section of the `TrainingWheels` class discussed in Chapter 8, in particular `actionPerformed` method. The code shown below is really only a simplified version of `actionPerformed`, but it does illustrate the concept being discussed.

```
public void actionPerformed(ActionEvent event)                   1
{                                                                 2
if(event.getSource() == inputButton)                             3
     ifButtonPressed();                                          4
if(event.getSource() == inputTextField)                          5
  try {                                                          6
       processInput(Integer.parseInt(inputTextField.getText())); 7
       }                                                          8
  catch(NumberFormatException nfe)                               9
       {                                                          10
       processInput(inputTextField.getText());                   11
       }                                                          12
} // End actionPerformed                                         13
```

The `try-catch` block above will call different methods depending on what the user supplies as input. The program assumes that the user will always supply an integer and tries to convert the string contained in the text field into an integer value (line 7). If this conversion succeeds, then the method `processInput` which takes an integer parameter is called. If the user does not enter an integer, then the conversion will generate an exception and the `processInput`, which takes an integer parameter will not be called. Instead, the `catch` block is executed and the `processInput` method which takes a string as a parameter is called.

9.4.4 Creating a custom exception

We have seen basic error handling in earlier chapters, that is, situations where input is checked or validated and the user informed if the input is incorrect. We have also seen how sentinel values are used to indicate that a certain event has taken place. Both of these mechanisms can also be facilitated using exceptions. The process is to define your own special exception. Your input validation routine can then generate the custom type of exception if the input is incorrect and you can use the try-catch block to handle this exception.

You create your own custom exception by declaring a class which inherits the Exception class. You can now create exception objects from this class. You generate an exception by 'throwing' an object of a particular exception type. You use a statement of the form:

```
throw new CustomExceptionClass();
```

where CustomExceptionClass is the name given to the class which extends Exception.

Once the throw statement is encountered, the remaining statements in the method which contains it will be ignored and an exception will be passed back to the point which called the method. Any method which contains a throw instruction must indicate this in its definition by placing throws CustomExceptionClass at the end of the methods declaration.

Let's look at an example search method. The program below will create an array of names which will be searched. The user inputs a name and the program starts to search the array (it calls the method named search on line 30 to do this). If the search method cannot find the name the user supplied in the array 'names' it will generate an exception (line 54) of type NotFoundException (defined on line 64). Therefore, line 57 will not be reached and the catch block at line 32 is executed as the statement generated an exception and a message is printed out. This message is contained within the exception object and is obtained by calling the method explain. If however, the string supplied by the user is found in the names array, then no exception is generated and line 30 will complete its execution by outputting the value returned from the search method.

```
import javax.swing.*;                                          1
import java.awt.event.*;                                       2
import java.awt.*;                                             3
                                                               4
public class SearchUsingException extends JApplet implements   5
ActionListener
{                                                              6
private String names[] = {"John","Joe","Jane","Jennie"};      7
private JTextArea output;                                      8
private JTextField input;                                      9
                                                               10
public void init()                                            11
    {                                                         12
    getContentPane().setLayout(new FlowLayout());             13
                                                               14
```

```
    output = new JTextArea(7,25);                           15
    getContentPane().add(output);                           16
                                                            17
    getContentPane().add(new JLabel("Input Name sought"));  18
    input = new JTextField(10);                             19
    getContentPane().add(input);                            20
    input.addActionListener(this);                          21
    } // End init                                           22
                                                            23
public void actionPerformed(ActionEvent eventObject)        24
    {                                                       25
    String nameSupplied = input.getText( );                 26
                                                            27
    try                                                     28
        {                                                   29
        output.append("Name found at index:"                30
        + search(nameSupplied));
        }                                                   31
    catch(NotFoundException exceptionObject)                32
        {                                                   33
        output.append(exceptionObject.explain());           34
        }                                                   35
    output.append("\n");                                    36
                                                            37
    } // End actionPerformed                                38
                                                            39
public int search(String nameParameter) throws NotFoundException  40
    {                                                       41
    int currentIndex = 0; // Start at the start of the array 42
    boolean found = false; // Item is not yet found         43
                                                            44
    while((currentIndex < names.length) && (!found))        45
        {                                                   46
        if(names[currentIndex].equals(nameParameter))       47
            found = true;                                   48
        else                                                49
            currentIndex ++;                                50
        }                                                   51
                                                            52
    if(!found)                                              53
        throw new NotFoundException();// Quit the method    54
                              // if not found               55
                                                            56
    return currentIndex; //If item found return its location 57
```

```
      } // End search                                    58
                                                         59
} // End SearchUsingException                            60
                                                         61
// Define the custom exception which is generated if the 62
// item cannot be found                                  63
class NotFoundException extends Exception                64
{                                                        65
public String explain()                                  66
    {                                                    67
    return "Error: the search term was not found";       68
    } // End explain                                     69
                                                         70
} // End NotFoundException exception                     71
```

An example of an error message output and its cause is shown in Figure 9.7.

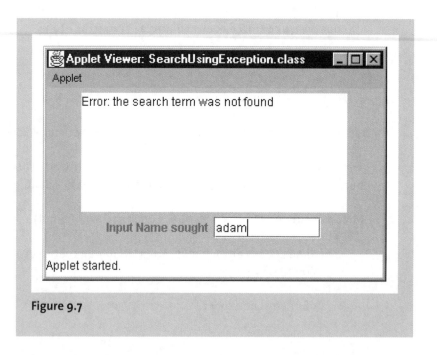

Figure 9.7

EXERCISE Rewrite the above program so that the case is not important (i.e. if the user typed in JANE, the program will return the index location for Jane).

9.5 EXTRACTING DIFFERENT PARTS OF A STRING: **StringTokenizer**

Suppose a string contain three pieces of data in the form:

`Name:Phone:OfficeNumber`

(i.e. this is the order of the elements and each element is separated by a colon), for example,

`John:1339:3.24`

How do you print out just the phone number, part of the string? You can go through each character of the string using the `getChar(int)` method contained in each string object to extract the relevant characters. This is the process that is carried out in other programming languages, but the developers of Java decided to produce an object called `StringTokenizer` which separates a string into distinct sections or 'tokens' and allows each token to be output on its own. So, the result of tokenising the above single string will be three separate strings:

```
John
1339
3.24
```

How can a `StringTokenizer` object tell which part of the string is which? Well, it needs to be informed what character or characters are used to separate the different sections of the string. Most strings containing multiple data elements separate them using particular characters (e.g. a space or a comma). Therefore you need to setup a `StringTokenizer` object with the characters which separate (or delimit) one token from another. In the example string, this character will be a colon ':'. In some strings, you may have several different characters which can separate a string and these can all be passed to the `StringTokenizer` object. The most common delimiters are: `,` `–` `:` and a space. Many databases export records using these delimiters.

The first part of breaking up a string into different parts is to initialise the `String-Tokenizer` object with the delimiter(s) used and the string which contains these delimiter(s). The delimiter(s) are supplied in the form of a string which can consist of a single character or many characters.

Declaration syntax is

`StringTokenizer objectName = new StringTokenizer(<string>,<delimiter(s)>);`

For example,

```
String Address = "Colin:3339:3.24";
StringTokenizer addressTokenizer = new StringTokenizer(Address,":");
```

`StringTokenizer` works by going through each character until it finds a character it has been told is a delimiter. Use the `nextToken` method in the `StringTokenizer` object you have created to extract the next token. When `nextToken` is called, the VM returns the section of the string it regards as a distinct section. The VM continues moving from the start of the tokens to the end of the string until the user stops asking for tokens or no more tokens are left.

Your original string is not changed as it is a copy of it that is given to the String-Tokenizer object.

You must import the java.util package as it contains StringTokenizer class. For example,

```
String theDate = "Dec 9 12:45";
String month,day,time; // Extract tokens into these strings
// A space is the delimiter
StringTokenizer dateToken = new StringTokenizer(TheDate," ");
month = dateToken.nextToken();// Extract the 1st token which is
                                // put in 'month'
day = dateToken.nextToken();// Extract the 2nd token which is
                                // put in 'day'
time = dateToken.nextToken();// Extract the 3rd token which is
                                // put in 'time'
```

9.5.1 hasMoreTokens

What happens if you do not know how many tokens are in a string? Well, if there are no more tokens, then the nextToken method will return a null value. Alternatively, you can check if there are any more tokens by calling the method hasMoreTokens.

You can use the hasMoreTokens method in a loop to process a StringTokenizer object until it runs out of tokens.

EXAMPLE   Process the string numbers until no more tokens exist. The tokens may be separated by a space, a comma or a colon so all of these are supplied to the StringTokenizer object as delimiters.

```
String numbers = "1,2,4,5:6:2:9:12";
StringTokenizer numberToken =
    new StringTokenizer(Numbers,",:");
    // 3 delimiters: comma, space and colon
while(numberToken.hasMoreTokens())
    textAreaObject.append( numberToken.nextToken());
```

9.5.2 countTokens

Another method in a StringTokenizer object is the countTokens method. This returns the number of tokens that a string contains and is quite useful if you want to create an array to hold the tokens extracted but are unsure how many tokens there will actually be.

In the following program, two strings are tokenised. One string has its tokens placed in three named strings (declared in line 15). The other string has its token placed in an array. Two methods extractDateTokens and extractNumberTokens do the extractions. The `extractDateTokens` method expects three tokens and expects their order to be month, day and time. The `extractNumberTokens` is unsure how many tokens there will be, and so it calls the `countTokens` method to count them and then creates an array to hold the number of tokens currently in the `StringTokenizer` object. A counter is used to track the next free location in the array used to hold the tokens extracted and converted into integers.

Both methods output the results of their tokenization.

```
import java.awt.*;                                              1
import javax.swing.*;                                          2
import java.util.*;                                            3
                                                               4
public class TokenizerExample extends JApplet               5
{                                                              6
// Setup the string to be tokenized                           7
private String theDate = "Dec 9 12:45";                       8
                                                               9
// Setup the object which will tokenize the string           10
private StringTokenizer dateToken = new                      11
StringTokenizer(theDate," ");
                                                              12
// Declare variables which will hold the tokens extracted    13
// from the above string                                     14
private String month,day,time;                               15
                                                              16
// Setup the string to be tokenized                          17
private String numbers = "21,52,34,55,36,12";                18
                                                              19
// Setup the object which will tokenize the string           20
private StringTokenizer numbersToken = new                   21
StringTokenizer(numbers,",");
                                                              22
// Declare the array which will hold the tokens extracted    23
// from the Numbers string                                   24
private int numbersArray[];                                  25
                                                              26
// Declare the output display areas                          27
private JtextArea dateResult;                                28
private JtextArea numbersResult;                             29
public void init()                                           30
    {                                                        31
    getContentPane().setLayout(new FlowLayout());            32
    dateResult = new JTextArea(5,25);                        33
    numbersResult = new JTextArea(10,25);                    34
```

```
                                                              35
    getContentPane().add(dateResult);                        36
    getContentPane().add(numbersResult);                     37
                                                              38
    extractDateTokens();                                     39
    extractNumberTokens();                                   40
    } // End init                                            41
                                                              42
public void extractDateTokens()                              43
    {                                                        44
    // Start tokenization for the first string              45
    // Assign the result of each token extraction to a variable  46
    month = dateToken.nextToken();// First token is the month  47
    day = dateToken.nextToken();// Second is the date        48
    time = dateToken.nextToken();// Third is the time        49
                                                              50
    dateResult.setText("The original string was "+theDate+"\n");  51
    dateResult.append("Tokens are: \n");                     52
    dateResult.append("Month:- " + month +"\n");             53
    dateResult.append("Day:- " + day +"\n");                 54
    dateResult.append("Time:- " + time +"\n");               55
    } // End extractDateTokens                               56
public void extractNumberTokens()                            57
    {                                                        58
    // Start tokenization for the second string             59
    numbersResult.setText("The original String was"          60
    + numbers +"\n");
                                                              61
    // Setup the array which will hold the tokens extracted  62
    numbersArray = new int[numbersToken.countTokens()];      63
                                                              64
    // Setup the counter which will hold the next free  array  65
    // location                                              66
    int counter = 0;                                         67
                                                              68
    // Process the string until it contains no more tokens  69
    // Output each token to the TextArea                     70
    while(numbersToken.hasMoreTokens())                      71
        {                                                    72
        // Extract the next token                            73
        String tokenExtracted = numbersToken.nextToken();   74
        numbersResult.append("token is "+tokenExtracted+"\n");  75
        // Place the token in the next free array location and  76
        // increase the value of the variable holding the next  77
        // free location                                     78
```

```
      numbersArray[counter++] = Integer.parseInt          79
      (tokenExtracted);
      }                                                    80
   // Output the contents of the array                     81
   for(counter = 0;counter < numbersArray.length;counter++) 82
      {                                                    83
      numbersResult.append("numberArray["+counter+"] = ");  84
      numbersResult.append(numbersArray[counter] + "\n");   85
      }                                                    86
   } // End extractNumberTokens                            87
} // End TokenizerExample                                  88
```

Figure 9.8 shows the results of the tokenization. As you can see the original strings do not change and the resultant tokens are completely separate from the original string.

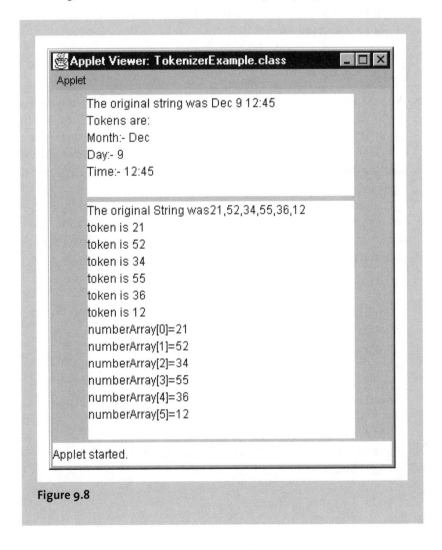

Figure 9.8

1   Write a method which will take as parameters a string of delimiters and a string containing tokens and return an array of tokens.

2   Write a method which checks the tokens being extracted to see if they are integers or doubles. (*Hint*: have a separate method which calls the method developed in the previous exercise to tell what values are returned.)

9.6 WORKING WITH DATES AND TIMES

The main class that the Java date managing system is based on, is the Date class. Two other classes, Calendar and GregorianCalendar are used in conjunction with this class in order to access and manipulate it.

In this section, you are introduced to another class called SimpleDateFormat which is easier to operate when dealing with basic operations associated with an object of type Date.

9.6.1 Date

We first look at an object of type Date. An object of this class represents a specific instant in time (measured in milliseconds from a particular starting point). The java.util package needs to be imported to work with the Date class.

A Date object used to be directly accessible in older versions of Java (e.g. you could supply a date as a constructor to a Date object) but now Date is formatted and altered using other classes, one of which is SimpleDateFormat.

You can still create and use a date object directly, for example, the following code creates a Date object and then outputs that object (line 9). Note that the VM will not output the address of the Date object in line 9 as you will expect but will convert (or cast) the contents of the Date object to a string which will be output.

```
import java.util.*;                                          1
                                                            2
public class TodaysDate                                      3
{                                                            4
                                                            5
public static void main(String arguments[])                 6
{                                                            7
Date today = new Date();                                     8
System.out.println("Todays Date  " + today);                9
} // End main                                               10
                                                            11
} // End TodaysDate                                         12
```

The above program will produce the string which represents the contents of the `Date` object, for example,

```
Todays Date Wed Jan 10 12:01:07 GMT 2002
```

The information produced is taken from the operating system which maintains the current time, date and time zone information.

Creating an object of type `Date` captures the date and time of the instant that the `Date` object is created (i.e. you can put line 9 in an infinite loop and its output will always be the same). This means that the contents of the `Date` object do not change as time progresses, it is a snapshot of the time it is created. It also means that any change to an object of type `Date` will not affect the system (computer) date from which the `Date` object derived its contents. You can even change the system date after creating a `Date` object and this would not affect the contents of the `Date` object.

To change the contents of the `Date` object, we work through another object which is of type `SimpleDateFormat`.

9.6.2 SimpleDateFormat

`SimpleDateFormat` is a class used to handle access to an object of type `Date`. `SimpleDateFormat` can be used to display the contents of a `Date` object in a specific format or to enter data into a `Date` object.

An object of type `SimpleDateFormat` will use a 'language' of special characters to represent certain sections of a date. For example, what if you just want to extract the current hour from a `Date` object? Well, you give the symbol which represents hour to the `SimpleDateFormat` object when it is created and it will return the current hour stored in the `Date` object it is supplied with.

The `SimpleDateFormat` class is contained in the `java.text` package so this must be imported in any program using it.

Some of the characters used and what they represent are shown in Table 9.1.

A `SimpleDateFormat` object is created with the required formatting instructions passed to its constructor. The symbols in Table 9.1 can be arranged in any order and can even be mixed with symbols not in the table which the programmer wishes to use to display the date formatted in some predetermined fashion (e.g. using ':' to separate hour from minute or '/' to separate day, month, year). Be careful to use non-alphabetic symbols to format your date, otherwise the `SimpleDateFormat` object may not be able to deal with the formatting string. If a `SimpleDateFormat` object has a problem with a formatting string, an exception of type `IllegalArgumentException` will be generated. You have the option of handling this exception or ignoring it. This exception is generated only when the `SimpleDateFormat` object is used, not when it is created. The syntax is:

```
SimpleDateFormat dateFormatObject = new SimpleDateFormat(formattingString);
```

For example,

```
SimpleDateFormat returnHours = new SimpleDateFormat("H");
```

The following will cause an exception if the object `returnMonthYear` is used:

```
SimpleDateFormat returnMonthYear = new SimpleDateFormat("Year = y");
```

Table 9.1

Symbol	Explanation	Format	Range	Example
a	AM/PM indicator	String	AM/PM	AM
d	Day of the month	Int	1–31	2
D	Day of the year	Int	1–365	33
E	Day of the week	String	Mon–Sun	Fri
h	Hour in 12 hour clock (AM/PM)	Int	1–12	10
H	Hour in 24 hour clock	Int	0–23	10
k	Hour in 24 hour day	Int	1–24	10
K	Hour in 12 hour day	Int	0–11	10
m	Minute in hour	Int	0–59	58
M	Month in year	Int	1–12	2
MMM	Month in year	String	Jan–Dec	February
s	Second in current minute	Int	0–59	2
S	Millisecond in current minute	Int	0–999	0
w	Week in year	Int	1–52	6
W	Week in month	Int	1–6	1
y	Year	Int		00
z	Time zone	String		GMT + 00:00

Note: The example column in the table is based on a date of 2/2/00 at 10:58:02 a.m.

9.6.2.1   Using SimpleDateFormat to extract elements of Date

As we have seen, a `SimpleDateFormat` object is created and has a string parameter passed to its constructor. This parameter will indicate what information will be extracted from the `Date` object which the `SimpleDateFormat` object will be passed later in the program.

You can ask for one single item to be extracted, for example, hours (symbol 'H') or you can ask for a number of items to be extracted and presented in a particular order and format. For example, you may like to see the name of the current month and whether it is AM or PM. You might like the symbol '-' to be placed between these two pieces of information. You can therefore setup a `SimpleDateFormat` object as follows:

```
SimpleDateFormat returnMonth = new SimpleDateFormat("MMM-a");
```

You extract an element of a `Date` object (such as an hour) by calling the `format` method in the `SimpleDateFormat` object with the `Date` object that you wish to format. For example,

```
Date today = new Date();
returnMonth.format(today);
```

The `format` method above returns a string which can be output or processed further (e.g. tokenised or parsed into an integer).

In the following program, three buttons are created and displayed on an applet window. Each of these buttons represents a particular type of date formatting. The `SimpleDateFormat` objects associated with these buttons are setup in the `init` method (lines 17–19). The first `SimpleDateFormat` object (line 17) will format a `Date` object to return a string which contains the date, month and year, each of which are separated using a '/'. The second `SimpleDateFormat` (line 18) formats a `Date` object to return the hour, minute and second each separated by a ':'. The third `SimpleDateFormat` object will format a `Date` object to return the number of minutes in the current hour.

When the user presses a button the `actionPerformed` method is called. This creates a new `Date` object each time it is called (line 39). Once it has been determined which button has been pressed the relevant `SimpleDateFormat` object is used on the newly created `Date` object and the result output. In the case of the `minutesLeftButton` being pressed the string returned from the `call` to the `format` method is converted into an integer and subtracted from 60 to give the number of minutes remaining in the hour (lines 47 and 48).

```
import java.util.*; // Needed if Date class used          1
import java.text.*; // Needed if simpleDateFormat used    2
import javax.swing.*;                                     3
import java.awt.*;                                        4
import java.awt.event.*;                                  5
                                                          6
public class DateFormatApplet extends JApplet implements  7
ActionListener
{                                                         8
private JTextArea outputArea;                             9
private JButton dayMonthYearButton,                      10
hourMinSecButton,minutesLeftButton;
private SimpleDateFormat dayMonthYear,                   11
hourMinSec,minutesLeft;
                                                         12
public void init()                                      13
```

```
    {                                                              14
    getContentPane().setLayout(new FlowLayout());                  15
                                                                   16
    dayMonthYear = new SimpleDateFormat("dd/MM/yy");               17
    hourMinSec = new SimpleDateFormat("HH:mm:ss");                 18
    minutesLeft = new SimpleDateFormat("m");                       19
                                                                   20
    dayMonthYearButton = new JButton("Day-Month-Year");            21
    hourMinSecButton = new JButton("Hour:Min:Sec");                22
    minutesLeftButton = new JButton("Minutes left in hour");       23
                                                                   24
    getContentPane().add(dayMonthYearButton);                      25
    getContentPane().add(hourMinSecButton);                        26
    getContentPane().add(minutesLeftButton);                       27
                                                                   28
    dayMonthYearButton.addActionListener(this);                    29
    hourMinSecButton.addActionListener(this);                      30
    minutesLeftButton.addActionListener(this);                     31
                                                                   32
    outputArea = new JTextArea(7,20);                              33
    getContentPane().add(outputArea);                              34
    } // End init                                                  35
                                                                   36
public void actionPerformed(ActionEvent eventObject)              37
    {                                                              38
    Date currentTime = new Date();                                 39
                                                                   40
    if(eventObject.getSource() == dayMonthYearButton)             41
        outputArea.append(dayMonthYear.format(currentTime) +      42
        "\n");
    if(eventObject.getSource() == hourMinSecButton)               43
        outputArea.append(hourMinSec.format(currentTime) + "\n"); 44
    if(eventObject.getSource() == minutesLeftButton)             45
        {                                                          46
        int minutesLeftValue = 60 - Integer.parseInt(minutesLeft  47
        .format(currentTime));
        outputArea.append(minutesLeftValue +" minutes left in     48
        the hour\n");
        }                                                          49
    } // End actionPerformed                                      50
                                                                   51
                                                                   52
    } // End DateFormatApplet                                     53
```

Figure 9.9 shows the applet following each of the buttons having being pressed.

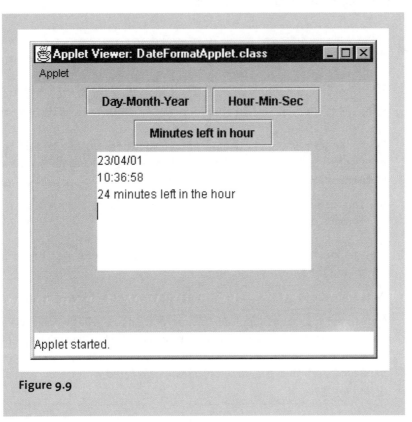

Figure 9.9

1 See what happens when a formatting string is of the form "Day=d".
2 Move the Date object creation into the init method. Does the output of the program change now?

9.6.2.2 Entering a date into a Date object with SimpleDateFormat

A SimpleDateFormat object can also be used for formatting date information in order to set up a Date object. The procedure is that you create the SimpleDateFormat object supplying, as above, the symbols indicating the format you intend to use. You then call the parse method in the SimpleDateFormat object and supply a string which contains date information in the format defined when the SimpleDateFormat object is setup. The call to the parse method will return a Date object which is setup to contain the relevant values obtained from the string supplied to the SimpleDateFormat object.

You will need to catch an exception as the parse may be incorrect (i.e. all the elements of the date as indicated when the SimpleDateFormat object has been created, are not present in the string supplied, or values exceeding permitted ranges are supplied, e.g. 32 o'clock). The exception object generated is of type ParseException.

A SimpleDateFormat object can therefore be used both for formatting an existing Date object and creating a new one.

Inserting information into a Date object

Step 1: Create the SimpleDateFormat object with the required format.

```
SimpleDateFormat createDate = new SimpleDateFormat("hh:mm");
```

Step 2: Setup a string containing the relevant portions of the date that you wish to insert into a Date object. The format of the string must agree with the format of the SimpleDateFormat object defined in step 1.

```
String timeString = "03:30"; // Fits format hh:mm as in SimpleDate-
// Format object
```

Step 3: Extract the Date object from the SimpleDateFormat object using the string containing the date information.

```
Date dateObjectRequired = createDate.parse(timeString);
```

Note that if you do not supply all the information to the Date object via a SimpleDate-Format object the missing elements of the date will be filled in using default values. For example, if you supply only the current hour when the Date object is created (using the parse method) then the Date object will be created with the current day set as the 1st of January 1970.

In the following example program, the user is asked to input the required date in a specific format (day/month/year). A SimpleDateFormat object is setup to convert the string supplied into a Date object (line 19). A Date object is then created using this string (line 37). This Date object is then output (line 38).

```
import java.util.*; // Needed if Date class used              1
import java.text.*; // Needed if SimpleDateFormat class used  2
                                                              3
import javax.swing.*;                                         4
import java.awt.*;                                            5
import java.awt.event.*;                                      6
                                                              7
public class SetDateApplet extends JApplet implements        8
ActionListener
{                                                             9
                                                              10
private JTextField input;                                     11
```

```
    private JTextArea output;                                    12
    private SimpleDateFormat formatTime;                         13
                                                                 14
    public void init()                                           15
        {                                                        16
        getContentPane().setLayout(new FlowLayout());            17
                                                                 18
        formatTime = new SimpleDateFormat("dd/MM/yy");           19
                                                                 20
        getContentPane().add(new JLabel("Enter time"));          21
        input = new JTextField(10);                              22
        input.setToolTipText("Enter time in the form: day/month/ 23
        year");
        getContentPane().add(input);                             24
        input.addActionListener(this);                           25
                                                                 26
        output = new JTextArea(5,20);                            27
        getContentPane().add(output);                            28
                                                                 29
        } // End init                                            30
                                                                 31
    public void actionPerformed(ActionEvent eventObject)         32
        {                                                        33
                                                                 34
        try                                                      35
            {                                                    36
            Date currentDate = formatTime.parse(input.getText());37
            output.append("Date is " + currentDate + "\n");      38
            }                                                    39
        catch(ParseException exceptionObject)                    40
            {                                                    41
            output.append("\nTime supplied in incorrect format\n");42
            output.append("should be day/month/year\n");         43
            }                                                    44
        } // End actionPerformed                                 45
                                                                 46
                                                                 47
    } // End SetDateApplet                                       48
```

Figure 9.10 in p. 414 shows what happens when the string entered in the text field is converted into a Date object. This Date object is then output in the text area. Note that the hour and second values are set to 0 (their default values) as these were not supplied when the date object was created.

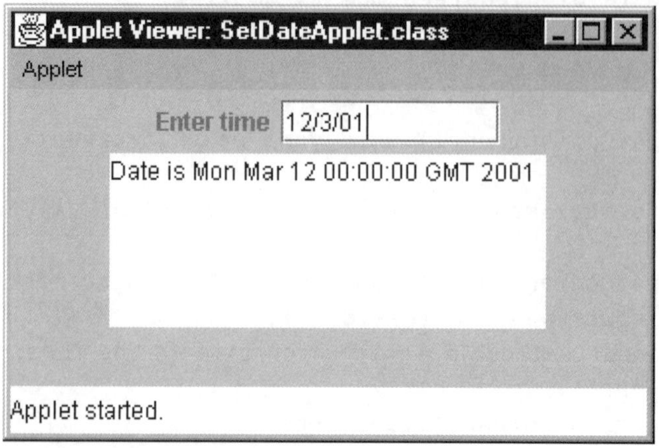

Figure 9.10

9.7   READING AND WRITING INFORMATION TO AND FROM DATA FILES ON A DISK DRIVE

A Java program can access files stored on a disk drive and read the contents of these files. These files contain simple text (produced by a program such as notepad or vi) and can be accessed by other applications (such as word processors, databases, editors).

We refer to 'streams' when talking about file access, a stream is the term for a source of data. Data can come from the local disk drive, a network or be typed in by the user, but the way data is treated when it comes into a program is independent of its physical source (just like a stream of liquid can come from a tap, a bottle, etc., the source is not important, it's what in the stream that is useful).

Imagine you are writing to a file, the process is like using a telephone and an answering machine (which stores your message). You use the telephone to dial the number you want, once the answering machine answers, it takes whatever is sent down the telephone line and stores it. Your telephone conversation is 'streaming' down the line to the answering machine. Once you have finished leaving the message you close the connection (hang up). You have now closed the stream.

Note that

1   Accessing files via an applet is subject to security restrictions, so VMs (particularly those in browsers) will, by default, not allow local file access. Therefore, the examples discussed are in the form of applications.

2   You need to import the java.io.* package to use the classes which will access files.

9.7.1 Writing information to a file

Writing to a file involves two objects. A `FileOutputStream` object is used to make the connection to a particular file to handle the output stream. The object of this type is created with the file name passed to its constructor. If no path information is passed with the file name, then the operating system assumes the file will be created in the directory in which the program is running. If the file name passed does not exist, the operating system creates a new file with the supplied name. If the file name passed already exists then the operating system deletes it and a new file with the same name is created.

A `PrintStream` object adds functionality to another output stream (such as `File-OutputStream`), mainly the ability to write data of differing types.

A `PrintStream` will be declared with a reference to another object which will connect to the actual file (e.g. an object of `FileOutputStream`). The `PrintStream` object is used to format the information and it depends on the other object to put the information into the correct destination.

So a declaration for the two objects needed would look like:

```
String filename = "result.dat";
FileOutputStream outputStream = new FileOutputStream(filename);
PrintStream output = new PrintStream(outputStream);
```

Alternatively, you could combine the above two lines to give:

```
PrintStream output = new PrintStream(new FileOutputStream(filename));
```

The filename string supplied can contain path information but make sure it is properly formatted. For example:

```
filename = "c:\\java\\files\\details.txt";
```

The `FileOutputStream` object creation statement could result in an exception of type `IOException` so this must be caught.

Once a `PrintStream` object has been created, you can write to the file by calling the methods `print` and `println`. Each of these methods will take as a parameter the data to output (most common data types can be passed as both methods are overloaded). The difference between the two is that `println` will move onto a new line in the file after the data has been written and `print` will not.

9.7.2 Reading from a file

We use objects of type `BufferedReader` and `FileReader` to read information from a file. An object of type FileReader will take the file name as a parameter to its constructor and will act as a link to the operating system for us. The `BufferedReader` object will use the `FileReader` object to extract the information from the file and format it for use in the program.

Again you can carry out both steps in a single line, that is, setup the stream and setup the object that communicates with the stream for you.

```
BufferedReader infile=new BufferedReader(new FileReader("details.txt"));
```

Again the exception thrown if there is a problem setting up the FileReader object is IOException.

When the BufferedReader object is setup, we now have an object that we can use to read information from the stream. There are methods in this object that will return values to us.

One of the methods is the readLine method which can read a single line from a file. This line is returned as a String object.

```
String aLine = BufferedReaderObject.readLine();
```

When the BufferedReader object is first declared, it points at the first line of the file that the BufferedReader object is attached to. When the readLine method is called, it returns this line as a string and moves onto the next line. When readLine is called again, it returns this line (the one it is currently pointing to) and moves its place marker (pointer) onto the next line, and so on all the way down the lines of the file until there are no more lines in the file to be read in.

If you want to test whether you have reached the end of a file (i.e. you can do no more reading), then check if the call to readLine returned a null value. For example,

```
if(BufferedReaderObject.readLine() == null)
```

Having a null value returned from a readLine usually means you have reached the end of the file (known as EOF).

The problem with the above statement is that the line has been read in order to check it, so the same line cannot be read again as the pointer has moved on to the next line.

How can you read a line from a file into a string and simultaneously check to see if that line is the last one in the file? Well, you can join both of the readLine commands shown above to give the statement:

```
String currentLineReadIn;
if((currentLineReadIn = BufferedReaderObject.readLine())!=null)
```

This statement has two stages, in the first stage the expression nested deepest in brackets is evaluated (currentLineReadIn = BufferedReaderObject.readLine()). This reads in the current line of the file and places it in the variable currentLineReadIn. Note that this value may or may not be null. In the next stage the result of this expression, which are the contents of the variable currentLineReadIn, are checked to see if they are not equal to the value of null. If they are equal to null, then we can stop reading and ignore the current contents of currentLineReadIn, if not, we can process the line (print it out, tokenise it, etc.).

Therefore, we can perform a read and a check to see if there is anymore to be read in the same line by using the output of one expression as the input for another.

When you are finished with a file it is good practice to indicate that you are done with the file by calling the close method in the BufferedReader or PrintStream object. This will tell the operating system that the file is finished with and it can close the file properly.

EXAMPLE The following program contains two methods. One, called write, writes two strings to a file and the other, read, reads the contents of the named file into memory and prints it out. The read method will read in lines from the named file until it runs out of lines.

```
import java.io.*;                                                    1
                                                                    2
public class FileIOExample                                          3
{                                                                   4
                                                                    5
private void write(String filename)                                 6
   {                                                                7
   PrintStream output;                                              8
   try                                                              9
      {                                                             10
      output=new PrintStream(new FileOutputStream(filename));       11
                                                                    12
      // Print out two strings to the file                          13
      output.println("hello");                                      14
      output.println("there");                                      15
                                                                    16
      output.close();// Close the file                              17
      }                                                             18
   catch(IOException exceptionObject)                               19
      {                                                             20
      System.out.println("Error writing to " +filename);            21
      System.out.println("Error message" +exceptionObject           22
      .toString ());
      }                                                             23
                                                                    24
   } // End write                                                   25
                                                                    26
private void read(String filename)                                  27
   {                                                                28
```

```
         BufferedReader input;                                    29
         String lineRead;                                         30
                                                                  31
         try                                                      32
            {                                                     33
            input = new BufferedReader(new FileReader(filename));  34
                                                                  35
            // Read in the contents of the file                  36
            while((lineRead = input.readLine())! = null)         37
            System.out.println("Line read is:  " + lineRead);     38
                                                                  39
            input.close();                                       40
            }                                                     41
                                                                  42
         catch(IOException exceptionObject)                       43
            {                                                     44
            System.out.println("Error reading from  " + filename); 45
            System.out.println("Error message  "                 46
             + exceptionObject.toString());
            }                                                     47
         } // End read                                           48
                                                                  49
      public static void main(String arguments[])                50
         {                                                        51
         FileIOExample application = new FileIOExample();          52
                                                                  53
         String fileToUse = "file.dat";                          54
                                                                  55
         application.write(fileToUse);                           56
         application.read(fileToUse);                            57
         } // End main                                           58
                                                                  59
      } // End FileIOExample                                     60
```

9.8   A METHOD FOR TRACING PROGRAM EXECUTION

If the FileOutputStream object is setup with the file name (in a string) and a boolean value of true, then it will not delete any file which already exists with the name supplied but will instead append to it.

You can use the output methods discussed above to build a class to help you debug your programs. This class can contain a static method which appends a file with the string you pass to it. You must also pass to the method the name of the file to use (the default extension is .dat).

```
class DebugUtils
{
public static void trace(String message,String file)
    {
    try
        {
        // Open the file for appending
        PrintWriter output = new PrintWriter(new
        FileOutputStream(file + ".dat",true));
        output.println(message); // Write the message to the file
        output.close();// Close the file
        }
    catch(IOException ioe)
        {
        System.out.println("Couldn't write to file" + file);
        }
    } // End trace

} // End DebugUtils
```

EXERCISE Can an input and output stream object have simultaneous access to a file, that is, can you add to a file while reading from it?

9.9 MULTIDIMENSIONAL ARRAYS

9.9.1 One dimensional array (1D)

So far the arrays we have used are what are called single dimension arrays (1D). The dimension of the array is the number of directions you can travel in it. In a one dimensional array we can travel forward or back (i.e. we could increase the index or decrease it). A one dimensional array is declared with only one parameter which is an integer that indicates the number of elements in the array (so you can go forward this number minus 1). The limit that you can go back to is usually taken to be 0.

It is possible to create arrays which have more than one dimension. The examples we look at are two dimensional and three dimensional arrays.

9.9.2 Two dimensional arrays (2D)

Two dimensional arrays involve the ability to travel up and down as well as forward and back. The easiest way to picture a two dimensional array is to think of it in terms of a table. In a table you have rows and columns, you can move from row to row (up and down) or from column to column (forward and back) and each cell in the table can store something.

	Columns →	
Rows	cell at row 0, column 0	cell at row 0, column 1
↓	cell at row 1, column 0	cell at row 1, column 1

Lets look at an example table. This table represents quarterly sales figures from three different departments of a business (we represent them using the numbers 0,1 and 2). We represent the four quarters using the numbers 0,1,2 and 3.

	0	1	2	3
0	390	595	234	602
1	440	304	290	292
2	634	233	455	530

We use the relevant rows and columns to store and access our data. For example, the sales figure for the first quarter (column 0) from the third department (row 2) is 634. This information can be stored in a two dimensional array exactly as it appears above. First we declare the 2D array. The declaration is of the form:

data_type array_name[][]=new data_type[rows][columns]

So we need to know how many rows and columns will be in our table. For our example above there are three rows and four columns so the declaration would be:

```
int salesFigures[][];
salesFigures = new int[3][4];
```

You would then place the values in their appropriate cells. Cells are accessed using the row and column numbers in square brackets.

arrayName[row][column]

So, for example, the statements which would initialise the first row (as in the table above) are:

```
salesFigures[0][0] = 390;
salesFigures[0][1] = 595;
salesFigures[0][2] = 234;
salesFigures[0][3] = 602;
```

9.9.2.1 Dynamic initialisation of a 2D array

If you have a large amount of data to place in a 2D array typing all the necessary assignment statements can be a bit tedious, however as with a 1D array you can use dynamic initialisation to setup a 2D array. The format is that you supply the elements of each row separated by commas enclosed within a set of curly brackets. Each row is then put in another set of curly brackets with the rows being separated by commas. The number of rows is the number of groups of brackets, the number of elements in the group corresponds to the number of columns.

For example, the above table can be inserted into an array in one of two ways:

1 If you are declaring the array and initialising it all in one line:

```
int salesFigures[][]={{390,595,234,602},{440,304,290,292},{634,233,
455,530}};
```

2 If you are declaring the array in one part of the program and creating it in another then you can use declarations of the form:

```
int salesFigures[][];
salesFigures=new int[][] {{390,595,234,602},{440,304,290,292},{634,
233,455,530}};
```

Make sure you do not put a semicolon after `new init[][]` as what follows is part of the array declaration. You do not have to supply actual values, variable names will also be acceptable (provided the variables match the type of value the array will hold). For example,

```
int jan,feb,mar,apr,jun,july,aug,sep;
// Statements to assign values to jan, feb, etc...
salesFigures=new int[] {{jan,feb,mar,apr},{jun,july,aug,sep}};
```

When the compiler sets up the array it will count the number of groups of elements within the main brackets (three in our first example). This is used as the number of rows. Then it counts the number of elements within the nested brackets (four in our first example). This is used as the number of columns. It then creates an array with these dimensions. You must be very careful to ensure that for the rows each group has the same number of elements in it. For example, the following declaration which has different numbers of elements declared in each row would not cause an error but could lead to problems when the array is used:

```
int salesFigures[][] = {{390,602},{440,304,292},{634,233,455,530}};
```

How do you figure out the length of a two dimensional array? With a one dimensional array you simply accessed the variable length (e.g. `myArray.length`). You can do the same thing with a 2D array, you just need to get both dimensions. To get the number of rows in the array you get the value of `arrayName.length`. To get the number of columns in an array you use one of the columns and get its length, that is, `arrayName[0].length`. The above works because a 2D array is essentially a 1D array of objects, each object is a 1D array of actual values.

You are still free to change any of the cell contents if you dynamically initialise an array, for example the statement:

```
salesFigures[1][2] = 99;
```

will cause the value of row 1 column 2 to change from 290 to 99.

EXAMPLE

You can arrange the contents that you are placing in a 2D array on different lines of the source code, as in the example below (line 23). The compiler will ignore the fact that you have different parts of the statement on different lines. The example program below will setup a 2D array and output its contents. One point of interest in the program below is the passing of the address of the 2D array object, salesFigures, to the method output - Array (which outputs the contents of the array it is supplied with) in line 17. Line 33 shows how a method which takes a 2D array reference as a parameter is written.

```
import javax.swing.*;                                    1
                                                         2
public class Array2DExample extends JApplet              3
{                                                        4
// Declare a 2D array called salesFigures                5
// which will be setup later in the program              6
private int salesFigures[][];                            7
                                                         8
private JTextArea output;                                9
                                                        10
public void init()                                      11
    {                                                   12
    output = new JTextArea(8,20);                       13
    getContentPane().add(output);                       14
                                                        15
    setupArray();                                       16
    outputArray(salesFigures);                          17
    } // End init                                       18
                                                        19
public void setupArray()                                20
    {                                                   21
    // Setup the array salesFigures                     22
    salesFigures = new int[][] {{390,595,234,602},      23
    {440,304,290,292},
    {634,233,455,530}
    };
                                                        24
```

```
// Output the number of rows and columns in the array    25
output.append("salesFigures.length (rows) is "          26
+ salesFigures.length);
output.append("\n");                                     27
output.append("salesFigures[0].length (columns) is");   28
output.append(" " + salesFigures[0].length);            29
output.append("\n");                                     30
} // End setupArray                                      31
                                                         32
public void outputArray(int arrayParameter[][])          33
   {                                                     34
   // Output each cell in the array                      35
   for(int row = 0;row<arrayParameter.length;row++)      36
     {                                                   37
     for(int column = 0;column<arrayParameter[0].length; 38
     column++)
         output.append(" "+arrayParameter[row][column]); 39
         output.append("\n");                            40
     }                                                   41
                                                         42
   } // End outputArray                                  43
                                                         44
                                                         45
} // End Array2DExample                                  46
```

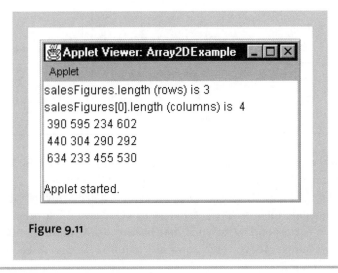

Figure 9.11

9.9.3 Three dimensional arrays (3D)

The easiest way to visualise a 3D array is as a 2D array of 1D arrays, that is, imagine a 2D array where each cell contains a 1D array (so it looks like a cube).

A three dimensional array is declared by simply adding an extra set of brackets and limit to a two dimensional declaration.

data_type array_name[][][]= new data_type[rows][columns][cell]

For example, suppose we wanted to store the following information in a table: we want to keep the quarterly sales figures for particular items for three different shops. We can represent the shops and items using a 2D array (in our example we have 2 shops and 3 items). Step one of the solution:

		Shops	
		0	1
Stock Items	0		
	1		
	2		

We can now store the four data items, representing the quarters, in each of the cells. Step two of the solution:

	0				1			
0	Quarters				Quarters			
	0	1	2	3	0	1	2	3
	78	34	32	44	22	12	9	11
1	Quarters				Quarters			
	0	1	2	3	0	1	2	3
	24	54	43	19	77	84	89	65
2	Quarters				Quarters			
	0	1	2	3	0	1	2	3
	34	49	33	21	22	9	14	45

So the sales figure for item 3 (index value 2) in shop 1 (index value 0) for quarter 2 (index value 1) is salesFigures[2][0][1] which is 49.

Like 2D and 1D arrays 3D arrays can be dynamically initialised. Again the best way to imagine them is like a 2D array of 1D arrays. First prepare the brackets for a 2D array corresponding to your dimensions (leave them empty for the moment). For the example above three rows are required so put three sets of empty {} in the declaration.

```
int salesFigures[][][]={{},{},{}};
```

Next put empty 1D arrays inside the deepest brackets (those represent the cells in a 2D array). In the example two columns will be present in each row so put two {} in the brackets representing each row:

```
int salesFigures[][][]={{{},{}},{{},{}},{{},{}}};
```

Finally put in the groups of values into the deepest brackets. In the example above four values go into each cell, so put each group of values inside the deepest brackets.

```
int salesFigures[][][]={{{78,34,32,44},{22,12,9,11}},
{{24,54,43,19},{77,84,89,65}},{{34,49,33,21},{22,9,14,45}}};
```

This may look a little confusing but you are permitted to arrange the elements on separate lines as in the example program shown below. You can use the length attribute to obtain each dimension of the sections of the 3D array.

```
arrayName.length will give you the number of rows
arrayName[0].length will give you the number of columns
arrayName[0][0].length will give you the number of elements in the
array in each cell.
```

EXAMPLE

The following example will setup a 3D array in the method called setupArray and output its contents in the method outputArray.

```
import javax.swing.*;                             1
                                                  2
public class Array3DExample extends JApplet       3
{                                                 4
// Declare a 3D array                             5
private int salesFigures[][][];                   6
                                                  7
private JTextArea output;                         8
                                                  9
public void init()                                10
   {                                              11
   output = new JTextArea(8,20);                  12
   getContentPane().add(output);                  13
                                                  14
   setupArray();                                  15
```

```
      outputArray();                                          16
   } // End init                                              17
                                                              18
      public void setupArray()                                19
      {                                                       20
      // Setup the array SalesFigures                         21
      salesFigures = new int[][][]{                           22
         {{78,34,32,44},{22,12,9,11}},                        23
         {{24,54,43,19},{77,84,89,65}},                       24
         {{34,49,33,21},{22,9,14,45}}                         25
         };                                                   26
                                                              27
      output.append("salesFigures.length (row) is"           28
      + salesFigures.length);
      output.append("\n");                                    29
      output.append("salesFigures[0].length (column) is"     30
      + salesFigures[0].length);
      output.append("\n");                                    31
      output.append("salesFigures[0][0].length (cells) is"   32
      + salesFigures[0][0].length);
      output.append("\n");                                    33
      } // End setupArray                                     34
                                                              35
   public void outputArray()                                 36
      {                                                       37
      // Output each cell in the array                        38
      for(int row = 0;row<salesFigures.length;row ++)         39
        {                                                     40
        for(int column=0;column<salesFigures[0].length;       41
        column ++)
           {                                                  42
           output.append("[");                                43
           for(int cell=0;cell<salesFigures[0][0].length;     44
           cell ++)
              output.append(" "+salesFigures[row][column]     45
              [cell]);
              output.append("]");                             46
           }                                                  47
        output.append("\n");                                  48
        }                                                     49
                                                              50
      } // End outputArray                                    51
                                                              52
                                                              53
   } // End Array3DExample                                    54
```

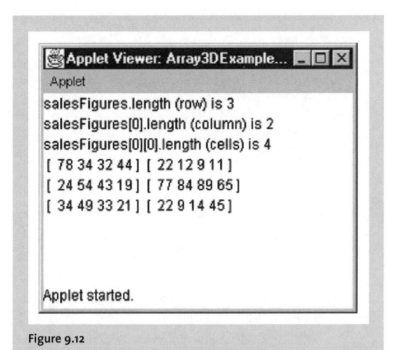

Figure 9.12

SUMMARY

The first topic examined was how to convert strings which contained numbers into a number type (int, double). We saw that class types corresponding to int and double existed (Integer and Double) and static methods contained in these classes can be passed strings which will return the value represented by the numbers contained in the string. Note that the string must contain only numbers (and a decimal point in the case of a double) otherwise no conversion can take place.

An exception occurs when some statement don't perform as expected. For example, if you try to open a file that does not exist. The compiler may require that a statement which can cause a problem (known as generating an exception) be placed in a try-catch block. This means that if an exception occurs, then the VM knows what to do (it executes the code in the catch block). If there is no try and catch block then the VM will report the exception to the user (who may not understand it) in the form of a runtime error

A string may be composed of several pieces of distinct data. These pieces of data, called tokens, can be extracted using an object called a StringTokenizer. Once a String-Tokenizer is given the contents of a string and information about how to tell one piece of data from another, the different tokens can be extracted, one at a time, starting from the front of the string.

A Date object will hold a time and a date. Date objects are not designed to be directly accessed, so instead an object of a class such as SimpleDateFormat is used. A Simple-DateFormat object can be used to extract only certain parts of a Date object (e.g. the minute part) or can be used to put information into a Date object.

We saw how to read data from a disk and write data to a file. We did this by making a connection to a file and setting up a stream object which handled the process of reading data from the file and writing data to it. Finally we looked at setting up and using multi-dimensional arrays.

KEYWORDS

▶ *Delimiter* – A character used to separate tokens in a string.

▶ *EOF* – End of file. A symbol which indicates that the end of the file being read has been reached.

▶ *Exception* – An unwelcome event, an instruction that does not complete execution through no fault of the program.

▶ *Exception handler* – Statements which will deal with an exception.

▶ *Path* – The directions supplied to the operating system so that it can precisely locate a particular file.

▶ *Token* – A piece of data.

KEY CONCEPTS

▶ Code for handling an exception

```
try
    {
    statements, one of which can cause an exception;
    the other statements depend on the statement which can
    cause an exception;
    }
catch(ClassWhichExceptionBelongsTo exceptionObject)
    {
    statements which explain to the user what has occurred;
    and discuss corrective action;
    }
```

▶ Opening a new file for output

```
PrintStream outputObject=new PrintStream(new FileOutputStream
(filename));
```

▶ Opening a file for appending

```
PrintStream outputObject=new PrintStream(new FileOutputStream
(filename,true));
```

▶ Writing a string to a file

```
outputObject.println(string);
```

▶ Opening a file for reading

```
BufferedReader input=new BufferedReader(new FileReader(filename));
```

▶ Reading a line of a file into a string

```
String line=input.readLine();
```

Note that the string `line` will be null if no lines are available for reading (i.e. either there is a problem with the file or the BufferedReader object has reached the end of the file).

EXERCISES

1 Write an applet to store information. The information will be provided in a string in the following format:

`Name:IDnumber:price`

where `:` is a delimiter.

   The user hits return after typing in this string to have the data processed by the applet. For example,

`Clock:D5:23`

Your applet should print out an error message if the data isn't in this format. You should also supply a button which, if pressed, will output all the entries input so far in a text area (they can be output in any order). Include in your applet a text field `Total` which displays the total of the prices read in. Assumptions you can make:

   ▶ Price can be treated as an integer value

   ▶ You do not need to protect against a number format error.

2 Write a calculator which will convert values from any European currency into Euros.

3 Extend the Euro calculator so that it converts from one European currency into another. The output should be formatted with the correct symbol for each currency.

Solutions to exercises and interactive exercises can be obtained at:
http://www.palgrave.com/resources

Chapter

Databases

In this chapter, we look at what a database is and how it is structured. We examine how to enter information into and extract information from a database using Java code. The examples assume that a Microsoft Access database is being used. The SQL and Java code discussed in this chapter are only a fraction of what is possible and for further information it is recommended that you consult more specialised textbooks.

10.1 WHAT IS A DATABASE?

A database is a repository of information, that is, a file on disk which contains information stored in a particular structure. It is also a term used for a Database Management System (DBMS) which is the program that manages a database file. So, the word database often denotes both the information stored and the program which manages this information.

How does a database store information? Databases come in a number of shapes and forms but the most popular form is called a relational database which stores information in tables. Each table contains related data in a row, called a record.

Example of a record:

Name	Phone	Email	Room
John Smith	3129	John@company.com	3.24

Each column represents a portion of the record called a field, the fields in the above record are:

`Name,Phone,Email,Room`.

When new entries are made, another row is added to the table and the new information is placed in that row:

Name	Phone	Email	Room
John Smith	3129	John@company.com	3.24
Jane Jones	3443	jane@myco.com	2.55

Each table has its own identifier (name). The name of the above table could be 'contacts'.

Most DBMS systems are very sophisticated as they may have to handle large amounts of data and deal with many different people wanting simultaneous access to data. It is therefore common to see a DBMS being used to hold all the information for an application layer and writing programs to use a DBMS instead of using objects to store data.

You can extract information from a database by writing an instruction, known as a 'query'. Queries can also be created using GUI tools contained in a DBMS program but ultimately all queries can be represented in a standard language called Structured Query Language (SQL) which is common to the majority DBMS packages (i.e. SQL code written for one database will work if entered in another, provided of course the same tables and names are used).

For example, here is a sample SQL query:

```
select phone from contacts where name = 'John Smith';
```

where I ask the DBMS to give me the contents of the field, named `phone`, for all the records which have the name `John Smith` stored in the `name` field. If there are more than one result, each will be output. The output for this query using the example table discussed in p. 431 will be '`3129`'.

Restrictions can be placed on the nature of data that is entered in tables, for example, a range (0–100) can be specified. If a database is given instructions to enter data in a field which conflict with the rules it has, it will refuse. Another common restriction is that a particular field is used to identify each record uniquely. This type of field is called a 'key'. In the sample table, we could have made the `Name` field a key so that no two names are the same. Therefore, when entering a new record, you must ensure that the value supplied for a key field is unique. These restrictions can cause problems for you when using a database from a Java program, so take very careful note of the tables you are accessing and make sure that any information you send to the database meets all the relevant rules.

10.2   SQL STATEMENTS

As introduced above, SQL is the 'programming' language used to manage databases. Most modern databases hide the SQL behind a GUI but it is necessary to have a basic idea of some SQL statements if you are bypassing the GUI, that is, if you are accessing the database through a Java program.

The two SQL statements that we look at are `select`, which is used to extract information from a database, and `insert`, which is used to put information into a database. There are many other types of SQL statements which deal with operations such as table creation, data deletion, and so on. SQL statements commonly end with a semicolon.

10.2.1   Selection – getting data from the database

The syntax of a select command is:

```
select [FieldNames] from [TableName];
```

Field names or table names are not case sensitive but they can contain spaces as part of their identifier which must be included when you reference them. It is best to automatically put field names and table names in square brackets as this will avoid problems if there are spaces in a table or field name.

If you use a wildcard (i.e. an *), all the field names will be selected (do not put the * in square brackets). For example, to output every cell in the table `CustomerTable`, use the following query:

```
select * from [CustomerTable];
```

This goes through each row in the table and prints out the contents.

EXAMPLE

Name	Phone	Address
Fred	555	12 High Street
Jane	123	1 Main Street
Jim	555	23 West Street

If the above represents the table `CustomerTable`, then `select * from [Customer-Table];` will output:

```
Fred    555    12 High Street
Jane    123    1 Main Street
Jim     555    23 West Street
```

You see that each record is accessed starting at the first row. Each cell in the row is then printed out and when there are no more cells, the next row is accessed.

You can select one particular field by giving its name:

```
select [Name] from [CustomerTable];
```

This will print out all the elements of the Name field:

```
Fred
Jane
Jim
```

You can further narrow what is returned by supplying a `where` condition, this will return only fields which match your criteria. For example,

```
select [Name] from [CustomerTable] where [phone] ='555';
```

This selects all the elements of the Name field which have as the contents of their phone field the string 555. The result of this query is:

```
Fred
Jim
```

Note that strings **must** be enclosed in single quotes ('). Some fields will hold numbers (integers, doubles) which do not need to be placed in quotes. How do you know whether the field you are dealing with is a string or a number? Look at the database file using the database program and examine the design of the table. This will tell you what each field holds and any restrictions that are associated with a field (range, key, etc.).

You can nest select statements by putting them in round brackets. The output from bracketed select statements will then be passed as the input to another. For example, in the query below the values for Month in 'WHERE [Month] = ' are generated from the query "SELECT [Month] FROM [TheReceipts] WHERE [Receipt] = '102'."

```
SELECT sales FROM [Total Sales] WHERE [Month]=(SELECT [Month] FROM
[TheReceipts] WHERE [Receipt] = '102');
```

10.2.2 Insertion – putting values into the database

You can place a new row in a table and put values into its cells using the insert statement. The syntax is:

insert into [Table Name] values ('value1','value2');

For example,

```
insert into [CustomerTable] values ('Joan','125','12 East Street');
```

Note that the number of values you insert should match the number of fields in the table (i.e. in the above example, I am inserting three strings into the cells Name, Phone and Address). Again be wary of dependencies, restrictions, field qualifiers, and so on, that have been built into the database as these rules must be followed by the insert statement.

For example, suppose that a table called Days Receipts has a rule that the value in the first field is a key (and therefore should be unique). If you try the following statements on that database, it will output an error message as you are not supplying a unique key in the second insert (i.e. the value Tuesday is already in the table and cannot be repeated).

```
insert into [Days Receipts] values ('Tuesday','55');
insert into [Days Receipts] values ('Tuesday','12');
```

If you are connecting your Java program to the database and passed it the above statements, then it will produce a message saying an error occurred but may not give much detail about what happened. Therefore, if such errors do occur, it may not be the fault of the Java program but the SQL statement. So, if you are having problems, print out the SQL statements being sent to the database and try them out on the database program itself.

10.3 WHY USE A DATABASE?

Why do we need to connect to a database? Can't objects be used to store all the relevant data? Well, databases are specifically designed to manage information and deal with constant requests for changes or access to that information. Database programs contain mechanisms to handle security, reporting, backups and accident prevention. We can write a Java class to do all this but this would be a case of reinventing the wheel (a common programming term meaning redoing what someone has already adequately done). Therefore, for any large scale program, we are best served by storing our data in a database and accessing this data from our Java program. Many different types of database are out there, for example, Microsoft's Access and SQL Server. Oracle and IBM also have relevant database management systems. This type of approach was discussed when the multi-tier system was introduced.

10.4 CONNECTING A JAVA PROGRAM WITH A DATABASE

How do we connect a Java program to a database? Well, fortunately the process has been made simpler for use by the use of existing standards. Any program we develop will talk (using a particular Java class library) to a program which will communicate with the database file on our behalf. The package Sun wrote to allow programmers to access any database from their Java program is the `java.sql` package, called the Java Database Connectivity package (JDBC). The JDBC package will allow you to connect your Java program with a database. You communicate with the database by sending it, via the JDBC, a statement written in SQL. This statement will then be executed and any result can be read by your Java program using a specific object.

How does the JDBC talk to the database? Well, it does not talk directly to the database, instead it can use a common standard called the Open Database Connectivity (ODBC), developed by Microsoft. Many programs talk to the ODBC which in turn will pass the information to and from the database.

So, to talk to a Microsoft Access database we go through Microsofts driver interface, the ODBC. A program which connects the JDBC to the ODBC (known as a bridge) has been created, this is known as the JDBC-ODBC bridge and this is the driver that you setup in your Java program to talk to the database. The JDBC-OBDC bridge will take the SQL commands and pass them to the OBDC which will access the database file and carry out the instructions contained in the SQL command. The OBDC will return any result of the SQL command.

The sequence can be seen in Figure 10.1. Instructions in the Java program setup the JDBC-ODBC bridge and establish a link to a specific database. The SQL instruction is assembled in the Java code and sent to the JDBC-ODBC bridge, which in turn will send it to the ODBC program which will carry out the instruction on the database file. If any information results from the instruction (e.g. if it were a `Select` statement), then this information is passed from the ODBC to the JDBC-ODBC bridge which in turn passes it to the Java program (Figure 10.1).

The Access database file must be located on the same computer as the Java program communicating with it. Other databases (e.g. ORACLE, SQL Server) can be contacted through the ODBC from remote computers.

Java applets have certain security restrictions associated with them, so the examples discussed will exclusively use applications.

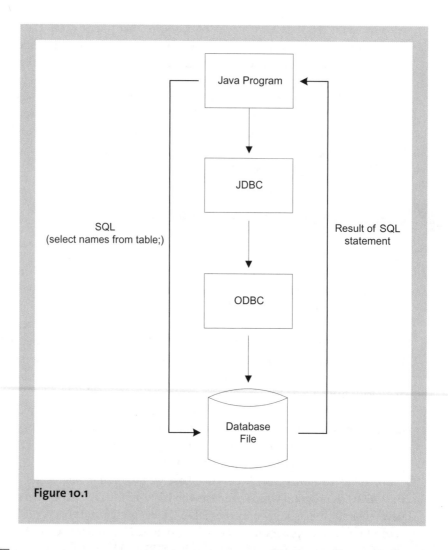

SQL
(select names from table;)

Result of SQL
statement

Figure 10.1

10.5 CREATING AN ODBC LINK FOR A DATABASE IN ACCESS

Before you can connect a Java program to a database, you must make the ODBC program aware of your database. This step is required because your Java program will need to refer to a particular database and many different databases may be stored on the same machine. The ODBC program will hold the name of the database that the Java program will use and will be aware of the actual location of that database file on the disk drive, so it can use the database when its name is invoked. It also knows what database program originally created the database file (e.g. Oracle, SQL server, etc.). If the ODBC program is not able to associate a name with a file of a particular database type then it cannot contact the database file and the query will fail. For the Access database program, you must setup a link between the ODBC and the Access database file (which has the extension mdb). You do this by setting up a data source name (DSN) in the ODBC program found in the control panel.

You can see the exact steps required described on the books website:
http://www.palgrave.com/resources

10.6 LINKING A JAVA PROGRAM WITH A DATABASE

Step 1: The first step is to setup the Java database drivers. You must put `import java.sql.*;` at the start of your program.

Before you try to connect to a database, you need to load the drivers into the VM. The following instructions will do this and must be executed first.

```
try
{
Class.forName("sun.jdbc.odbc.JdbcOdbcDriver");
}

catch(Exception e)
{
System.out.println("Failed to load JDBC/ODBC driver.");
}
```

It is possible that the drivers for connection to a particular database may not be found, so you must handle the exception from the driver setup. In the above example, the error handling process simply outputs a message to the console window although in practice you can perform other activities such as setting a flag. Instructions which depend on the drivers being loaded correctly can thus be prevented from executing.

Step 2: Setup your connection to the database you wish to work with. You need three things to make the connection, the URL for the database and a username and password for the database. The username and password are not needed if the database is not password protected and can therefore be empty strings (" ").

The URL consists of the following sections:

- The protocol you wish to use for establishing a link to the database or its interface. *A protocol is a set of rules.*
- The name of the computer which contains the database.
- The port number on which that computer is listening. *A port number is like a telephone number.*
- The name of the database you wish to access (you set this up in the ODBC program).

If you are accessing a database on the same computer as your program is running on, then you can leave out the name and port number. For instance, to communicate with a Microsoft Access database called `Accounts`, your URL will take the form:

```
jdbc:obdc:Accounts
```

Remember that the name `Accounts` is the DSN you defined for the database in the OBDC setup program you used in the control panel, not the name of your database file.

There are two parts to the connection setup:

a. Setup the connection object for the drivers to connect to the database identified:

```
Connection connectionObject = DriverManager.getConnection(URL,
username,password);
```

b. Create a Statement object using this connection:

```
Statement statementObject = connectionObject.createStatement();
```

Step 3: Assemble your query (in SQL). For example,

```
String SQLquery = "insert into SalesTable values('Joe Smith','50');";
```

The query should use correct SQL, samples of which you would have tested in the database program. You can assemble an SQL query from variables using string concatenation. For example,

```
String SQLquery="insert into "+tableName+" values('"+Name+"','"+Amount+"');";
```

Be careful about where you put your single quote ' (part of SQL) and double quotes " (part of the string). If in doubt print out the contents of the `SQLquery` string, so you can see what is being passed to the database, that is,

```
System.out.println("SQL is :"+SQLquery);
```

If the query causes problems when your Java program is executed, then you can copy it from the output console and place it directly in the database to get a more detailed idea of where the problem is (i.e. whether it is in the program, the database file or in the SQL statement).

EXAMPLE   Example of setting up the objects

```
String URL = "jdbc:odbc:Accounts";
String username = "";
String password = "";

Connection connectionObject;
Statement statementObject;
try
    {
    Class.forName("sun.jdbc.odbc.JdbcOdbcDriver");
    connectionObject = DriverManager.getConnection(URL,
    username,password);
    statementObject = con.createStatement();
    }
```

```
catch(Exception e)
    {
    System.err.println("problems connecting to " + URL);
    }
```

`Class.forName` loads the JDBC-ODBC driver into the VM which will use it to connect to the ODBC program. `DriverManager` is a class, `getConnection` is a static method which will return an object of type `Connection`.

The `Connection` object uses the driver, it manages a session with a database file. The SQL queries and their results are passed via this object. The `Statement` object sends your SQL query and holds the object which contains its result (that object is of class type `ResultSet`).

IMPORTANT! Do not leave an Access database file open (i.e. loaded into the Access program) when attempting to communicate with it through a Java program as this may block your program from accessing the database file.

Step 4: Execute your statement. This can take two forms:

- Fire and forget statements, such as insertions, whose results you are not interested in.
- Statements that will return data, such as selections, whose results you will want your Java program to read in.

Fire and forget statements can be executed using:

`statementObject.executeUpdate(SQLquery);`

To read whatever data a statement returns you need to setup an object of type `ResultSet` to hold the data sent back from the ODBC.

`ResultSet queryResults = stmt.executeQuery(SQLquery);`

You can then call methods in this `ResultSet` object to extract the data returned by the query. Results of SQL queries are placed (in the order they have been extracted) into the `ResultSet` object and can be extracted one at a time.

10.6.1 Using the ResultSet object

The `ResultSet` object works like a `StringTokenizer` object. Information is held in it and individual parts are pulled out by using particular instructions to position the object at the next piece of information and extract 'tokens' which represent the fields. One way to visualise how the `ResultSet` object works is to imagine that it holds the contents of the cells that were returned as part of the query in a 2D array of strings. You move from the starting row to the final row and extract the cells in each row one at a time.

The first operation that must be carried out with a ResultSet object is to move it onto the first row of the contents of the table returned:

```
ResultSetObject.next();
```

You also carry out this instruction when you have finished extracting the contents of the current row and want to move on to the next one.

You can check if there are any results currently available for extraction by checking if ResultSetObject.next() returns a false value.

Once you have moved to a row you can extract the cells from that row. Results are associated with the column they occupied in the table returned from the ODBC. The first column is always column number 1. For example, we can extract the contents of the first two cells of the current row as strings by using:

```
String cell1row0=queryResults.getString(1); // will get the contents
//  of column 1
String cell2row0=queryResults.getString(2); // will get the contents
//  of column 2
```

To move onto the next row give the command:

```
queryResults.next();
```

The cells in the current row can then be extracted

```
String cell1row1=queryResults.getString(1); // will get the contents
//  of column 1
String cell2row1=queryResults.getString(2); // will get the contents
//  of column 2
```

EXAMPLE The following is the table which is currently present in a ResultSet object called queryResults.

Name	Phone number
Joe Smith	6321
Jane Jones	2345

The output for the following statements:

```
while(queryResults.next())
{
// Get the first column
System.out.println(queryResults.getString(1));
// Get the second column
System.out.println(queryResults.getString(2));
}
```

will be:

```
Joe Smith  // First row first column, returned by getString(1)
6321  // First row second column, returned by getString(2)
Jane Jones  // Second row first column, returned by getString(1)
2345  // Second row second column, returned by getString(2)
```

The `while` statement above does two operations at once, it moves onto the next row and it returns a true value if there are values contained in the row (so the `getString` instruction will be executed) or a false value if no rows are left to be processed (so the `getString` instructions will be skipped).

Remember `ResultSetObject.next()` must be carried out before you try to extract the result of a query. This is carried out by the `while(queryResults.next())` statement in the example. The `next` method is called in order to 'prime' the query result. If this is not done, then the result of `getString` will be null.

10.6.2 Example: extracting values from a database

The following program shows an example of supplying a `select` query to a database (whose name as defined in the ODBC is `Accounts`) and outputting the results of the query. The program starts at the `main` method which creates an object of `select-Example`. This results in the constructor being called, this is where all the operations of the program are performed. The first job in the constructor is to load in the classes to handle communication with the database (line 21). These classes may not be found by the VM so the loading commands are placed in a `try-catch` block.

The next step is to setup the connection and statement objects (lines 35 and 37). The SQL query is sent to the database in line 44 and its result is returned from the database and put in the `ResultSet` object called `statementResult`. A `while` loop is setup to go through each row of returned results (line 50). At each row, the two cells present in the query result (name and address) are extracted and output (lines 54 and 57). Finally, the connection to the database is closed (line 62). There is no real need to close the connection as the VM will close it for you when the program finishes, however, it is a good habit to get into.

```
import java.sql.*; // import all the JDBC classes          1
                                                           2
class SelectExample                                        3
{                                                          4
                                                           5
private String SQLquery = "select [Name],[Address] from    6
[CustomerTable];";
private String URL = "jdbc:odbc:Accounts";                 7
private String username = "";                              8
```

```
    private String password = "";                              9
                                                               10
                                                               11
    public static void main(String arguments[])               12
       {                                                       13
       SelectExample application = new SelectExample();        14
       } // End main                                           15
                                                               16
    public SelectExample()                                    17
       {                                                       18
       try                                                     19
       {// Initialise drivers                                 20
       Class.forName("sun.jdbc.odbc.JdbcOdbcDriver");          21
       }                                                       22
                                                               23
    catch(Exception e)                                         24
       {                                                       25
       System.out.println("Failed to load JDBC/ODBC driver.");26
       }                                                       27
                                                               28
    Connection connectionObject;                               29
    Statement statementObject;                                 30
                                                               31
    // Setup connection to database                            32
    try                                                        33
       {// Make connection to database                        34
       connectionObject = DriverManager.getConnection (URL,   35
       username,password);
       // Setup statement stream                               36
       statementObject = connectionObject.createStatement();   37
                                                               38
       // Execute statement and process results of the execution 39
                                                               40
       // execute SQL commands to select data                  41
       ResultSet statementResult = statementObject.execute     42
       Query(SQLquery);
                                                               43
       // The command will be executed and the result put into 44
       // a ResultSet object. This will return the next result upon 45
       // a call to 'getString'                                46
       // If there are no more results then a call to 'next'   47
       // will be false                                        48
                                                               49
       while(statementResult.next())// While there are rows to 50
       // process                                              51
```

```
            {                                                        52
            // Get the first cell in the current row                 53
            System.out.println("Name :"+statementResult.getString(1)); 54
                                                                     55
            // Get the second cell in the current row                56
            System.out.println("Address:" +                          57
            statementResult.getString(2));
                                                                     58
            System.out.println();// Print a blank line               59
            }                                                        60
        // Close the link to the database when finished              61
        connectionObject.close();                                    62
        }                                                            63
                                                                     64
    catch(Exception e)                                               65
        {                                                            66
        System.err.println("problems with SQL sent to               67
        " + URL + ":" + e.getMessage());
        }                                                            68
    } // End selectExample constructor                               69
                                                                     70
    } // End SelectExample                                           71
```

The output of the above program is:

```
Name :Fred
Address :12 High Street
Name :Jane
Address :1 Main Street
Name :Jim
Address :1 West Street
Name :Joan
Address :12 East Street
Name :John
Address :1 North Street
```

10.6.2.1 Error messages which can result from extraction

As mentioned earlier, it is very important for you to check any SQL query you are passing to the ODBC for correctness. Some of the possible errors, if mistakes are made, are listed in Table 10.1.

Table 10.1

Error message from program	Likely cause
Data source name not found and no default driver specified	The name of the database given in the URL cannot be found in the ODBC program
Invalid cursor state	You forgot to put a `ResultSetObject.next()` statement before a `ResultSetObject.getString()`
The Microsoft Jet database engine cannot find the input table or query `CustomersTable`. Make sure it exists and that its name is spelled correctly	Name of table misspelled in SQL query string
Too few parameters. Expected 2	The field name identifiers referenced in the select statement were misspelled or omitted
Invalid descriptor index	Tried to extract more columns than were returned from the database, e.g. if you had the statement `ResultSetObject.getString(3)` but no column 3 existed in the table returned

10.6.3 Example: inserting values into a database

The following example shows the execution of an SQL command which will insert three strings into the table `CustomerTable` contained in the database known to the ODBC as `Accounts`. The setup steps are identical to the last example, the major difference being when the SQL statement is executed (line 42). We are not interested in what is returned from the execution so the statement is executed and we close the database.

```
import java.sql.*; //import all the JDBC classes          1
                                                          2
class InsertExample                                       3
{// Setup database SQL statement                          4
private String SQLinsert = "insert into [CustomerTable]   5
values ('John','535','1 North Street');";
private String URL = "jdbc:odbc:Accounts";                6
private String username = "";                             7
private String password = "";                             8
                                                          9
public static void main(String arguments[])              10
   {                                                      11
   InsertExample application = new InsertExample();       12
   } // End main                                          13
                                                          14
public InsertExample()                                    15
```

```
{                                                          16
    // Setup database connection details                  17
                                                           18
                                                           19
    try                                                    20
        {// Initialise drivers                             21
        Class.forName("sun.jdbc.odbc.JdbcOdbcDriver");     22
        }                                                  23
                                                           24
    catch(Exception exceptionObject)                       25
        {                                                  26
        System.out.println("Failed to load JDBC/ODBC driver.");  27
        }                                                  28
                                                           29
    try                                                    30
        {                                                  31
        Statement statementObject;                         32
        Connection connectionObject;                       33
                                                           34
        // Establish connection to database                35
        connectionObject=DriverManager.getConnection(URL,  36
        username,password);
                                                           37
        // Setup statement object                          38
        statementObject=connectionObject.createStatement();  39
                                                           40
        // execute SQL commands to insert data             41
        statementObject.executeUpdate(SQLinsert);          42
        connectionObject.close();                          43
        }                                                  44
                                                           45
    catch(SQLException exceptionObject)                    46
        {                                                  47
        System.out.println("Problem with "+SQLinsert+" sent to"  48
        +URL);
        System.out.println("Problem is :"                  49
        +exceptionObject.getMessage());
                                                           50
        System.out.println("Insertion successful");        51
        }                                                  52
    } // End InsertExample constructor                     53
                                                           54
} // End InsertExample                                     55
```

The new contents of the table `CustomerTable` after the above program are:

Name	Phone	Address
Fred	555	12 High Street
Jane	123	1 Main Street
Jim	555	23 West Street
John	535	1 North Street

10.6.3.1 Error messages which can result from insertion

Error message from program	Likely cause
Number of query values and destination fields are not the same	The SQL statement does not insert the same number of values as there were fields in the table, for example, if in the above example line 5 changed to `insert into [CustomerTable] values ('John', '535');` then this error would result as the database expects three values (name, phone and address) to be supplied for insertion into the table
General Error	The SQL statement may have conflicted with the rules associated with a field, for example, if a field is defined as a key and two similar values are inserted into the field
Could not find output table	The table named in the SQL insert could not be found in the database

SUMMARY

A database is the name given to a file which stores information in a formatted fashion or the program which manages such a file. A Java program can communicate with files produced by most modern databases by using the ODBC interface program. A library, called JDBC is supplied to Java programmers in order to connect to the ODBC and interact with database files.

Database files are manipulated using a language called SQL. Commands in this language are sent from the Java program to the ODBC which carries out the command on the relevant database file. Each database file must be made known to the ODBC, a process known as setting up a data source name. The Java programmer therefore needs to know only the name given to the database, not its location on disk (which is the business of the ODBC).

SQL commands can act on the database file in order to yield results. These results are read back into the Java program using a `ResultSet` object. This stores the result produced by the SQL command which is sent to the program by the JDBC-ODBC bridge. This information is stored in tabular form and can be extracted one row at a time (and then on a cell per cell basis).

KEYWORDS

▶ *Field* – A cell in a record (the equivalent of a column in a table).

▶ *Key* – A value stored as part of a record which must be unique, that is, no other record can contain the same value in the same field.

▶ *Record* – The storage unit for a table, each record is essentially a row of a table. The record consists of fields which contain data which may be of any type.

▶ *Relational* – A type of database which works using tables.

▶ *SQL* – Structured Query Language, the language used by database programs to access and alter data stores.

KEY CONCEPTS

▶ SQL `select` statement

```
select [fieldName] from [tableName] where conditions;
```

`fieldName` may be * denoting all fields. Conditions may be another `select` statement contained within brackets ( ).

▶ SQL `insert` statement

```
insert into [tableName] values ('value','value');
```

The number of values and their types must match the number of fields in the table you are inserting into.

▶ Reading from a `ResultSet` object
First you need to prime the object:

```
resultSetObject.next();
```

You then need to extract each field in the current row (the fields start at 1), for example,

```
resultSetObject.getString(1);
```

If there is nothing in the field the above will evaluate to null.

▶ Once all the fields are extracted time to move onto the next row

```
resultSetObject.next();
```

If there are no rows left, the above will evaluate to null.

EXERCISES

1 Marley & Marley operate a property letting agency. They keep a database of how much each customer has paid them each quarter and how much they should pay in total. Sometimes their customers do not pay them the total due, in that case they are usually added to a delinquent table. However, if the customer is already in the delinquent table, then they are added to an eviction table.

Given the above conditions, you are to write the application that computes what each customer has paid, compares it to what they should have paid and updates the relevant tables.

Main Table: Payments
Fields:
Tenant – name of customer
Q1 Rent – rent paid for first quarter
Q2 Rent – rent paid for second
Q3 Rent – rent paid for third
Q4 Rent – rent paid for fourth
Total Due – the value that Quarters 1 – 4 should amount to.

2   A company wishes you to write them a program which will extract each of their divisions sales figures from their database and compute the average sales figure (which should be output). If a division is performing below the average of the others, then you should print out the relevant divisions name.

   The figures are stored in a table with the following structure:
Name: Results

Division	Sales

Solutions to exercises and interactive exercises can be obtained at:
http://www.palgrave.com/resources

Chapter

Software development

INTRODUCTION

Software design and development is an area which has had an enormous amount written about it over the years. This chapter is intended to act as a very brief introduction to some of the relevant topics.

Software design and development aims to answer the following questions:

▶ What does the user want?

▶ What exactly should the program do?

▶ What parts should the program be divided into?

▶ What programming language (or languages) should be used?

▶ How does the user want to use the system (the User Interface)?

▶ What parts of previous projects can be reused?

▶ What training material/help facilities does the user need?

The people involved in software design and development have very different viewpoints and this must be appreciated in order to avoid confusion and conflict.

For example, you can generalise about what each group wants by saying:

▶ The user wants the system to do certain things and be easy to use.

▶ The users manager wants a system which is cheap, has no frills and can be ready quickly.

▶ The systems analyst wants to communicate exactly what the user wants to the programmer by means of designs and diagrams. This is the area with the most problems as customers often want more than can be achieved with the available time, technology or budget.

▶ The programmer wants a solution which is efficient (i.e. uses the minimum of memory and processor) and modern.

> ▶ The programmer's manager wants code that is cheap, reliable and can be reused for other problems.

In this chapter, we look at some of the issues in software development. For a proper introduction, you should consult a more specialised textbook.

11.1 / PHASED DEVELOPMENT

When working on a large software problem, the best approach (as mentioned earlier in Chapter 1, Section 1.3.3) is to break up the problem into smaller problems. You can plan various phases of the project with certain deliverables (programs, designs, etc.) for each phase. The point of dividing into phases is that the program is assembled piece by piece and there is usually something to show the user early on in the process.

Different tiers can be constructed as part of each phase. Dummy tiers can be used to simulate the presence of a finished tier, so the parties involved can get a better idea of how the system will work when completed.

11.2 / VERSION NUMBERS

Most software developers associate a unique 'version number' with their programs. This version number is often used to indicate how old a piece of code is or how reliable it is. Code changes as it is being developed and it can become hard to keep track of what the latest version of the code is if a large project is being worked on. Therefore, some sort of numbering system is needed to keep track of the versions so that each new piece of code gets a new number. That way if you have two pieces of code which may look the same but if one has a number that is 'older' than the other you know which is the most recent piece of code. Unfortunately, there is no particular standard for version numbering.

The usual system is to have a single number, which represents a major phase of the project, followed by a second number (sometimes called a revision number) which represents some minor change. For example, code with the number 2.3 indicates that it is newer than any code with the number 1 (e.g. 1.40) and is revision version 3 (or version 4 depending on whether the programmer started at 0 or 1) of the code. This number is often further divided up into another level which denotes some finer division, for example, 1.4.3.

Another possibility is to simply use a date/time marker, that is, when finished altering the code put the current date and time in a comment at the top of the code:

```
// 4/5/01 20:45
```

What about when a file is saved, a time stamp is kept recording when the file was saved? Why not use the date of the files? This is not a reliable version system to use for three reasons.

1 A programmer could change a comment and resave the file, giving it a newer file stamp without it actually being a newer version.

2 File stamps may be changed when files are copied from one location to another.

3 File stamps use the current time as defined by the computer being used, different computers may be on different times (e.g. one computer may be a week behind the other).

If you are planning on using a version number system (and it's a good idea to keep track of code this way) the main thing to remember is to be consistent. Settle on a particular numbering system to denote relevant versions of the code and stick with it, because if you change your mind from program to program you may forget what system you used and become confused when cataloguing your code.

Example of a versioning system:

- *Main number* – used for major changes to the code, that is, new features added, user interface changed substantially.

- *Second number* – used for minor changes to the code, bug fixes, and so on.

- *Third number* – used to represent cosmetic changes, changes in the comments, code layout, variable method names, and so on. In other words any change to the appearance of the source code which is not a change to the code itself.

Many programs whose source code is available for public use contain a history of their versions in comments at the start of the program. This is very useful for long time users of the program as they can figure out whether problems they previously experienced have been fixed or see what the latest changes to the code are without having to work through the program itself. This would be a good policy for you to adopt in your programs.

11.3 UNIFIED MODELLING LANGUAGE (UML)

The best way to learn is to learn by your mistakes. About now, if you have been doing the exercises you've made a lot of mistakes. You've also realised what a complicated process putting together a large program is and why you should plan out your program before you even write a line of code.

This process is called software design and consists of a number of parts, including

▶ GUI design
▶ Database design
▶ Program design
▶ Deployment design
▶ Testing

Software design is not only important to get an idea of what should be done, it is necessary to have some way of representing a paper solution, so people who are not familiar with programming can acquaint themselves with what is going on (and as these are the people who pay the bills at the end of the day you should try and keep them happy).

11.3.1 Introduction to UML

Software development is not a solo process. How do you coordinate and communicate with a lot of people from different backgrounds in order to develop a solution, record that solution and test it out? The whole process is like building a large building. You need a blueprint, diagrams for the electrical wiring, symbols to represent the plumbing, the walls, door, and so on. All this needs to be trashed out before the building is built. It also needs to be gone through carefully to make sure that you don't have the software equivalent of a door in an outside wall three stories up. All the people involved in the building, the planners, the builders, the client and the architects must be able to look at relevant parts of the plan and understand them. And of course all the plans need to fit together to produce a building at the end.

The software industries equivalent of a blueprint is a notation standard called UML. UML has been designed to be many different things to many different types of people. You have notation (symbols, boxes, lines) for representing: who interacts with the program, what parts the program is divided into, how these parts communicate, what classes inherit other classes, and so on. You can also model some of the more general aspects of the problem such as the business process. UML can be used for every stage of the system development and we will be looking at some relevant UML notation later in this chapter.

UML replaces other design notations and is intended to cope with the fact that system development often involves non-technical people, for example, operator, store manager, accountant. Diagrams are needed for these people to show them how system will be used when it is finished. If they don't understand how the new system is supposed to work, they can't make suggestions and if they can't make suggestions, you may get it wrong. Diagrams are also drawn for programmers so they can see what they have to do. UML is actually intended to be independent of a programming language. Indeed you could use a combination of programming languages to implement a UML design.

The first stage of any software development is to analyse what is needed and diagram what is proposed. You should try and do this even for the smallest project as it gives you a chance to take a calm look at the problem and the proposed solution before the hurly burly of coding breaks out.

11.3.2 Use cases

As we work through Java and OO, we looked at how programs are planned and designed. We now look at the first level of UML, the Use-Case diagram.

A Use-Case diagram shows who is going to be using our program and what parts of it they use. It indicates (in vague terms) what the program is expected to do for each different type of user.

The diagram to show this is called a Use-Case diagram and the parts of it are as follows:

- *An actor* – represented by a stick figure – is intended to indicate a particular type of user.
- *Use-Case* – represented by an oval – is intended to show what the system will do for the actor (i.e. the user).
- *Arrows* – each actor can have one or more arrows pointing to particular use cases indicating that the system will do this particular task for this particular user. The arrow can have a direction which indicates the source and destination of information (information can come from the user or the program).

For example, say we are writing a computer program that will allow a stock broker to put in a value for a stock and allow potential customers to view that stock value. We will have two use cases, enter stock value and view stock value. We will have two actors, stock broker and customer. Finally, we will have two different information flows, the stock broker will be sending information into our system and the customer will be getting information out of it. This simple system could be modelled using Figure 11.1.

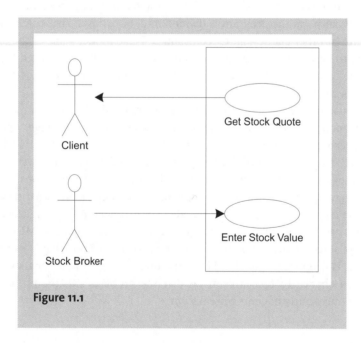

Client

Get Stock Quote

Stock Broker

Enter Stock Value

Figure 11.1

11.3.3 UML and decision making

Another element of the design process that need to be represented is any decision making. If you have complicated decisions, it's best to draw them out graphically first and then write if statements to represent your diagram (we have seen the example of a decision tree in Chapter 7). In UML you can draw what is called an activity diagram which illustrates how your program works, what choices are present in the program and what happens for each choice.

The symbols that are used are shown in Table 11.1.

Table 11.1

Symbol	What it means
●	The program starts at this point, just follow the arrows
◉	The program stops at this point
⟶	The program goes from one part to another (it goes in the direction of the arrow)
▭	An activity, the general description of the activity is contained within it

Let's have a look at an activity diagram that represents the creation of a bank account. We can express it in words first: The customer comes into the bank and asks the teller to open an account. The teller asks the customer their name and then checks to see if an account with that name already exists. If the account exists, then the teller tells the customer that they cannot have an account. If no account with that name exists, then the teller creates the account (i.e. does the paperwork). The teller then asks the customer if they want to lodge money to their account. If they do, the teller lodges money. If they don't, the teller does nothing. At the end of the transaction, the teller hands the customer their bank book.

This example is of course very restrictive (why must every account name be different for example) and a real world situation will be more complicated.

The diagram which represents the activity description is shown in Figure 11.2 in p. 456. Note that the activities usually start at the top and proceed down the page.

11.3.4 Class diagrams

The last part of UML that we look at is a class diagram. A class diagram is composed of two main parts. The description of each individual class involved and a diagram showing the relationships classes have with each other. Classes can use other classes (i.e. create objects from them) as well as extending other classes and each form of relationship has a different symbol.

Let's look at the form of a class description first. A class is drawn as a table with three rows. In the first row is the name of the class. In the second row are the attributes (variables) and in the third row is the list of operations (the methods).

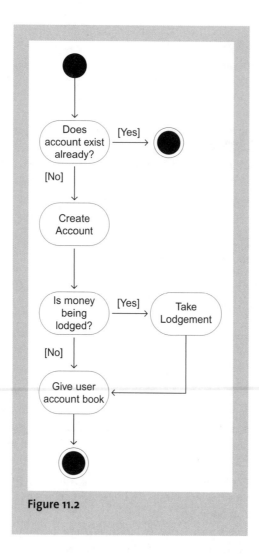

Figure 11.2

For the variables and methods the question of visibility comes into play. The visibility of an element is denoted by a symbol, + for public, – for private and # for protected.

Variables are written with their visibility, then their name, followed by a semicolon and their type.

Methods are also written in a particular way. A method must be described in the following form:

visibility name (parameters) : return type

If any of these are not present, then they are omitted (e.g. if the return type is void then omit it).

For example, the class below

```
class UserData
{
private int ID;
protected String Name;
public String getName()
    {
    }
public void setName(String nameParameter)
    {
    }
}
```

will be represented by the following diagram. The names of the parameters can be omitted or included.

UserData
– ID : int
Name : String
+ getName() : String
+ setName(String)

The other aspect of a class is how it relates to other classes. There are several types of relationship but we look at just two, inheritance and use.

11.3.4.1 Inheritance

If one class inherits another, then they are shown on a diagram linked via an arrow. The arrow (which is an outlined triangle) goes from the subclass to the superclass. The subclass is said to be a generalisation of the superclass.

For example, if a class, `UserDataDated`, which extends `UserData` is declared, its definition is the following:

```
class UserDataDated extends UserData
{
private Date today;

public Date getDate()
    {}

public void setDate(Date dateParameter)
    {}
}
```

If the class `UserDataDated` and its relationships are drawn as diagrams, they will look like Figure 11.3.

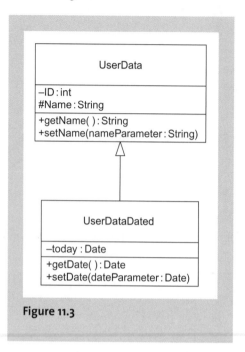

Figure 11.3

As we have said before, classes can inherit only one single other class. A description of the relationship between classes (what class inherits what class) is known as a class hierarchy. You can use the diagramming system above to draw a set of relationships between classes, for example, if there is a chain of inheritance this can be represented. This sort of information is useful since it shows which classes are depending on each other, so if you are considering changes to a class you can ascertain which classes these changes may affect.

11.3.4.2　Association

If one class is used by another class (e.g. if one class creates and uses an object of another class) then they are said to have an association. Associations are usually indicated by a single line between two class diagrams. There can be several different types of associations, for example, one class can use another class once or many times (e.g. in an array). These are different types of association and are represented in different ways.

11.4　DOCUMENTATION

Documenting code is another area which is often neglected in the rush to complete a project. Documentation usually involves the following:

▸ Training manuals for the beginner (new users)
▸ Operating manuals for the administrator/programmer
▸ Commented code for the maintenance team
▸ Design specifications of the software.

11.4.1 Help facilities

The provision of help facilities are a priority if the users of the program are not comfortable with new technology. Help facilities can take the form of:

▶ Hover messages (tool tip text messages)
▶ Help buttons
▶ Help screens (which feature indices of topics, search features)
▶ FAQ – Frequently Asked Questions, a compendium of all the commonly asked questions regarding the software and what usually goes wrong.

11.4.2 Code documentation and javadoc

Code documentation principally takes the form of commenting, however, you can automate some of the documentation for your Java programs by using a program called javadoc.

The javadoc program, which is part of the Sun JDK, processes java source code and produces HTML files based on what it finds in the source code. It extracts the name of any class inherited and the names of the methods (and their parameters).

You can also supply information to the javadoc program to add to its automatic description of the class file. This information takes the form of a group of 'tags' which denote various relevant items of information.

For example, a 'version' tag indicates the version number of the class, an 'author' tag identifies who is responsible for the code and another tag called 'see' can be used to provide a link to a web page for the code. These tags must be placed inside a block which starts with the characters '/**' and ends with '*/' (it is not strictly a comment so be careful not to leave out one of the *). You must place this block at the start of the source code file, before you begin the class definition but after any import commands. You can also place HTML inside the block which will be reproduced when the documentation page is generated.

A reference page for javadoc is available at:
http://java.sun.com/products/jdk/javadoc/index.html

An example of a block is shown below. Place this block at the beginning of a source code file and issue the command (where `fileName.java` is the name of your source code file):

```
javadoc -author -version fileName.java
/**
@version 2.4
@author UNKnown
@see <a href="http://www.codesite.org/help/"> Help info</a>
<h3>Welcome to my class</h3>
The purpose of this class is to provide a data structure for dates.
*/
```

The tags and the code will be processed and a number of HTML pages will be created which will hold the documentation about your class. Load the page called 'index.htm' into your browser as this is the main documentation page. An example of such a page is shown in Figure 11.4 in p. 460.

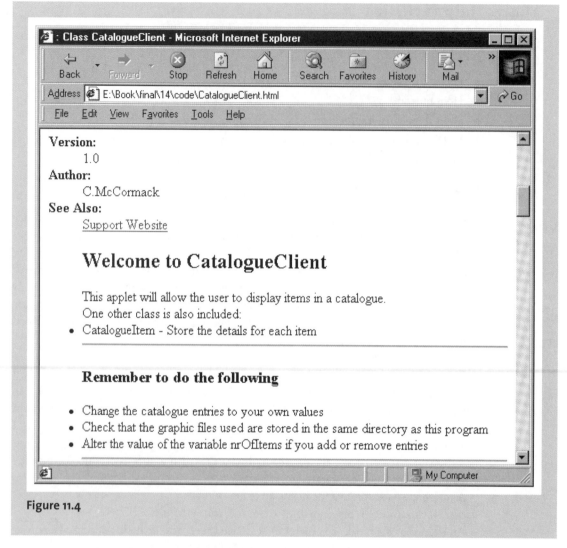

Figure 11.4

11.4.2.1 Commenting methods

Javadoc comments can also be placed before methods and will be added to the description of the method in the HTML page produced by javadoc. To add a method comment simply put the comment in the javadoc comment format and place this comment immediately before the method declaration. For example,

```
/** This method will setup the object used in the program */
public void setupObjects()
```

Two other tags which are useful when commenting methods are @param, which describes the methods parameters and @return which describes what is returned by the method. The format of the tags are:

```
@param <name of parameter> <description of parameter>
@return <description of what is returned from the method>
```

```
/** This method will setup the array of usernames
@param fileName The name of the file on disk which contains the
data
@return Array of strings containing the names of users
*/
public String[] setupNames(String fileName)
{
String result[];
....
return result;
}
```

The result of the above comments are shown in the documentation page reproduced in Figure 11.5.

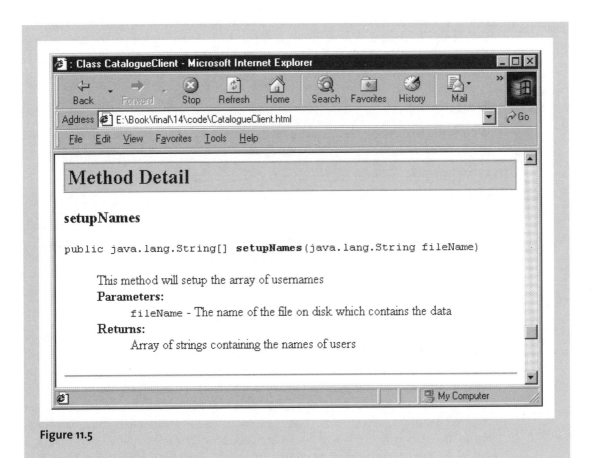

Figure 11.5

11.5 TESTING

As you no doubt appreciate the fact that a program will work correctly for one set of data doesn't guarantee that it will work for them all. Therefore, it is important to get into the habit of testing the code for reliability. In this section, we look at the possibilities for testing.

11.5.1 Forms of testing

The two main forms of testing are known as black box and white box.

11.5.1.1 Black box

Black box testing tests from the users point of view, that is, the software is viewed as a 'black box' which the user (in this case the tester) has no knowledge of or interest in. What the tester is interested in is how the software performs in response to various inputs (i.e. does it perform the computations and operations it should). The tests are therefore designed to see if the software reacts correctly to different types of user input. The software can be written so that test scenarios can be generated automatically and run through the software (i.e. you bypass the user interface and call the relevant methods with the test values and then compare what the methods return to what you expected them to return).

11.5.1.2 White box

With white box testing the tests are built using knowledge of the code structure and operation. The test cases are produced so that:

▸ All paths are executed at least once (i.e. no commands are left unexecuted)
▸ All conditions are tried for their true/false values.

White box testing means that all the possible situations that the code can find itself will be explored, this is important as some paths may be executed so infrequently that they may be overlooked in black box testing.

11.5.2 Dummy classes

When developing tiers of classes it is common to use a dummy class to represent a completed layer. This class will have all of the relevant methods that the final product will have but these methods will have very limited (if any) functionality. Usually these methods return some default value to simulate their intended result.

For example, the class BankAccount, as defined below, can be used by another class in its current state. It is not complete (variables and statements must be added) but to any class using it, it will be indistinguishable from a complete class, that is, a call to the getBalance method will return a double value. The difference is clear to the programmer and user since the same value will be constantly returned but they will generally accept this until the final version of a tier can be completed.

```
class BankAccount
{
public double getBalance()
    {
    return 22.3;
    }
public void setBalance(double currentBalance)
    {}
} // End dummy class
```

11.5.3 Adding and subtracting sections

If you wish to remove sections of code, in order to test if they are causing problems or not, then one option is to comment them out. Another option is to declare globally accessible boolean variables representing all the sections you are working on. You can enclose the relevant trial code in if conditions and switch on and off the sections via the boolean variables. This can be extended so that your program can read in a file which describes which sections to switch on and off, thus saving on having to recompile the program each time you want to switch on and off a section.

An example of such a switch is

```
boolean sectionAOn = true;
// Rest of the program
if(sectionAOn)
{
// Section A
}
```

11.5.4 Random number generation

Random numbers can be generated using the Random class. Random numbers can be used as test terms on their own or they can select from an array of possible test items. For example, you can create an array of possible test values (such as doubles) and select the array location using a random number generator. You need to import java.util to bring in the Random class.

Mechanism

1 Setup a random number object.

```
Random randomObject=new Random();
```

2 Call the nextInt method in the random number object with the maximum number you want to be returned plus one. For example, if you want numbers in the range 0–20 to be returned, you use the instruction:

```
randomObject.nextInt(21);
```

This returns your random number in integer form.

The following program will select a random number in the range 0–9 and output it.

```
import java.util.*;                                              1
                                                                2
public class randomExample                                      3
{                                                               4
                                                                5
public static void main(String arguments[])                     6
    {                                                           7
        // Setup the random number object                       8
    Random randomObject = new Random();                         9
                                                                10
        // Pick an integer in the range 0 to 9                  11
    int randomNumber = randomObject.nextInt(10);                12
                                                                13
        // Output the number picked                             14
    System.out.println("Random Number is " + randomNumber);     15
    } // End main                                               16
                                                                17
} // End randomExample                                          18
```

11.6   PACKAGES

How are the various classes in Java grouped? Are they all thrown into one directory or is there some sort of a hierarchy? Well, each class that is used in Java has its own particular place. Packages are a way of grouping class files, they are grouped in a directory hierarchy. A package is a name for a related set of class files. You denote that a class you are writing belongs to a particular package (and where in that package hierarchy it is located) by using a package statement which precedes the class definition. Packages are like libraries, there are particular categories (fiction, reference, etc.) and sub-categories.

Each class has a full name which denotes what package it belongs and the hierarchy of that package. You were introduced to the full name for a class at the start of Chapter 7, for example, java.awt.Graphics. The very last part of the name denotes the class (`Graphics`). The rest of the name indicates which package the class belongs to (java) and what sub-category the `Graphics` class is a part of (awt).

To declare that a class which follows is part of a particular package, use a command of the form:

package directory.subdirectory. subdirectory . . . ;

This must be the first statement in the program (i.e. you can put comments before it but no other statements such as import, these must be placed after the package statement). For example,

```
package main.example;

class ExampleClass
{ // Code for class
}
```

The above states that the class following the statement `package main.example` belongs to the `main.example` package. The class `ExampleClass` can be referenced in other programs by putting:

`import main.example.*;` at the start of the relevant program.

When a compiler encounters a reference to the class called `ExampleClass`, then one of the places to look will be in this package.

Classes which are part of packages are stored in the relevant directory tree which corresponds to their name: for example, `main\example\`, or in an archive format called a JAR file which contains a similar hierarchy.

Note that package names starting with 'java' are reserved for the programming language itself.

Package names are hierarchical, like a directory tree. Packages can have similar sub-trees and final class names as long as they are different in some aspect. For example, the class names

```
\main\io\readText.class
\main\gui\readText.class
```

refer to two distinct classes which happen to share the same name. These classes will be referred to in a program as:

```
main.io.readText
main.gui.readText
```

The convention for package names is that the start of the package name contains the reverse of the main internet address of the company or organisation that created the code. Domain names are guaranteed to be unique so theoretically all the packages in the world can be stored on the same computer without any possibility of confusion.

For example, for an organisation with the website www.codesite.org, the start of their package names will be org.codesite.www.

So, a unique name for our package will be:

```
org.codesite.www.readText
```

The directory that will be searched for this class will be:

```
org\codesite\www\io\
```

To get a program to find classes stored in a package, you not only have to import the package (which simply tells the compiler to look through that package for unidentified classes) but you either have to put it somewhere that the compiler is guaranteed to find it or supply specific guidance on how to get the classes in the package.

Option 1

Put the package in a directory in the JVM hierarchy with the default packages (this means you have to go into the directory which stores your Java VM).

Option 2

Alter the environment variable CLASSPATH to reflect the starting position of your package. On the windows operating system this would entail altering the class path environment variable, for example, for Windows NT change the classpath:

```
SET CLASSPATH=c:\java\code;d:\examples\java
```

Option 3

A final alternative is to put the package underneath the directory in which you are compiling your program, the compiler will look in the current directory by default.

EXAMPLE   The following class file will use a static method in the class message contained in the package org.codesite.www. We place the package in the current directory so that the JVM will find it when executing. So, in the current directory we create a new directory org, in that we create a directory codesite, inside that www and inside that a directory called example. Inside the example directory, all the way down the directory tree, we put the file which is part of the package, that is,

```java
// Package file
// Place the class defined herein in:
// <current directory>\org\codesite\www\example

package org.codesite.www.example;
public class message
{

    public static String print()
```

```
    {
    return "This is a message from org.codesite.www.example.
       message";
    } // End print

} // End class message
```

The instruction at the start of the file tells the compiler it belongs in this package.

Go back up the tree until you get back to where you started and create the file listed below.

```
// Main program
// Run this program in current directory

import org.codesite.www.example.*;
public class usePackage
{

public static void main(String arguments[])
    {
    System.out.println("Message from imported package:"
    + message.print());
    } // End main

} // End class usePackage
```

You can compile this file and the compiler will go looking for the class definition message. One of the areas it will look for message is in the sub directory org\codesite\www\example where it should find it. It will compile the source code if a .class file is not present.

The above program, when executed, will show the result of accessing the class stored in the package, that is,

```
Message from imported package: This is a message from org.code-
site.www example.message.
```

11.7   ABSTRACT

Like an interface, abstract is intended to enforce some sort of user defined standard. Whereas an interface is empty as regards statements, the class which contains abstract can contain valid methods which do not need to be redefined. The primary purpose of abstract is to allow the programmer to specify that a particular method should be declared by a subclass, that is, the programmer is issuing instructions that the method should be defined later.

An abstract method has no statements associated with it, these will be provided by the subclass. Obviously an abstract method cannot be used if the class which contains it is turned into an object as no method contents exist, a subclass must be used instead. Indeed the compiler will not permit an object which consists only of the abstract class to be created. A class must be declared as abstract if you intend to have an abstract method in it.

EXAMPLE   The following piece of code will declare a class with an abstract method, ComputeBalance.

```
public abstract class Account
{

public abstract void ComputeBalance();
// Note no statements

public void printDetails()
    { // Statements
    }
} // End class account
```

The following class, CurrentAccount, inherits the class above and defines the abstract method. This class can be turned into an object and the ComputeBalance method can be called. The printDetails method, defined in the superclass, can also be called as it does not have to be defined.

```
class CurrentAccount extends Account
{

// You MUST define the method ComputeBalance here
public void ComputeBalance()
    {// Statements
    }
} // End class current account
```

11.8 JAVA ARCHIVE FILES (JAR)

Projects which contain multiple class files and other related information (like data stores or pictures) can be more difficult to keep track of and manage than a smaller number of large files. It is also the case that sending many small class files over a network connection is less efficient than transmitting a smaller number of large files.

Since it is not a good policy to create larger class files just to gain a slight advantage in performance terms another mechanism was developed to facilitate combining many files into one. Java projects can be placed in single archive files, called JAR (Java ARchive) files. These have the extension .jar.

JAR files use an algorithm called zip as a compression mechanism. JAR files can be created with the JAR program (distributed with JDK) or using any program which supports the zip algorithm. The format is:

JAR ‹options› destination-file input-file1 input-file2....

The usual options used are:

cvf (c – create new archive, v – view trace, f – specify the archive file name)

You can use a wild card (e.g. *.class) to select multiple input files. Type 'jar' on its own to get an option list.

A manifest is a file which contains details about the contents of the archive and how it is to be used. The manifest will be automatically generated.

The following command will create a JAR file called hello.jar and will place in it all the files in the current directory with the extension .class.

```
jar cvf hello.jar *.class
```

The jar program will output its progress in a form similar to the example below.

```
added manifest
adding: hello.class (in=426) (out=298) (deflated 30%)
adding: Information.class (in=354) (out=258) (deflated 27%)
```

This information tells the user which files have been added to the JAR file and by how much they have been reduced in size (deflated). Reducing a file in size (compressing) means there is less to store and transmit over a network. However, work must be done to recreate (inflate) the file before its contents can be executed.

11.8.1 Storing applets in a JAR file

EXAMPLE The following applet will print out a simple message which is contained in an object.

```
import java.awt.*;                        1
import javax.swing.*;                     2
                                          3
public class hello extends JApplet        4
{                                         5
                                          6
public void paint(Graphics screen)        7
```

```
    {                                                        8
    Information InfoObject = new Information();               9
    screen.drawString(InfoObject.getMessage(),10,10);       10
    } // End paint                                          11
                                                            12
} // End applet                                             13
                                                            14
class Information                                           15
{                                                           16
private String content = "Hello";                           17
                                                            18
public String getMessage()                                  19
    {                                                       20
    return content;                                         21
    } // End getMessage                                     22
                                                            23
} // End class Information                                  24
```

Compile the above applet (which also compiles the class `Information`). Place it and the `Information.class` file generated into a jar file called `hello.jar` (use the example JAR file creation commands shown in the previous section).

The name of the JAR file and the principal file to use is placed in the HTML file used to load the applet (note that this applet tag only works with the appletviewer program and swing enabled browsers).

```
<applet
archive = hello.jar
code = hello.class
height = 200 width = 100>
</applet>
```

This applet tag specifies, by using an archive attribute, the name of the jar file to download. When this file is downloaded, the VM will automatically open it and look for the class file mentioned, namely `hello.class`.

11.8.2 Storing applications in a JAR file

Applications can be stored in JAR files in the same way as applets. However, applications are not started through a HTML file, therefore, how is it to be made known which file in the JAR should be executed first?

The answer is to identify the name of the relevant starting file and place it in the manifest. When the JAR file is executed, the manifest is opened first and the file specified as the main file is executed first.

Procedure

Prepare a file which has instructions about which class file to start first (we could call it `wheretostart.txt`).

The form of the instruction contained in the file is:

```
Main-Class: <class file to start>
```

For example,

```
Main-Class: JARExample
```

Create the JAR file with this file (`wheretostart.txt`) included with the manifest (use the option 'm' to make an addition to the manifest). For example,

```
jar cvmf wheretostart.txt JARExample.jar JARExample.class Information.class
```

The code for the relevant application class and the class it uses are supplied below.

```
class JARExample
{
public static void main(String arguments[])
    {
    Information InfoObject = new Information();
    System.out.println("Output is " + InfoObject.getMessage());
    } // End main
} // End JARExample

class Information
{
private String content = "Hello";

public String getMessage()
    {
    return content;
    } // End getMessage

} // End class Information
```

When the program is run, via an instruction of the form:

```
java -jar JARExample.jar
```

The manifest is queried as to the starting file and `JARExample` is executed first (i.e. the VM goes looking for its `main` method and executes it).The result of execution is:

```
Output is Hello
```

11.9 DEPRECATION: MAINTAINING COMPATIBILITY WHILE IMPROVING A LANGUAGE

With any library based language, changes will eventually be made to the code in the libraries. Sometimes the changes which need to be made are so radical that the old methods and their parameters are no longer deemed suitable for use. Library designers therefore have two choices for implementing their changes:

1 Scrap the old methods, this means that any programmer compiling their existing code with the new libraries and compiler must rewrite their code. This means the designer has accomplished their goal of improving the language but by forcing a programmer to rewrite code they may alienate developers who incur extra cost (because any code you want to reuse must be rewritten).

2 Put in the new methods/classes but leave the old ones there to maintain compatibility. This way if you reuse old code with the new libraries and compiler your code will still compile (this is called backward compatibility). Therefore, developers are sure that any investment made in writing Java code will be protected in future releases of Java VMs and compilers. This was seems to keep the developers and the library designers happy but the problem is the programmers may not realise that improvements have been made and they may continue to use the old methods and mechanisms meaning that the language doesn't develop and progress as fast as it should. That is, they will be relying on a voluntary change, something which is unlikely unless there are clear benefits.

Java designers took the second approach to development of the libraries but they attached a mechanism that signals obsolescence to the programmer when they are compiling the code. This is called deprecation. By deprecating elements the programmer is notified that an element has been altered or replaced and they are encouraged to change their code accordingly to use the new element. They may continue to use the old element but it may disappear in future releases.

Two important notes about deprecation:

1 Deprecated methods may disappear in future releases of Java, therefore this acts as an incentive to rewrite code to use the latest methods.

2 If you replace your deprecated methods with the latest versions, you need to make sure that anyone running your Java code has an up to date VM which can handle the new elements, otherwise their VM may not be able to run the program and the 'latest' code will be unusable.

EXAMPLE The method `appendText` in the `TextArea` class has been deprecated, programmers are now expected to use the method `append` which accomplishes the same result.

```
import java.awt.*;
import java.applet.*;
public class example extends Applet
```

```
    {
    private TextArea output;
    public void init()
        {
        output = new TextArea(5,10);
        add(output);
        output.appendText("Hi there");
        } // End init
    } // End example
```

Compiling the above code will produce a warning message indicating that the compiler has found that a method or class in your program is obsolete. This deprecated item has been marked by the library developers so that the compiler will bring it to the programmers attention.

The output from the compiler for the command:

```
javac example.java
```

will be:

```
Note: example.java uses or overrides a deprecated API. Recompile
with "-deprecation" for details.
1 warning
```

Note that the use of a deprecated method produces a 'Warning' which means that the code will still compile and run. It is only when the compiler generates an Error that the compilation process is stopped and no class file is produced.

You can find out what methods or classes have been replaced by supplying the deprecation flag to the compiler:

```
javac -deprecation example.java
example.java:14:    Note:    The    method    void    appendText
(java.lang.String) in class java.awt.TextArea has been depre-
cated.
output.appendText("Hi there");

Note: example.java uses or overrides a deprecated API. Please
consult the documentation for a better alternative.
1 warning
```

You can now look up the documentation which says:

```
public synchronized void appendText(String str)
Note: appendText() is deprecated. As of JDK version 1.1,
replaced by append(String).
```

You can replace the appendText by append and the compiler will no longer complain when compiling the program.

SUMMARY

In this chapter we examined, briefly, some of the topics pertinent to software development. The main points to emphasise are that the user must be involved in the development process, the development must be planned carefully and proper testing must be carried out, preferably at different stages in the development rather than at the end. Keeping these three points in mind should help reduce the trauma associated with software development and deployment.

Unified Modelling Language is a way of diagramming and documenting the development process so that all the parties involved can follow what is happening. UML is not the only notation format, many others are still in day-to-day use, but it has been developed to address the shortcomings of earlier formats.

We have also examined some of the Java features that can be used to assist the developer. Version numbers and detailed comments can be included in special comments which can be picked up by a Java code documenting program called javadoc. Packages can be used to group related classes and simplify coding. JAR files can contain complete projects for easy transportation and storage. Finally, we saw that deprecation is a useful mechanism to encourage developers to conform to change in the language without causing them undue hardship.

KEYWORDS

▶ *Black box testing* – Testing without any interest in how the program actually works.

▶ *Deprecation* – A mechanism designed to mark that a particular method or class is now obsolete and may be removed from future releases of a language.

▶ *JAR* – Java Archive, a single file which will store multiple class files. A JAR file is compressed using the ZIP algorithm.

▶ *UML* – Unified Modelling Language, a set of symbols and rules which can be used to design and implement software.

▶ *White box testing* – A test which is developed so that all the instructions in the program on will be executed.

KEY CONCEPTS

▶ javadoc comment
```
/** comment */
```

▶ Writing a javadoc heading for a class file
Make sure that the javadoc comment is placed **after** the imports, but **before** the declaration of the class.

▶ Packages
Marking a class as being part of a package

```
package org.codesite.www.example;
```

This must be the first statement in the class file. The class file must be placed in a subdirectory `example` contained in a subdirectory www contained in a subdirectory `codesite` contained in a subdirectory `org`.

▶ Using a class contained in a package

```
import org.codesite.www.example.*;
```

Make sure that the compiler can 'see' the package, that is, it must be contained in the current path or as a subdirectory of the directory in which you are compiling the program.

Appendix

Java Development Kit guide

Suns Java Development Kit (JDK) provides all the tools you need to build Java applets and applications. The main programs contained within it are:

▶ *javac* – the compiler, suitable for both applets and applications

▶ *appletviewer* – the applet VM, for applets only

▶ *java* – the application VM (for applications only)

▶ *javap* – a program which displays details about a class

A.1 GETTING THE JDK

The JDK is available at http://www.javasoft.com. It is usually available in a single file which contains all the relevant programs archived in it. Once you have downloaded (or acquired) the file run it and it should install the relevant programs on your computer.

The documentation for the various classes you will use is usually not included with the JDK. This is available from the same site and it is recommended that you download this as it contains useful information.

A.1.1   Using the JDK on Windows

Open an MS-DOS window (if no MS-DOS icon is present in the start menu, then press the Start button and Select 'Run'. Type in `cmd.exe` or `command.com` and press OK. This should bring up an MS-DOS window).

Select the drive that you wish to work in, for example, if you want to work on the d: drive, type

```
d: <return>
```

You may need to move to the root directory of the drive that you are working on:

```
cd\
```

Move into the directory that you wish to create a Java project in or create a new directory. For example, to create a directory called `example`:

```
mkdir example
```

To move into a directory called `example`:

```
cd example
```

Open up the notepad application with the name of the file that you want to create using the command:

```
call notepad Example.java
```

The notepad window will open up and allow you to edit the file. When you have finished editing the file save it, go back to the MS-DOS window and type

```
javac Example.java
```

If you get an error when calling javac which says 'Bad command or file' then the OS is unable to find the javac program as it hasn't been added to the path. To create a path for the operating system type:

```
path=c:\winnt;d:\jdk1.2\bin
```

where `d:\jdk1.2\bin` is the location of javac. If this is not the location of javac, then use the find program to locate it (its full name is javac.exe).

See the instructions provided with the Java distribution for a discussion of altering your environment to accommodate Java:

```
http://java.sun.com/j2se/1.3/install-windows.html
```

When the program is compiled, the bytecode will be written out to the current directory, so one or more files with the extension `.class` will appear.

If the program you write is an application, then type

```
java Example
```

to execute the program. If the program doesn't terminate itself (e.g. if you open a frame but don't listen for a window closing event), then you need to go back to the DOS window and press CTRL-C to exit application.

Note that javac and java do not print messages if all goes well (see Figure A.1 for a typical output).

If the program you have compiled is an applet, then you must create a HTML file which contains instructions that will load the applet. Use notepad to create a HTML file by issuing a command such as:

```
call notepad example.htm
```

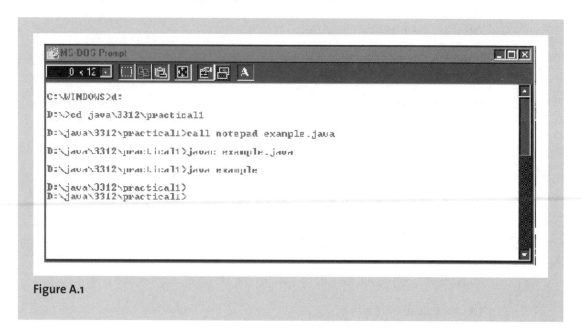

Figure A.1

A HTML file which contains the following:

```
<applet code="example.class" height=300 width=300> </applet>
```

should be placed in the notepad and saved. Remember to put the name of the file in the exact same case as defined in the class file, for example, if the class file is called ExampleProg, then make sure the same filename is placed in the HTML file.

Once you have the HTML file, you can execute it by typing

```
appletviewer filename.htm
```

This will open up a window into which your applet will be loaded and executed. Appletviewer will execute an applet regardless of whether it is written in swing or using the AWT (see Chapter 7). If you use the code in the book and want to execute an applet by loading the HTML file into a browser, then you should place the following into the HTML file to tell the browser exactly what sort of a file is being used:

```
<objectclassid="clsid:8AD9C840-044E-11D1-B3E9-00805F499D93"
width="300"    height="500"    codebase="http://java.sun.com/
products/plugin/1.2.2/jinstall-1_2_2-win.cab#Version=1,2,2,0">

<param name="code" value="example.class">

<param name="type" value="application/x-java-applet;version=1.2.2">

No JDK 1.2 support for applet, attempting to download plugin

</object>
```

Table A.1 List of MS-DOS commands

Command	Meaning	Example
CD	Change directory	`CD h:\project1`
		`CD\ {return to the root of the disk}`
mkdir	Make directory	`mkdir project1`
h:	Drive letter – change drive	`d: {Changes from the current drive to the d drive}`
call	Execute or call a program	`call notepad.exe {calls the NotePad application}`
path	displays and sets the locations for the operating system to search when the user supplies the name of a file they wish to be executed	`path {path on its own displays the current path settings} path=c:\winnt;c:\winnt\system32; d:\jdk1.2\bin {tells the operating system to search the listed directories when the user tries to execute a file that is not in the current directory}`
copy	Copy files from one directory to another	`copy d:\temp\project1\* h:\project1 {copy all the files from the directory d:\temp\project1 to h:\project1}`
dir	list the contents of the current directory	`TRB41E5 TMP  0 15/01/01 14:20 trb41e5.TMP TRB43B3 TMP  0 15/01/01 14:21 trb43b3.TMP ~WRA0635 WBK 24,576 1/01/01 20:07 ~WRA0635.wbk 159 file(s) 7,108,842 bytes 6 dir(s) 639,270,912 bytes free`

Appendix B

INTRODUCTION

This appendix discusses how to get the programs in the book working and how to change the way the programs work to suit your circumstances.

The first section discusses how to get the programs working, the second section deals with a situation where you may wish to use Applications instead of Applets and the final section deals with a situation whereby you may have an older Java VM (or wish to use the AWT instead of Swing) and may not be in a position to update it.

B.1   GETTING APPLETS WORKING

The programs in the book which makes use of the TrainingWheels class are applets. If you wish to make use of the programs as applications, then see Section B.2.
To get the programs to work do the following.

1   Obtain the code for the TrainingWheels class. This can be found at the books website or you can type in the code listed in Chapter 7.

2 Write the program which uses the `TrainingWheels` class.

3 Save this program on disk.

4 Take the `TrainingWheels` class source file (`TrainingWheels.java`) and place it in the same directory as the program you have written. If you are using an Integrated Development Environment (IDE) such as `JBuilder`, then add the `TrainingWheels` source code file to the current project. Do not put the code for the `TrainingWheels` class in the same file as the program you are writing (i.e. do not copy and paste the code).

5 Compile your program.

6 If the program compiles correctly then write the html file that will load the applet you have written. This html file will take one of two forms depending on your circumstances.

Form 1

Write the following code and put in it your html file. Replace the word `program` with the name of the class file you have in step **2** above.

```
<APPLET CODE="program.class" WIDTH=350 HEIGHT=300>
</APPLET>
```

Run the above class file by loading it into a web browser or by using the appletviewer program if you are making use of the Sun JDK.

Form 2

If your web browser does not display the program, then you will have to put the following in your html file

```
<objectclassid = "clsid:8AD9C840-044E-11D1-B3E9-00805F499D93"
width = "300"    height = "500"    codebase = "http://java.sun.com/
products/plugin/1.2.2/jinstall-1_2_2-win.cab#Version = 1,2,2,0">
<param name = "code" value = "program.class">
<param name = "type" value = "application/x-java-
applet;version =1.2.2">
No JDK 1.2 support for applet, attempting to download plugin
</object>
```

Again replace the name `program` with the name of your file.

B.2   USING APPLICATIONS

If you want to use Java applications instead of applets, then use the following code and replace references to `TrainingWheels` with `TrainingWheelsApplication`.

You should add the following method to the sample programs discussed in the text:

```
public static void main(String arguments[])
    {
    className application = new className();
    }
```

Replace the phrase `className` in the above method with the name of the class that you defined (i.e. the name of your program).

Make sure the above method is contained within your class definition.

Java Applications are run using a different VM to that used for Applets, for example, the VM supplied with the JDK is called java. So, to get a Java application running if you have Suns JDK you will type:

java ClassName

on the command line.

B.2.1 TrainingWheels code for applications

```
import java.awt.*;                                            1
import java.awt.event.*;                                      2
import javax.swing.*;                                         3
                                                              4
public class TrainingWheelsApplication implements            5
ActionListener,WindowListener
{                                                             6
private JButton inputButton;                                 7
private JTextArea outputArea;                                8
private JTextField inputTextField;                           9
private JScrollPane outputPane;                              10
private JFrame outputWindow;                                 11
                                                             12
public TrainingWheelsApplication()                          13
    {                                                        14
    outputWindow = new JFrame("Application");                15
    outputWindow.setSize(350,300);                           16
    outputWindow.getContentPane().setLayout(new FlowLayout());  17
    outputArea = new JTextArea("[Output will be displayed    18
    here]\n",10,30);

                                                             19
    outputPane = new JScrollPane(outputArea);                20
                                                             21
    outputWindow.getContentPane().add(outputPane);           22
    outputWindow.show();                                     23
```

```
    outputWindow.addWindowListener(this);                       24
    entryPoint();                                                25
    } // End init                                                26
                                                                 27
public void init()                                               28
    {                                                            29
    outputWindow.getContentPane().setLayout(new FlowLayout());   30
    outputArea=new JTextArea("[Output will be displayed          31
    here]\n",10,30);
                                                                 32
    outputPane = new JScrollPane(outputArea);                    33
                                                                 34
    outputWindow.getContentPane().add(outputPane);               35
    entryPoint();                                                36
    } // End init                                                37
                                                                 38
// Methods which manage input and output                         39
// The methods below are used for adding and processing          40
// input elements                                                41
public void addButton(String ButtonLabel)                        42
    {                                                            43
    inputButton = new JButton(ButtonLabel);                      44
    outputWindow.getContentPane().add(inputButton);              45
    inputButton.addActionListener(this);                         46
    outputWindow.validate();                                     47
    } // End addButton                                           48
                                                                 49
// Add an text field to the screen and place the string          50
// supplied before it                                            51
public void addInputElement(String InputLabel)                   52
    {                                                            53
    // Add the label                                             54
    JLabel Description = new JLabel(InputLabel);                 55
    outputWindow.getContentPane().add(Description);              56
                                                                 57
    // Add the text field                                        58
    inputTextField = new JTextField(10);                         59
    outputWindow.getContentPane().add(inputTextField);           60
    inputTextField.addActionListener(this);                      61
    outputWindow.validate();                                     62
    } // End addInputElement                                     63
                                                                 64
// Called if the user presses the button or presses return       65
// in the text field                                             66
public void actionPerformed(ActionEvent event)                   67
```

```
{                                                             68
    // If the user pressed the button then call the method    69
    ifButtonPressed                                           70
    if(event.getSource() == inputButton)                      71
        ifButtonPressed();                                    72
                                                              73
    // If the user pressed enter in the text field try and figure out  74
    // the contents of the text field and call the relevant methods    75
    if(event.getSource() == inputTextField)                   76
        try {                                                 77
            // Try to convert input to integer form           78
            processInput(Integer.parseInt(inputTextField.     79
            getText()));
                                                              80
        }                                                     81
        catch(NumberFormatException nfeInteger)               82
        {                                                     83
        try                                                   84
            {                                                 85
            // Try to convert input to double                 86
            processInput(Double.parseDouble(inputTextField    87
            .getText()));
            }                                                 88
        catch(NumberFormatException nfeDouble)                89
        {                                                     90
        // If conversion processes fail, treat input as a string  91
        processInput(inputTextField.getText());               92
        }                                                     93
    }                                                         94
} // end actionPerformed                                      95
                                                              96
// Clear the output area of its current contents              97
public void clearScreen()                                     98
    {                                                         99
    outputArea.setText("");                                   100
    } // End clearScreen                                      101
                                                              102
// Method executed if outputOnScreen is called with a string  103
// actual parameter                                           104
public void outputOnScreen(String stringToOutput)             105
    {                                                         106
    outputArea.append(stringToOutput +"\n");                  107
    } // End outputOnScreen(string)                           108
                                                              109
```

```
// Method executed if outputOnScreen is called with an int      110
// actual parameter                                             111
public void outputOnScreen(int intToOutput)                     112
    {                                                           113
    outputArea.append(intToOutput +"\n");                       114
    } // End outputOnScreen(int)                                115
                                                                116
// Method executed if outputOnScreen is called with a double    117
// actual parameter                                             118
public void outputOnScreen(double doubleToOutput)               119
    {                                                           120
    outputArea.append(doubleToOutput +"\n");                    121
    } // End outputOnScreen(double)                             122
                                                                123
// Method executed if outputOnScreen is called with a          124
// boolean actual parameter                                     125
public void outputOnScreen(boolean booleanToOutput)            126
    {                                                           127
    outputArea.append(booleanToOutput +"\n");                   128
    } // End outputOnScreen(boolean)                            129
                                                                130
// Backup methods                                               131
// The methods below are likely to be used in your program      132
// (i.e. they are overridden in your program). If you do not     133
// declare them in your program then the virtual machine will   134
// execute the ones below, the purpose of these is to          135
// tell you that you need to put in the relevant methods.       136
public void entryPoint()                                        137
    {                                                           138
    missingMethodMessage("public void entryPoint()");           139
    } // End entryPoint                                         140
                                                                141
public void ifButtonPressed()                                   142
    {                                                           143
    missingMethodMessage("public void ifButtonPressed()");      144
    } // End ifButtonPressed                                    145
                                                                146
public void processInput(String inputSupplied)                  147
    {                                                           148
    missingMethodMessage("public void processInput(String       149
    inputSupplied)");
    } // End processInput(string)                               150
                                                                151
public void processInput(int inputSupplied)                     152
```

```
    {                                                              153
    missingMethodMessage("public void processInput(int            154
    inputSupplied)\n");
    } // End processInput(int)                                     155
                                                                   156
public void processInput(double inputSupplied)                     157
    {                                                              158
    missingMethodMessage("public void processInput(double          159
    inputSupplied)\n");
    } // End processInput(double)                                  160
                                                                   161
public void missingMethodMessage(String message)                   162
    {                                                              163
    message="You have not written a method called:\n"              164
    + message+ "\n";
    message+="This means your program won't work properly\n";      165
    message+="Please write this method, compile your program      166
    again \nand execute it.";
                                                                   167
    JOptionPane messagePane = new JOptionPane();                   168
    messagePane.showMessageDialog(null,message,"Status",           169
    JOptionPane.INFORMATION_MESSAGE);
    } // End missingMethodMessage                                  170
                                                                   171
// Methods to handle a closing window                              172
public void windowClosing(WindowEvent e) {System.exit(0);}         173
public void windowClosed(WindowEvent e) {}                         174
public void windowOpened(WindowEvent e) {}                         175
public void windowIconified(WindowEvent e) {}                      176
public void windowDeiconified(WindowEvent e) {}                    177
public void windowActivated(WindowEvent e) {}                      178
public void windowDeactivated(WindowEvent e) {}                    179
                                                                   180
} // End TrainingWheelsApplication                                 181
```

B.2.2 Example for applications

The following program shows the first example program converted to operate as an application.

```
// The purpose of this program is to output a message on the screen    1
// You must look at appendix B to get this program to work properly    2
```

```
                                                                    3
                                                                    4
public class MyFirstApplet extends TrainingWheelsApplication        5
{                                                                   6
                                                                    7
public void entryPoint()                                            8
    {                                                               9
    outputOnScreen("This is my first program");                   10
    } // End of entryPoint                                         11
                                                                   12
public static void main(String args[])                            13
    {                                                              14
    MyFirstApplet application = new MyFirstApplet();               15
    }                                                              16
                                                                   17
} // End of MyFirstApplet                                          18
```

B.3   CODE FOR AWT

If you wish to use the older Java GUI components (known as the AWT) instead of the Swing components (see Chapter 7 for further discussion), then obtain the code below and substitute it for the TrainingWheels source code. You should change any references in the sample programs from TrainingWheels to TrainingWheelsAwt.

With some older development environments a change to the TrainingWheelsAWT class is necessary as they will not support the Swing libraries.

```
import java.awt.*;                                                  1
import java.applet.*;                                               2
import java.awt.event.*;                                            3
                                                                    4
public class TrainingWheelsAwt extends Applet implements            5
ActionListener
{                                                                   6
                                                                    7
private Button inputButton;                                         8
private TextArea outputArea;                                        9
private TextField inputTextField;                                  10
                                                                   11
public void init()                                                 12
    {                                                              13
    setLayout(new FlowLayout());                                   14
    outputArea = new TextArea("[Output will be displayed          15
```

```
        here]\n",10,30);
                                                                16
        add(outputArea);                                        17
        entryPoint();                                           18
        } // End init                                           19
                                                                20
    // Methods which manage input and output                    21
    // The methods below are used for adding and processing     22
    // input elements                                           23
    public void addButton(String ButtonLabel)                   24
        {                                                       25
        inputButton = new Button(ButtonLabel);                  26
        add(inputButton);                                       27
        inputButton.addActionListener(this);                    28
        validate();                                             29
        } // End addButton                                      30
                                                                31
    public void addInputElement(String InputLabel)              32
        {                                                       33
        // Add the label                                        34
        Label Description = new Label(InputLabel);              35
        add(Description);                                       36
                                                                37
        // Add the text field                                   38
        inputTextField = new TextField(10);                     39
        add(inputTextField);                                    40
        inputTextField.addActionListener(this);                 41
        validate();                                             42
        } // End addInputElement                                43
                                                                44
    // Called if the user presses the button or presses return  45
    // in the textfield                                         46
    public void actionPerformed(ActionEvent event)              47
        {                                                       48
        // If the user pressed the button then call the method  49
        // ifButtonPressed                                      50
        if(event.getSource() == inputButton)                    51
            ifButtonPressed();                                  52
                                                                53
        // If the user pressed enter in the textfield try and figure  54
        // out the contents of the textfield and call the       55
        // relevant methods                                     56
        if(event.getSource() == inputTextField)                 57
            try {                                               58
```

```
        // Try to convert input to integer form       59
        processInput(Integer.parseInt(inputTextField.  60
        getText()));

                                                        61
        }                                               62
    catch(NumberFormatException nfeInteger)             63
        {                                               64
        try                                             65
            {                                           66
            // Try to convert input to double           67
            processInput(Double.parseDouble(inputTextField  68
            .getText()));
            }                                           69
        catch(NumberFormatException nfeDouble)          70
            {                                           71
            // If conversion processes fail, treat input as  72
            // a string                                 73
            processInput(inputTextField.getText());     74
            }                                           75
        }                                               76
    } // End actionPerformed                            77
                                                        78
// Clear the output area of its current contents        79
public void clearScreen()                               80
    {                                                   81
    outputArea.setText("");                             82
    } // End clearScreen                                83
                                                        84
// Method executed if outputOnScreen is called with a string  85
// actual parameter                                     86
public void outputOnScreen(String stringToOutput)       87
    {                                                   88
    outputArea.append(stringToOutput +"\n");            89
    } // End outputOnScreen(string)                     90
                                                        91
// Method executed if outputOnScreen is called with an int  92
// actual parameter                                     93
public void outputOnScreen(int intToOutput)             94
    {                                                   95
    outputArea.append(intToOutput +"\n");               96
    } // End outputOnScreen(int)                        97
                                                        98
// Method executed if outputOnScreen is called with a double  99
// actual parameter                                     100
```

```
public void outputOnScreen(double doubleToOutput)          101
    {                                                      102
    outputArea.append(doubleToOutput +"\n");               103
    } // End outputOnScreen(double)                        104
                                                           105
// Method executed if outputOnScreen is called with a      106
// boolean actual parameter                                107
public void outputOnScreen(boolean booleanToOutput)        108
    {                                                      109
    outputArea.append(booleanToOutput +"\n");              110
    } // End outputOnScreen(boolean)                       111
                                                           112
// Backup methods                                          113
// The methods below are likely to be used in your program 114
// (i.e. they are overridden in your program)              115
// if you do not declare them in your program then the virtual 116
// machine will execute the ones below, the purpose of these is to 117
// tell you that you need to put in the relevant methods.  118
public void entryPoint()                                   119
    {                                                      120
    missingMethodMessage("public void entryPoint()");      121
    } // End entryPoint                                    122
                                                           123
public void ifButtonPressed()                              124
    {                                                      125
    missingMethodMessage("public void ifButtonPressed()"); 126
    } // End ifButtonPressed                               127
                                                           128
public void processInput(String inputSupplied)             129
    {                                                      130
    missingMethodMessage("public void processInput(String  131
    inputSupplied)");
    } // End processInput(string)                          132
                                                           133
public void processInput(int inputSupplied)                134
    {                                                      135
    missingMethodMessage("public void processInput(int     136
    inputSupplied)\n");
    } // End processInput(int)                             137
                                                           138
public void processInput(double inputSupplied)             139
    {                                                      140
    missingMethodMessage("public void processInput(double  141
    inputSupplied)\n");
```

```
} // End processInput(double)                                  142
                                                               143
public void missingMethodMessage(String message)              144
   {                                                          145
   message = "You have not written a method                   146
   called:\n" + message+ "\n";
   message += "This means your program won't work properly\n"; 147
   message += "Please write this method, compile your program 148
   again\n and execute it.";

                                                               149
   outputArea.append("\n"+ message);                          150
   } // End missingMethodMessage                              151
                                                               152
} // End TrainingWheelsAwt                                     153
```

Bibliography

TEXTBOOKS

Introductory

Not Just Java. Peter van der Linden. Prentice-Hall; ISBN: 0-13-079660-3

Advanced

Just Java. Peter van der Linden. Prentice-Hall; ISBN 0-13-010534-1
Java How to Program. Paul and Harvey Deitel. Prentice Hall; ISBN: 0-13-012507-5
Core Java 2, Volume 1: *Fundamentals*. Cay S. Horstmann and Gary Cornell. Prentice Hall; ISBN: 0-13-089468-0
Core Java 2, Volume 2: *Advanced Features*. Cay S. Horstmann and Gary Cornell. Prentice Hall; ISBN: 0-13-081934-4

Reference websites

http://www.dejanews.com – archive site for usenet newsgroups, a valuable source of information
http://www.afu.com/javafaq.html – The Java FAQ (Frequently Asked Questions)
http://www.pcwebopedia.com – General computing resource
http://www.gamelan.com – Example Java programs
http://www.jars.com – Java application rating service

http://www.ibm.com/java – IBMs Java resource page

http://www.javasoft.com – Worthwhile not just as a source of Java development programs but also for reference documentation and a questions and answer bulletin board.

Index